Local C
The First Fi... **S0-EVD-252**

Local Color
The First Five Years

*Stories by Western Massachusetts Senior Citizens
about life as they remember it*

Edited by Anna Viadero

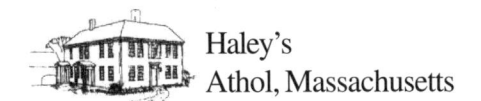

Haley's
Athol, Massachusetts

Copyright 2003 by Anna Viadero

All rights reserved. No part of this book may be reproduced or transmitted in any form or by any means, electronic or mechanical, including photocopying, recording, or by any information storage and retrieval system, without permission in writing from Anna Viadero. The proprietary trade dress, including the format, is the property of Anna Viadero and may not be reproduced without the expressed permission of Anna Viadero obtained in writing through the publisher.

"Never Too Young to Fall in Love" reprinted by permission from *Clarion Chronicles: A Garden Along the Railroad Tracks*, published by The Daily Hampshire Gazette, 115 Conz Street, Northampton, MA, 01060. Copyright 1994.

Published by
Haley's
PO Box 248
Athol, MA 01331
1.800.215.8805
haley.antique@verizon.net

Book and cover design by Anna Viadero.
Copy editing by Toni Brandmill & Ann McNelly
Printed by McNaughton & Gunn, Saline, Michigan
Printed in the United States of America

ISBN 1-884540-72-4

Library of Congress Cataloging-in-Publication Data
Local color, the first five years : stories by western Massachusetts senior citizens about life as they remember it / edited by Anna Viadero.
    p. cm.
Consists of: The stories of our lives (based on an eight week writing course for seniors in Montague, Mass.), the first five vols. of Local color (less three contributions), and thirty three additional stories.
  ISBN 1-884540-72-4
  1. Massachusetts--Social life and customs--20th century--Anecdotes. 2. Massachusetts--Biography--Anecdotes. 3. Aged--Massachusetts--Biography--Anecdotes. I. Viadero, Anna. II. Local color. III. Stories of our lives.
  F70.L63 2003
  974.4'043--dc22

Contents

Introduction..xv
Acknowledgements..xvi

The Stories of Our Lives (Spring 1998)
Kitchen Dances by Edna Baublis, Athol...1
Lost Dream by Edna Baublis, Athol...2
My Experimental Tomatoes by Edna Baublis, Athol.......................3
My Neighborhood by Alice Brough, Montague Center....................5
Self Portrait I by Estelle Cade, Turners Falls....................................8
Self Portrait II by Estelle Cade, Turners Falls...................................9
My Father's Hands by Estelle Cade, Turners Falls.........................10
Ice Skates for Christmas and Another Surprise!
    by Estelle Cade, Turners Falls...11
The Day I Had My Tonsils Out
    by Mary Ciechomski, Turners Falls...12
I Remember by Mary Ciechomski, Turners Falls............................14
Lilacs by Margaret M. "Pat" Currie, Turners Falls.........................15
Mary E. by Margaret M. "Pat" Currie, Turners Falls......................16
Memories by Jane Daignault, Turners Falls...................................17
Memories II by Jane Daignault, Turners Falls................................18
Aunt Katie Because by Warren LeMon, Turners Falls...................19
Aunt Katie's Kitchen by Warren LeMon, Turners Falls.................20
Keep Cool with Coolidge
    by Warren LeMon, Turners Falls...21
My Father by Warren LeMon, Turners Falls...................................23
Mother's Spring Cleaning by Phyllis Loomis, Ashfield.................23
Today I Danced at the Unitarian Church!
    by Phyllis Loomis, Ashfield...28
The Last Visit by Eileen Marguet, Greenfield.................................30

Ma Going through WWI by Joseph A. Parzych, Gill......................33
The War Years by Charlotte Potter, Turners Falls............................42
My Inspiration by Leona Robert, Turners Falls................................45
My Earliest Memory by Charlotte Robinson, Turners Falls...............48
Sex Education by Charlotte Robinson, Turners Falls........................49
World War II by Charlotte Robinson, Turners Falls.........................50

Local Color (aka Local Color #1, published in 1999)
Sunday Drives by Helen G. Adzema, Greenfield..............................57
Sunday Downfall by Edna Baublis, Athol...59
The McShane Family by Alice Brough, Montague Center................60
My New England Grandfather
    by Estelle Cade, Turners Falls...62
Mother's Kitchen by Guy Carey, Jr., Warwick.................................65
Christmas Past by Mary Ciechomski, Turners Falls.........................67
School Days in a One-Room Schoolhouse
    by Dorothy Clark, Charlemont..69
The Ladder by Margaret M. "Pat" Currie, Turners Falls..................72
The Homes of My Youth
    by Jane Daignault, Turners Falls...74
The Mail Must Go Through
    by William R. Fitzgerald, Ashfield...76
A Hunting She Will Go
    by Margaret "Peg" Folgmann, Shelburne Falls........................78
Life in Orange, Massachusetts
    by Katherine L. Forster, Orange..79
One Hometown through a Child's Eyes
    by Phyllis Hamilton, Turners Falls...81
The Great Depression by Irmarie Jones, Greenfield.........................83
A Dream by Elisabeth Leete, Ashfield...86
Gladys by Warren LeMon, Turners Falls..88

Memories by Janice Howard Lepore, Greenfield..............................90
War Years by Betty Lockwood, Charlemont......................................92
The Dollhouse Christmas by Phyllis Loomis, Ashfield.....................95
WWII from the Vantage Point of One Family
       by Eileen Marguet, Greenfield..97
The Pioneer Valley Women's Rifle Club
       by Louise Bowen O'Brien, Colrain...98
A Room at the Inn by Joseph A. Parzych, Gill.................................100
A Different Memorial Day
       by Charlotte Potter, Turners Falls...102
The Montague Inn by Leona Robert, Turners Falls........................103
Investigating Grandma's Trunks
       by Charlotte Robinson, Turners Falls...................................106
The Depression Years by Doris Shirtcliff, Greenfield....................108
Going to Grandpa's by Priscilla Tromblay, Turners Falls................110

Local Color #2 (2000)
By the Water's Edge and Beyond
       by Helen G. Adzema, Greenfield..115
My Mother and I by Edna Baublis, Athol...116
To My Grandmother, Whom I Never Really Knew
       by Estelle Cade, Turners Falls..119
Thoughts About 1930s Greenfield
       by Margaret M. "Pat" Currie, Turners Falls.........................121
Remembering Peanuts by Guy Carey, Jr., Warwick......................123
South Hadley Summers
       by Mary Ciechomski, Turners Falls......................................125
Camping at the Mohawk Trail Campground
       by Jane Daignault, Turners Falls..127
Northfield Farms in Retrospect by Vera Farris, Northfield............129
A Hide and Go Seek Story by Edith J. Fisher, Leyden...................133

A Move to Heaven by Suzanne Gluck-Sosis, Greenfield..................134
The 1938 Hurricane by Dorothy G. Hmieleski, South Deerfield......136
A Bear in Our Backyard by Jean Kozlowski, Northfield.................137
Mother, the Illuminator by Warren LeMon, Turners Falls...............138
Reverse Roles by Janice Howard Lepore, Greenfield.....................140
Senior Year, 1929 by Betty Lockwood, Charlemont........................142
Neighbors by William R. Fitzgerald, Ashfield................................145
Dear David by Phyllis Loomis, Ashfield..146
Not for a Million Dollars by Eileen Marguet, Greenfield.................149
Colrain Memories by Louise Bowen O'Brien, Colrain....................153
Bikes and D.O. Paul's Store by Joseph A. Parzych, Gill...............154
The Wedding by Charlotte Potter, Turners Falls.............................158
The Cousins by Charlotte Robinson, Turners Falls........................159
Fun & Games in Turners Falls
     by Juliana Sivik Samoriski, Shelburne......................................161
The Cat by Doris Shirtcliff, Greenfield..165
Aniwa by Norah (Noreen) Torrey, Greenfield.................................167
The Wedding by Leona Robert, Turners Falls................................172
Back Home to the Farm for Christmas
     by Ellen C. Tosi, Northfield..173
Fond Memories of My Father
     by Priscilla Tromblay, Turners Falls..176
Dear Enzo by Robert Viarengo, Heath...179
Asolo, Italy by Hélène Sullivan Walker, Ashfield............................181

Local Color #3 (2001)
Pieces of My Past by Allan D. Adie, Gill..187
School Traumas by Edna Baublis, Athol.......................................189
The Baby Carriage by Rosalie Bolton, Greenfield.........................190
Who Remembers "The Gables"?
     by Estelle Cade, Turners Falls..192

A Dog Named Captain by Guy Carey, Jr., Warwick..........................195
The Hurricane by Mary Ciechomski, Turners Falls.........................199
Ice Cream, Anyone?
    by Margaret M. "Pat" Currie, Turners Falls...........................201
My Story by Robert A. Desilets, Gill...203
Childhood and Leisure by Elisabeth R. Donaj, Greenfield..............206
Myrtle's Gun Shy by Vera Farris, Northfield....................................208
A Trip to a Wilmington, Vermont Square Dance
    by Edith J. Fisher, Leyden..209
Our First T.V. by William R. Fitzgerald, Ashfield...........................210
Christmas with Uncle Frank and Aunt Ruby
    by Margaret "Peg" Folgmann, Shelburne Falls......................211
When Rover Saved the Day
    by Jane L. Gilbert, Turners Falls...214
Halloween Capers
    by Dorothy G. Hmieleski, South Deerfield............................215
Playing Paper Dolls by Irmarie Jones, Greenfield...........................216
Reflections by Jean Kozlowski, Northfield.......................................219
Twenty Minutes a Day by Elisabeth Leete, Ashfield........................222
Lafayette, I am Where? by Warren LeMon, Turners Falls...............224
In Memory of Nellie Doran
    by Janice Howard Lepore, Greenfield...................................226
Trabili by Phyllis Loomis, Ashfield...230
A Snowbird Story by Lorraine Madden, Greenfield........................231
When Greenfield was a Seaport
    by Eileen Marguet, Greenfield...233
Ma's "Watchdog" by Marjorie Naida, Gill.......................................235
Little Church on Christian Hill
    by Louise Bowen O'Brien, Colrain.......................................237
Immunity, Love and Learning in a Red Brick Schoolhouse
    by Joseph A. Parzych, Gill...238

The USS Montague AKA-98
      by Nicholas Prokowich, Turners Falls..................242
Gardening by Leona Robert, Turners Falls..................244
The Picture as Posed
      by Charlotte Robinson, Turners Falls..................246
The Grocery Store circa 1939
      by Juliana Sivik Samoriski, Shelburne..................248
Moving by Doris Shirtcliff, Greenfield..................251

Local Color #4 (Published in 2001)
The Civilian Conservation Corps
      by Allan D. Adie, Gill..................257
Through the Eyes of a Child
      by Joanne Balzarini, Bernardston..................259
Learning to Drive by Edna Baublis, Athol..................260
The Necklace by Rosalie Bolton, Greenfield..................262
The General Store by Estelle Cade, Turners Falls..................264
The Henderson Ice Company by Guy Carey, Jr., Warwick..................266
Girl Scout Camp by Mary Ciechomski, Turners Falls..................269
Cornstalk by Genevieve Clark, Northfield..................271
The Boat Train by Margaret M. "Pat" Currie, Turners Falls..................273
Gratitude by Elisabeth R. Donaj, Greenfield..................274
The Picture by Rena Finch, Northfield..................276
An Apple Pie Story by Edith J. Fisher, Leyden..................277
Getting Juiced Up by William R. Fitzgerald, Ashfield..................278
Coon Hunting by Margaret "Peg" Folgmann, Shelburne Falls..................282
The Farm by Katherine L. Forster, Orange..................284
A Dog's Tale by Henry Gabriel, Northfield..................287
Pud: A Cat's Tale by Jane L. Gilbert, Turners Falls..................288
Heaven Continues to Open Up
      by Suzanne Gluck-Sosis, Greenfield..................290

The New Schoolteacher
    by Dorothy G. Hmieleski, South Deerfield..................291
That's the Way It Was by Leona Jarvi, Athol..................292
Living with a Limited Amount of Water
    by Irmarie Jones, Greenfield..................296
Josie by Jean Kozlowski, Northfield..................299
My First Cello Lesson by Elisabeth Leete, Ashfield..................302
Memories of When I Was Ten
    by Janice Howard Lepore, Greenfield..................304
Winter Squash by Phyllis Loomis, Ashfield..................306
The Radio by Lorraine Madden, Greenfield..................307
Soft Shell Crabs by Eileen Marguet, Greenfield..................308
The Player Piano by Marjorie Naida, Gill..................309
Castle in Wales by Louise Bowen O'Brien, Colrain..................313
Working on the Railroad by Joseph A. Parzych, Gill..................315
Spring Fling by Dorothy M. Persons, Northfield..................321
A Magic Spring by Marilyn M. Pinson, Bernardston..................322
A Childhood in Turners Falls
    by Francis R. Pleasant, Erving..................323
Christmas 2001 Perspective
    by Marjorie Reid, Greenfield..................326
Mother's Apron by Leona Robert, Turners Falls..................327
A Night to Remember
    by Charlotte Robinson, Turners Falls..................328
The Past Revisited
    by Juliana Sivik Samoriski, Shelburne..................331
Just Passing By by Doris Shirtcliff, Greenfield..................333
Tamie by Margaret D. Smolen, Bernardston..................334
Remembering Mr. Lyman
    by Helen Carey Tatro, Baldwinville..................335

A Bottle Full of Memories by Lynne Warrin, Northfield..............337

Local Color #5 (Published in 2003)
The Grocery Store by Allan D. Adie, Gill.........................341
Memory Lane by Edna Baublis, Athol..............................344
It's Freezing Out There! by Rosalie Bolton, Greenfield..................348
The Magical Surprise by Estelle Cade, Turners Falls.....................350
The Fire by Guy Carey, Jr., Warwick................................351
My First Car by Mary Ciechomski, Turners Falls.........................354
Gramma's Kitchen by Genevieve Clark, Northfield.......................355
Our Easter: 1942 by Elisabeth R. Donaj, Greenfield....................358
Yellow Butterflies by Edith J. Fisher, Leyden..............................359
Montague Memories by Alice Fisk, Greenfield.........................360
A Ride is a Ride by William R. Fitzgerald, Ashfield.......................366
Bill Daniels by Margaret "Peg" Folgmann, Shelburne Falls..............368
Spring by Katherine L. Forster, Orange..............................372
After My Phil by Suzanne Gluck-Sosis, Greenfield..........................373
Field Days Revisited
    by Dorothy G. Hmieleski, South Deerfield.......................374
Liederkranz Cheese:
Or Why Mrs. Furman Stopped Parking at the Loading Dock
    by Dick Hoyt, Winchendon..................................375
That's the Way It Was in the City by Leona Jarvi, Athol..............378
Radio by Irmarie Jones, Greenfield..................................383
I Remember by Jean Kozlowski, Northfield........................386
Surprise at the Iron Bridge
    by Florence M. Lanfair, Turners Falls..........................387
Death of a Refrigerator by Elisabeth Leete, Ashfield.....................388
Memories by Janice Howard Lepore, Greenfield..........................391
Memorials by Janice Howard Lepore, Greenfield.........................392

xii   *Contents*

A Gift was Given by Phyllis Loomis, Ashfield..................................392
Memories of the Depression
      by Lorraine Madden, Greenfield..394
The Pencil Sharpener by Eileen Marguet, Greenfield......................395
Life on the Farm by Louise Bowen O'Brien, Colrain......................396
Bedbugs and Root Beer by Joseph A. Parzych, Gill.......................399
Remembrance by Dorothy M. Persons, Northfield..........................401
Stars in the Water of Star by Dorothy M. Persons, Northfield.........402
The Iceboat by Marjorie Reid, Greenfield..403
The Brookside Maple by Theresa Richards, Orange......................404
Memories and Gifts by Leona Robert, Turners Falls......................405
The Book Bag by Charlotte Robinson, Turners Falls......................407
Memories of Play by Constance Sokoloski, Greenfield..................408
Musings by Virginia Taylor, Charlemont..409

Extras: Previously Unpublished Stories
2 Fer, 3 Fer by Edna Baublis, Athol..417
Orchard Days by Estelle Cade, Turners Falls..................................418
Getting My License by Mary Ciechomski, Turners Falls................420
Inflation by Elisabeth R. Donaj, Greenfield....................................421
Inflation Caused a Turning Point
      by Elisabeth R. Donaj, Greenfield..423
Night Flying by William R. Fitzgerald, Ashfield............................424
The One-Room Schoolhouse, District Number One
      by Jane L. Gilbert, Turners Falls..426
Comet Teaches Me a Little Horse Sense
      by Jane L. Gilbert, Turners Falls..428
Memories of the Family's Grain Mill
      by Jane L. Gilbert, Turners Falls..429
Going to Christian Hill by Jane L. Gilbert, Turners Falls................430

Contents xiii

Christmas at Apple Valley School in the Twenties
 by Barbara R. Graves, West Springfield..................431
The "Wash" by Barbara R. Graves, West Springfield..................434
Oh, Tithonia! by Barbara R. Graves, West Springfield..................438
Grandfather and the Model T
 by Dorothy G. Hmieleski, South Deerfield..................439
Prospecting for Gold on Maple Street
 by Dick Hoyt, Winchendon..................440
Enjoyable Journey by Florence M. Lanfair, Turners Falls..................442
Resurrection by Elisabeth Leete, Ashfield..................444
Lincoln School—1936 by Warren LeMon, York, Maine..................446
Home to Paris by Warren LeMon, York, Maine..................447
York Beach by Warren LeMon, York, Maine..................448
Never Rarely Often Always by Warren LeMon, York, Maine..................449
A Day at Greenfield Pool by Eileen Marguet, Greenfield..................450
The Dining Room Table by Eileen Marguet, Greenfield..................452
My First Job by Eileen Marguet, Greenfield..................453
The Front Porch by Eileen Marguet, Greenfield..................454
Childhood's End by Joseph A. Parzych, Gill..................456
First Day in Church by Joseph A. Parzych, Gill..................461
Never Too Young to Fall in Love by Jack Perry, Shutesbury..................464
The Parade of Pots by Charlotte Robinson, Turners Falls..................468
My First Job by Charlotte Robinson, Turners Falls..................471
Funerals by Charlotte Robinson, Turners Falls..................473
Our Blue Jewett by Juliana Sivik Samoriski, Shelburne..................473

About the Authors..................477
Photo captions..................488

Introduction: The Story Behind Local Color

In 1998, encouraged by my writing mentor Gene Zeiger, I applied for a Massachusetts Cultural Council arts grant to teach one, 8-week memoir writing course for seniors at Montague Senior Center in Montague, Massachusetts.

The first time the class met, most of the twelve participants came in hesitantly. I heard quite a few people say "I'm only here because my daughter/son *made* me come." Many more said "I'm not a writer."

Over the next eight weeks these shy seniors opened their hearts and minds and created some incredible works prompted by phrases or photos or family heirlooms. The more stories that came out, the more other writers were reminded of similar incidents in their own life and more stories were generated.

What struck me was how skilled and comfortable these people, aged 70-95, were with words and how clear their stories were. They were, in fact, writers and historians with a compassionate commitment to helping "the generations that follow" to understand how they had lived their lives.

As a grand finale I "published" some of their works under the title *The Stories of Our Lives*. Copies of these booklets went to the authors as well as three local libraries. At about the time I believed this project should be opened up to other seniors in our county I started getting calls from people asking where they could buy *The Stories of Our Lives*.

The next year, thanks to another Massachusetts Cultural Council arts grant, *Local Color* was born. Named to reflect what stories like these add to local history (like watercolor paint over a pencil sketch) issue number one had twenty-seven authors all age 65 or older. Supported by area businesses and individuals, *Local Color* has been published in a limited run each year since 1999.

Local Color: The First Five Years is *The Stories of Our Lives* plus the first five volumes of *Local Color"*(less three authors who couldn't be found to give permission for their work to be included) plus thirty-two stories that showed up on my doorstep over the years.

I once heard a news reporter say "A community is best described by the stories its people tell." I couldn't agree more.

Anna Viadero
September 2003
Montague, MA

Acknowledgments

Thanks, first, to my husband Joey and sons, Jason and Dominic, for their patience and understanding with all the "projects" I get myself into.

Thanks to Gene Zeiger for her encouragement over the years. It has been with Genie's help that I've come to call myself a writer and writing teacher.

Without ongoing support of the following area businesses and individuals in the pre-publication phase I wouldn't have the funds needed to print each year's edition. (✭denotes five years of support): ✭Connecticut River Internists; ✭Connecticut Valley Oral Surgery Associates; ✭Steven Goldsher, DDS; ✭Joel P. Gordon, MD; ✭James Grubman, PhD; ✭J. Lincoln Hirst, II, CPA; ✭Dr. Bruce Schwartz; ✭Howard L. Tice, MD; ✭Norma & Donald Tower; ✭Richard Warner MD; James A. Andreas; Austen Family Eye Care; Robert W. Averill, MD; Reneé L. Billel; Laura & Stephen Coelen; Alberta Cronen; Ervingside Library; Timothy C. Fish; Franklin Medical Center; Friends on Council, Turners Falls, MA; Greenfield Savings Bank; Helen L. Hall; David Johnson, PsyD; Suzanne Keller, DMD; Alan Langburd, MD; Ann Lilly, Librarian, Academy at Charlemont; Linden Hill School; Julie Lowensberg; Frederick D. Mesloh, DDS; Robert J. Miller; Montague Dental, Daniel Cohen, DMD; Montague Old Home Days Committee; Lorraine Mosca; Network Chiropractic of Franklin County; Jean O'Hara; Barry Poret, MD and Mary Jo Korfange-Poret; Ruth Ryan; Charles Saunders & Associates; Dr. Robert Speth; Mike and Ruth Swanson; West County Physicians; Dr. Mark Wisniewski.

Volunteers, like Mary Beth Forton (*"Local Color #1"* editing), Agnes Temesvari (*Local Color #1"* cover design) and Sarah Gavryk (*"Local Color #2"* cover design) have been generous with their time and talents.

Book sellers at Baker Office Supply, Boswell's Books, Gill Store, Sawyer News Co., Upper Pioneer Valley Visitors Center, Wilson's, and World Eye Bookshop have been enthusiastic, helpful and patient.

Thanks, finally, to all the people who see *"Local Color"* in their doctor's or dentist's office and acquire a copy of their own. Little by little your interest helps get these important works out to a larger and larger audience.

The Stories of Our Lives

❖ Kitchen Dances ❖
by Edna Baublis, Athol, Massachusetts

One evening back in the 1930s, I heard my mother tell my father that the Beroni's were having a dance on Saturday night and that we were going—all of us—father, mother, me and my brother. My father would rather play cards with his buddies, but my mother was a very good dancer. Light on her feet—always in demand. She used to tell us, with a bit of braggadocio, that she won prizes for dancing when she was younger.

The dance was to be held in the Beroni's kitchen in Athol, Massachusetts. The Beroni's house was small—typical of the era—a story and a half, but the kitchen was rectangular and ran almost the length of the house. It was a good sized room.

At one end was the entry door and at the other end two windows looked out on to the backyard where they had a garden and some fruit trees. The musicians set up in front of the windows.

They had hired an accordionist, Ray, and a violin player, Joe, who would play old Italian songs that reminded them of their homes in the old country. Some of the men and women who had good voices would sing along; soon the ones with the not so good voices would join in as they danced or sat around visiting.

The furniture had been moved into the other rooms and the floor had been sprinkled with cornmeal. This was done so that dancers' feet would slide easily and shoes would not stick to the linoleum.

Most of the younger kids would race around the house and sometimes we would dance with our mothers, fathers, aunts, uncles or the neighbors. I think most of my friends and I learned to dance at the kitchen dances.

As I grew older the kitchen dances stopped. For years I always thought how nice the Beroni's were and so rich to have everybody over on a Saturday to dance and have a good time and to have a glass of wine.

Now I know why the dances stopped and I know that the Beroni's were not rich. Prohibition had been repealed—drinking was legal. They had been running a "speak easy." They hadn't been giving away the drinks—people had been buying them! We had been breaking the law!

Thankfully we were never raided. It had always been enjoyable, sociable evenings. Now when we gather and reminisce, we chuckle over how innocent we had been.

❖ Lost Dream ❖
by Edna Baublis, Athol, Massachusetts

Our neighborhood was diverse. We were all immigrant families—all different accents. When a mother called for "Yonnie" we all knew that John's mother wanted him; Bonnum was Leon's mother calling him.

I grew up in an Italian Catholic home in Athol, Massachusetts. I was reared the old-fashioned, old country way. I didn't know I had rights. My father had rights. One look from him and that was it.

In my neighborhood, we had a coterie of six girls—all the same ages—and we would meet periodically to discuss future plans. From one of these meetings was born a grand plan. After graduation, we would all go to Florida to work. WOW! This was it! Florida here we come!

So one night at supper (if I close my eyes I can still see the scene!) I told my family that I was going to Florida to work for the winter with the girls.

Without stopping eating, not even breaking his rhythm—spoon to plate to mouth to plate to mouth—my father just said "No." When I asked why not he responded "Because I say so." End of discussion, end of Florida—no recourse!

At the next meeting, I sadly told the girls that I couldn't go. My father had said no. And one by one the rest admitted that they couldn't go either.

❖ My Experimental Tomatoes ❖
by Edna Baublis, Athol, Massachusetts

I have a small postage stamp sized backyard. In one corner I have a small garden—enough for a few tomato plants, cukes, zucchini and some flowers.

One spring, my middle son came home from the University of Massachusetts at Amherst with all his possessions accumulated during the year and a gift for me—nine small tomato plants which he told me were an experimental breed being developed at the university.

I was so pleased! I thought, "Well, he's finally growing up. How thoughtful."

I offered to plant them, but he said no, he would take care of that. And he did. I noticed that he planted them right in front where they would get the most sunshine.

Several days later, I noticed the plants had been moved to the back row of the garden and from my vast knowledge of gardening I told him it wasn't good to keep moving the plants. He told me there would not be any more moves.

He took very good care of them. He watered them. He fertilized them and they responded beautifully.

My father always pulled the suckers off the tomato plants and I did the same. I noticed that my son Terry did not do so, so I volunteered to do it for him. He said no—this kind of tomato did not need to have the suckers trimmed off. After all, his plants were doing better than mine.

Little yellow flowers appeared on my plants, but even though his plants were bigger—no little yellow blossoms appeared on his. When I mentioned this to him, he didn't seem concerned.

One morning, as I stood looking at the garden, a niggling thought entered my mind. The plants looked like "tomatoes" but something was different. Also, Terry was acting out of character. He never cared whether anything was planted or not. But I shook my head, no, and went back inside.

However I couldn't shake the feeling that something was wrong, so I went back to the garden. I looked, walked around the "tomatoes" and looked again. And then a light began to flicker.

I raced back to the house, got the dictionary down and looked up marijuana. The dictionary said "See hashish." When I looked up hashish, there was a picture of my experimental "tomato plants."

All of a sudden the sky darkened and I thought I heard state police helicopters coming. I envisioned the next day's headlines: "School Committee member and Gardner School teacher arrested for growing marijuana in her garden."

What to do? I couldn't bring it to the dump and we weren't allowed to burn. I burned anyway.

When Terry came home from work, we had a shouting match. They could have heard us two streets over. I never, ever received any more experimental tomato plants from Amherst.

P.S. His brothers and sisters knew what the plants were, but the sibling Mafia is a very close knit organization.

❖ My Neighborhood ❖
by Alice Brough, Montague Center, Massachusetts

While going through my desk, I came across a letter written to me by my sister Anna in 1987. It was about the neighborhood near Boston where we grew up. Anna passed away in 1993 at age 95. She loved to write letters and kept in touch with many old friends. She was interested in everything and everyone. She mentioned the ethnic neighborhood we lived in—Danish, German, Greek, Irish, Scottish, Swedish—except for French or Polish.

Our next door neighbors came from Greece. Very religious people, they attend the Church of All Nations in back of the State House in Boston. The woman of the house had been brought up by missionaries and became a teacher. I attended many Greek weddings and picnics.

Across the street were the McHughs from Ireland. They owned a monument business. Their two sons continued the business. Theirs was a very strict Catholic family as ours was strict Protestant. The mother never missed mass early in the morning. One daughter was to be a nun, but married instead. The oldest girl sang and played the organ at many churches. Another girl became principal of our little four-grade school. Another, a college graduate and talented harpist, married a prominent lawyer.

In our neighborhood, in the big Catholic families, there usually was a priest and in the Protestant families there had to be a minister, which was true in our family.

Downstreet was a German family who made sauerkraut for a living and with their team of horses, took it to Fanueil Hall in Boston to sell. One thing which was quite funny was the time the "meter reader" or "quarter collector," while collecting at the German home, slipped and fell into the sauerkraut. What a mess!

Another Irish family across from them had a son. He was a lovable young man who liked to sample, as my mother said, "the fire water."

There were many Scandinavian families—Swedish, Norwegian, Danish. Oh! I loved their pastry and their Christmas celebrations and their customs!

In those families, one mother's day of rest was to sit and knit after she had served her family dinner. We all thought it so sinful as we considered it "breaking the Sabbath." As little as I was I always considered it "the better the day, the better the deed." She made beautiful sweaters.

A Jewish family owned their own business. Their daughter loved to sing and wanted to be an opera star, but in high school she tried out for the Glee Club and wasn't accepted. She did eventually succeed.

We had only one Italian family where my brother had to deliver papers. In summer I admired their beautiful garden and their tomato patch.

Another big family like ours had their dream come true when one of their sons became a priest and did good work with the people in the Bowery.

We had a colored family—we did not say 'black' in those days. Their grandparents had been slaves. They were such fine people. The men all had jobs at the State House.

In a family from Nova Scotia, all the brothers were fishermen and when they came ashore they stayed in our neighborhood with their sister. We always had nice fresh fish. I think that is why I always order fish when I eat out.

One man had some kind of affliction. He was born with it, but still was able to go to work everyday. He carried a paper with him to verify that he was not intoxicated. We children would sometimes meet him at the trolley and walk the hill with him.

We had many neighbors from Scotland who came as weavers and wove rugs. There was a family from the South who received a sack of paper thin pecans every year which we bought for 25 cents a bag. You could never get this quality in the stores.

My younger sister who is eighty-seven and in a nursing home had fine childhood friends who always kept in touch. Now there are still three of them living.

In our neighborhood we all respected each other's religion and customs and for so many nationalities we got along just fine.

❖ Self Portrait, Part I ❖
by Estelle Cade, Turners Falls, Massachusetts

When I was young, in fit of pique
I'd loudly declare I'm too unique
For this family.
I know I'm adopted
But in my ear the Voice of Reason would whisper
Not!
You know you're the image of
Your dear Aunt Dot!

Not for me the dimpled smiles
And bouncy curls
Of little girls in the 30's;
I faced my world with straight blonde hair,
Green-gray eyes with thoughtful gaze—
Never Flirty.

"Shorty", "Short Stuff", "Squirt",
and "Live Bait", too,
are names that I was called by.
Always lovingly, it's true—Never meant with hate.
But inside me, till the day I die
I'll know
That although I stand
Less than five foot two,
I'm really five foot eight!

In this era of models
as thin as any birdy,
I find it hard to be grateful
For legs and ankles so sturdy,
Four generations of women so blessed;
My daughters and granddaughters say they're hexed!

❖ Self Portrait, Part II ❖
by Estelle Cade, Turners Falls, Massachusetts

The Bookish Life
Placing no faith in my good looks,
I sought a wider world in books.
Tales of whales—and fairy tales;
<u>Little Women</u> and Nancy Drew,
<u>The Five Little Peppers and How They Grew.</u>

Millay, Dickinson, the search for the Grail;
Wizards and heroes whose powers could not fail.
<u>Gone With the Wind</u> (I hated Scarlett);
The nuggets I found in quotations from Bartlett!
<u>Alice Through the Looking Glass,</u>
Walt Whitman and his <u>Leaves of Grass</u>;
Alice again, in Wonderland; Robin Hood
And his merry band;
ALL of the Oz books, Dorothy Parker—
Robert Frost, and my view became darker.
Yet Thurber and Ferber and the like, kept at hand,
Lightened my life with their humor and dash—
And no one could rhyme like Ogden Nash!
The Dr. Spock, Dr. Seuss, and <u>Good Night Moon.</u>
Sweet days that ended all too soon.

For my work I read and read—
Freud and Jung and Bettelheim and such;
And pondered, amazed as I clutched my aching head,
That I'd managed to raise three children
Before I'd learned so much!

My reading tastes remain eclectic;
The smell of a new book still electric,
And my idea of hell; dear friends, pay heed—
Is to be put in a place where there's
Nothing to Read!

❖ My Father's Hands ❖
by Estelle Cade, Turners Falls, Massachusetts

My father's hands were quite long and slender. Because he smoked I also recall nicotine stains on the fingers of his right hand.

He used to draw funny pictures for me as I sat on his lap. I'd name something and he'd do a drawing—a horse, a cow, a cat sitting on a fence. I, of course, considered this high art and thought he was extremely talented.

His hands were clever—he made me a wooden doll house when I was three or four (I believed for many years that Santa had brought it, of course); his hands were adept at mending a broken plate from my doll's tea set or gluing the leg back on a piece of doll furniture.

His were the hands that made shadow pictures on the wall of my bedroom when I was ill with measles and forbidden to read at all for fear of damage to my eyes.

He gardened—we had a large "Victory Garden" and I can see his hands weeding the rows of vegetables—or picking string beans. He greatly enjoyed fishing for trout in the brook on our land, and I can see him happily arranging his gear, preparing for the first day of fishing season.

His were the strong hands that sewed the buckles back on our patent leather Mary Janes, and the buttons on our heavy winter coats. I might add, the only two spankings I ever remember getting were administered by those same hands, for the crime of being mean to my younger sister!

The only jewelry he wore was his Masonic ring, given to him by my mother one Christmas, and his wedding ring—a thin gold band that was never off of his finger until he died. I can still see how it looked on his hand.

When my younger son, Jonathan, was planning to be married, his fiancée, Kelly, told me one day that Jonathan had not been able to find a wedding ring for himself that he really liked. I mentioned rather diffidently that I had his grandfather's wedding ring and wondered if he might like to have that to wear, and gave it to her for him to try on. Not only was he delighted and touched to have it, it fit him perfectly. He had his and Kelly's initials and the date engraved inside, to go with his grandparents' initials and date.

Now when Jonathan steps to the podium and raises his hands to have his band start the first piece on the program, I see his long slender fingers with a simple gold band on the left hand—and see once again, my father's hands.

❖ Ice Skates for Christmas...and Another Surprise! ❖
by Estelle Cade, Turners Falls, Massachusetts

How I longed for a pair of white shoe skates! I was eight or nine years old. Sonja Henie was the Tara Lipinski of my 1930s childhood, and there was a pond within walking distance of my home where we'd all go, if not to skate, then to run up and down, sliding on our boot clad feet. My dream, of course, was to lace on beautiful white skates and glide gracefully around and around on the ice. Leaps would come later, I thought.

Christmas was coming. Each shopping trip with my mother found me gazing more and more longingly at *skates,* pristine in their boxes. Surely one pair would find its way to my Christmas tree! Meanwhile, my sister Carole had come down with the chicken pox. Itchy and feverish, she could have cared less, for a few days at least, about anything to do with Christmas.

Christmas morning Carole was better and there, under the tree, amid the other packages, was a square box with my name on it which surely had to be the much-desired skates. I opened the box with great excitement and sure enough—there was indeed, nestled in tissue paper, a pair of white shoe skates! What joy! I looked forward to lacing them on and trying them out for the first time the very next day.

And then—what disappointment! My hopes were dashed Christmas night at bedtime when Mother gave me 'that look,' checked my neck and behind my ears and stated, "Estelle, now you have the chicken pox!"

Now, picture this: The next day *I* was the one hot and itchy and covered with spots and calamine lotion, but I sat bolt upright in my bed and laced on those shiny new skates. By peering out my bedroom window at just the right angle I could see my friends without me in the vacant lot across the street. They were out playing and skating on a little patch of ice left by a recent rain. At home I could only scratch (when Mom wasn't looking) and dream.

Ice skates for Christmas—and chicken pox, too! I learned that prayers can often be answered by the people who love you—but it was my dear little sister who gave me chicken pox for Christmas!

❖ The Day I Had My Tonsils Out ❖
by Mary Ciechomski, Turners Falls, Massachusetts

On a day in late August when I was almost five, Mom said to me, "Come, Mary, freshen up. We are going for a walk." I can't remember now if she told me where we were going, but I always was happy to go somewhere with Mom. Of course, we went on foot because we had no car and there was very little money for the trolley.

It was a nice day and we took our time walking the two miles down to South Hadley Falls from our home in South Hadley, Massachusetts and eventually reached Doctor Doonan's office. He was a country doctor and a real friend to everyone. After checking my throat, he and my mother talked about things but I didn't pay much attention to them. Leaving the doctor's office we stopped to visit Veronica who lived on the second floor of a corner house on Lamb and School Streets. Veronica, Mom told me, had been her maid of honor at her wedding.

After visiting a spell, Mom and I started home. It was then that she told me I would have my tonsils out the next day. Not only was I to have my tonsils out, but my older brother, Cas, and younger brother Fred, would also join in the fun. This fun was to occur in our home, with the actual removal of our tonsils to be done in the kitchen.

Preparations for the big event started as soon as we got home. The kitchen window, in front of which we were to be "done," was washed sparkling clean and my Mom scoured the floor and made the kitchen immaculate.

We were up early the next morning. Mom bathed the three of us and put us in clean pajamas and nightie. We did not have any breakfast. I noticed that someone had set up a bed in the parlor and I wondered what that was for.

At about eight o'clock, there was a flurry of excitement because the doctor had arrived accompanied by an anesthesiologist and a nurse. Mom took the rest of the children outside and Cas (my older brother) and I were put into the parlor to await our turn. My younger brother, Fred, was the first to undergo the procedure of having his tonsils removed. It took quite a while and my Mom kept coming to the window, asking me if Freddie was done. After what seemed like forever, the nurse carried Fred into the parlor and laid him in bed. He seemed to be sleeping so I guessed that having your tonsils out wasn't too bad.

The nurse then said, "All right, Mary, come with me." She took me through the kitchen into the back room where there was a bench and another doctor. Of course, I didn't know that he was the one to put me to sleep. I looked around wide-eyed and the nurse told me to lie down on the bench—not bad so far. She then put a cloth that smelled really awful over my face. I didn't like it at all and struggled to get off that bench. Then I got the bright idea that if I stopped struggling, they would leave me alone. This I did and I heard the nurse say, "She's asleep!" She took the cloth off my face and I jumped up off the bench—but the nurse was too quick for me and before I could get away she had me back on the bench with that dreaded cloth on my face. Blessedly I must have been overcome by the ether at that point.

The next thing I was aware of was that I was in bed with my brothers and that my throat hurt. Mom was by the bedside which was much better than that "bad nurse."

Mom asked us if we would like some ice cream. Now this was Depression time and ice cream was a rare treat, but both my brothers and I all agreed that we didn't want any with our throats hurting the way they did. Mom, however, got each of us to eat a few spoonfuls which did, in fact, soothe our throats.

The next day we were as good as new—minus our tonsils—and had some stories to tell our friends.

❖ I Remember ❖
by Mary Ciechomski, Turners Falls, Massachusetts

I remember the day my youngest sister Rosalie was born. I was going on eight at the time.

It was a beautiful summer day in July and I didn't know there was anything unusual about the day when my father told me to take all of my younger siblings (three of them) and go across the street to play. We owned the lot across the street and it was used for an extension of the sizeable garden my parents maintained. There was also a coop for the geese we were raising at the time. The lot was a playground for us kids and had a large swing that my father had erected—the seat was long enough for two or three kids. I think it was a seat from a horse buggy. We kids had a ball on this swing, but it was usually my chore to push the younger ones. The geese we had that summer sometimes chased my brothers and nipped them in the buttocks. A lot of the time was spent collecting the down from the geese which later went into a feather cover for my Mom's bed.

I had no idea that this was going to be a special day as I often had to tend my younger siblings, but at some point I looked up and saw the doctor carrying his usual bag, rushing into our yard across the street. At this moment I heard a baby's cry and just knew that the doctor was bringing us a new baby in that bag of his!

I got quite excited and rushed to tell my brothers about the baby. I said, "The doctor just brought us a new baby." Brother Eugene's comment was "Oh great! Now we will have another christening!" This was the Depression years when we never tasted soda unless it was at a christening when all the family relations gathered for a big party.

It was interesting that brother Eugene associated the birth of a new baby to a party complete with soda. It was also interesting that I associated the birth of Rosalie as the baby coming to us in the doctor's bag.

❖ Lilacs ❖
by Margaret M. "Pat" Currie, Turners Falls, Massachusetts

I attended a confirmation Monday evening. It was raining as I entered the church. The pascal candle was banked with lilacs from the floor to the center of the candle—so simple, but so elegant.

I told my pastor how impressed I was. He asked me how I liked the centerpiece and other florist arrangements on the altar. I had to admit, I didn't notice them.

The lilacs reminded me of graduations—especially of one in the movie "Our Town" and when Billy Bigelow comes back in the dream scene in the movie "Carousel." Again—simple but elegant.

❖ Mary E. ❖
by Margaret M. "Pat" Currie, Turners Falls, Massachusetts

I walked down the nursing home hall again. Mary E. had been there four years. As I passed other rooms I would wave or greet other guests as I saw them.

When I entered her room I was greeted with a bright "Hello Patsy." This was a good day. We could talk.

"Do you realize in a few days you'll be one hundred, Mary? Imagine a century of living! Let's discuss how we'll celebrate," I said.

"Just quietly," she said.

"How about a few friends and some of the staff?"

"No, just my sisters and you."

The next question: "Anything special?" I asked.

"Perhaps cocktails—little appetizers—no dip (emphatically!) Plain cake and good coffee."

Emphasis on the "good," I thought. Just like she'd want.

I prepared a small basket with four cordial glasses—a small bottle of chardonnay (didn't know how a cocktail would affect her), spread small crackers with a cream cheese mixture, purchased a small pound cake and one candle.

The birthday arrived—my two aunts—her sisters (96 and 89) and I drove to the nursing home. I carried the small basket to her room. When we arrived she was sleeping which happened often now. I arranged a large embossed linen napkin on her bedside table while her sisters spoke to her. No luck—she still slept. After an hour or so with no response I poured the wine into the four glasses, put the cheese crackers on my aunts laps on their pretty napkins. We all took our glasses and toasted the centurion. Then I put the single candle on the cake as we softly sang "Happy Birthday." My aunts both kissed her as I packed and straightened everything up.

The next day when I visited her she was awake and never mentioned her birthday. Neither did I. It was past—past is yesterday. Now it's present. Future—uncertain.

❖ Memories ❖
by Jane Daignault, Turners Falls, Massachusetts

I never dreamed after both our parents died within six months of each other what would happen to us five children. We were never told what plans they had for us. But before school started, it was all arranged that we were going to an orphanage. On the way down, the priest kept us amused talking about the animals in the pastures and the beautiful scenery.

We were too young to think of taking, or to have a guardian save, certain pieces that belonged to our parents. At that time, because of our young age and the confusion surrounding their untimely deaths, that meant nothing to us.

But I remembered one piece of jewelry. It was a heart shaped locket with my mother's initials on it. I don't know how I got it. I was very proud to have one precious thing that belonged to my mother.

While visiting our guardian in later years, in the shed was a bathroom which I visited and saw a large, framed picture of our parents. My father was a handsome looking man and my mother was a beautiful woman. I took the picture and had it refinished. I also had copies made for the rest of the family (three sisters and one brother) so each one had one thing that is precious to all.

❖ Memories II ❖
by Jane Daignault, Turners Falls, Massachusetts

I remember one Fourth of July down on Cape Cod. I was five years old, dressed in a beautiful yellow dress trimmed with black velvet ribbon. I wore black, patent leather shoes. We were warned not to take any kind of fireworks from anyone. We would be punished and have no fireworks of our own. One of the neighbors, a five-year-old boy, came over to our house and offered me a fire sparkler which I refused. He begged me to take one—he had plenty. I still refused. So he threw the sparkler at me. Naturally my dress caught fire.

I screamed. The neighbors came out. All I remember was someone wrapped me in a white sheet. I only had my panties and shoes on. Then I remembered a cooling salve being put on my arm by someone. Then a doctor spoke to me. I remember how cool my arm felt. The left side of my hair was burnt.

The doctor came every day to change my dressing. I was scared. Someone paid me fifty cents to keep me from screaming so they could change the dressing. I don't know how long it took to heal, but I do know I couldn't start school that fall and was disappointed.

To get back to the boy, he was severely punished by both his parents. I can remember my mother saying to them, "Please stop. He's only a child." I do not remember ever seeing that family again.

What a Fourth of July in 1920.

❖ Aunt Katie Because ❖
by Warren LeMon, Turners Falls, Massachusetts

When my mother was twelve years old her mother died suddenly of a heart attack. My mother had an older brother and a younger sister. Since it was not considered suitable in 1908 that my grandfather raise three children as a lone widower, an arrangement was made whereby the maternal grandparents, the Bartnetts, took the boy. My mother's Aunt Katie and Uncle Johnny took her into their home, and the younger sister who was then about four years old was placed in a home at College Point, Long Island, conducted by nuns.

This last placement has always seemed to me a very cold-blooded measure, but I also must bear in mind that I am not in possession of all the pertinent facts, and that it is better to reserve judgment on matters enshrouded by time.

Thus my mother grew up with her aunt and uncle at their home in New York City which was an elegant four-story brownstone mansion on the upper East Side. During my childhood she called Aunt Katie several times a week, and we visited 185 East 64th Street each week. Thus this woman who had been born in Ireland when Victoria was queen and Abraham Lincoln was first elected president became part of my early years.

When the Triboro Bridge opened in 1936 and we took Aunt Katie across it as a treat, I thought it was very funny to tell her that our car was going to ride across the tops of the suspension towers. She became very upset at this outlandish prospect, and my mother dealt with me later at home.

❖ Aunt Katie's Kitchen ❖
by Warren LeMon, Turners Falls, Massachusetts

The kitchen in my Grand-Aunt Katie's house was in the back on the first floor. There were tubs for washing on the left-hand side covered with checkered oilcloth. When I was very little I used to take my afternoon naps there. Next to the tubs was an ice-box. Its wood was honey-colored and it had sturdy brass fittings. The blocks of ice from the ice-house in the backyard were put into the top of the box and there was a drip-pan underneath that Delia would empty.

Delia was a tiny Irish woman who had worked and lived with Aunt Katie for more than forty years.

Opposite the ice box was the big black kitchen range which was lit by either wood or coal. The stovetop had round heavy metal lids I was cautioned never to touch. I never got over how different all the things there were from the kitchen in our home, which was modern in terms of the 1930's. In Aunt Katie's kitchen everything worked and was of the finest quality, but it dated from the turn of the century.

There was a wonderful wall clock which bonged regularly, and at four every afternoon Delia served the family tea and hot buttered biscuits. The back door of the kitchen opened onto a stone courtyard where I rode my tricycle and fire engine. This courtyard was protected on all sides by high stone walls.

❖ "Keep Cool with Coolidge" ❖
by Warren LeMon, Turners Falls, Massachusetts

The year was 1928.

My Aunt Bobbie had great difficulty in balancing the family checkbook. I surmised from listening to her tales that she really didn't want to be bothered with the figures. She didn't want to count it; she just wanted to spend it.

Periodically there were scenes, tears, promises, sudden transfers of funds, letters from branch managers, and statements of account. The name of the Lord was frequently taken, and, apparently in vain for there was rarely any improvement.

Except once. It seemed that everything was in order—no voids, no inky smudges or scribbles, or crossed-out entries. And then the phone rang. It was the telephone company manager for Queens County. He explained to Aunt Bobbie that regrettably the company had made a little mistake with her last bill, and he was going to send her a corrected bill.

"Don't you dare!" she screamed. "I just sent you a check to pay that bill."

"Well, Mrs. Martin, just stop payment on your check and write a new check when you get our corrected bill."

"I will not do any such thing! I just got my account in balance—not that it's any of your business—and you just keep my check and forget all about it! We'll both forget about it! And don't you dare call my husband! And why do you fools send out incorrect bills?"

So enraged was she that she tugged on the phone so hard that she wrenched the wire out of its socket and hurled the entire apparatus against the wall. In an absolute fury, she grabbed her eldest child—a girl of two—and jumped into the car and headed for New York City. She screamed at

Lulu, their maid, to watch the other children and to keep an ear peeled for calls from Mr. Martin. She neglected to tell her that the phone was out of order.

Crossing the Queensboro Bridge into Manhattan, she drove like a madwoman and got stopped by a motorcycle patrolman. To his mild inquiry if she were all right, she replied with a screech that she was a mother, an unprotected woman alone in the big city with a child with a raging fever, and how could she get to the doctor if every overgrown bully with a badge and a club stopped her in broad daylight? Why didn't he go catch a racketeer or a pervert?

The police officer wisely waved her on and went his way, searching for calmer criminals, a mild murderer, a placid pyromaniac.

When Aunt Bobbie reached the doctor's office he gave her a heavy sedative and had her lie down. Her child, who was perfectly fine, played in the waiting room, and the nurse called my uncle at his office.

When they all got home later in the afternoon my aunt and uncle agreed that she had done a wonderful job with the checkbook, that the phone company was a bad old phone company, and that perhaps Lulu—in addition to her other duties—could manage the checkbook. This quickly became another family secret.

Lulu did a splendid job, Aunt Bobbie signed the checks Lulu prepared, and Uncle Jimmy rewarded them both suitable for helping him "Keep Cool with Coolidge".

❖ My Father ❖
by Warren LeMon, Turners Falls, Massachusetts

It is not extravagant to say that I adored my father. Love was understood. He was enthusiastic, energetic, and intelligent. Time in his company was always well-spent. He loved to organize outings.

From the age of ten I went with him to football games, baseball games, prizefights, horse races, restaurants, movie palaces, and the Broadway theater.

With other youngsters and their fathers we went to visit fascinating places such as the New York Daily News plant, and the private viewing room high up in the ceiling of Radio City Music Hall, where the Rockefellers would drop in to catch a movie without standing in line to buy a ticket.

Penn Station was demolished in 1963, but Grand Central Terminal still stands. My memories of jaunts with my father are so intense that whenever I pass through the station I hurry up, because to linger would be fatal to my composure and peace of mind.

❖ Mother's Spring Cleaning ❖
by Phyllis Loomis, Ashfield, Massachusetts

I expect the weather in Erie, Pennsylvania has changed little since I left there fifty-five years ago. Being located on the lower fourth of the downwind edge of Lake Erie, that poor city suffered from very long, cold winters. It was common to have three feet of snow for Thanksgiving and to be shoveling driveways and sidewalks several times each week until mid April. Mother always made us new spring outfits for Easter, but we were never sure of wearing those clothes before Memorial Day (that being the official day to put away all winter togs and to don a bathing suit for your first swim of the year). The lake was always defrosted by then. In fact, spring had passed. Even the fruit trees had blossomed and summer was upon us. Once the ice was off the lake, summer came in a rush—hot and humid—leaving spring a very short memory.

Still, Spring was a busy time. We kids knew it was here because, on one particular Saturday, Dad did not go to the office as usual, but stayed home to spend the entire day removing the storm windows, brushing the screens, and after Mother had washed the windows, attaching each screen to its proper summer working location. Then, Dad's spring family chores were over. The windows were open on warm days. The breezes blew through the house, and Mother began her spring cleaning in earnest.

Each day, upon returning from school, we would discover another room had been attacked by a woman struck with "spring fever." Mother usually began in the bedrooms and moved downstairs only after all the eiderdown comforters had spent a day on the outdoor clothesline and were safely stored for the summer in cardboard boxes in the attic. The flannel sheets were replaced with white cotton sheets. Colored and printed sheets were a marvel that happened after the Second World War. Each child's own beloved patchwork quilt spread its glory throughout the room, for it replaced the eiderdown and a white chenille spread that belonged to winter.

Mother and Dad had quilts of the tulip pattern. I cannot remember the boys' quilts though I am sure they were as attached to theirs as my sister, Martha, and I were to ours. We had the wedding ring pattern made of materials left over from all the clothes Mother had made for the family. Our quilts had a beautiful deep, dusty pink background behind all the wedding rings. Mother was very apologetic about the dusty pink background. She was sure all quilts should have a white background, but she had had a large quantity of that material and no white. She felt compelled to use it and to apologize regularly for having done so. She made our quilts during the Depression. I suspect there was no money anywhere to buy even a yard of material, but Mother never would have brought her financial secrets into the light of day.

Martha and I accepted Mother's apologies and went on loving our dusty rose quilts as being very special. We spent hours finding fabrics in our quilts that brought back memories: Dad's pajamas that Grandma made for him each Christmas; my plaid dress that got caught on the chain link fence when I took the short cut to Norm Sitter's grocery store; Bob's green shirt that never did anything for his blue eyes; Martha's doll dress made of a daisy print, and bits of all those gingham jumpers from our younger days, were splashed all over the quilts.

When we were growing up, Mother always had a bit of hand work ready to pick up should she ever find time to sit a few minutes. She was a strong believer that idle hands tended to get into trouble. She always kept her hands busy. So, we all had beautiful handmade quilts. Later, we each had a hooked rug at our bedside. Then came the crocheted table clothes. Of course we always wore handknit sweaters, mittens, scarves and caps. Martha and I were taught how to create all the lovely things that Mother enjoyed making. My entire life under my parents' roof is underlined with pleasant memories of the women in the family working together, each on her own "busy hands" project, as we quietly sat in the living room and listened to the Saturday opera on our radio. Martha and I also worked while Mother read the book of the day to Dad each evening after dinner. For the reading, we children were not permitted in the living room for it bothered Dad. We sat on the stairs out of sight, but certainly within hearing distance, and listened intently.

Those projects of my youth have remained an important part of my entire life. I almost always have a craft project to fill in those "what will I do?" minutes. For years, whenever I picked up knitting or quilting I felt like I was back in that big living room with my mother and sister. Sometimes I can even smell the wood burning in the fireplace, and hear Caruso's beautiful voice crackle an aria through the radio static of many years ago.

While changing the personalities of the bedrooms, Mother attacked our closets and wardrobes with equal vigor. She hand washed all wool skirts and boys trousers, sweaters, mittens, scarves and hats, hung them outside to dry, and then pressed them before packing them in the cedar chest for the summer. The middy blouses that were girls' winter wear, and the boys' flannel shirts were stored in cardboard boxes. The same boxes were used for years. In the summer they held winter clothes. In the winter they held summer clothes.

On an unannounced afternoon, upon returning from school, each person's Spring bedecked bed would be filled with last year's summer clothing. That was the "trying on" afternoon. One after another, last year's dresses, shorts and skirts would be tried on, carefully examined by Mother's eagle eye and pronounced too small, passed down to a younger sibling, or possibly kept so she could let out the hem and a little bit in this seam, or dub them just fine— "you can wear that again this year." Always my best loved pieces of last year needed to go to Martha. Still, Jean, a cousin who lived next door, was four years older than I and although her clothing had rested several years in a box in our attic, some of them would be mine this summer.

When the upstairs was finished, it and we, looked and smelled, as if we no longer belonged to ourselves. It was magic.

Mother simply moved her scrub buckets, wall paper cleaner, furniture wax and enthusiasm to the first floor and began again in the living room.

The drapes came down and were replaced with tea dyed lace curtains. The dark gray mohair couch and overstuffed chairs were covered with brightly printed chintz slipcovers. The windows were opened. The breezes blew in, billowing the lacy window covering into the room in a delicate wing-like fashion that was far beyond the ability of heavy winter drapes.

The dining room and kitchen showed little visual change, but the products that were produced in the kitchen and served in the dining room were suddenly light and filled with dandelion greens, fresh asparagus and rhubarb from Grandma's garden. Heavy hot meals, gradually faded into memory as more and more fruits and vegetables matured in everyone's garden. Our food pantry was filled with empty mason jars by late spring. It was always hard to believe we had eaten a hundred quarts of tomatoes, fifty jars of jam, and two shelves of peaches, pears, plums, and strawberries that Mother had put up the last summer. By early June the grocery stores were selling fresh vegetables again. They were shipped in from down South. Days of wiggly carrots, parsnips, turnips and sprouting potatoes, were over and we were all delighted.

The last room Mother tackled was the back porch. We lived on that screened-in porch all summer and of course it was closed off and forgotten from September through May. The linoleum on the porch floor was old when I was new. It tended to buckle and cloud over with the extremes of temperature. Each year Mother worried about that floor. Would it last just one more summer? She spent many an hour on her hands and knees scrubbing, polishing, and tacking down tattered edges. She never would have been so bold as to come right out and ask Dad to think about replacing that flooring, but she certainly would have been a happy woman had he ever realized her desire.

I wonder if the people who bought the house after both my parents died are still living with that well cared for porch floor?

❖ Today I Danced in the Unitarian Church ❖
by Phyllis Loomis, Ashfield, Massachusetts

I danced in the Unitarian Church in Greenfield, Massachusetts this noon. I, Phyllis Loomis, almost seventy four years old, DANCED IN THE UNITARIAN CHURCH IN GREENFIELD TODAY!————————————I cannot believe it!——I DANCED——IN A CHURCH—TODAY!

There was a time, in my teen years, when I danced a lot. I loved to dance. I felt so light and dreamy in the arms of a dancing partner. The music could be live or canned or hummed by the dancers. The magic was there if we, the dancers, were dreaming—drifting—letting the music carry us along. We floated like a feather or a speck of dust just letting the music take us together, as one, into a very special world of lightness and oneness.

The Second World War put a sudden stop to my dancing life when it took all the men to war. Our lives on the homefront were serious then, too—filled with ration books, blackout curtains, double daylight savings time, and around-the-clock eight-hour work shifts.

When the war was over, the men came home. Mine went to college. I had long since finished college and was having and supporting a family while he went to school. He was "much busier" with school work than I had ever been. No day was long enough for me to reach the bottom of my "must be done" list before the day was over. For years there wasn't even time to dream of dancing.

Then one day, I joined a modern dance class and discovered how to be a floating piece of dust all by myself. I was in my thirties then with a working husband, two children in school and two still at home. One night each week, daddy read the good night story and tucked everyone in while I when to dancing class. When the Christmas season came around, two classmates and I danced, in black leotards, at a Sunday school holiday party in the local Unitarian Church. Things like that were not done by New England college faculty wives in 1957.

At last everyone was more or less grown up, and there was time some days to do something that was just he and me. We decided to try dancing. Now my man had a good heart. He wanted to please me. Remembering feeling light as a feather once, I wanted to dance. He had played in dance bands while in high school and had never once been on the dance floor.

We took lessons. How odd that was. I had never before realized there were steps one learned to become a dancer. For me it had just HAPPENED. For him it was memorizing, counting, thinking hard, holding tight, watching his feet. Ballroom dancing, for us, just didn't work. We took up square dancing.

That was better for he could hang onto his counting and I could let it happen. The rest of the square helped each of us to let our partner be whatever was right to be. We square danced weekly for several years. It was a solidly structured, merry-go-round kind of activity. Fun, but certainly not soft, floating, and other worldly.

My second husband had been into books and classical music while in high school and indeed for his entire life. He also was tall and huggable. He would have been a wonderful speck of dust to drift away with—if only he could have tolerated the music. He was such a great hugger. I often felt like a baby in his arms, and even loved watching him hug others—but we never danced.

Two weeks ago my son was looking for dancers to dance to his rendition of J.S. Bach's Suite #1 in G major to be played at the All Souls Church in Greenfield for their midweek noonday concert. A teenager and her mother volunteered to dance and before I knew what I was doing, I had volunteered to be number three.

We had three rehearsals. Things just happened. We got together and talked. There was no direction. There was only Bach, a musician and three generations of women. Led by Bach himself, we laughed and played and had a wonderful time just letting it happen. And so——today——I danced——in the Unitarian Church in Greenfield——and I have been walking on a cloud ever since.

❖ The Last Visit ❖
by Eileen Marguet, Greenfield, Massachusetts

You may have heard it said that a drowning person, before he goes down for the third time, sees his whole life flash before him. Whatever his age at that time his memory is very keen.

I couldn't say for sure if that's true since I never had a near-death experience. I do thank God every day for the gift of memory, remembering the good times of the past. There are unhappy memories too, but we have the ability to put them behind us. I do feel a deep nostalgia for a major part of my life lived out in one large house we called "home."

We built our house nearly forty years ago. I spent more than half of my life here, and I never realized all the messages it contained.

The day of my last visit, the white dogwood was in bloom. I wondered if the new people who would move in could imagine what it looked like when it was just a little stick plant near the front door.

Local Color   31

I was there to "do over" the whole house. My husband had passed away. All my children had left and I was getting ready for the painter. I had agreed to paint the whole place white for the new owners. I took a minute to visit each room and remember.

We had redone just about every room of the house several times. Each time we repapered a room we scraped off most of the paper. I say, "most," because in every room even though we soaked and scraped there were pieces left behind. We sanded and sanded but telltale swatches remained.

Starting in my room I uncovered the original paper that we had when we bought the house. It was so lovely I hated to change it when we did. I thought of how we selected the paper in the wallpaper store, our two little children hanging onto us impatiently. It had pink roses and purple lilacs on a white background. I still don't think we ever had any nicer.

As I walked from one room to another, each room its own story to remind me of the four children we raised there. The kitchen sink had served as a bathtub when the kids were very small. The sanitas had red and blue fruits. The counter was adequate for all the splashing. Inside the closet door was a list of phone numbers frequently called. Faded and old each number represented some person or incident.

All the ceilings were white. In the living room the ceiling had a scratch that had been spackled and touched up, but I could still see the scratch. It was where the Christmas tree left a mark. On one of our first Christmases, my friend and I made cookies with a cookie press. We decorated them and put a string in each one before they were baked. They came out great so we hung them on the tree. Christmas Eve night we were awakened by a noise in the living room. We got up to find our Airedale, Andy, had pulled the tree down and was happily munching on the cookies.

That was one Christmas Eve that was different.

When our daughter Sue was starting kindergarten we papered her walls in pink paper with dolls on it. We got a bureau and painted it green and cut out the dolls and pasted them on. We had a bed in her room that was called a three-quarter size—bigger than a twin, but not as large as a double.

Our little girl Mary Anne's room was painted turquoise. I painted huge daisies on the walls and made a yellow corduroy spread. It looked so inviting!

Most of the furniture we had at that time came from odd sources, like the curb. People used to put out really nice things. We did buy something new. It was a Boston rocker from Macy's that cost $17, and did we ever savor it! We tried it in every corner of the living room.

I papered the bathroom with a pattern that had blue and gray bubbles, ceiling and all. What a job to hang that one.

The boys' room originally had the Walt Disney dog Pluto. When that paper got shabby we did it over in a geometric pattern. Their walls had shelves for all their trophies and models and mobiles.

The first three of our children, Sue, Greg and Mary Anne, were born without any physical problems. Then two little boys never made it home from the hospital. I just could not get reconciled to their deaths. I cried for weeks for each one. I think the death of a child is worse than losing a parent or sibling. Somehow it seems so unfair that two little guys never got a chance to make their mark on the world.

But we had a son a few years later. We called him Jonathan, which means gift of God. He was healthy and strong.

The basketball hoop is still in the backyard. When we used to watch TV, Jonathan would run outside to shoot baskets during the commercials.

When I look back at all the things that happened to us I know God had His reasons. I've had occasion to help other young mothers in their grief, including two nieces whose babies died. Nobody could empathize with someone who hadn't also suffered in this way.

The house is empty now and I'm moving to my summer place in Vermont near three of my children. I was just talking things over with the painter, taking care of some details.

He said as he was leaving, "You have company."

"No," I said. "Nobody knows I'm here since I planned to be in Vermont."

"Well," he said. "There's a van just pulled up. There's someone coming up the walk."

I was surprised to see my daughter Sue with a new minivan. For a moment, though, I saw instead—a big red station wagon filled with baggage, kids getting in, our big dog, the cat carrier; my husband, Bill, saying, "Hurry up. Aren't you finished packing?" I was recalling instead all those times we were getting ready for our annual trek to Vermont.

I had to go inside for the last time to smile at the little faces looking out at me from behind the wallpaper.

❖ Ma Going Through World War I ❖
by Joseph A. Parzych, Gill, Massachusetts

It gave me a good feeling to hear my mother tell stories as we all sat around our kitchen table in Gill, Massachusetts. A cheerful circle of light fell around us, cast by the kerosene lamp hanging from the ceiling. "Tell us about the old days, Ma," we'd say, and she'd begin.

"My husband Franz (she was married once before marrying my father) have a good job working for school in Housatonic, Massachusetts.

He help teacher when boys exercise, play baseball and football. Nights, he works with plumber. A volunteer fireman, too." Ma said and continued.

"Mary born just before Christmas, December 11, 1912. All I can think is to go back to Poland so see my family—show them my baby."

My mother's parents had brought her to the US as a child, then left her as a teen when they returned to Poland.

Ma and Mary, my older sister, left for Poland in the spring of 1913 when Ma was twenty-one and Mary was about six months old. As she prepared to leave Franz said, "You must take plenty money with you. No one knows what can happen." So she made a little sack for the extra money and pinned it to her underwear and left for New York where she and Mary boarded a ship for Poland. It must have been the Lusitania, because she planned to return on it.

After two weeks crossing the Atlantic, a long train trip, and then a horse and wagon ride, she and Mary arrived at her ancestral home in the village of Bialka, in the province of Nowy Targ. It was cause for celebration.

"It first time I see my two baby sisters, born after Mama and Tata go back to Poland. Whole village come to visit. So nice to see friends and relatives. Everyone brings food and drink—open bottle and throw away cork. One fella' play accordion and another bagpipes.

"They play polkas and mazurkas. Mary fall asleep. We singing many songs. Happy songs, first—then sad songs. Everybody singing.

"At the end, they play Polish National Anthem—'Poland will never vanish as long as we alive . . .'" Tears wet her cheeks.

"Austria and Russia say there no more Poland—but Polaks say Poland lives in people's hearts.

"We have such a happy time. But in June 1914 somebody shoots somebody and fighting starts. I afraid fighting come to us. I tell my Mama,

I want to go back to Ameryka before winter storms make big waves on ocean. But she say, "Stay, stay. Winter is far away. It just a border fight—it will soon be over—you'll see. I stay another year. But fighting is worse."

On the first of May 1915, Austro-German forces launched an offensive to drive the Russian-Polish forces out of the Carpathian Mountains in the region of my mother's village.

"Such a crazy time. Everybody fighting each other," my mother said shaking her head.

Back in the US, Franz had all but given up hope of ever seeing his wife and daughter again.

One day, Ma said she made up her mind. It had been over two years since she'd seen her husband and she decided she was going back to America, war or no war. Her parents were aghast.

"How will you get to Holland to board ship? The Army has taken over railroads. You can't take a two year old baby and travel on troops trains filled with soldiers. It is insanity. You are just a girl. Who knows what can happen—men go crazy in war. And now the Germans use poison gas; there's land mines, machine guns and shelling. You never get there alive."

My mother gathered what possessions and food she could carry, pinned her remaining money in her corset and got ready to leave. Parting was heart wrenching. In their sorrow, her parents looked older than their years. My mother knew there was a good chance her family would be killed in the war. But even if everyone survived the war, both my mother and her parents knew in their hearts that they would never see each other again. Grandfather refused to come out of the house to give his blessing or even bid them farewell.

"Hair will grow from the palm of my hand before you get to Ameryka alive. I will not come out to see you and my granddaughter going to meet your death." My mother left that day, never to see her parents again. And it would be more than 50 years before she saw her two little sisters, again—by then, gray-haired, old grandmothers.

A neighbor gave them a horse and wagon ride to the railroad depot.

"The Army has taken over the trains," the station master said. "There's a possibility you can find a place on a train going to the front. No one wants to go in that direction."

A troop train stood by the depot. Railcar after railcar was filled with men in uniform—somber men headed for the front. My mother said she prayed to Mary, Jesus and all the saints to help her. She walked along the train until she came to a rail car where a soldier stood smoking on the platform between cars.

"Can we ride with you?"

"Come aboard," he said, reaching down to help her up. "Where are you going?"

"To Ameryka."

"To Ameryka! Are you glupa? There's a war on." He shook his head. "You would have to go through the lines—through the fighting. This train is going to the fighting. You would do well to go back to your village if you value your life."

The train whistle sounded a warning toot. The soldier found a seat facing Ma and Mary. He smiled to Mary and asked her age.

"She is not yet three years," Ma said.

"I, too, have a child," he said. He opened his wallet to show her. Soon other soldiers gathered to show pictures of their families. They held Mary, shared food and blankets. After many starts and stops, and long waits, the train arrived at a town near the front. Artillery fire rumbled in the distance. An Army officer approached. "All civilians—off the train."

My mother turned to her protector. "What do I do now?" she asked. "How will I get through the fighting?"

"It is very dangerous, but it can be done. There are those who will guide you through the lines for a price. But you must be careful. My advice—go back to your village before it is too late. But if you must go forward with your plan, hire a food peddler as a guide. They often sell to both sides and can get you through, if anyone can. May God bless you and your child."

Soldiers and civilians milled about the train depot. In the rest room, Ma took Mary inside a toilet stall and latched the door. She transferred some of her money from her underclothing to her coat pocket. If they were robbed, they would not get it all. Looking into Mary's trusting eyes, Ma prayed God would help her find someone to get them through the fighting somehow.

Outside, food vendors hawked food. Refugees swarmed in all directions like a disturbed ant colony. People trying to barter family heirlooms for food had few takers. Flinty-eyed peddlers looked on the ragtag hordes with disdain, driving hard bargains and demanding gold watches, wedding rings or US dollars.

One peddler selling loaves of crusty rye bread seemed to look trustworthy. She wondered if she could trust him.

"Proze pan, to ile?" she asked pointing to the bread. When he told her the price, she bought a loaf and struck up a conversation.

"Do you sell to the soldiers on the front lines?"

"Oh, yes."

"Do you sell to the Germans, too?"

"Sometimes. In these times, one must do what one must do to say alive."

My mother told him she'd heard rumors that the German soldiers and the allies sometimes traded food and even beer.

"It is said they sometimes do," the peddler agreed.

My mother tore off a chunk of the crusty bread. She gave Mary a chunk as she sized up the peddler.

"You have a family?"

"Oh, yes. I have a fine woman and three little ones. The factory where I worked—closed now. So I peddle bread."

"Would you guide us through the fighting?"

He shook his head. "Too dangerous."

"Please? I have American money I will pay you good."

"I can use the money, but there is great danger for you and the little one," he said. "I can bring you just so far. And we have to go under cover of darkness and wait for a lull in the fighting. But you must think about it. It is a great risk."

He paused and looked away. After a few minutes, he said, "I must be honest with you. I don't want your death or the death of your daughter on my conscience. You must understand, in war, men go mad. They become like animals, sometimes looting robbing, raping and killing—even women and children."

He turned to go. "If you still want to go in the morning, meet me here. We will talk."

That night, Ma held Mary close. She slept fitfully. Doubts began to assail her. She prayed to God, Jesus, Mary and Joseph and to Saint Jude patron saint of the hopeless.

In the morning her mind was made up. She would continue to America. She waited for the peddler having only the sun to tell time. Just as she was about to give up hope, he arrived with a large sack of bread slung over his shoulder.

"The baker was late getting the bread. This is our passport," he said with a laugh. "The soldiers love fresh bread, after eating stale crackers and food with bugs in it."

Ma tried to pay him the agreed upon amount of money. He returned nearly half of it.

"Keep your money," he said. "You'll need it before you are done."

By afternoon they neared the front lines. The peddler passed loaves out to soldiers in the trenches. With a few loaves left they crossed over into no man's land. He turned to my mother. "We wait until dark."

At dusk he roused them from a fitful sleep, and they began their trek through the woods. Suddenly—BOOM—an artillery shell exploded lighting up the sky.

"To the earth, to the earth," the peddler cried out. They dropped to the ground.

"I get more and more scared," my mother recalled. "My hands shake. I cover our heads and wait for bomb to fall. Boom, boom! Then everything quiet.

"They sometimes do that to end the day," the peddler said. "We go now."

Branches whipped her face as she stuck close to her guide in near darkness. She held the branches from hitting Mary who clung to her skirt, half running to keep up. They walked for what seemed forever then rested fitfully until daybreak.

When the sun finally began to show light on the horizon, the peddler spoke solemnly. "Wait here. If there's shooting, go back the way we came. Don't wait for me. Just go. Go back and don't try to cross again."

He walked to an open place on the hill, stood upright with bread sack displayed in full view, took off his hat, and whistled with two fingers thrust between his teeth. He waved his hat back and forth. Soon a returning whistle sounded.

"Come quickly," he said.

At the outpost, the German soldier wore a gray uniform. He wore a helmet while Polish soldiers wore only cloth army hats. Like my mother he was little more than a teenager.

"Just a boy really," Ma remembered. "Dressed up in a soldier suit playing war."

The peddler pointed to Ma and Mary, then began speaking to the soldier in a mixture of German, Polish and gestures, pointing to my mother and Mary and the church spire barely visible in the distance. The soldier nodded. "Yah, yah," he said.

The peddler handed the sack of remaining bread to my mother. He told her to walk towards the trenches she had to cross to get to the town in the background.

"Don't stoop or run—stand straight and walk not too fast. God go with you."

She walked, standing as tall as her slight figure would allow under the burden of her bundles, Mary holding tight to her skirt.

"I pray to Holy Mary—we have the same name, maybe that help some," she recalled.

When she got to the trenches, she passed out bread. She encountered German soldiers who greeted her with smiles saying "Dankue." Some gave her German marks or franks, but getting through the line, moving forward was all she cared about.

She saved a loaf for herself and Mary and the bread was soon gone. As she moved through the war torn countryside German soldiers were everywhere. At the depot in town a troop train filled with wounded

Local Color 41

stood waiting. At last she got the courage to ask about being taken aboard. The response was so positive she was taken aback. Along with troops she moved towards Rotterdam.

Once in Rotterdam, Ma learned the Lusitania had been sunk on the way to Liverpool. Dejected she walked along the waterfront with Mary. The Dutch freighter, Nieuw Amsterdam, sat tied up at the dock. When a sailor came down the gang plank, through gestures and broken English she told him she was headed for America. He took them on board in the steerage area for eight dollars, leaving her only twelve dollars for the remainder of her trip.

In steerage there was no privacy; sailors walked through the open hold at will. Brackish bilge water sloshed back and forth under the duck boards, Mary held her nose. Three more women boarded the ship and departed. Mary was the only child.

The ship seemed to wallow through the sea forever. After thirteen miserable days, the ship docked in New York.

Without the papers to disembark Ma had to enlist the help of the sailor again. After nightfall she and Mary descended the gangplank lugging their bundles.

After Ma bought a train ticket for Housatonic, she had just one dollar left. She blessed her husband for insisting she take extra money. And she blessed those generous souls who had not accepted money when she offered it.

When they got to Housatonic, the apartment was dark. The thought that Franz might have moved away alarmed her. She knocked on the landlady's door. "Ghost, ghost," the landlady screamed, slamming the door in Ma's face. After much coaxing and reassurances that they were indeed alive, the landlady opened the door.

"I so sure you both killed in war. I thought you come to haunt me," she said. "Franz down at the tavern. I send somebody to get him."

When they said, "Hey Franz, your wife's home," Franz took them to task for trying to play such a cruel prank. At closing time, Franz came back home to a joyous reunion. Ma was happy to be back with her husband. But Mary, who hadn't seen her father since infancy, was not at all sure she wanted to be around this stranger who was hugging and kissing her mother, and she wouldn't go to him.

"I so happy to be home safe again," she said.

❖ The War Years ❖
by Charlotte Potter, Turners Falls, Massachusetts

On December 7, 1941, my future husband, Ed, was taking me back to Norridgewalk, Maine, where I was a teacher in the public school. We did not say much when the announcement came over the car radio. We had hoped and prayed that this day would never come. Somehow one clings to the hope of avoiding war—especially modern war.

At first there were few changes in our lives. Eddie continued his work as a 4-H club agent and I went on teaching. In September 1942, I took a position in a small high school in West Paris, Maine so we could be nearer each other. The high school was then struggling against consolidation and the cooperation from the parents was total. If a problem arose with the pupils, a word to the parents was all it took for a solution. My schedule was heavy. I taught Latin, French, English, history and home economics (of all things!).

Meanwhile the war machine ground on, and Eddie was drafted and sent to Fort Benning, Georgia. We went through all the common experience of having no letters for several days and then getting five at once. Sometime during that very cold and snowy winter we decided to be married during his first leave. The leave came in May and the weeks before were hectic. Somehow I bought a long, white dress and veil, rounded up a best friend and two cousins as bridesmaids, planned a home reception (largely my mother's work) and tended to the myriad of details of a country church wedding.

When Eddie finally arrived from Georgia, two days before the wedding, we discovered that Maine would not accept a blood test taken in Georgia. So we spent the day before the wedding hunting down a superior court judge to waive the ruling. We finally found one several miles from my home. A few weeks later the rule was changed. Evidently too many young people found themselves in the same difficulty we had.

On May 21, 1943, we were married in a small country church. The words "In God We Trust" were printed in large letters above the altar. Everything fell into place—thanks largely to my mother's diligence. The reception at my home went without a hitch. My uncle was an amateur photographer, so we have a picture record of the events. Some of the pictures are faded now, but they have served to remind us all these years of that day.

All the omens were bad, however. We were married in May (supposedly an unlucky month), it was a Friday and it rained! However, the marriage has endured for 55 years, so we "beat the odds," we might say.

That summer I worked on my father's farm, driving a tractor for the haying crew and helping my mother with the picking and canning of fruits and vegetables. In the fall, I returned to West Paris to help with registrations for ration stamps and to join a drill team where I learned the simple mechanics of an automobile and how to change a tire. (Today I would call AAA.) All of this was in addition to my regular school work.

During the fall, word came that Eddie was in the hospital in Fort Benning. He was having difficulties with his heart—a supposedly harmless murmur had turned into a problem. In time, he was sent home with an honorable discharge. These had been hard months. It seemed that almost everything was rationed: sugar, shoes, meat, gasoline. Items like cars and refrigerators or washing machines were not available at all. Also we were bombarded with rumors of submarines off our coast, so blackout curtains were a must. And for my generation there was the aching loneliness of having our men in possible danger and not knowing from day to day what was happening. Gold stars began to appear in windows; women went to work in factories; and there were shortages of everything!

Eddie came home around Thanksgiving and after a month's rest began hunting for a job. With labor shortages everywhere it was not difficult to find one, but he was restricted to work that did not make physical demands on his heart. He became a county agent with the Extension Service in Washington County, Maine. This was as far "down east" as a traveler can go without being in Canada. The headquarters were in Machias, Maine.

We were fortunate to find a furnished apartment. I resigned my teaching position at mid-year, and with the boundless faith of youth we embarked on a new adventure.

Machias, Maine was very good to us. By now the housing shortage was in full swing and we lived in a furnished apartment, then a house and a then half-house in the almost three years we were there. The people were friendly and we felt quite at home, even though it was a five hour drive to see our parents. Our son, Noel, was born there in a small maternity home which a nurse ran in her own residence.

Noel was born on the day after V-E day which we had celebrated with neighbors, having ginger ale and cookies. In those days new mothers stayed in the hospital for a week or ten days. My mother came to help with Noel after that. He howled most of the daytime hours for about six weeks because we were told he should be fed only once in four hours. After listening to him for over a month, I decided that perhaps my mother's instinct was better than the baby books, and I fed him some cereal. From then on, he was the happiest baby one could have.

I remember one day when I was hanging out diapers a neighbor went by and, looking enviously at my washing, remarked that I must be able to get soap somewhere! Soap was one of the rationed items, but new babies got a little extra. The diapers were all washed by hand, since washing machines were unavailable.

In August 1945 peace finally came with Japan after the atomic bombs were dropped. Gradually our lives became more normal. Eddie took a new position in Rockland, Maine with a cooperative grain company. We acquired a refrigerator, washing machine, and an electric iron. The war years had left a mark on our generation that exists among the survivors still.

❖ My Inspiration ❖
by Leona Robert, Turners Falls, Massachusetts

"Hi, Mom! I'm back home," was the greeting from our brother Philip as he and his wife arrived from California on September 8, 1983. It was his fifty-third birthday.

Mother's nine children (six boys and three girls) had not been together all at one time for nearly thirty years. Also included was Buster, a cousin who had lived with us from his mid-teens and was more like a brother. Five of Mom's sons, and Buster, had all served in the military during WWII, and the Korean War. Gerry, our youngest brother had served in the Air

Force for twenty-four years. My sister Myrtle had moved to California where her husband, a Naval career man was stationed. Eventually brother Pat and his wife headed west, then Philip to escape our harsh New England winter cold, snow and ice.

Philip had pushed diligently for months to set a date for a family reunion at sister Ina's home in Leeds, Massachusetts. He, Myrtle and Pat, with their spouses all flew in together from California, for the event. What a great day it was! The weather was warm and sunny. Foliage was already beginning to turn color. Everything was so perfect, what more could we ask.

Of course, aunts, uncles and cousins were all included. They arrived with folding tables, chairs and food enough to start a restaurant. The only one missing was my husband, Phil, who was in a Greenfield, Massachusetts hospital with another of his numerous heart attacks.

There was much hugging, kissing and reminiscing.

"Remember when Mom went to a PTA meeting uptown and the neighborhood guys came in to play cards and we ate her homemade bread? Boy was she mad!"

Mother, then ninety-one, piped up, "You didn't even leave a slice for breakfast."

"What about the time we threw Myrtle out in the snow bank, because she wouldn't fix our breakfast?"

Myrtle added, "I just had on my housecoat and slippers!" (Myrtle never let Mother know during the reunion that she was being treated for cancer and had stopped her chemotherapy treatments to come home for the reunion. She felt Mother had enough heartaches and worries what with raising eight of her children alone. Dad had died when the youngest was seven months old.)

When he was a strapping six foot tall, sixteen-year-old, mid-November, Philip was stricken with polio. Not another case was reported in the state. Philip was admitted to the isolation building of the Franklin County Public Hospital in Greenfield and an iron lung was brought in and stood outside his room in the hall as a last minute resort. Thankfully, it never had to be used. The isolation building was located where the parking lot is now, to the left of the building, opposite the Greenfield Tap and Die building on Sanderson Street. There was a porch on the back of the building and we were allowed to go up and talk to him through the window. Myrtle, by then an RN, left her job as supervisor at Boston Lying-In Hospital, in the middle of the night and came home to "special" Philip around the clock. Friends of hers at the hospital would come in when their shift ended and put in time to relieve her for a few hours.

Eventually he was transferred to Lakeville Sanitarium in Middleboro, Massachusetts where he remained for six and a half years. His biggest complaint of the long trip was the ambulance never blew the siren for him.

For nearly nine months he couldn't even hold a spoon to feed himself. He couldn't sit up for almost fourteen months. But with sheer determination he showed the doctors, who said he would never walk again, that he would succeed.

When he finally left the hospital he was in a full length body brace, full length leg braces and on crutches. One by one he eliminated all of them and got down to a cane. He married and supported a wife. She had great courage and understanding to overlook his disabilities.

"Hi Mom, I'm back home," Philip cried that day. He must have had a premonition that pushed him to organize the reunion. We buried him two weeks later. Four weeks after that we buried my husband and the next day Buster.

Such a difficult period in our family's life but there were such wonderful memories to sustain us.

❖ My Earliest Memory ❖
by Charlotte Robinson, Turners Falls, Massachusetts

I was probably 2 or 2½ years old. I was in the small hall that was created when my father converted the run-around porch into a larger living room and extra bedroom. My mother was at her sewing machine in the dining room which was between this hall and the kitchen. The location of the sewing machine in the dining room was appropriate as my mother spent so much time at the machine making new clothes, remodeling old clothes for the next child and creating crafts and doll clothes.

If our kitchen was the center of the home, the dining room was next in importance. We ate all our meals there. We usually lingered long after the evening meal discussing the day. The coat closet within this room held more sewing materials than coats.

I had been climbing on the piano bench in that hall. The bench was usually brought into that area for someone to stand on while clothing was being hemmed. It was a flat, rectangularly shaped bench and I suspect that I had been delegated to return it to its usual spot in front of the piano in the living room. Instead, I had stopped to play for a little before completing my assigned task. It was a rather short bench although large enough for a teacher and student of the piano to sit comfortably. Because it was short, my lower legs extended beyond its limits. I had already practiced rolling over instead of off and somersaulting carefully and controlled because of its hard wood surface. I can't remember what happened next, but I began to wonder why I had this free time.

We were usually busy, even at my tender age. I have always remembered the thought, as clear as a bell, that jumped into my mind just then—"I'm wasting time!" I have always remembered that moment.

Even now I try to have something to do at all times, if only a pencil and paper for writing. That is why I have special "car books," crossword puzzle books, and plenty of pencils stored in the car—as necessary to me as an extra sweater or umbrella. Crafts and jigsaw puzzles clutter most of the rooms in my home. Parlor games and toy boxes are always available for younger visitors. And I am always available to help them use them.

❖ Sex Education ❖
by Charlotte Robinson, Turners Falls, Massachusetts

We really didn't need any additional or organized sexual education. We always had cats and kittens. We knew where the kittens came from and how they got there. We also knew that Ma would have ready the big milk pail, the cloth sugar bag, a needle and thread and the cover to her largest kettle. When all of the kittens had been born my mother would select one for the mother cat to keep and the rest went into the cloth bag which was sewed shut and into the milking pail by now full of water and were held down by the kettle lid until life was over. This was the method of controlling the cat population then. Later the bag and its contents were tenderly buried. My father almost always had an old tom cat whose main job was to continue giving my mother practice at the above.

I always spent a week or more with my Aunt Bessie and Uncle Ira each summer on their farm, often coinciding with the haying season. Once when I was there a cow came into season and was ready to be bred. Uncle Ira tied her outside the barn then said to me, "I'm going to bring the bull out now so you had better go into the house where it is safer." I knew that the bull was not going to bother me with that cow so close by but I went into the house anyway and I had a much better view of the succeeding events.

Another year and another "vacation." Because Aunt Bessie had no sons to help on the farm, my oldest brothers Theron and Sumner often spent time there helping Uncle Ira with haying and other farm activities. I was there when one of the cows came to full term. Theron greeted me at breakfast with this wonderful news and I could hardly wait to get out to the barn. The cow sure took her time in producing an offspring. When she finally laid herself down I noticed two little blue things protruding from her hind quarters. It sure didn't look like a calf appearing. A worried question to Theron eased my concern. It seems that cows and horses and perhaps other large animals are born forefeet first with the head nestled between the legs most of the time. The little blue things were the calf's hooves.

Watching that cow having a hard time delivering her calf and then seeing the little calf jump up faltering after only seven or eight minutes is a memory that I'll never forget.

❖ World War II ❖
by Charlotte Robinson, Turners Falls, Massachusetts

The prospect of being drawn into war seemed very remote in the mind of a ten and a half year old girl. I knew that terrible things were going on in Europe but that knowledge had little effect on me. I remember how angry my father was at the Lend/Lease agreement with England and Russia. "We are actually part of this war *now*. They are using our ships of all kinds. The ships are manned by American sailors. We are lending them all kinds of military and survival supplies. They don't have to pay us 'til the war is over and twenty years beyond. That means we will never be repaid."

I remember that Sunday afternoon in December during the Christian Endeavor Meeting. The conversation was "What is Pearl Harbor?" and then "Where is Pearl Harbor?"

Even Thanksgiving Day was affected in 1939. The holiday had always been on the last Thursday in November even though the first Thanksgiving Day with the Pilgrims had been in October. November 1939 had five Thursdays and President Roosevelt wanted to give the merchants a longer selling season until Christmas so he decreed that Thanksgiving Day would be the fourth Thursday in November. All of the New England states also celebrated Thanksgiving on the fifth Thursday. Many of the other states celebrated on the fifth Thursday. In 1941 Congress set the fourth Thursday in November as the only Thanksgiving Holiday.

Living in Stoneham, Massachusetts which is only about eight to ten miles from the coast, we were required to have blackout curtains in all of the windows—and to make sure to use them! This was because if everything was dark the enemy planes that would surely fly over couldn't take bearings to find the big cities.

Later, we had to have buckets of sand placed strategically within the house, particularly upstairs. Rumors were rampant of German planes dropping incendiary bombs all over the East Coast. I guess the sand was for stifling the ensuing fires. Certainly we wouldn't be able to pick up any such bomb after it fell through the roof and put it into the sand pail. Maybe the bombs were of delayed ignition.

Everything was rationed. Recycling then was most important. Even the silk and nylon stockings were used by the services as batting for certain types of ammunition. All of the metal packaging was turned in to the war effort. Books of rations sheets of various denominations were allotted from the OPA to each family for food, clothes, gasoline and tires. I remember that crushed pineapple, being a delicacy and from out of the country, cost too much in stamps for us to afford. In order to buy a tube of toothpaste one had to have an empty one to turn in because the tubes were made of metal. Remember "Lucky Strike Green has gone to war?" The green coloring material had some chemical in it that the war effort needed. People made great balls of the tiny amount of tin foil found in cigarette packages. Everything was saved. What had been the outhouse that was attached to the old hen house now became a locked storehouse with a big metal container for the gasoline that wasn't used on a daily basis but might be needed in an emergency. Everyone stored or hid the excess from a daily ration and then went and got the next daily ration rather than just a top off. When we wanted to visit my grandmother in Nelson, New Hampshire my father would borrow a tire or two from a friendly filling station acquaintance in case of a blow out which happened frequently in those days. When word got out that a certain store had received a supply of butter, cheese, meat of any kind or even peanut butter the lines soon formed and you hoped that you were near enough to the front of the line to be able to buy the allotted amount.

    I remember when we lost the privilege of saluting our flag. We only pledge allegiance now. Before Hitler's "Seig Heil" we always extended our right arms palm up towards the flag on the words "to the flag." Someone of importance decided that our salute was too much like the German salute, so of course we had to adapt to only a pledge. Since then, our hand has remained on our heart to the end and the number of words in the pledge has also been increased.

    Soon after the Japanese attacked Pearl Harbor, we lost our red sun within a white star within a blue circle, the symbol painted on all of our aircraft. Unfortunately our red sun looked too much like the symbol of the Rising Sun that the Japanese used to denote the spread of their empire. So, of course, someone in authority required us to adapt again.

Women didn't enter the services until later, but they did take over many jobs that were always considered only for men. "Rosie the Riveter" was one example. Closer to home, my cousin Dorothy Thompson had a job in a filling station in Stoneham. She pumped gas. Totally unheard of. Also, gas stations at that time were called "filling stations" because that was where they filled your car with gas. I still call gas stations filling stations.

Miss Spinney, my French teacher, applied for and received a commission in the army because of her expertise in the language.

Two things of importance emerged after the war: Spam, from the Army "C-Rations" and white oleo margarine with the little orange pill included that would surely make the oleo look like butter.

Local Color
(aka Local Color #1)

❖ Sunday Drives ❖
by Helen G. Adzema, Greenfield, Massachusetts

I was raised by my mother and lived with her and my maternal grandparents in Greenfield, Massachusetts as a child. I don't remember my father who died when I was only a year and a half old from wounds suffered fighting World War One in France. So, my family was really my mother, my grandparents, and a local aunt, uncle and cousin.

After my mother, grandparents and I came home from church on Sundays we would have our dinner. Then about two o'clock in the afternoon we would climb into our car and drive to Turners Falls, Massachusetts where we would call for my aunt (my mother's sister), my uncle and my cousin Buddy. There were seven of us in a six-passenger Buick and it was quite crowded.

As I was the youngest I had to either sit on Grandpa's lap or between his legs and lean back against him. I do not think that he was very comfortable, but he never complained.

One Sunday we drove to Vermont. There were roadside stands along the way which sold maple syrup and wonderful Vermont cheese. The cheese was cut to order from huge wheels of cheese and had a flavor you would never forget. There was also maple fudge with black walnuts that was really melt-in-your-mouth good.

Grandma was always on the lookout for a vegetable and fruit stand, and when we came to one, Mother would stop without fail. Grandma loved to select all the vegetables and fruits she would use in the next week's meals. If it was cantaloupe season she would have to have one. She'd always choose one that was big, juicy and ripe and then Auntie would have to have one, too.

Did you ever ride for miles with two cantaloupes in the car along with a couple of pounds of strong cheese? It was all you could smell, but as long as Grandma and Auntie were happy that was all that mattered.

On some Sundays Grandpa would take us to an amusement park in Holyoke, Massachusetts. It was called Mountain Park and what fun that was! My cousin and I would ride around in small battery-powered cars on a round track and when we were tired of that we went to the bumper cars. My favorite was the Merry-Go-Round. We got on the horses and tried to catch the brass ring as we rode up and down but we were too small to reach it.

One Sunday in autumn we started west up the Mohawk Trail to view the fall foliage. We zipped along until we got to Shelburne, Massachusetts where the cars were bumper to bumper all the way to Whitcomb Summit. There was no way you could turn around, so we had to travel about five miles an hour for miles. That was the last time we went viewing leaves on a Sunday in October.

On another Sunday drive we took a picnic lunch with us. We packed fried chicken, potato salad, cole slaw and my aunt made some lovely rolls to go with the meal. We had a thermos of milk for my cousin and me, and one of coffee for the grown-ups.

We drove until we found a place to stop and have our lunch. We put down a blanket to put our food on and all at once caterpillars started to drop down from the trees. They were the Gypsy Moth caterpillars and that year they were everywhere! You never saw a basket repacked as fast as ours was, but not one caterpillar found its way into our basket!

My youth was filled with love and caring. We always did things together.

❖ Sunday Downfall ❖
by Edna Baublis, Athol, Massachusetts

Now in Athol, Massachusetts, back in "the good old days," the Chief of Police knew everyone in town and where they lived. Chief Murphy would ride around in our one cruiser, driven by a patrolman. He did this periodically—checking out the neighborhoods. He even did this on Sunday.

One Sunday morning—either I overslept or I dawdled—and the girls went to church without me. This meant I had to go alone. I remember trying to convince my parents that I should stay home because I was going to be late anyway. My efforts earned me a push out the door and a "walk fast."

As I was walking to church, I was mad so I thought—I'll show them. I'll skip mass! And so I did.

I leisurely wandered around the other neighborhoods. I was dressed in my Sunday best—hat, gloves, Sunday dress—swinging my purse and looking at the houses and gardens. I was just meandering and looking and pausing when something looked interesting. I wandered until I thought that enough time had elapsed and I could start for home.

I was walking down Cottage Street which is two streets from where I lived. I was definitely out of my neighborhood here. I was in front of the "bird lady's" and Representative Cooke's house when the cruiser pulled to a stop by me.

The Chief rolled his window down (by hand) and asked me my name. I told him. Then he asked me what I was doing in this neighborhood. I didn't live up here.

I told him I was going home from church.

"Mass isn't out yet," said the Chief.

"I know," I said. "I left after communion." (I knew that sometimes people did this.)

He looked at me. I'm not sure he believed me.

"O.K.," he said. "Go right home and don't let me catch you up here again."

I nodded and started to walk a little faster.

I thought for sure I was going to go to **HELL**. I not only disobeyed my parents—I skipped church *and* I lied to the Chief of Police! All in one hour! On a Sunday morning! I was petrified! I just knew he would tell my parents and if he did I might as well die now because my life would not be worth living, but first I would have to go to confession.

If he did tell them, I never heard about it. For weeks I was very obedient—never causing a ripple. I just waited—and waited—and waited. I couldn't ask if they knew and they never said. I don't know to this day if they ever knew. Eventually I relaxed—but I never pulled a stunt like that again.

❖ The McShane Family ❖
by Alice Brough, Montague Center, Massachusetts

The McShane family lived across the street from us in Malden, Massachusetts. Malden was my husband's family home and we lived there before we came to the farm in Montague.

The McShanes had six children: John and Marie, then the twins Peter and Paul and a few years later more twins, Linda and Larry.

The two older boys had worn a path across the street to our house. They were interested in learning to cook so they would come borrow my little *Swifting Cookbook*. It had a recipe for a mix that you could make most anything from. Finally, tired of lending it out, I sent away for a copy that I gave them for their own.

Their parents had separated so they didn't have an abundance of things, but they always shared what they had.

One time a Sister of the church asked their mother if she would care for some children from a needy family for about a week. It turned out to be much longer, but still the McShanes shared what they had.

It was a few days before Christmas in 1948. My husband and I were living on the farm. I had to leave the farm to go back to Malden because tenants we had in our house across from the McShanes had moved. It being winter, I didn't want anything to happen to the property. I packed up a few things to tide us over until we could sell the house (sleeping bag, card table, folding chairs, coffee pot, etc…). I told my husband to pack up as we might be there for weeks. He got ready and brought with him my brother Arthur whom I cared for as he was a WWI veteran who had been in the Veteran's Administration hospital.

We got to Malden and settled in the day before Christmas. Our little neighbors, Linda and Larry, came over to our house all smiles and excited. "It's a surprise!" they said. They were inviting us to their house for Christmas eve supper. They took Arthur and I by the hand and took us to their home. What a surprise for us! The house was decorated, a table set with shiny glasses, beautiful dishes, and silverware. All on a pretty Christmas tablecloth. I was so surprised by the beautiful table setting and asked where it all came from. They said all these things were returned to John by his fiancée when she broke off their engagement.

After a delicious supper, the two older children left the house and my husband, brother and I crossed the road to our own house where we found, set up on the card table, a Christmas tree that a local florist had donated to us. Mrs. McShane brought over a big box of Christmas decorations. We had to separate the balls from the icicles and tinsel and other beautiful items. I asked where she had accumulated such a beautiful assortment of decorations. She explained these decorations came from the Holy Cross Cemetery dump. Back then people used to decorate the cemetery with wreaths and flowers every season. When the season was over the decorations were removed by the cemetery workers. The workers wanted a clean area on which to do their lawn work, so the decorations went to the dump.

Mrs. McShane and a friend had taken their children in strollers or walked them through the cemetery as it was a safe and quiet place. The grave diggers always enjoyed the childrens' visits and looked forward to the second set of twins visiting when they got old enough. One day Mrs. McShane and her friend found out about the treasures at the dump and decided not to let such beautiful things go to waste.

Mrs. McShane let me keep the decorations from that wonderful night. I had them for many years and each time I saw them I thought of the McShane family and it brought back so many happy memories of the kindness of the McShane family and the fact that that Christmas with the McShanes, in an empty house on Byron Street, was the last one we had at that address.

❖ My New England Grandfather ❖
by Estelle Cade, Turners Falls, Massachusetts

If I were to paint a picture called "Still Life With Grandfather," the background would be a soft mélange of nebulous figures, while standing firmly in the foreground would be my Grandfather Burton, the only grandparent I ever knew. Both of his wives died before I was even thought of. His first wife, my grandmother, was gone when her two sons were babies; his second wife died before my parents were married. My mother's father died when she was only eleven years old, and his wife, my grandmother, is a shadowy figure, seen in old photos, holding me as an infant. She died when I was about four and I have no memory of her as my Nana.

So, there is Grandpa—William Augustus Burton—such a dignified name. To his friends he was "Will." To many people in Ashfield, Massachusetts whose lives he had touched in some manner he was "Uncle Will." My dad always addressed him as "Father," which my sister and I thought rather quaint. To us, of course, he was "Grandpa."

He was a tall man, as were his two sons, and a burly man even in his later years. He had grey hair and a neatly trimmed, bristly mustache. I remember him always wearing a cap when he was outside and one of those grayish or brownish "grandpa" cardigans buttoned over a blue workshirt. Dark trousers with suspenders and black leather high-topped boots completed his usual ensemble.

I must digress about his cap. Once I came home from school and saw Grandpa sitting on the front porch smoking his pipe. Curled on top of the cap which was still on his head was our tiny black kitten. "Oh he got up there," he explained, "and I didn't want to disturb the little tyke."

My sister and I were fascinated by the fact that Grandpa was missing his left index finger. He explained to us that one bitterly cold day when he was young, he was splitting wood with an ax and didn't get his finger out of the way on the chopping block quick enough.

Also, when we would complain about having to go to the dentist, he would tell us about sitting on that very same chopping block (which was still in our woodshed) when the itinerant dentist came around and pulled any offending teeth with the tools he carried with him. The only novocaine was a shot of whiskey! Carole and I would grimace in sympathy and look more favorably upon our dental care.

Grandpa was born in 1862 and died in 1945. I wish people had been more into doing oral histories when I was in school, because he had interesting tales to tell. He recalled when horse thieves would come through town and how the men would turn out to catch them—and actually did punish "bad guys" by "running them out of town on a rail."

He had some wonderful expressions. He enjoyed listening to the Red Sox and the fights on his radio which he referred to as his "gig wheel." When it was time for his Saturday night bath (ah, tradition) he'd say to dad, "Well Charles, time to get out the scalding tub." A scalding tub is a large copper tub filled with boiling water that the butchered pigs were dipped into to make them easier to skin. He always referred to my bike as "your wheel" which is what old bikes with the enormous front wheel were called in his younger days. At one point we had one up in our attic. In the afternoons when we came home from school, grandpa would often say, "Well girls, did they hang you up on a hook today?" We thought this was quite funny, but in reading about education in the olden days I learned that naughty pupils actually were hung on a hook by the back of their jackets. Their toes would barely touch the floor.

He loved to tell us tall tales like the one about a neighbor who fed his horses sawdust because he was too cheap to buy feed. By the time the horse got used to the sawdust, it up and died on him. Carole and I were so gullible we'd say, "Really, Grandpa?" Then how he'd chuckle. He had truly blue eyes and they would just twinkle when he knew he'd put something over on us.

One thing he taught us was to be wary of a blue sky. No matter what season, the sky would be a brilliant cloudless sparkling blue, and Grandpa would cast an eye skyward and invariably say, "Pretty blue out, Charles. We'll pay for this." My sister and I would look at each other and roll our eyes, "What could he be thinking of?" But indeed, within twenty-four hours, we'd surely have a complete change of weather—clouds, rain, snowstorm, or something stormy. And today I find myself looking at a clear, cloudless sky saying, "Pretty blue out—we'll pay for this."

Although I was resentful at times that we left the city to move to the country to be near my grandfather in his old age, I've always been grateful that I had the chance to spend time with my only grandparent.

❖ Mother's Kitchen ❖
by Guy Carey, Jr., Warwick, Massachusetts

There are times when a special dream or goal becomes a dominating factor in one's life. Dominating perhaps for a fleeting moment or until the dream is realized. This is my memory of such a dream.

As a boy I often heard Mother speak of "her dream." It was to have a sparkling, white modern kitchen. She held onto her dream at a time when, in our small town, some of the households had only recently obtained electricity; a time when neighborhood children could swipe a chunk of ice off of the iceman's delivery truck.

I am sure father never really thought mother's dream would be realized. There were nine children to support not to mention the bad ecomony. Mother would ask father about remodeling the kitchen.

"Maybe someday, Mother, maybe someday," he'd say.

This was before World War Two and after the hurricanes of 1936 and 1938. During the hurricanes, much of the town's trees had been laid to waste, especially on the mountain side behind our home. What had once been a stately forest was now uprooted with trees piled upon one another. The fire tower at the top of the mountain blew down. What was left was a mass of twisted steel with the little observation house from the top strewn over the mountain side.

Portable sawmills and their crews moved to the mountain to salvage what they could. After the logging was completed, the Civilian Conservation Corps (CCC) boys were brought in to clean up what was unusable for lumber. My sisters, brothers and I spent many days watching the men cutting and burning waste. At night we would sit on our lawn looking with wonder at what seemed to be hundreds of little fires burning on the mountainside. It was great fun watching the fires and listening to the fire watchers as they sang and called to each other.

It was this combination of events that produced the opportunity for mother to start realizing her dream. Every year mother did much canning and preserving, not only of our garden crops but of the wild berries from the woodland around our home. We journeyed forth every year in a family group to gather raspberries and blackberries for our jellies and jams and the sweet blueberries to can so we would have pies during the long New England winters.

The clearing on the mountainside and the burning of the brush had made a very fertile field for wild blueberries. They were in such abundance and of such good quality that it was no trick at all to pick a quart without even changing position. This gave mother an idea: with her crew of pickers we would go into business selling blueberries.

She organized the family. Some would do the picking while others sorted and packed berries. Many days we would pick sixty-four quarts of blueberries, equaling two crates. Every morning Mother would take the old Model A car and deliver berries to hotels and bakeries in the surrounding towns. Sometimes if she failed to sell them all, we would go out in the evening and peddle what was left door to door.

Mother's savings grew enough, even in the first year, to begin working on her "dream." First a new kitchen floor, then a new white cabinet sink. As the seasons went by, blueberries were picked, packed and sold and more of mother's dream came true. There were gleaming white cabinets on the walls and the pantry was converted into a bedroom for my sisters. Plans were made for running a pipe from the spring and putting in a pump for running water. The icebox was replaced with an electric refrigerator and the kitchen range was replaced with a new fancier one, still a wood burner, though. The oven doors and warmers had porcelain fronts and bright metal handles. The front and side of the hot water reservoir were porcelain like the oven, and at each end of the stove, there were fenders that matched the oven door handles.

Thus, by working hard and using what Mother Nature provided, my mother made her dream a reality.

❖ Christmas Past ❖
by Mary Ciechomski, Turners Falls, Massachusetts

Christmas was and still is a joyous time—a time when we get ready to welcome the birth of the Child, Jesus, and a time filled with the fun and work of buying and wrapping gifts.

When I was a child we experienced the excitement of Christmas preparations in our Polish household. My mom bought or made, wrapped and hid gifts—one for each of us. Usually, it was a pair of mittens or long cotton stockings, but somehow, with money so scarce, Mom still managed to have a gift for each of us.

The day before Christmas was a flurry of work and excitement with Mom cooking all day for our traditional Wiegelia supper. The stove was covered with pots and pans of food—all vegetables and cereal dishes and of course, borsch, but no meat.

I can still remember Mom cautioning the boys (who were rascals) that if they merited a licking on that day, they would have a licking every day of the coming year. That, of course, made them behave.

Our Wiegelia dinner was impressive—so different from our regular meals. There was a sparkling white tablecloth with a bit of hay in the middle of the table, and candles on both sides of the hay. An opatek, or holy wafer, was placed on the hay. Each dish of food was placed on the opatek for a moment as a form of blessing before being served.

Before we started eating, we each were given a piece of the opatek and then went around sharing the same with our parents, brothers and sisters, wishing them health and happiness for the coming year.

We then sat down and proceeded to enjoy our meal one dish at a time, each being placed on the center opatek set on hay before it was served. The food wasn't the greatest—all vegetables and cereals—but the solemnity of the occasion was overpowering and we all had to take a little of every dish and eat it whether we liked it or not.

After our Christmas evening meal and after all the dishes were cleaned up, we all went into the parlor where we sat around singing carols—both in English and Polish.

I can vividly remember one particular Christmas Eve. We were in the living room or parlor as it was called in those days, enjoying our carolling. I sat with my back to the door that opened into an enclosed porch. At some point, I felt a cold draft on my back and realized the door was open. I closed it and went on with our singing. Again, I felt cold air and found the door open again. Before I closed it, I noticed a man on the porch. His arms were full of bags of presents. He explained to my folks that he was from the Red Men's Club in South Hadley, Massachusetts and had gifts for each one of the children in the family. What a wonderful Christmas that was! A gift of a toy and an article of clothing for each and every one of us. We really had something to be thankful for that year.

❖ School Days in a One Room Schoolhouse ❖
by Dorothy Clark, Charlemont, Massachusetts

My school days began at the Bozrah School in August of 1929. I was six years old. The reason we started in August was that we didn't have snow days off—we had mud days in the spring. Bozrah School was named for a farmer in Hawley, Massachusetts.

My first grade teacher was Miss Helen Sawyer. My second grade teacher was Mrs. Ruth Hawkes. My third through eighth grade teacher was Mrs. Estella Carter. I was an honor student and also called "Teacher's Pet," which hurt me very much. The superintendent was Mr. David Malcomb, who visited the school once a month.

The school exterior was painted white with green trim and the door was green. There were five windows in the front to let light in, two on the side and two in the back.

As you walked into the school there was a cloak room and a wood shed and then the one-room school.

The teacher's desk was in the front of the room and the desks of the pupils were screwed to the floor. First grade was in the front of the room through eighth grade at the back.

There was a small supply cupboard and also a large wood stove with a large steel jacket to keep us warm.

We had two large blackboards for the teacher to write on. It was an honor if she asked us to clap the erasers to make them clean. We also had maps that came down from the ceiling, like pulling a window shade.

In the back of the school we had a two-holer outhouse, or as we would call it now a privy. The boys were on the left and the girls on the right.

Every day we had to have a clean handkerchief, folded and put up in the left hand corner of our desk. We didn't have Kleenex back then.

We made our own ink out of water and a black substance, which was very, very messy if we spilled it.

We got our own drinking water from an old man across the road. We put the water in a crock and made folded-paper cups to drink it. When cider making time came, the old man would give us some. It was quite a treat!

Our school started with "Good Morning, Mrs. So-and-So." Then we would bow our heads and say "The Lord's Prayer" followed by saluting the flag.

We had many subjects: Reading, Arithmetic, Spelling, History, Geography, Health, Music and Rhinehart Penmanship. The music teacher came once a week.

We celebrated many holidays. At Memorial Day we would march down to a small cemetery nearby and decorate graves with wild flowers and flags. At Valentines Day we would make a large decorated box and fill it with our homemade valentines.

Christmas time was very special. We would have a tree and exchange small gifts. We would also sing carols, recite poems, or have a small skit. We would invite our parents, but mostly the mothers would come because the fathers would be at work. One year, our school caught fire at Christmas time, so we had to go to a neighbor's house to have our party.

We had an average of 18 pupils including State Wards. Our school day started at 9 a.m. and went to 3:30 p.m. We played many games. They were tag, duck on rock, hide and seek, hopscotch, football, and in winter, fox and geese. We would also slide a lot. We would have an hour for lunch and two fifteen minute recesses.

My husband, who went to the same school, told me that once a boy put a dead woodchuck in the teacher's desk. When she put her hand in the drawer, how she did scream!

I remember when the boys had to stay after school. They would sneak out the back window and go home.

At the end of the school year, we would have a picnic at Mohawk Park on the Mohawk Trail. We would have a hot dog roast under the pine trees and also go to the Wishing Well and throw pennies in. We would go to the river for a swim and go into the gift shop to buy small souvenirs.

As I was the only one to graduate from eighth grade, I went to Pudding Hollow School and graduated with the children there.

P.S. The superintendent and teacher wanted to skip me ahead in fourth and eighth grade, but my parents wouldn't let them.

I also went for four years without being absent!

❖ The Ladder ❖

by Margaret M. "Pat" Currie, Turners Falls, Massachusetts

I was on the front porch playing jacks with my best friend Mary. She was good. She had just picked up six and the ball. That was always the hardest. Just then my dad came from the garage after coming home from working at his railroad job in Greenfield, Massachusetts.

"Mary just made sixes Dad," I called. "Now it's my turn, want to watch?"

"Later, babe. Later."

Probably thought I couldn't make it. Mary was good. Then I heard him from the kitchen. He was crying. I looked at Mary.

"My father is crying," I said.

I went into the house through the dining room and into the kitchen. He was sitting in his chair, his head down on his chest. My mother was in a chair close to the table and leaning toward him, her hands on his knees.

"He missed the last step and the wheel went right over him," he said.

Who? I thought. Who?

My mother motioned me to go back outside.

Mary and I sat down on the front steps, the game of jacks forgotten.

"What happened?" Mary wanted to know.

"I don't know," I said.

"Guess I've got to go home. See you later," she said. She picked up her jacks and crossed the street.

I went back into the house. Dad had gone upstairs to clean up. My mother was preparing supper in the kitchen. She called to me.

"What happened?" Of course I wanted to know. I had to know.

Local Color 73

My mother took both my hands. One of Dad's best friends on the railroad, Tom Matthews, had been killed that day.

"How?"

The train was pulling into the station and somehow Tom slipped on the ladder, fell under the train and was killed.

"What ladder? Where was the ladder?" I thought.

This was my main thought along with my sympathy for Betty, Tom's daughter.

At school the next day, there were all kinds of stories and rumors. Betty's father was walking on top of the train—he fell off and six, seven eight, ten even more freight cars ran over him. But I knew different. It was because of the ladder.

That day after school, I asked Mary to walk down to the station with me. She couldn't. She had to go right home after school, but I had to see the ladder. I didn't know they had ladders on freight trains. What for?

When I got to the station there were no freight cars and only one passenger train. I had been to the station many times with my dad—seen many passenger and freight cars, but never noticed a ladder on any of them. The passenger train was going south. The conductor called,

"Northampton, Holyoke, Springfield. Change for Hartford, New Haven, New York and points west." No one was in the station. I was the only one outside.

"All aboard!" the conductor called, then he swung up the steps. No ladder there.

I went inside, looked at the clock. It was four o'clock. The couple of people sitting at the lunch counter had probably come up from the street. The ticket agent was just sitting in the office. I went outside again. I heard a train whistle, then a long wail, "All Clear."

A freight train was pulling in two tracks over: the engine, the coal car, the box car then another. A man was walking across the top of the train. I watched him, fascinated. I had never seen this before. Then I saw the ladder. It went right down the side of the train car with rungs or steps to the bottom.

The man reached over and lowered himself to the bottom and then walked across the tracks to the freight office. I couldn't move. I was fixed. It was my father. When he came out of the office he headed for his car which was parked near the end of the parking area near the tunnel. I called out, "Dad! Wait!"

"What are you doing here today?"

I couldn't talk. I just hugged him.

"I didn't know what you did—just that you worked on the railroad like Mr. Matthews. Please stop!" I said.

"Can't. That's what I do," he said. "Mr. Matthews just had an accident. Remember I always told you, safety first."

❖ The Homes of My Youth ❖
by Jane Daignault, Turners Falls, Massachusetts

My father died November 15, 1928 and my mother followed on May 4, 1929 leaving behind four girls and one boy ages three to twelve years. We had no idea where we were going or who was going to take care of us. For the moment we were still in our home together in the eastern part of Massachusetts.

After my mother's funeral all the relatives were told by our pastor that they couldn't separate us—that we were to remain together as a family.

On a beautiful day in September, the pastor, Father Riley, came and picked all of us up and off we went not knowing our destination. He kept us busy on our drive looking at the beautiful scenery, counting cows and horses grazing in the fields. Finally one hour or so after we had left our home we arrived at our first stop: Brightside Orphanage in Holyoke, Massachusetts.

My three-year-old brother was left at Brightside. He was left with nuns he didn't know and had never seen. I'm not sure he even knew they were nuns. I don't remember what his reaction was when we left him.

My sisters and I were then driven to nearby Mount Saint Vincent's Orphanage for Girls. We were greeted by nuns who I didn't know and had never seen before. I had no idea why we were there. No one took time to explain it to me. I didn't know that we were in our new home.

I stayed for two years and to this day have very little recollection of my time there. One thing I do remember is bedtime at the orphanage. My sisters and I were allowed to stay together. We slept in four beds all together in a row. At night the nun in charge would come, tuck each one of us into our own bed, and kiss us good night.

I remember in school how you could not miss an answer to any question asked. If you did, you were punished with a slap of a ruler to your hands.

There were some true nuns there, though, who I remember. Nuns that loved children and took good care of us.

We were expected to be up every morning at six for Mass, then breakfast, then chores, then school. I don't remember what I did for chores.

There isn't much I can say about my time at the orphanage. I think I was grieving the loss of my parents, so I didn't really understand what we were doing there or what it was all about.

I left in August 1931 to go to Worcester, Massachusetts and start high school at Ascension High with the Notre Dame sisters. There, I worked in a day care called the Saint Agnes Guild run by the Sisters of Providence. The Superior at the Saint Agnes Guild was understanding, helpful and caring. My work there allowed me to make money to pay my own way through high school.

Living with the nuns we had strict rules to follow. There were set times to be in, no boyfriends allowed. We were all girls in this orphanage, too.

I had four enjoyable years there.

❖ The Mail Must Go Through ❖
by William R. Fitzgerald, Ashfield, Massachusetts

It was the winter of 1933 or 1934 in Conway, Massachusetts and our road, Main Poland, was plugged tight with eight foot snow drifts for several days. The hill had been washed out each spring for many years until it became six to eight feet deep between the banks. It didn't stop washing until the town put stone walls alongside into the roadbed and covered them with gravel. After a big snow storm, a northwest wind would come and fill that canyon bank deep with snow.

The two small two-wheeled-drive town trucks could hardly keep the village streets open and maybe the Shelburne Falls Road open. So we, along with the rest of the town, would have to wait days until the small town Cletrac with its huge V-plow could ponderously get to all of the rest of the roads. Schools were seldom closed because kids walked to school or out to the main roads to meet the bus. Besides, they didn't have an efficient system of notification. In fact, Albert Cranson from up the road walked more than a legal mile and could have been bussed or paid to walk, but his father would have none of that. "The taxpayers paid for a good school. They don't have to pay to get him there."

Albert's father, Mr. Cranson, had been sledding the milk for the neighborhood to the covered bridge with his team and down through relatively snow-free fields. The tractor came up the sleigh track so he could buck the drifts going downhill. Behind the tractor came mailman Henry Wells carrying his leather mailbag, ready to walk the four miles in deep snow through Poland District to Burnetts Corner on Route 116. I suspect someone met him on 116. Sometimes his horse substituted for his Model T in the mud, but until there was a trail broken, the poor horse would flounder in the deep drifts, so Henry walked.

Henry did lots of errands for people along the route that were above and beyond the call of duty and would be frowned on these days. He brought medicine and groceries to shut-ins (Conway had three groceries, a meat market and a druggist in the thirties). I know he brought home a lot of apples, potatoes and all kinds of produce. He carried the neighborhood cabbage shredder, the lard press and even the dehorners with nary a postage stamp. I still have that cabbage shredder, though I'm sure no one has made sauerkraut with it for more than fifty years.

Henry lived in the third home on the left, up on Elm Street, in a small house that must have been crowded with his wife and seven kids. They kept their horse in a small barn. This was during the Depression and he must have considered himself lucky to have a steady job. Nonetheless, I imagine he performed all of those services out of old fashioned conscientiousness and because of the fact that everyone pulled together then in time of need.

❖ A Hunting She Will Go ❖

by Margaret "Peg" Folgmann, Shelburne Falls, Massachusetts

The usual open season for deer hunting in November 1924 brought much excitement in anticipation of the hunt before the first day. As a child, I ate more venison than beef. It was expected that the season would surely prove successful. There was almost no waste in using the deer meat. Even the neck was canned to make the best mince pies ever.

What makes memories of this particular deer season so special? My dear mother. She registered interest in hunting and asked my father if she might join the family men-folk for the hunt.

"Unheard of, it's no place for a woman," my father said.

This was not the answer Mom wanted. She was determined. Unbeknownst to my father, she applied for a hunting license, collected some old World War I uniform pants, made sure she had a "hired girl" for us and set the alarm to go off soon after she knew that my father would be long gone. You see, it is very important to get into the woods before daybreak for a successful hunt.

My mother had her own little Model T Ford Coupe, and she headed for Mount Toby in nearby Sunderland, Massachusetts with her sixteen gauge double barreled shotgun and enough shells along beside her.

My mother followed the rules and regulations of the hunt, and soon, by mid-morning, her prize made an appearance. Taking aim, she fired, taking down her first deer. That was seventy-three years ago. I was seven. She pinned her hunting license to the deer's ear and headed down the mountain to a nearby farm. The farmer helped her dress the deer, pack the cavity with snow and drag it down the mountain and into his Model T pickup truck and home.

When my father came home that night, tired and after a day of not even a close look, he asked whose deer hung outside the shed. Naturally, he did not accept Mother's answer. He was finally convinced as the conversation continued. From then on, she was welcome to tag along on yearly hunts.

My mother had taken a course in taxidermy and so she mounted her own deer head. She developed a shoulder problem before she was through, however, and since the shoulder problem persisted, the deer head was finished by someone else. Mother tanned the hide, though.

That old eight point buck hung on the wall in our living room with the sixteen gauge shotgun resting on the mounted hooves below. This was a constant reminder of my mother's skill and determination.

The deerhead now hangs in the home of her great grandson and family.

❖ Life in Orange, Massachusetts ❖
by Katherine L. Forster, Orange, Massachusetts

I was born on February 15, 1907 in Chico, California in a house built by dad, Albert Foster. My dad, mother Sue, and I lived there until 1909 when we rode the "choo-choo" train back to their native Orange, Massachusetts on tracks that my father had helped lay all the way to the Pacific Coast.

In Orange we moved into the house that my Grandpa Foster had built for his family just before he walked to Vermont to join their militia to fight the Civil War.

That home in Orange became my home through my school years.

When I was a freshman, my neighbor, Betty Campbell, who was a senior, invited me to ride with her and her father who was driving some high school baseball players to an out-of-town game. There were no buses in those days. It was 1921 and the Orange High School (OHS) baseball team were Franklin County Champions. On that ride the team captain, Clifford Forster, kissed my cheek as we went under the covered bridge in Millers Falls. What a thrill! He being a senior and me a freshman! Later, after graduation services which were held on a platform erected on the OHS lawn, the same Clifford Forster walked me home. We were married in August, 1926 and moved to the farm in Orange that Clifford had bought in January of that year.

In spite of there being no modern conveniences, I enjoyed every minute in that big ten room house. There were two barns—a horse barn and a long cow barn. At first our wedding gifts of Dinah, the horse, and Molly, the cow, were the only occupants. In time, though, the long cow barn was full of cows and Clifford was supplying their milk to customers in Orange. He also supplied half-pint bottles of milk to the elementary schools.

When the Depression hit, many milk customers were unable to pay. However, our family, which had added "Jack" (Clifford, Jr.) in 1927 and "Jill" (Suzanne) in 1929, was able to have sufficient food, thanks to our farm. The farm provided maple syrup, raspberries, Baldwin apples and vegetables as well as plenty of dairy products.

The development of the Quabbin Reservoir brought an asset to the farm. The relocation of many homes resulted in an electric pole being built up Chestnut Hill through to New Salem. In 1936 our farm saw its first electric lights!

That joyous occasion was followed two years later by a tragedy—the 1938 hurricane. The roof of the cow barn shifted in the winds and the barn might have gone, too, had the cows not been in it at the time.

That disaster began a three-year downward financial spiral: the barn roof could not be repaired; the hired man of twelve years left to go to work in a defense factory; we had two poor hay crops in a row and, in 1941, the town passed an ordinance that only pasteurized milk could be sold in town. So, in the fall of 1941, the milk route herd was sold and Clifford went to work in the foundry at Leavitt Machine Company.

Work was plentiful during World War Two, but gasoline, sugar, lard and so many other items were scarce so there was rationing. There were no school buses for the high school, so Jack and Jill had to find other means of transportation or walk the three miles to school.

Then our big surprise came in the summer of 1944 when our second daughter Dorothy was born.

After the war, Clifford's and my efforts were concentrated on getting our three children through college. This was ultimately accomplished with Clifford, Jr. becoming an electrical engineer; Suzanne, a school teacher; and Dorothy a pediatric nurse.

Our biggest joy has been the eight grandchildren who all enjoy visiting "The Farm" as our place on Chestnut Hill is now known.

Though I lost Clifford in 1985 at the age of eighty-three, I'm kept young by the visits to "The Farm" by thirteen great-grandchildren ranging in age from two to sixteen.

❖ One Hometown Through a Child's Eyes ❖
by Phyllis Hamilton, Turners Falls, Massachusetts

We moved from Barre, Massachusetts to Westboro, Massachusetts in 1938. Both were small, rural New England towns. Pretty typical of the time with farms and orchards a short distance in any direction from the small center of the town. Well, on second thought Westboro wasn't so typical. Out of a town population of 8,000, half were mental hospital patients and reform school boys from their respective facilities in town.

Parts of the mental hospital must have been pretty nice to live in. When one of our local doctors had a nervous breakdown he went there to recover and decided to stay. He lived there until he died.

My girlfriend's father worked there in the kitchen and had patients for helpers. When we visited him once we couldn't tell they were patients. He did tell us they weren't allowed to work in the kitchen when there was a full moon, but he didn't explain why.

Once a week some of the patients were brought into town for a little shopping at our Woolworth's and to see a movie. The patients were certainly funny looking based on the prim and proper standards for dress and conduct in the mid 1940s. Their makeup could be anywhere on their faces and sometimes even their hands. It was usually lavishly applied. One lady made round red circles on her cheeks with lipstick. They wore prints and plaids together and ankle socks with high heels. We had heard about one lady who loved fur and would sew little pieces of it onto her clothes. She put strips of fur up the seams of her nylon stockings, and on her shoes. Of course her dresses got their share of decorations. She'd even fastened some onto her hair with bobby pins.

Our town offered summer theatre with live performances in the Town Hall auditorium. Actors and actresses came from Hollywood to great fanfare. They'd arrive in town sitting on the top of the back seat of a convertible waving to the crowd gathered to watch the festivities. It was like a small parade. There might have been a band.

The Hollywood star or starlet would alight in front of the Town Hall to be greeted by town dignitaries and honored in some way, probably with speeches, before being escorted past the Baptist Church to the Merrie

M where they would stay. The Merrie M was the equivalent of a Bed & Breakfast except that three meals a day were served in the dining room.

Some of the famous people who came were C. Aubrey Smith, and Gloria Stuart. (Ms. Stuart played the old lady in the recent blockbuster movie *Titanic*.) There were others whose identity is lost to memory as are the plays they performed. I do remember, though, that the most normal looking star in the troupe was C. Aubrey Smith. The rest, including the crew, wore heavy makeup and outlandish clothes (by Westboro standards) all hours of the day. For example, one short chubby man wore khaki shorts, argyle knee socks, sandals, a sweater that clashed with the socks. On top of his head he wore a plaid tam o'shanter.

On the days the hospital patients came into town and the theater people were out for a stroll it was hard to tell some of them apart.

❖ The Great Depression ❖
by Irmarie Jones, Greenfield, Massachusetts

Less than half of the Americans now alive lived during the Great Depression of the 1930s.

For me, at five years of age, the "Depression" meant that my father was home a lot as he was dropped as a salesman after fifteen years with Norton Grinding Wheel Co. of Worcester.

In 1930 there were "relief" payments. My mother and father never applied. My father managed to find one salesman job after another, never making ends meet.

Mom babysat for fifty cents an afternoon or evening. Somehow from that income she managed to give my sister and me piano lessons and dancing lessons, experiences she felt were essential to a well-rounded life.

Because our mother could sew beautifully, we always had lovely clothes. She could take women's discarded clothes and use the cloth to make dresses for my sister Maydee and me.

Shoes were another story. We had one pair of shoes a year for school. By spring our toes were cramped. Then, in the summer, we would get cheap sneakers. Does anyone remember the rubber soles that you could buy in Woolworth's? You'd put them on with rubber cement. When we had holes in our soles, Daddy would keep putting on those rubber things, which often would begin coming off when we were playing.

One of my favorite lunches was bread dipped in molasses, with plenty of milk to drink. Now that I think back to it, I'm sure that was probably all my mother had in the house. Years later she told me about the day when there was no money at all. She was doing the wash and crying the whole time; when she finished and emptied the washer, she found a dime in the bottom and sent one of us to the store for a loaf of bread. When Daddy came home that night, he had a little money, too.

I remember a scissors grinder who came through the neighborhood, his sharpening tools strapped to his back. Mom bartered with him. He kept her scissors sharp and she fed him lunch on the backs steps—a bowl of homemade soup and a piece of bread.

Oleo margarine was introduced as a cheap substitute for butter. Oleo was sold in white pound blocks with a little envelope of yellow food coloring included. My mother would set the block out to soften and then some family member would have the chore of mixing in the food coloring. "Do it evenly to make it look like butter," was my mom's admonition. She didn't want neighbors to know she used oleo. I know now that they used oleo, too.

There were no visits to the dentist unless absolutely necessary. When my sister had to have seven of her baby teeth pulled, my mother took her to a nearby dentist and he never sent a bill. She cried a little to think of how thoughtful he had been. Oh, we had fun, all right. There were the kick-the-can or run-sheep-run games at night with the whole neighborhood, all ages playing together from kindergartners to junior high age kids. We played hopscotch, jump rope and jacks. We roller skated. I never could have the bicycle I wanted, but sometimes I could ride one of my friends' bikes.

And then there were the movies, another whole story in itself. If we had a dime, a Saturday afternoon could mean one episode of a continuing serial, a cartoon, plus a double feature. It took a whole afternoon.

Radio was just as popular as television is today. Everyday, just before supper, we would sit spellbound, often with friends, as we listened to the fifteen minute dramas of "Jack Armstrong, the All-American Boy," "Little Orphan Annie," and "Buck Rogers." You didn't dare miss one day, even though the adventures moved at a slow pace, because, all of a sudden, in one episode a mystery would be solved or an adventure would end and the program would move on to a new event.

On Sunday evenings, my folks, my sister and I would play Parchese, and listen to Joe Penner or Jack Benny or Eddie Cantor before we went to bed. Fred Allen and Fibber McGee & Molly were on in the middle of the week. Sometimes my sister Maydee and I would roll on the floor laughing, they were so funny.

The hardships of the Depression certainly shaped my life, but I'm not sure it was not a good influence.

❖ A Dream ❖
by Elisabeth Leete, Ashfield, Massachusetts

"So, my child, what have you done with the life I gave you?"

In my dream, my father is lying in an open casket, wearing the black robe and white bow of a Calvinist minister. I had seen him dressed like this so many times during the first nine years of my life, as he stood in the pulpit of the golden church in Geneva, Switzerland. His curly hair, pulled back from his tall forehead, rests on the pillow in this dream. His eyes in the emaciated forty-five year old face are open, twinkling with humor and wit. He is smiling.

My veiled mother, my uncles and aunts, dressed in black, my two older sisters, twelve and ten years old, and I, wearing identical black and white plaid skirts, white blouses, gray socks and black shoes, stand around the coffin. The room is dark, but pale rays of sun filter through the curtains forming a halo around the coffin.

"You don't know, Father?" I ask.

"Where I am, I can think about you, pray for you, love you, but I do not know mundane details about your life since my death. Do you go to church and pray?"

"I do not go to church and rarely pray."

"So what do you do about spirituality?"

"I think about you, Father, and try to emulate you. I try to be honest and loyal, to help my neighbor, to laugh at myself from time to time."

"What do you remember about me?"

"I remember you wearing a long white nightgown in your bed upstairs in the parsonage. Every morning I came to your room to say goodbye before leaving for school. We had a ritual: I handed you my glasses and you wiped them with a white handkerchief from under your pillow. I remember the morning you installed a rope on the banister at the top of the stairs, attached the bottle of hated goat milk your doctor wanted you to drink and sent it down so I would have to drink it with my breakfast. I remember walking with you to school, before you became ill; the road was just a country trail then. I held your hand, leaving it from time to time to jump or run or pick up pods from linden trees. I stuck those pods on my nose! I remember you, standing at the gate of the school and waving until I got safely inside."

"*Do people still talk about me?*"

"They do, with a reverence that would make your humility cringe. They say you were a saint."

"*What do you remember about my death?*"

"I remember a dark room in a chalet at Le Sépey in the Swiss Alps. You were lying in bed, in your white nightgown, coughing and perspiring from the tuberculosis. An ambulance appeared one snowy winter morning. I was standing against the house when your stretcher was loaded into the ambulance. Your eyes were red and puffy, your cheeks wet when I kissed them gently. I never saw your face again. In a sunny Geneva living room filled with flowers, I was told your suffering had ended, and I did not comprehend at first. A few days later, I sat on the third row of the golden church when your flower bedecked coffin, followed by a long procession of men in black, was brought in as the organ played Bach. One after the other, solemn men in long black gowns climbed into the pulpit and eulogized you. My favorite was your French friend, Pastor Vidal, who had lost an arm during World War Two. He had a big mustache. As I cried and cried, he seemed to be looking at me when he said: 'He was a saint.'"

❖ Gladys ❖
by Warren LeMon, Turners Falls, Massachusetts

In 1936, you move into apartment 5H of the Park Plaza Apartments in Mount Vernon, New York. You will live there for ten years, from your seventh to your seventeenth birthday. You will live there until you join the army in August 1946. Your life will never be the same thereafter.

In 1936—unbeknownst to you—on the second floor in apartment 2E lives Gladys. Gladys is also a pupil in the third grade at Lincoln School.

During your morning walks to Lincoln—about three blocks away—you suddenly discover this very pretty, very nice girl walking in the same direction with several books tied securely in a book strap.

Who is this person? Who can she be?

She is Gladys.

Jean Wilson, who lived up the street on Cottage Avenue, was a friend, and in our home there was Dick Dwyer who lived on the third floor, and Geoffrey Bullard who lived above us in 6H.

We all walked to school together mornings and afternoons. There was no cafeteria at school, but there was a lunch room where children who brought brown bag lunches ate. I believe milk was available for a penny.

Almost every day we walked home and our mothers made our lunches. We were back at school by one o'clock.

Mostly we played in the leaves in the fall, in the snow in the winter, and in the green grass in the spring. When we boys crossed the street to the large lot where we played Robin Hood and Jesse James, it was clearly understood that girls were not invited. And that was no problem. We were vaguely aware that there was a private girl's world they inhabited every so often that was foreign and forbidden to us.

In 1939, when we were all in the fifth grade, a wonderful thing happened. There was a junior dance one Friday evening at the Mount Vernon YMCA. I invited Gladys, and Dick invited Jean.

We walked to the Y, each girl wearing a short, white cape, their hair nicely arranged, and in new dresses they had picked out at Genung's on Fourth Avenue—accompanied by their mothers, no doubt.

Our dancing was extremely tentative, but we did hold each other and we did move around the floor. The adults kept things moving, there was punch and cookies, and that was the first time I was involved in dancing a John Paul Jones.

On our way home we discussed, rather seriously, the possibility of stopping at the Bee Hive on Fourth Street, a wonderful ice cream parlor where the high school kids went on weekends.

Common sense prevailed and we settled for sundaes at Columbus', a luncheonette-soda fountain in our neighborhood on Prospect Avenue. I had the pleasure of spending my entire weekly allowance of twenty-five cents on Gladys buying her a sundae and watching her eat it, delicious spoon after spoon.

We were all safely home by eight o'clock, and nobody got any funny ideas about kissing anybody. After all, we were in the fifth grade.

That was in June 1939, a shimmering spring, and my last at Lincoln School. About that time my parents discovered that I couldn't count.

That September I was enrolled in Our Lady of Victory in the grip of the Dominican nuns. Also, World War Two began.

❖ Memories ❖
by Janice Howard Lepore, Greenfield, Massachusetts

It seems like a vision. A gentle face framed by a halo of white hair. A frail body in soft bedclothes propped up on pillows. Day after day she would lie in the double-sized bed facing the door which separated the bedroom and the seldom used living room. The room always seemed to be an oasis of peace and quiet to me. At the age of four or five, time had no meaning. I now wonder how she felt, all alone in that room, when daily activity ceased and the house was quiet.

This vision is actually one of my first memories of my great grandmother, Mary Jane Holland Doran. Her family emigrated from Ireland and eventually settled in Shelby County, Iowa and Emerson, Nebraska via Wisconsin, to the best of my knowledge. Whatever records there may have been of her family, the Doran family and/or my grandfather's family (the Howards), were destroyed by fire or lost in the rigors of homesteading in Iowa, Nebraska and eventually the plains of South Dakota.

I wish I could remember her voice. I do remember the three generations—her daughter Nellie, Nellie's son Francis Howard and wife Edith and us kids—kneeling nightly around her bed to say the rosary by the light of kerosene lamps that had a vivid smell. I also remember being more interested in the shadows in the room than the prayers.

Being allowed to unpin and brush her long, white hair daily was my badge of "grownupness." How she passed the long hours or how long she lived with us, I do not know. My parents had lived with her on her farm after Grandpa John Doran died. There are pictures of my brother, Patrick, and me as toddlers on the front porch. I have also inherited a picture of Patrick and me helping her walk in the yard, probably to view the garden that took so much effort with minimal results. This was the late thirties when the Depression was tangible and prayer the only consolation.

When she was dying, more family gathered in silence when the priest came to administer last rites. He was escorted by my father to her bedside by the light of a blessed candle from a special crucifix box that also contained holy water and oil. I don't recall the burial or any other activities except that the north room was suddenly the private domain of my parents.

As many times as I have visited her grave at the St. Wilfred's Cemetery in Woonsocket, South Dakota, I don't recall what years are engraved on the headstone. It seems most of Dad's family lived into their late eighties, despite the lack of medical attention and nutritious eating as we know it.

Ironically, over fifty years later, a half dozen unframed portraits were found abandoned in the attic of another farm house. (This farm will remain in the family for at least the rest of my lifetime.) Fortunately, there was one person still living who could possibly identify the face.

One of my youngest brothers, Douglas, and I carefully removed at least one layer of dust from the portraits and transported them to the Weskota Manor Nursing Home in Wessington Springs, South Dakota. On an ordinary, hot summer day, nattily dressed in Western attire: pearl buttons, bolo tie, Black Hills gold belt buckle and ring, Uncle Charlie Doran, 104 years old, had no trouble identifying these family members: his father John, his mother (Mary Jane Holland Doran) at three different stages in her life, Mary's brother Thomas and my grandfather, Patrick Howard, both who died as young men in Iowa. He regaled us with some stories about unexpected guests at Grandpa Doran's farm, horses, saloons, the Dust Bowl days, hard times and Saturday night dances. He also chastised us for expecting him to remember such things at his age and invited us to his birthday party in August. Uncle Charlie was a younger brother of my G'ma Nellie. He was a Cavalry hero and farmer. Crediting his longevity to potatoes—on the table or from the bottle—Uncle Charlie may have traded his horse for a wheelchair, but his spirit was still indomitable.

Unfortunately, I wasn't able to join his family in celebrating Charlie and Leona's seventy-fifth wedding anniversary, February 14, 1999 when they once again shared their original Valentine card, but I will always be grateful to Uncle Charlie for his help in bringing reality to my vision of Great Grandma Mary Jane Holland Doran.

❖ War Years ❖
by Betty Lockwood, Charlemont, Massachusetts

A four year old girl is still alive in this eighty-five year old body, sitting with my sister and mother around the dining room table, playing a word game. Daddy is at the railroad where he works. Baby brother is napping.

We play "My father owns a grocery store, and in it he keeps something that begins with—"

Ruth is the oldest so she starts, "…begins with B."

Clarice says, "Bacon!"

"No!"

Mother says, "Brown sugar!"

"No!"

I say, "Bread!"

"Yes!"

Now it is my turn. I cannot spell, so I'm allowed to use letter sounds. My sisters groan. That makes it harder to guess. I say, "…starts with guh-guh."

"Grits?"

"No!"

"Gravy?"

"No!"

Cookies, milk, sugar—they guess anything; finally, they give up reluctantly. I proudly give the answer: "Ground glass—like the Germans put in sugar for the Belgian children." It was 1917, the war in Europe was on, and even at four I had heard propaganda.

When my sisters came home from school every afternoon, we'd sit on the top step of the back porch, and they would tell me about school. Ruth on one side of the step, and I on the other. Clarice always in the middle. She was best friend to us both. When we were on walks, she always walked in between us and held our hands.

Soon the war intruded more decisively on us with influenza—"the plague." Every day, someone we knew was sick. Then one day we were all sick in bed except Daddy who still went to work. A nurse came to help. She took care of Tommy, the baby, and all of us. Then one day mother was out of bed and the nurse left to help some other family where she said, "There is no one on their feet."

Soon Ruth was well and started school again. I was well and helped with Tommy. Eight-year-old Clarice was still sick in bed. Only Mother and Daddy and the doctor went into her room.

One day, sitting in the rocker with Tommy on my lap, watching my mother wash dishes, I heard Clarice call out and ask for a glass of water. Mother called back, "Just a minute, honey."

Mother emptied the dishwater, wiped the sink, took a glass, filled it with cold water and went upstairs. I sat and held Tommy and waited.

I can only imagine now what happened to her when she went into that room and found her little girl dead. If she cried out it was in silence. She came downstairs and did not say anything. She went to the phone and tried to make a call. Finally, she got through and talked to someone. Then she began to walk back and forth between the two front rooms. I laid Tommy on a blanket on the floor and followed her in that tragic pacing. I don't even think she knew I was there.

Then people came. No one spoke to me. I sat and watched people and patted Tommy lying on the blanket.

I don't remember when anyone told me that Clarice was dead. No one talked to me, just to each other. Dishes of food were left by the door—mute sympathy and love, I know now.

A purple crepe bow and a long ribbon were hung on the outside door. I knew what it meant.

The day of the funeral I was sent to a neighbor's. That night, Daddy came and carried me home to my own bed.

One night later I had a dream. It was the first dream I recall ever having. I guess I did not really know it was a dream. In it I went to Heaven looking for Clarice. Someone said, "Oh, she's not here anymore. She has gone further on to a better place." I woke up and knew I would never see her again. I would never catch up to her.

I don't remember anyone ever talking about Clarice. Ruth stopped sitting on the porch steps with me. Mother did not sit at the piano and sing songs with us the way she had when there were three of us.

Even now I think sometimes I can hear Clarice laughing, and I feel the warm sun on the back porch steps where we sat. Ruth on one side. Me on the other side. Clarice always in the middle. Always laughing.

❖ The Dollhouse Christmas ❖
by Phyllis Loomis, Ashfield, Massachusetts

The boys had grown beyond Santa Claus. It was time for them to become his helpers.

The girls, on the other hand, were true believers. Weeks before Christmas they began worrying about the cleanliness of our fireplace following the occasional fire, and planning what foods they would give Santa to help him along his way.

As usual, I helped each group make their dreams come true.

The boys had great hopes of building a playhouse for their sisters. For several evenings, after the girls were in bed, we four older members of the family planned how we could make a playhouse big enough for a five and seven-year-old to be in together *and* that would fit into their shared nine by twelve foot bedroom which already held two twin beds and far too many toys.

We settled on raising the beds four feet off the floor and using the beds themselves for the playhouse roof. Building twin cottages under flat roofs seemed to be the perfect answer.

Once our ideas gelled we were all greatly excited. Each night through December we more or less pushed the girls off to bed at an increasingly early hour. Then, to the basement we went with saws, hammers, nails, paint brushes, wallpaper, cloth, sewing machine, plastic flowers, doorknobs, curtain rods, and anything else that came to mind as our dream houses took shape.

When the night before Christmas arrived, each house wall was finished and furnished both outside and inside, but each stood alone. The windows had curtains on the inside and flower-filled window boxes on the outside; there was wallpaper inside, bright yellow paint outside. We were ready to carry everything to the girls' bedroom if they would ever get themselves camped out in the living room next to the small table set with Santa's midnight snack.

Eventually, both girls were quiet. We each quickly put our books—which were little more than decoys—aside and rapidly retreated to the basement. We rather noisily moved the cumbersome sections of the playhouses up two flights of stairs to the girls' room. That room was located directly above the living room where the girls were sleeping. Once everything had been transported, we began assembling out project. We had made the girls' beds in the first place so that plywood would take the place of springs. It was easy enough to remove the current twelve inch legs and replace them with four foot legs. The walls were in place in no time and all the toys that used to fill the room were put in their new locations within the houses.

Santa's helpers then tiptoed downstairs and ate Santa's snack while they laughed and congratulated each other. Through it all the girls continued to sleep.

We were all awakened early in the morning by two excited girls who reported Santa had eaten everything that had been left, but they had missed his visit. Still pajama clad, we all gathered in the living room, lit the tree lights and opened our gifts. No one said anything, but the atmosphere was not the same as Christmases had been in the past. The boys were in a hurry to finish unwrapping. The girls opened their gifts one by one and played with each item in turn.

When the wrapping papers were somewhat pushed aside and the boys were almost too antsy to sit still, I suggested we all help ourselves to a bowl of cereal and take it up to the girls' room for breakfast. In no time at all, all six of us were sitting around a table built for children inside one of the two dollhouses.

The Christmas spirit of lovingly giving and receiving had come alive once again.

❖ World War II from the Vantage Point of One Family ❖
by Eileen Marguet, Greenfield, Massachusetts

It was December 7, 1941. There was a bridal shower for me near my Brooklyn, New York home. That was the same day that the shattering news came over the radio, "Japan has attacked us at Pearl Harbor and we are officially at war." Roosevelt declared war on Germany the next day.

My brother Jimmy had been drafted a few months earlier. I was married a month later and my husband was drafted four months after that. My sister Anne's husband left for New Guinea shortly afterward. My sister Peggy got word that her fiancée who was living in Singapore was captured by the Japanese. He spent the next three years in a prison camp. My brother Arthur joined the Navy and was sent to Alaska.

It was like that in every family. The men left one after another leaving the women at home. Many of the women went to work in factories making war materials.

"The war on the home front," as it was called, was quite different from pre-war life. There were ration books for sugar, butter, meat and even gasoline. Each person was allowed two pairs of leather shoes.

When the war ended in 1945 we faced another set of problems: finding jobs for the returning men and housing for them and their families. Nothing had been built for four years. Returning servicemen needed both jobs and housing.

The Government offered builders loans to be used for housing for veterans. One man, William Leavitt, accepted the challenge and built 10,000 single family homes. These homes were functional, charming, and available to servicemen with no down payment.

Mr. Leavitt became the "fairy godfather" of the American housewife by providing every one of the homes he built with an automatic washing machine!

❖ The Pioneer Valley Women's Rifle Club ❖
by Louise Bowen O'Brien, Colrain, Massachusetts

During the Second World War, Americans proved their patriotism and love of our country in many ways. Perhaps the most unusual act of patriotism was the organization of the Pioneer Valley Women's Rifle Club in the hilltowns of Western Massachusetts.

It had an impressive name, but actually there were only about a dozen women from Buckland, Ashfield, Colrain and Shelburne who comprised the club. My sister and I were among the first members. We had handled guns and target practiced with our brothers.

We both had young children, so there was no way we could join the women's military services. The rifle club seemed something we could do for the defense effort.

We used 22 caliber rifles to train and I had my own 22 rifle. Most of the women had handled guns, but a few were novices.

We trained evenings on the upper floor of a barn in Buckland. We used paper targets and it was fun to see who the best shot was. One night we were reloading when we heard a loud "Squawk!"

"There are chickens down below!" Our instructor told us. To the newer members he added, "Be careful!"

We had shooting matches with area groups, mostly men. Once we went all the way to Adams, Massachusetts to shoot against a men's rifle club. It was a successful match and we held our own, but the appearance of my rifle caused the men to chuckle. As I had been leaving my home for the trip to Adams, a strap on the gun sling had parted and I needed something to tie it together. There was no time to look for a piece of leather, so I knotted it up with a ribbon that was handy on the counter. It happened to be a pink ribbon.

A few weeks ago I was sorting through some old papers and found a newspaper clipping I had saved. It read, "Pioneer Valley shooters win over deer hunters by a score of 818 to 804. Highest scorer for Pioneer Valley was L. O'Brien: 96, 64, 160." The best part of that match was that we defeated men who were experienced deer hunters.

We practiced through the years of conflict and told each other that we could protect our homes from enemies.

Now, at this late date, it all seems silly that we were planning to repel the German invaders with our little 22's. However, it does show the spirit of American women.

❖ A Room at the Inn ❖
by Joseph A. Parzych, Gill, Massachusetts

The week before New Year's Day 1999, I read about the closing of the Macano Inn in Housatonic, Massachusetts. My mother, Maria, had once worked there as a cook.

She was twenty-six when her husband, Franz "Frank" Zagata, died in the flu epidemic of 1918. Left with two young children and pregnant with a third, she had no money, no job, and no family to help her. There was no Social Security, no welfare, and the country was sliding into recession. The words of the song, "You picked a fine time to leave me," fit the situation well.

My mother first got a job as a seamstress. Forced to leave her children alone, she left food ready to heat for Mary who was six, and two-year-old John. One day the fire in the coal cook stove died down. The food wouldn't heat and the house got cold. Mary poured kerosene on the coals. The explosion blew the stove lids off and singed Mary's hair.

When it came time to give birth, Mother gave up her apartment, sold her furniture and stayed with friends. After the birth of baby Bessie, Mother got a job as cook at the Macano Inn. The arrangement included one tiny room on the third floor. Mary watched over her brother John and sister Bessie. She heated the baby's bottle on a hot plate, fed and changed her.

I telephoned Mary, now eighty-six, and Bess, eighty. Mary lives in Greenfield, Massachusetts and Bess lives in Great Barrington next to Housatonic. Neither had ever been back to the inn.

"Why don't we have lunch at the Macano before they close?" I asked.

I didn't have to ask twice. Mary and I headed out on the twenty-ninth. It began snowing on the Mass Pike—heavier in the hills—but we were on our way and nothing was going to stop us. We picked up Bess and soon arrived at the Macano.

I'd called owner Peter Del Grande the previous day to tell him we were coming. He and his wife, Robin, welcomed us. They talked with us, posed for pictures and served us cream of celery soup with turkey club sandwiches.

Mary well remembered living in the small room upstairs and heating the baby bottles.

"But," she said. "The downstairs was much bigger when we stayed here."

The rooms had apparently shrunk with age!

We were the first to write in a book of patrons' remembrances which the Del Grandes were collecting. My sisters told of the innkeeper's son getting married and his bride running off with another man. The heartbroken man generously gave Mother all his lovely new household furnishings so she could rent an apartment and go back to her better paying seamstress job.

After leaving the Macano, my sisters showed me an empty lot next door where the apartment house once stood. A highway ran in front; the Housatonic River ran in back. Bess once had a wild ride towards the river in a runaway carriage a baby sitter had left unattended. The carriage tipped over and Bess rolled to the brink of the river, uninjured.

They pointed out railroad tracks across the road where John had sat with a train bearing down on him, its whistle shrieking. Mother had a premonition of danger while at work and jumped up suddenly from her job, ran home and snatched John away from death at the last second.

One day the landlord's son accidentally chopped off Mary's finger when she held a piece of wood he was splitting. The landlady threw the finger in the river, hoping Mother wouldn't notice it was gone.

After these three long years of struggling alone, friends introduced Mother to Jozef Parzych, whose wife had died leaving him with three young children. He proposed to Mother and she accepted on the first date. I was the fourth of seven more children of that marriage of desperation.

We concluded our enjoyable day of reminiscing with a visit to Mama's grave. But her spirit seemed to have gone from there, perhaps to a livelier place—such as the Macano Inn.

❖ A Different Memorial Day ❖
by Charlotte Potter, Turners Falls, Massachusetts

All spring my husband, two children and I had looked forward to the Memorial Day weekend when we would go to Maine to visit grandparents. We were finally packed and ready to start on our trip when I noticed my daughter Nedine was not her usual, cheerful self. Upon feeling her forehead I decided that she must have a fever. Sure enough, the thermometer registered 104 degrees!

My husband and I easily decided that there was no way this child was going to travel. We immediately made some necessary phone calls, including one to our regular doctor. In those days, doctors made house calls, and it wasn't long before he got to our house to check Nedine out. Unfortunately, I didn't find his visit very reassuring because he admitted he had no idea what was causing Nedine's fever.

We spent an anxious week looking after her and finally she broke out in a red rash. It was then that we knew she had somehow contracted measles which had the potential, back then, of being a very dangerous disease. It was a very good thing that we didn't go to Maine, because she would have passed her germs on to her cousins. In time, we learned that a little girl who had visited with my husband Ed's brother and wife had come down with the measles and could have passed them on to Nedine through that visit. I guess I never quite forgave the wife for not warning us. It would have saved us a very worrisome week.

Since my children never caught anything at the same time, we had to wait three weeks before my son Noel came down with the disease. By then, the summer had become very hot and our small house often heated up to ninety degrees in the heat of the day. I shall never forget how uncomfortable Noel was. He broke out not in spots, but a solid, total body rash.

By the middle of July, everyone had recovered and we were able to embark on our long delayed trip to Maine. Thankfully, I thought, my children will never fear catching measles again!

❖ The Montague Inn ❖
by Leona Robert, Turners Falls, Massachusetts

The original Montague Inn (Montague Center, Massachusetts) was located where the Montague Post Office is today. The Inn was a beautiful long, yellow building with a porch along the front and left side on both the ground floor and second story.

The Inn's office, a pool and game room, and ice cream parlor were on the right half of the building. In the center was a lovely, comfortable living room with a fireplace. The room was furnished with antiques. At the left end was a large combination living area and bedroom reserved for special guests.

Beyond the sitting room, to the back, was a pleasant dining room. The tables were always set with white tablecloths, real cloth napkins and fresh bouquets of flowers from Mrs. Ward's garden which was to the back and left side of the Inn. Mrs. Ward and her husband were the owners then.

On the second floor were guest rooms. Some people came for an overnight visit, some for the weekend, others for more extended visits.

From the time I was fifteen, I worked at the Inn in the summers. After I was married, at age eighteen, I continued on weekends and for parties. For part of the mornings I worked as a chamber maid and at mealtimes I worked as a waitress.

Helen was the head waitress. She was responsible for the dining room—washing the windows and floors, dusting and polishing the furniture and doing the floral arrangements.

Beyond the dining room you entered a large room. Directly to the left was a sink with a wide counter at each end where waitresses piled dirty dishes. In the center of that room there was a large table with two shelves above it. On those shelves would be desserts—dozens of homemade pies including the Inn's famous mince meat pie. The mince pies were on the menu every day.

An extra person was hired to help with dishes on the weekends, but in between waiting on customers we all pitched in and did dishes. There was no job description for us to use to get out of doing the dirty work!

Beyond that room was the kitchen where Mrs. Kudukey, the cook, reigned. She did it all. Prepared the meals from soups to desserts. No recipes in sight. She just did it her way. She was a small, quiet woman who could never be replaced.

Mrs. Kudukey saved every scrap of leftover meat. When she

had enough, she made huge pots of real mince meat. It smelled so good! It was canned for the famous mince meat pies that the Inn was known for—served, of course, with cheese. Mr. Ward made trips to Plymouth, Vermont to buy large rounds of sharp cheese that weighed twenty-five pounds each!

Upstairs, to the right of the building, was a spring floor dance hall. The floor sort of swayed as you walked on it. Benches were built along the sides of the hall. If a party was scheduled, I had to clean the hall. Cleaning the dance hall was the usual routine: washing the benches, dusting, and sweeping.

Mrs. Kudukey saved fat and drippings which were rendered and strained and used to make soap. I know lye was added. I don't recall what else was used in that recipe. Soap was made on a quiet afternoon and I remember we would stir and stir the soap pot until it was smooth, thick and light. That soap was used for scrubbing everything from chickens to floors.

A retired couple from the Eastern part of the state came every summer for a month or six-week stay. When they left, I, as chambermaid, received a $5.00 tip. Great money for those days!

The Esleeks, from Turners Falls Paper, in Turners Falls, Massachusetts were frequent Sunday dinner guests. Usually a party of five—and good for a $1.00 tip. Mrs. Ward assigned us, usually by turns, to wait on them as most tables left only twenty-five or fifty cent tips.

The summer of 1931, I lived at the Inn and received $5.00 a week plus room and board. I was saving to get married in February 1932, so it looked like big money to me then.

I stopped working at the Inn when I was pregnant with my second child.

The Inn, built in 1830, was destroyed by fire in March 1953.

❖ Investigating Grandma's Trunks ❖
by Charlotte Robinson, Turners Falls, Massachusetts

Once when we were young teenagers, my sister Priscilla and I were staying at my grandmother's house in Nelson, New Hampshire. No adult was in the house. For some strange reason we decided to investigate one of the "bangways"—an area previously off limits to us. Bangways were storage areas built under the eaves of a house. They were walk-in areas with no doors and no lights. We knew all about the large trunks stored in a line in the bangway. We also knew there was one small trunk about the size of a suitcase. We had been told that these trunks held the possessions that Grandma and Grandpa (my mother's parents) accumulated from the time of their marriage in 1879 onward. This day seemed to be a good time to look into some of the trunks.

We went to the bangway and had no trouble opening the first trunk. All of the trunks were backed up against the room side of the bangway, so the trunk lids could be easily opened. The steeply slanted ceiling was only inches from our heads.

We found many vestiges of a life gone by in the trunks. Items found were indicative of the trappings of a farm family of reasonable means. There were a lot of clothes for men and women for every type of weather or season. The clothes were all carefully folded with paper between the layers. We found garments of velvet, wool and some linen of dark colors. There were a few ornate white shirts and several colored blouses; many long skirts and trousers of different dark colors; white collars and cuffs to be worn over the heaviest clothes to protect them from stains. There was a bundle of *Youth Companion* magazines tied with string. There were horse and cow magazines and feed and forage offers.

The trunk tray held lots of small boxes. Some contained pseudo-heirloom pins, bracelets and necklaces. Other boxes held needles and pins. Still others held buttons of all sizes and colors. All the boxes were tied with string to secure the contents. There were undergarments, hose, slippers, long slim ivory stays to be inserted into various garments, combs for holding hair in place—almost everything for day-to-day life was found in those trunks.

The deep drawers were stuffed with fading letters and a few pictures. Some of the pictures were in envelopes; some were free in the trunk and beginning to fade. Delicate dried flowers tied with slender, fraying ribbons were wrapped in a kind of tissue paper for storage in the trunk.

The oddest articles, of which there were a large number, were the little two-inch squares of folded paper. Each one had a name and date written on the outside. When unfolded, each contained a curl or length of hair. We found out later that the hair had been snipped from the head of an individual at the time of their death. This was the custom at the time. The curls were from babies or little children. The longer strands might have been from any adult, but mostly older men and women. I recognized several of the names as those of friends or family. Along with these parcels there were many brass plates etched with the name of the deceased. These plates had been removed from the casket before burial and were carefully stored in the trunks.

The dainty posies fell apart in our hands and the fragile materials were easily torn. As we continued exploring, we found that all of the trunks contained similar items. The further into the bangway we went, the darker it became and we carried armfuls of history out into the light to investigate. When we dumped them back into the trunks in the dark I'm sure many of the delicate articles were damaged or even destroyed.

The one small trunk the size of a suitcase contained the clothing and one or two toys that had belonged to William, my mother's brother who had died at the age of four. The sight of the stockings and little shoes brought a catch to our breath.

I now regret our foray into the trunks and leaving the contents in disheveled order. Certainly, we didn't put the contents away as we had found them. In retrospect, it seems like a sacrilege. At a much later date we admitted our day's activity to my mother and she didn't seem too angry. We asked her about one beautiful blouse with leg-o-mutton sleeves and intricate embroidery around the neck, shoulders and wrists. It was finished so short it wouldn't even tuck into a skirt and we wondered why. Her answer after several minutes (and with a wink) was, "It wasn't a blouse. It was Grandma's wedding night gown."

I guess the trunks were moved to Aunt Grace's house in Sullivan, New Hampshire where Grandma Barker spent her last years. Grandma's house was destroyed by age, weather and lack of occupancy.

❖ The Depression Years ❖
by Doris Shirtcliff, Greenfield, Massachusetts

My father went to work in the morning and came home late in the afternoon. I assumed that was what all fathers did.

My mother was a homemaker. She kept house, made the meals, baked bread, and canned the things our garden provided. She also canned the blueberries we picked and made jams and jellies that we used during the long winter months. The damp, dark cellar always had a stone crock of sauerkraut.

Local Color 109

I was about eight years old when the Depression started. I don't remember any great transition from wealth to poverty. There were other things that were more important to me and I had never heard of the stock market. My world consisted of school, roller skating, hopscotch and all the other activities of kids that age.

But that Depression thing stole its way into every household, gradually, one way or another. Later, there was a change in our house. My father didn't go to work anymore, but he was kept busy doing odd jobs for different people. Things seemed to be getting leaner. I didn't have the clothes I had before; we made-do with hand-me-downs. My father resoled my shoes with a kit from Woolworth's. I couldn't take music lessons any more, but the piano remained and that satisfied me to some degree.

The need to save every penny and use things not once but twice, became the rule. Dad was out of work for the first time I ever knew about. Christmas time changed. Presents were not toys or frivolous things. They were needed things, like mittens, sweaters, scarves, and ugly, black, overshoes with buckles that clacked if you didn't fasten them up. There would usually be a game or two for all of us to share. One year I received a harmonica and drove everyone crazy with it!

My father finally went to work for the town on the WPA. This was the Work Progress Administration, a project put in operation by the government to afford people jobs so they would not be on welfare.

It was mid-winter when my father was assigned to the Greenfield Massachusetts Water Department. Frozen and broken water pipes required digging into frozen ground with picks and shovels. The men carried their own lunches and their meals sometimes froze to the point where they had to heat them over the small fire they kept going to warm their hands. Sometimes the boss would come around in his truck and have hot coffee or soup for them. Each man had his own tin cup. They usually worked six full days a week for $11.80 in wages! I remember my mother rubbing my father's back and shoulders at night and the whole house smelling of Raleigh's liniment.

There were things I wanted but could not have. I didn't like it, but I understood why. I was in the seventh grade when President Roosevelt enacted the National Recovery Act (NRA). The Depression was supposedly over. Then came the big NRA parade. With a banner across my chest proclaiming "Greenfield Junior High School," I marched with every other student in town. The parade was so long I often wondered who was left over at the end to view it all.

All in all, I think those years were good for me. (I can say that partly because they are behind me!) They *had* to make me a better, stronger person. They gave me a sense of what was really important. We shared. We cared. There was more togetherness.

❖ Going to Grandpa's ❖
by Priscilla Tromblay, Turners Falls, Massachusetts

In the early 1920s, when I was only five years old, my family would go to Westhampton, Massachusetts where my grandparents lived.

To get there, we would sometimes go by train from Springfield, Massachusetts to Northampton, Massachusetts. This was a great trip, going north along the Connecticut River. My father, being a Boston & Maine railroad engineer, knew all the important things for us to see. There was a signboard for Ne-Hi Soda that was always marked with the height to which the river rose during the spring floods. There was the Northampton Fairgrounds, and the place where Smith Ferry went across the river. We would also go by the Oxbow, which was a great fishing place.

Being the smallest, I got to sit on my father's lap, so I had the best view. When we arrived in Northampton, Dad would go to the livery stable to hire a pair of white horses and a carriage with a fringe all around the top. In that carriage we rode the ten miles to Westhampton over a dirt road that was little more than one lane wide. Today it is Route 66. If we met someone back then, one driver would have to pull over to the side and let the other one pass.

My grandfather had a large farm with lots of apples trees, chickens, cows, pigs and horses. The farm buildings were set on the flat land at the bottom of Perry Hill. Back then that hill seemed like a mountain to me.

At the far end of Grampa's land there was a beautiful waterfall that we played in during the summer. The house and barn were large. There were six rooms downstairs in the house and five bedrooms upstairs, so when the whole family came there was room for everyone. Us kids would sleep crosswise, five to a bed. What a great time we had!

When we woke up in the morning, Gramma would have a task for each of us to do. She would send some of us out to the barn to get the milk from the uncles who were doing the milking; some were sent out to the chicken coop to gather the eggs. The big kids got to go down in the cellar where the well was and the meats and food that needed to be kept cold. They would bring up the ham, bacon, sausage that had been prepared from the pigs that had grown fat all summer long in the pigpen out in back of the barn.

Gramma did the cooking with the help of her daughters-in-law. My father was the third son of seven.

In Gramma's house there were two large tables: one in the kitchen and one in the dining room. The kitchen was for the kids and the dining room for the adults. Gram never sat down until all the food was on the table and everyone else was served

What a great time was had by all! Lots of talking and laughter. One could feel the love that was flowing in that house.

Local Color #2

❖ By the Water's Edge and Beyond ❖
by Helen G. Adzema, Greenfield, Massachusetts

Quite a few years ago, my mother and I decided to take a day off and go for a ride on country back roads near our Greenfield, Massachusetts home. We stopped the car and walked along one road finding a shady glen. We sat there and listened to the sound of water in a stream as it rippled over stones and bounced against the banks. It was such a restful sound.

We heard birds singing, frogs croaking, bees buzzing, the twang of a dragonfly and chirp of crickets each "playing their own instrument." Looking into the water we could see fish swimming and a few snails making their way slowly over the bottom of the stream.

We walked along the water's edge and then into the woods. The sky was beautiful—a heavenly blue. Big, leafy trees spread their branches wide and their leaves waved gently in the warm summer breeze.

Under one tree we saw Lady Slippers which must not be disturbed if you want them to bloom again the following year. The air smelled so clean; the warm sun felt wonderful shining down on us. The whole world seemed at peace.

Suddenly, we heard a sound coming from the edge of the woods. Click, clack, click, clack. When we went to investigate, we saw it was a farmer on a tractor with a hay rake turning over the hay so it would dry. The hay would be useful to feed his cattle in the winter. From a distance we could hear another sound of hammering. Someone was putting up a fence to keep cattle from straying into the woods.

With the sun high in the sky, we found a big, flat rock for our picnic table and a lower flat rock for our seat. Everything seemed to be made-to-order for us! We unpacked our lunch basket and had a wonderful time watching the clouds drifting by. They looked like gobs of whipped cream!

Before we knew it, the sky had started to change into a beautiful sunset. We packed our basket into the car and knew we had spent a day that we both would long remember.

On that day we had seen a small part of God's creations. We heard the sounds of nature and saw the things that made those sounds, too.

Never take miracles for granted. Take care of them. Once gone, they can never be brought back. Taken care of, these treasures will be around for future generations to enjoy too.

So walk by the water's edge and beyond and be grateful for all of nature's gifts.

❖ My Mother and I ❖
by Edna Baublis, Athol, Massachusetts

I read somewhere that a woman said she put her arm in her coat and her mother's hand came out the sleeve. Growing up I can remember watching my mother and saying to myself, "When I grow up I'm never going to do that…" or "When I get to be a mother I'm never going to behave like that!" But, you know what? I find myself doing the same things that my mother used to do that aggravated me so much!

My mother was a superstitious person. She had so many different superstitions that it's a wonder we grew up with any degree of sanity. We never could start anything on a Friday—that was a bad luck day. You never started a vacation or bought a car or a house or any big item on a Friday. God forbid you started a vacation on Friday! You might as well have stayed home for all the good time you would have had on it. I remember once the doctor saw her and wanted her to go into the hospital the next day. She refused because it was a Friday. She went in on Saturday. In case you might be interested, I will neither start a vacation on a Friday nor take possession of a new car on a Friday.

My mother said we had to eat everything on our plate because, "God came down from the cross for a crust of bread." My brother used to tease her and ask where she read this marvelous bit of information and then he'd say something like, "Maybe for a hot dog, but not just a crust of bread." This would make her so angry! I can see her finger now, pointing at the accused. My mother would say, "God will punish you!"

When I was pregnant there were so many taboos, it's a wonder I lived through them. I could not wear a necklace because that would cause the umbilical cord to wrap itself around the baby's neck. I had five children so you see I did not wear necklaces very often. I couldn't eat salami because it might make me choke and I would die. There were many more superstitions I've since forgotten.

My mother was a sale shopper, especially for bed linen. Whenever Grant's Store had a white sale, you could be sure that she would buy *sheets* and *sheets* and *sheets!* They were marked down from $1.98 to $1.35. Now, to pay even a dollar and a half back then for 100% cotton percale sheets was a good buy.

My mother's been dead now for thirty years and I am just now down to my last white sheet and I may save that one instead of using it. I get a charge out of the price tag. Imagine, $1.50 for a white, cotton, 220 count percale sheet. They were always all white because back in those days that was the only color sheets came in.

I have continued the practice of buying on sale, only I can't resist towels. I have drawers full of towels. I don't think my children will have thirty years full of towels, the way I had with my mother's sale sheets, but I bet they have a good five years' worth.

When my mother put her sheets and her good nighties away (for special occasions), or if she was going to the hospital, she would wrap things in tissue paper. If you wanted to know what was in the package you had to unwrap it. I looked in the bureau drawer the other day and what did I find but packages that I had wrapped in tissue paper! I went a step further, however, and put little pink Post-it notes on the packages so you would not have to open them up to find out what was in the package. I can't believe I do that!

My mother also had a habit of hiding money in weird places. If you went into a drawer to get a blouse that you hadn't worn for a long time, when you put your arm in the sleeves, there was the possibility that a five dollar bill would fall out. Or, if you unrolled a tablecloth to use that hadn't been used for a long time, a ten spot might fall out. In those days that was a lot of money and it was saved from her "house money" that my father gave her for things for the house, like groceries. You had to be careful when you went into certain places in the house like that bureau. It was like a treasure hunt.

She didn't want my father to know she was hiding money and "saving it for a rainy day," but I'm sure he must have known. Not much escaped his eyes. She always said it felt nice to have some money of her own.

She would cry at sad movies or at a sad story on television and I would shake my head. Now I cry at movies and over television stories that are sad. I cry when the necrology list is read at our high school class reunions, especially for those who where killed in the "Big War."

I don't hide dollar bills in the sleeves of shirts that have not been worn for a long time, but I do say and do the same things as my mother did—Heaven forbid! But I could do a lot worse.

❖ To My Grandmother, Whom I Never Really Knew ❖
by Estelle Cade, Turners Falls, Massachusetts

Dear Nana, Estelle M. (Heard) Robinson, born near Digby, Nova Scotia on April 12, 1861,

There you are in this formal portrait holding on your lap the "mythical Gracie," born on January 30, 1891. She looks to be about two years of age as she sits there so nicely, dressed in her best. As you hold her, you could not have foreseen what a loss you'd suffer in a few short months. Her obituary reads, "Captain and Mrs. John F. Robinson have suffered the loss of their dear little daughter Gracie, dead of diphtheria on December 30, 1895."

You suffered many losses in your life, my Nana. Although your eldest child and only son, Harold (b. 12/14/82) survived and outlived you, the list I found written in someone's loving copperplate script (yours, perhaps?) reads sadly:

Edith Gertrude b. 12/10/89—d. 1/16/90

Grace b. 1/30/91—d. 12/31/95

Ruth b. 6/15/95—d. 6/19/95

Such brief lives! How you must have grieved each little lost one.

Then came Dorothy Estelle b. 2/9/03 who died in the 1980s and my mother Asenath Mae b. 7/15/06 who died in 1977.

My mother told my sister Carole and me, of her growing up in Rockland, Maine. I remember her telling us of the wooden sidewalks and of going to sea in the summer during vacation times on whatever ship your husband, Captain Robinson, was Master. The ships then were three-masted schooners, carrying lumber, granite, and other merchandise up and down the coast, from Rockland to Newport News, New York, Boston and so on. Fascinating family tales!

My mother and aunt also often spoke of the little sister who died so young, and whom they never knew. Do you know that the little tea table my sister and I played with growing up came down through the family as "Gracie's table?" My children played with it and soon my youngest granddaughter, your great-great-granddaughter, will play tea parties at that same wooden table. You and Gracie are not forgotten.

When my mother was just eleven, you suffered another loss. Your dear husband fell ill with what used to be called Bright's Disease (kidney failure) and died in 1916 after a period of failing health.

There you were, Nana, a fairly young widow—fifty-six, I believe—with two young daughters to raise and provide for. Your son, working in the city then, was able to help some, but you did have to go to work for the telephone company. How frightened you must have been, but in all the photos I have of you, you seem a lady with a very determined looking jaw line (which I inherited!).

My mother never spoke of you being anything but a loving, caring mother. You and your girls went to church. You sewed for your girls and made a home for them. A diary that my mother kept tells of "helping Mama with the housework," and going to "Girl's Friendly meetings"; "Mama made my new dress for the Christmas party!"(Growing up with a working mother is not a new idea then, is it?)

Other losses came to you over time like the move from Rockland, leaving all that was familiar to you. You moved to Waterbury, Connecticut to be nearer your son, Harry. There were other moves later on, like the move to Boston with Dorothy and Asenath when they were working there. You were always loved and admired by your daughters and their friends. You were a delightful lady.

And then, in your later years, a final loss. I was a small child when

I saw you lost in the mists of dementia, not knowing any of us, until you died of pneumonia and we lost you forever. The day you died was the first time I ever saw an adult cry. Your younger daughter, my mother, wept for her loss.

I can only pray that you moved on to that good place where there are no more losses to be suffered.

Your loving granddaughter, and namesake,

Estelle

❖ Thoughts About 1930s Greenfield ❖
by Margaret M. "Pat" Currie, Turners Falls, Massachusetts

With the coming of the millennium, I read newspaper interviews with people aged eighty to one hundred years old. They talk about their lives in the past century. Reading those interviews made me remember, while I still could, and write down my memories for the coming century.

As I think back, one of the first things I can remember was the flurry of activity on Sunday nights which meant we were getting ready for Monday wash day. If Dad was home from his job on the railroad, he filled the wash boiler with water. It was a large, tin or copper kettle placed over the front burner on the kitchen stove. The stove was used to heat the kitchen as well as for cooking and heating water. The stove was "powered" by burning wood or coal.

If Dad was not there, my mother and I filled pails of water and then poured them into the boiler to fill it that way. Then we'd put in sheets (which were stripped from the beds on Saturday), Dad's long underwear, towels and more. Soap was added by cutting or slicing pieces from a larger bar. Then these items were boiled together in the kettle all night.

In the morning, these articles were lifted out of the cooling (but still hot) water by using a cut-off broom handle. The clothes were placed, a few at a time, into a washing machine. The fuel-powered washer was turned on and tumbled the clothes for about twenty minutes.

Next, the clothes were put through a ringer and into rinse water in a "set tub" (a tub on the wall in the kitchen with two faucets running into it). After that, the clothes went into another tub to which bluing had been added.

While this was going on, another load was put into the washing machine. Then these were put through the same cycle described above. The last load was probably work clothes. No doubt, at some point, more hot water had to be added to the original kettle. The water would have to be heated on the woodstove or in a tall tank in the kitchen which was heated with gas.

Finally, all the clothes had to be hung outside to dry. No wonder they called it Wash *DAY*! It really took that long!

I also remember the ice man. If Mother needed ice, she put a card in the window of our house. On the card was written the number of pounds of ice she wanted. Each side of the card had a number, such as ten, twenty or even fifty. The ice truck came different days each week. The ice man would bring the ice into the house and put it in the ice box (refrigerator) and collect the money from Mother. If she wasn't going to be at home she could just leave the ice money on the table for him or even pay him the next time he delivered ice.

Doors were always open back then.

❖ Remembering Peanuts ❖
by Guy Carey, Jr., Warwick, Massachusetts

I never really knew how or why she became known as "Peanuts," but at that time, Peanuts the cow had been part of our family for all ten years of my life. Now, as I think about it, I wonder about that name. Back then I never thought to question it.

The night we lost Peanuts, two of my sisters, Joan and Louise, were sitting in the parlor listening to the radio with Jack Reed, one of the neighbor boys. I was supposed to be in my room sleeping, but I had slipped into my sisters' room so I could spy on them. I was listening through the open air register in their bedroom floor. The register was over the parlor. I don't know how late it was, but hearing my father speak to the girls I knew they would be coming up to bed soon. I heard Joan start upstairs, so I scurried back to my own room and slipped into my bed.

Louise went to the door with Jack. She must have taken too long to say good-night, because I heard my father's voice again. Then Louise closed the door and started for the stairs. Suddenly, Jack ran back onto the porch and banged on the door. There was a lot of excited conversation as my father went outside with Jack. Mother went to the door and was talking with Louise, but I couldn't make out what they were saying. I wanted to go downstairs, but the fear of being punished for being out of bed so late kept me upstairs. I waited with my ear to the door for Louise to come up. When she finally came upstairs, Joan asked, "What happened? Why all the excitement?"

"Peanuts. It's Peanuts. Jack found her under the apple tree dead," Louise said.

I reeled away from the door. My insides knotted with pain as a lump formed in my throat and tears trickled down my face. I crawled back into bed, my body writhing with sobs.

Sleep wouldn't come. I just kept thinking about Peanuts and why she had come to mean so much to me. She had been a part of the family all my life and though it might seem strange to some to think of a cow as family, Peanuts was family to me.

My first memory of Peanuts was how dangerous she first appeared to my young eyes. She was a big animal with wicked looking horns and bulging eyes. She was constantly chewing on something. My sisters soon taught me that Peanuts was quite gentle; she was to be enjoyed, not feared. Soon, I walked by Peanuts' side and held her halter as my sisters led her to water, all the while imagining I was one of the world's great Western cowboys.

As I grew older, I was allowed to lead Peanuts to the spring and back by myself. My pride and joy at being able to lead Peanuts to water were insurmountable. I cannot recall being too happy about being initiated into the chore of cleaning her stable, but I did enjoy cleaning and currying her. I had fun throwing hay down to her from the loft.

At milking time, I would watch with envy as my sister Louise sat on the milking stool and, like magic, brought forth frothy milk from Peanuts' udder to fill the big pail. As soon as my hands were big enough, my sister started to teach me how to get the long, steady streams of milk from Peanuts. After many lessons and much practice, I finally mastered the technique. Then the day came when I was sent to milk Peanuts alone. There I was all by myself doing the milking! I poised myself upon the stool with the pail between my legs making it sing with the long steady streams of milk that I had enviously watched my sister produce. Now I was the milker! This was the pinnacle of my success with Peanuts. I had learned to feed her and water her, how to curry and clean her. I had mastered the enviable task of cleaning her stable and finishing it with fresh bedding. Now I was the milker, able to bring forth the big pail of milk that was so important to the well being of our big family.

It is true that as time went by, I did these chores with less joyful imagination than I had at first. Still, I enjoyed working with Peanuts, for it was with her that I learned to conquer fear and envy; how to handle an unpleasant task along with learning the joy of accomplishment.

Wondering where cows go when they die, I knelt and asked God if there was a place in heaven for cows. It is clear to me, that even after she died, I was still learning from Peanuts.

❖ South Hadley Summers ❖
by Mary Ciechomski, Turners Falls, Massachusetts

When our children were young, summers were always fun and interesting in our South Hadley, Massachusetts neighborhood. The children never went to the school playground because it was over a mile away. Their dad took our only car to work each day, so the neighborhood became their playground.

After their chores, the kids got involved in many activities, like plays and shows. Many shows were performed in our basement. A memorable one was Rumplestiltskin, staged by Holly, Lynne and a few neighborhood kids. This was performed before a small audience that netted the group about sixty three cents which they donated to charity.

A trapeze over a large ditch provided many hours of pleasure, too. It was a heavy rope attached to a tree. The tree hung over a small brook so kids could swing out over the water on the trapeze. The fun ended the day Holly decided to swing doubles with a friend. She failed to hang on and plummeted fifteen feet to the edge of the brook. Fortunately, she only received a cut near her eye. Dad took that trapeze down right after work that day.

One of the most memorable summer moments involved the White Birches Golf Course. My son Steve and his friend Jimmy were into golf and decided to build a nine-hole golf course on our side lot. Actually, it had one hole and nine different tees. That one hole was on the other side of our house, so the boys had to drive *over* our house to get to the hole.

For days they worked diligently raking the area, smoothing the dirt and cutting grass. Finally, the day came to dedicate the White Birches Golf Course. The neighborhood kids were invited, as was our neighbor from across the street, and myself. We all gathered that fine morning about ten o'clock and solemnly paraded around the "course" with one of the kids carrying the American flag. We then stood at attention while Steve played the Star Spangled Banner on his trumpet. That was followed by a treat of donuts and drinks that were my gift to the occasion.

After refreshments, Steve and Jimmy announced that there would be a contest to see who could get closest to the hole in one stroke. The prize was to be ten dollars. Of course, everyone was thrilled to try for the prize and we all took a shot. We did not know that Steve and Jimmy would also be competing. Naturally, one of them won and we all left the course fuming that the contest was a "put-up job."

Summers rolled by with the golf course being replaced by a large above-ground pool which I believed could never be as much fun as the activities the kids created themselves.

❖ Camping at Mohawk Trail Campground, 1945 ❖
by Jane Daignault, Turners Falls, Massachusetts

Sunday, August 6

Wilfred and family arrived. We're all glad to see them full of pep. Helen brought a nice chicken dinner. Wilfred, Jr. is having a good snooze. In the meantime, it is sprinkling a little to cool us off. We left at 2:30 and looked like campers, all right—a cot tied to the top of the car! The ride was a treat after being so warm on Saturday.

We arrived at camp at 3:15 p.m. and it started to rain, but Jane had a classy umbrella on hand. Luckily the camp was already vacant, so we started to settle in right away. The place was rather dusty, but we were prepared. The men got ice and oil and soon we had hot water for dishes and coffee. It was swell! The precooked ham made delicious sandwiches with tomatoes, pickles, fresh corn and cake.

We brought cards, so after the dishes were done we played Rummy and I won! Then I came "home" to write. Others went for a boat ride. It is getting quite cool. We'll have to cover up tonight.

Monday, August 7

Cloudy, a little rain and damp. No bathing today—too bad for the children. Everyone had a boat ride. We cleaned cupboards. This afternoon played cards or read. Finally, the weather cleared. The boys had a ballgame with other men down the line—the boys lost. Had chicken for supper, then the sun came out. Whooppee!! Let's hope it's nice and warm tomorrow. The men went out for crawlers. We stayed in and wrote cards. Two couples decided to go to the dance down the street at the general store. We heard music there this afternoon and went for a time.

Tuesday, August 8

Glorious morning! Cool breeze in the pines. Men and children gone bathing. Our housework is done. The ladies did their marketing and came home loaded down with watermelon, corn, bread and rolls. We'll have hot dogs and corn and cold drinks out at the picnic table today. The kids turned in early. We had dinner, then one of the men picked me up and carried me into the pond and gave me a good wetting! All around laughed and laughed. Took pictures and sat on the beach—nice and warm. Played cards.

Wednesday, August 9

Nice and bright again. Thank heaven! Everybody's out swimming, playing ball, baking on the beach. I took my knitting down to the beach. I wonder how much I'll do? Had toast, donuts, jam, coffee and cocoa for breakfast. Played Monopoly (TM) and was in jail all the time! Sandwiches, corn and cold drinks later—if I don't get fat now I never will!

Thursday, August 10

Everybody sore from sunburns. Guess we'll have to buy another bottle of vinegar to soothe burnt skin. Took the baby to the beach where we built a dam and an Indian Reservation. Later we went to see the Knights of Columbus (K of C) Camp in Hawley, Massachusetts. Had ice cream at Packard's Store on the way back. Stopped at the band concert where Little Wilfred asked Helen to dance.

Friday, August 11

Peanut butter and marshmallow sandwiches, donuts, jam and coffee for breakfast. Went on a boat ride. Little Wilfred wanted to row (and also his mother!). Played Monopoly(TM) and got beat! It was 112 in Adams,

Massachusetts yesterday.

Sunday, August 13

Back from mass at the K of C chapel. Got lumbago, I guess from having my feet in cool water. Had dinner in bed and was waited on like a queen. Jane's birthday so we sang to her at breakfast. Camp is straightened out, clothes packed. A good thing, too, because the other campers are waiting to get in! Arrived home at 7:30 p.m. All tired out!

❖ Northfield Farms in Retrospect ❖
by Vera Farris, Northfield, Massachusetts

The following could be appropriately captioned, "The Changing Scene." Nostalgia seems to appear more frequently on the "scene" nowadays. It's the "in" thing.

So…if I may, I would like to acquaint you with my ol' hometown of Northfield Farms, Massachusetts. It is a little clustered settlement on Route 63, between the Erving town line, Northfield proper and the changes "Father Time" has wrought over the years.

As I was growing up, when I told people outside my town limits where I lived, they always said they'd never heard of it. Some even laughed. To avoid ridicule, I simply started answering that I lived in Greenfield, Massachusetts. Today, since the Northfield Mountain project was built in our front yard, Northfield Farms is very well known to most people.

The village and its inhabitants were self-sufficient in my time. We had the Number Four Community Schoolhouse within short walking distance to enlighten and enliven our young days. Miss Brailey and Miss Fish were at the helm of that institution of learning. They were also the guardians of the single file of youngsters heading for the nearby cemetery every Memorial Day to place wild flowers on the graves.

Mrs. Nettie Gilbert was the librarian at the Farms Library. She also substituted for the absent teacher when the school needed her. When I first learned to read, I devoured every word in the books. In due time I graduated to my older brother's tastes in Horatio Alger books and read them with interest. River Boys, Aesop's Fables and Arabian Nights held me in paralyzed fascination.

With each school grade, my fancies wavered and by the time I reached seventh grade, I was wading brow deep in Edgar Rice Burroughs' books and tingling with the horrors and adventures of the mighty Tarzan. Soon, Zane Grey and Max Brand with their galloping cowboys replaced my jungle interests. Budding womanhood found me engrossed in love stories.

The library is still with us and brings back many moments made enjoyable for me through reading. Books were my only option since my family couldn't afford luxuries like radio, television, transportation or small change for the children's matinee.

Our self-reliance wouldn't be complete without mention of the rustic railroad station, the quaint post office and variety store neighboring our family home's boundary line.

I can't forget Mr. Wood, an elderly gentleman and proprietor of the variety store—a rural establishment. When business ebbed low, he would retire to his home across the dirt road and settle down in his comfortable rocking chair. He was always "on call," though. When a homemaker needed an item that she forgot to pick up on her semi-monthly shopping trip to the larger towns, a knock on Mr. Wood's door would bring him out to meet any need. How he would grumble at times!

"I hope you kids aren't getting me out for a few measly penny candies," he might say. Some prankish children would purposely get him out to the store and then run away.

Mr. Nash, the milkman, was right across the road. He could help you when the family cow was dry or if you needed ice to make your weekend treat of ice cream.

A walk to Tenny's filling station years later was how we satisfied our appetite for homemade ice cream. Mr. Hammond, the meat man, was also handy when the family supply of fresh meat dwindled.

The Raleigh man would come by weekly to leave vanilla extract, coffee, tea, and more in exchange for eggs and produce. Neighbors were close, warm, friendly and helpful in times of need. There was much sharing.

These people and their occupations have long gone. The schoolhouse facilities were terminated years ago. The post office was eliminated. The railroad station has been neglected. The small town store was torn down out of necessity and our latter day gas station is out of business. All these changes in my short years of existence I find almost impossible to believe.

Today's landscape may be a thing of beauty to travelers passing through on Route 63 near the site of the Northfield Mountain Project, but that's because they haven't been long term residents of Northfield Farms. To the natives the area looks unlike anything they remember being born into and brought up in for years.

I'm still young and broad-minded enough to appreciate progress, but is it necessary to eradicate a village in the process? I've always stood in awe of a building going up—being born so to speak—but always saddened by its demise. Old and sturdy homes which withstand the ravages of time and the elements crumble under the wheels of bulldozers—all in the name of progress.

When a house is "laid to rest" it's a heart wrenching site. Its windows are plucked out one by one. It's encircled by a heavy chain tied to tractors. The driver drives and the house trembles, groans and finally, with a heavy sigh, succumbs, collapsing like a house of cards. The speed of this process can take your breath away. A bulldozer then pushes the brick, wood, plaster, aged dreams and hidden memories into a pit and covers it over with dirt. So far, seven homes and five cottages in Northfield Farms have gotten in the way of progress and suffered the consequences.

Progress can be a cold, cruel, eradicator of warm, fond memories. Ghandi once said "There is more to life than increasing its speed." So sadly true.

Elaborate steps have been taken by those in charge of this progress to beautify the area of leveled homesteads. The area is seeded with grass and dotted with picturesque evergreens. Unfortunately, it doesn't even come close to being the same. This nostalgia and sentiment may not mean much to some, but when one gets older, places and things with which they weathered so many years of life get to be a part of them.

As I've gotten to be fairly aged, I feel affectionately close to all people, almost every animal, bush, tree and building. I'm nostalgic about a silly old apple tree, for example. I grew up with that tree and did indeed see it, as poet Joyce Kilmer did, "in summer wear a nest of robins in her hair." The apple tree shared its fragrance and beauty in the spring. It gave off shade in the sweltering heat of summer. There was an abundance of apples for pies and jellies to relish in the fall. In its branches there was the makeshift tire swing for youngsters to enjoy.

I can't forget the sight I witnessed during a severe wind storm several years ago. I was watching out of my kitchen window and saw every blade of grass, every bush and tree swaying in the wind. I had been preparing supper and left the window for a second to check on my boiling potatoes. When I returned I was stunned, horrified, close to tears: the tree was gone! My gnarled and stalwart apple tree had been uprooted and was down in a horizontal position. It had bowed and broken under the pressure of the high winds.

If we ever wanted to give this land back to the Indians who once inhabited it, I doubt if at this point, even they would take it back.

❖ A Hide and Go Seek Story ❖
by Edith J. Fisher, Leyden, Massachusetts

When I was about four years old, my sister Christine (seventeen months younger) and I were playing hide and go seek around our home at Denison's Mill in Colrain, Massachusetts. I was "it."

I counted out and went to find my sister. I looked and looked for her for a long time and couldn't seem to find her. I knew I needed to go in and tell my mother. She and an aunt, who had come to visit, came out to help me.

I remember walking with my aunt who had on high button shoes and a long skirt. I think those details stand out because I remember at that moment being scared about not finding my sister.

The three of us looked and looked, but still we couldn't find her so we got my father who worked just across the way at the sawmill. Since we had looked for so long and couldn't find her, people began to become afraid that she had fallen into the Green River which ran just in back of our house. Soon, the other mill workers had left their jobs and come out to help us look for her.

When it began to get dark, hope began to fade. My father asked one hired man to go to Greenfield, Massachusetts and bring back help to drag the river. The hired man went out into the barn to hitch up our horse to our buggy. When he looked into the buggy he found my sister. She was asleep under the seat! It was a happy ending to a scary situation.

❖ A Move to Heaven ❖
by Suzanne Gluck-Sosis, Greenfield, Massachusetts

In April of 1995, Phil and I were married. He was eighty three and I was seventy.

It was a love match and we were joined spiritually at Beth Israel Hospital in Newark, New Jersey while Phil was waiting to have triple bypass surgery. That was in November of 1994, Thanksgiving actually. My son and his wife left their Thanksgiving festivities in Vermont to be with us. We were so touched by their love.

We were married officially five months later with all our children, grandchildren and friends by our side helping us celebrate. It was lovely and delicious. Afterward, we were able to sell my house in New Jersey. We used that money to buy our "log cabin" here in Greenfield, Massachusetts in November 1996.

The house is perfect for us. It has only one floor and a huge basement which holds our still unopened or partially unpacked boxes of books and memorabilia. Across the street from us is Highland Park where one can walk on many wooded trails in all seasons.

We are surrounded by tall, old, stately evergreens and when it snows it looks like a white fairyland. Once a red cardinal perched amid the braches of a snow covered hemlock. It looked exactly like a greeting card or painting. Heavenly!

    Phil and I both grew up in the New York City area. It buzzed with activity. It was full of tall, cramped buildings where sun rarely shone its full radiance. We loved the hustle and bustle of living in the "Great Metropolis" until we moved to Greenfield.

    What caused us to move here? We concluded that being close to family was more important than the conveniences a big city could offer. My son, his wife and my granddaughter Sonya live in Vermont. Phil has Parkinson's disease and I couldn't drive so far anymore. I felt it so important for us to bond with Sonya. Grandparents are important people in the life of a child.

    Today we are happily embedded in our new environment. We love the slower pace of our community which has everything we could want. We love being close to downtown and close to the woods. We love the friends we've made and the activities we are devoted to, like our church and the Restorative Justice program. When I recently broke my arm, I was overwhelmed at the thoughtful, helping-hands that came to my aid from the time of my fall through the surgery. We hardly missed a step in our lives thanks to the help of friends.

    Right now we are planning to have an eighty-sixth birthday celebration for Phil in the fall of 2000. We're inviting all our relatives and friends from here and from many other states. Children and grandchildren are cooking up skits, music, poems and more. It's wonderful to remember and reinforce family ties—both biological and those added along the way. They are one of the most basic and deepest meanings of life.

❖ The 1938 Hurricane ❖
by Dorothy G. Hmieleski, South Deerfield, Massachusetts

The day had been extremely hot and humid for fall. The sky was overcast and the air was still. There was almost a palpable weight to it.

My sister, brother and I watched out the window as my father made a last minute check to see that everything was secured outside. He checked the barn, the woodshed and the hen house.

My grandmother sat in the kitchen and peeled peaches. She was preparing them for canning. She gently chided my mother for not helping her.

In the distance, we heard the low rumble of thunder. The wind came up and lightening flashed. Staccato drops of rain sounded on the old tin roof. My brother and sister and I stood transfixed at the window. Our familiar yard was transformed. Great torrents of rain fell. The last of the season's leaves were ripped prematurely from the trees. The trees were writhing and bending in the wind. The dirt driveway was rapidly turning into a river. Small branches joined the other debris being swept away in the swirling water.

Suddenly, loud screams rent the air. Joshua, our baby pig, ran about the yard terrified because his house had just blown away. My father and brother quickly donned their bathing suits and went out into the storm. Within a few minutes they had captured Joshua and shut him safely in the barn.

We grew accustom to the raging of the storm. My grandmother had finished the peaches and had taken up her crocheting. Our complacence was shattered, however, by a crash and then the lights went out. The oak tree, which graced the entrance to our driveway, had fallen. My parents lit kerosene lamps and, as the storm abated, we went to bed.

We woke in the morning to a new world. The sun shone brightly and the air was fresh and clean. Outside, the ground was littered with twigs, branches and leaves. The small pine grove behind the barn had been damaged to an extent that would take nature years to repair. It was many days before we were to have electricity again, but we were safe and our house was intact.

❖ A Bear in Our Backyard ❖
by Jean Kozlowski, Northfield, Massachusetts

I happened to glance out my back door one summer to see a bear at my birdfeeder.

I yelled at my husband, "You won't believe it, but there's a bear in our backyard!"

Quickly, I rushed upstairs for my camera to capture a shot before it disappeared. Standing on my deck, I felt safe enough to snap a few pictures. As I stood there, I noticed branches moving on one of the tall trees. To my amazement, there were two bear cubs swaying back and forth on those branches!

Although I was hesitant to walk off the deck, I clapped my hands trying to scare the mother bear away. She wore a tracker around her neck, which told me she had been spotted before.

My hand clapping did not discourage her in the least. She merely backed up a little to get a better look at me. Then she decided to continue eating the black oil sunflower seeds in the feeder. Standing on her hind feet, she popped the seeds rapidly into her mouth. When she was finished, she must have used a silent signal because her two cubs hustled down the tree to follow her. In the meantime, I alerted our local police that a mother bear with two cubs was in our backyard, but by the time the police arrived she had taken off with her offspring.

The following day, my next door neighbor informed me that the bear had visited his feeder on his back porch! He had reported it to the police who told him it was probably the same bear that had visited me the day before.

I kept a sharp eye out for her as we had fairly dense woods in the back of our house that extended up South Mountain Road.

While I was watering the garden that evening, I saw her ambling up our dirt road with her two cubs behind her. Unafraid, she sauntered quietly into the woods.

Since then she has been sighted in Erving, Massachusetts numerous times. I felt it was the same mother bear that had visited me because of her tracker and her two cubs. It was an unusual and exciting event, but I did not continue to feed the birds in the summer. That seemed to be a definite attraction to bear.

I always secretly hoped she would come tramping into the area again, but she didn't visit our place. I do have a snapshot, though!

❖ Mother, the Illuminator ❖
by Warren LeMon, Turners Falls, Massachusetts

When the Greyhound bus pulled out of the Los Angeles depot, a mother and her three children settled themselves in two rows of seats. The children's names were Angeline, Dawon and Buddha. Their ages were seven, six and five.

The bus' final destination was New York City. The family was traveling to Chicago where they would separate. The mother would continue

Local Color 139

on to Michigan and the children to Ohio.

The children's playful talk was delightful, graceful, and full of fancy and imagination. I, a single traveler on that same bus, stretched my legs in the aisle while the bus plowed through the California desert. I saw the mother sitting behind her children. Her eyes were squeezed shut, her hand lay across her face, and tears flowed beneath her fingers. She made no sound.

Later in the darkness the mother settled the children in their seats and covered them with their coats.

"Now it's time to hush," she told them. "I love you all."

The boy began to hum and stir about.

"Buddha," his mother called.

"Yes, Momma?"

"Do you want to feel my hand on your behind?"

"No, Momma."

"Then, hush and stay hushed."

In Arizona the older girl awoke.

"I want to see the Grand Canyon. It's right out there, but it's too dark to see," the girl said.

"What do you want? Your Momma to run alongside this bus waving a flashlight so you can see it all?" her mother teased.

"Yes!" the girl cried out.

Across the desert and the mountains and the plains the mother sheparded her trio, feeding and tending and guarding them. I had no idea why the family was making this trip, why they had separate destinations or what the future might hold for each of them. I did know, though, that I did not want to witness their farewells.

At one point the mother told her children that someday they'd be riding the bus together again, that they'd have lots of money and whenever any one of them saw something exciting out the window she'd stop the bus so they could all get out and stay there as long as they wanted. Someday.

There were about fifty passengers on that express bus. From this traveler went a prayer to the prairie stars that by a divine dispensation these three children would one night watch with adoring eyes from the bus window as their own true mother raced along the highway waving a flashlight, illuminating for her children the peaks and gorges and thrilling colors of old Arizona.

The young deserve a little heaven on earth, do they not?

❖ Reverse Roles ❖
by Janice Howard Lepore, Greenfield, Massachusetts

As Ilene replaced the brush on the vacuum for storage, Papa dozed off. It was dusk and time for his snooze.

Ilene could feel that it was also time for a major change. Change always evoked long lost memories for Papa and Ilene. Scenes, events, popped into their conversations like watching an old slide show.

"Remember the time I found the doll furniture hidden under my bed and thought the good fairy had put it there?" Ilene would ask hoping Papa would show some glimmer of recollection. So long ago he had put so much time and energy into making the dollhouse. He had intended for it to be a Christmas gift. When it wasn't finished to his satisfaction, Momma suggested it could be a Valentine surprise. She also rationalized with him that by February, most of Santa's toys would be old hat. At least that was Momma's version. Her stories always included comments about what she thought at the time. Remembering this, Ilene was beginning to understand why Momma talked like that; even then, her conversations with Papa happened with her "home alone."

Papa's gnarled hands no longer fashioned wood into works of art. Instead, they lay folded lifeless in his lap. Shortly after Papa's doctor delivered the crushing news—Alzheimer's—Ilene took time off work under the Family Leave Act. At first it was like an extended vacation—day trips to the theater, museum, and lunches with her sister, brother-in-law or old friends. She helped out with community projects and took weekends at the beach with Gretta's twin boys—the only grandchildren. Days stretched into weeks, though, and then weeks into months and the year changed on the calendar again.

Soon, Papa could no longer be left alone. His friends didn't ask to speak to him when they called inquiring about his condition. Occasionally someone asked, "Are you OK, Ilene?" It was getting more and more difficult to respond good-naturedly. All the glib remarks had evaporated. Actually, sometimes she felt like her sense of humor was drowning in a deep pool of varying shades of blue. It was similar to how Papa's mind had disappeared into the shadows of time.

Ilene recalled that Papa had always joked with his card playing buddies saying, "Age isn't important unless you're cheese." He hadn't wasted time worrying about getting old, even after Momma died of cancer. His disease now, kept him alive, but not living. He would never have wanted to be idle, hour after hour. It seemed cruel to deprive the grandchildren of both grandparents.

Ilene also recalled another of Papa's sayings which he repeated when things hadn't gone quite as expected: "Opportunities are often things you haven't noticed the first time around."

Papa had always been so wise and patient, especially with his daughters. Being his caregiver had been an easy decision for Ilene to make and now she realized that the experience had really been one of those unforeseen opportunities.

Full of resolve, Ilene excitedly dialed Gretta's phone number. It was time for a change. Ilene knew it was time for her to get on with her life. It was time to share Papa's care with professionals. Papa had enjoyed life and he would have wanted the same for her.

❖ Senior Year: 1929 ❖
by Betty Lockwood, Charlemont, Massachusetts

Sometime in August, we moved into Harvey, Illinois. It was thirty-five miles from Cal City where we'd lived for four years. I'd been in high school there for three years. Now I'd attend a much larger school for my senior year, not knowing anyone—students or teachers.

Classes were not that different in subject matter, but teachers were a mystery to be discovered. French was new to me and so was American History. I knew I'd miss my "old" teachers, especially Miss Rice. I adored her, but Mr. Richards in my new English class was a love. The French teacher was intense and cross and banged a ruler on the desk at our faulty pronunciation. Soon, however, Mr. Turner, who taught American History, had most of my attention.

American History was very exciting. I was won over by the way Mr. Turner taught, presenting different points of view, questioning political decisions, challenging us to be skeptics. He asked our opinions almost as often as he gave his. He insisted we justify our opinions. I was completely bewitched by him as a teacher, and suddenly I realized I was also mesmerized by him as a "male person." That's when I fell in love with him. He was handsome with dark protruding eyes and dark hair. He had a serious voice but a nice smile. My eyes never wandered. I knew his every facial expression. My mind did wander, though. I daydreamed about marrying him and having a baby boy who would look just like him.

Dinner time at my home was family time with all of us talking faster than we ate. That year I'd start talking before anyone else every night.

"Today Mr. Turner said…" I'd begin

One night my father, as he started serving the first plate, grinned and spoke before I could.

"Well, what did *HE* say today?" Daddy teased me.

It was okay. I jumped into my favorite topic. "He said…" I began again.

Well, senior year ended and I wondered what life would hold for me. Weeks of summer stretched before me, but no plans at all. A few days after graduation I came home to be greeted by my mother.

"George Turner called while you were out. He asked permission to ask you for a date," she said.

"WHAT?!?!" I said.

I felt fireworks and fear. Joy and terror. Astonishment. I'd daydreamed of bearing his son, but NEVER of being asked out on a date! Mother, usually strict, gave permission. When he called back, I accepted the invitation.

We went to a beach with a couple of his friends: a reporter for the Chicago Tribune and his girlfriend. They were nice, friendly people and we had a fine afternoon. Mr. Turner asked me to call him, "George." Did I dare? I tried, and my voice didn't even squeak. We swam and then sat on the beach and talked. George asked me questions about myself while he massaged my feet and told me how beautiful they were. Wonderful! Foot massage is more pleasurable and, to me, more intimate than a hug or even a kiss.

Other dates followed: to movies or Bohemian-type nightclubs in Chicago where intellectuals gathered for talk and argument both serious and amusing—lots of shouting and laughing. I was over my head in terms of conversation, I knew, but I was always an avid listener.

George accompanied us when my family drove to Cleveland to visit Daddy's family. They were our German relatives and we didn't get to see them often. My aunt disapproved of George: "Too old." Cousins looked amazed. Grossmutter and Grossvater were hospitable and I had no idea what they thought.

George took me to see "An American Tragedy." I think he was trying to help me grow up faster. I suspect he hoped we could talk about the story and perhaps get inside my private fears and shyness, but I stayed silent. He was a dear man who moved so carefully. He was gentle, loving and considerate as he watched me, sat close to me and talked only safely to me.

One night, at my home, when we were alone (a very unusual thing for my mother to have allowed), we danced to records. George held me close and kissed me gently on the cheek. I froze, panicked. A sweet, soft kiss, not even on the mouth, but I was afraid. My mother's sex education talk from years before had been brutally effective. That terror held me.

Oh dear, Mr. Turner. He finally gave up on me. A few years later he married a much younger woman who was also a former student. He lived for only a few more years. I heard they were happy years. I hope they were. Still I wonder what my life would have been like. I almost wish…

❖ Neighbors ❖
by William R. Fitzgerald, Ashfield, Massachusetts

We were a young family in June 1960, with a new farm (a full-time job), a good sized mortgage and the need for a new barn to be built. The stress sent me to the hospital for a week with a case of ulcers. Dr. Whittier ordered me not to do anything until further notice and to try and stop worrying so much. That was about the first of June and the hay was almost ready to cut. During that month, hay nutrients can be halved—but "not to worry."

Between shivering in the hospital's basement hall outside the x-ray department awaiting a GI series and trying to "relax," the folks back at my home assured me that everything was going "OK". They told me "not to worry." Even their encouragement could only stop me from worrying sometimes.

Upon returning home, a quart of Maalox by my side, I found all the hay on the farm had been mowed and the farmyard was full of tractors, machinery and neighbors. With two more days of sunshine all of our hay was in the barn.

I recovered and I didn't know if a miracle cured the ulcers or put the hay in the barn. I'm sure all those friends just thought they were doing the neighborly thing and went home with their machinery and a warm spot in their hearts.

I've had many chances to pay back since then. When there were many and smaller farms, there was always an opportunity. Over the years I've been able to participate in fixing a barn cave-in, completing a corn harvest, three clean-ups after barn fires and a roof shoveling.

People call these helping projects "work bees" and anyone who hasn't participated in one or been the recipient of one doesn't know the feeling. It's the equivalent of bringing a casserole or pie when there is a death or sickness in a home. It makes the giver and receiver both feel good. After all, the Old English definition of "neighbor" is "the farm near you."

❖ Dear David... ❖
by Phyllis Loomis, Ashfield, Massachusetts

How well I remember when you and your wife Alice returned to my life. You had both resigned from teaching some years earlier. Your children were living far away, beginning families of their own and shaping their working lives. Their mother's illness was something they were not ready to accept. Alice was coping with advancing Alzheimer's disease and you had called on a number of your friends for help and support. You wanted help for her—to keep her living her life on whatever level was appropriate for her at the moment. I doubt, David that you had any idea of the strain those years of caring for Alice had on you. In a short time you both aged far beyond your sixty years. She still smiled and retained her upper middle class manners, but she seemed to look far away and wild. You just looked old and worn out. When we reconnected back then you hugged me in a desperate and lost way. I wondered which one of you was more in need of help.

I took my turn helping you both by spending a month each year as a member of your family. Each time upon my return, Alice had slipped further into her own world, but you, with the support of twelve, one-month-a-year extended family members, you were slowly finding the David we all remembered.

Bear hugs were your trademark and over time I felt them turn from desperation back to "Welcome, old friend!" Your sense of humor returned. Together we kept finding new and interesting ways to reach Alice.

Then Alice was gone and you and I became a lifetime family of two. Since we were both already in our sixties when we began our life together, we figured we'd have about twelve years left to share before we might begin to go downhill. We promised each other that those twelve years would be good years. In the end we had twelve years nine months. They went by much too fast, but they certainly were good.

I know that throughout our twelve years we often told each other of the joys we experienced sharing our lives together. Our recorder playing grew and introduced us to a large and interesting group of new friends. Our outdoor bathtub for four was also expanded by friendships, as was my interest in the night sky. Even you found it wonderful to look up at your heavenly friends on winter nights while sitting up to your chin in hot bath water.

We built a screened-in porch so we could sleep outdoors all year round. Each morning we took an hour-long walk before breakfast. The dogs ran in and out of the woods coming back to the road to check on us every now and then. The cats followed at a safe distance behind. You were interested in the stories told by footprints in the snow or mud, by a field of daffodils at the forest's edge, by the road crew who insisted on breaking the beaver dam near the roadside and by the beavers that quickly rebuilt the same dam. I just enjoyed the behaviors of all my walking pals.

Off and on throughout each day something would please you. You brought that pleasure to me and shared it very often. How we enjoyed smiling or laughing over something we had seen or read or just imagined. Those warm times were always accompanied by a big bear hug and usually a kiss on the top of my head. I always felt small and protected in your arms. Were you so gentle and caring because you were so very tall?

I was not the only one you hugged. You were a natural hugger.

You hugged everyone in greeting and saying good-bye. You held babies and little children in your comfortable big arms and cradled them in tenderness. You even hugged people as you were being introduced to them. Everyone seemed to know that being hugged by you was the right thing to happen. I loved that tenderness in you.

Each morning you were up making yet another exotic cereal in our old and dented double boiler. Our coffee perked on another burner, and I continued to sleep deep and snug beneath our feather quilt. You always served me my cup before climbing back into bed. There, snug and together, we planned our day or perhaps worried about the distance between our moon and Jupiter which we measured by odd things like the distance each traveled in a certain number of minutes past the checks in our window screen.

We kept learning from each other as the days passed—even deep into some nights when everyone should have been asleep. How many times did we stay up listening to the piano scores of Beethoven's symphonies or Wagner's operas and finish too exhilarated to even think of going to bed?

Many times while we were living it, I thanked you for all you gave me, but I never got to tell you that you taught me how to die in control of even this last project that we all one day complete. When you left me I knew somehow that I'd hear from you again with more positive and fun-loving experiences from wherever you were.

Soon after Alice died, you and I both promised our bodies to Harvard Medical School for medical research. You liked to say you were going to Harvard! That was fine with me, but although I had applied I was not as sincere as you until a year after you had gone. It was when I was invited to a communal service in honor of the over one hundred

Massachusetts citizens who had also donated their bodies to science and in doing so taught at least one more person something long after other "dearly departeds" were in their final resting place.

That day when I stood in the rain with a large crowd of celebrants, we all looked down the forty-foot line of commemorative white plastic name tags stuck into the damp earth. They were about twelve inches apart and bore the names of those who had donated their bodies to science that year. Your tag was one of few that had two beautifully lettered names in that small space: Maria Gongales, on top, and David Dickinson, below.

With an entire year between your death and this service I found it very pleasing to know that you will spend eternity, not cold and alone, but with your arms wrapped around Maria Gongales in a bear hug.

❖ Not for a Million Dollars ❖
by Eileen Marguet, Greenfield, Massachusetts

It was December 1943, a year after WWII started. I had just spent four days in the coach of a train traveling from New York to the west coast. It was great to finally arrive in California. My husband Bill had gotten us a place to live in Monterey as he was stationed at Fort Ord.

Money was very scarce—almost nonexistent since his pay was held up because his name was misspelled on the payroll. We were eking out a living, so far, but were down to crumbs.

There was an announcement over the radio urging people to work in the fish canneries. I heard that some society ladies from Carmel were applying for the jobs. They were replacing some cannery workers who left to go into military service.

The next morning I went to the union hall to get information about being hired.

"What are you? A packer or a cutter?" the man asked me.

"Which pays more?" I inquired.

"A cutter gets eighty-nine cents an hour," he said. "A packer gets seventy-five."

"Oh," I answered eagerly. "Put me down for a cutter."

That eighty nine cents an hour sounded very good. I was a kid from Brooklyn who used to travel on the subway to an office job in New York City. I didn't have a clue as to what was in store for me at the canneries.

We could see the Pacific Ocean from a window where we lived. I remarked to Bill, "You can tell when the fish are in because the seagulls are so numerous around the ships."

"I understand the seagulls follow the girls home that work in the canneries," Bill said. I pictured myself sitting in the bus with seagulls flapping at my window. I had a slight case of cold feet, but that eighty-nine cents an hour held me like a magnet.

Each cannery had its own whistle sound. My cannery, E.B. Gross, had two long and three short blasts. When this signal sounded, the girls started lining up to get on the bus.

The first day I arrived for work, the foreman said, "What about your boots?"

"What boots?" I asked. Nobody had told me that I needed to have boots.

"We'll loan you a pair 'til you get your own," he answered.

Hip boots are not exactly comfortable. We had to walk out on a long pier in them. Then up tall stairs to the cannery. I held onto the banister for dear life. Looking down I saw big waves splashing into the pier below.

When I reached the top of the stairs, the foreman told me to stand on one side of a big trough containing fish. There was another person on the other side. At the end was a conveyor belt with grooves to hold the fish. We were to pick up the fish and put one in each groove.

"Sardines," I said to myself, expecting to see little fish the size of goldfish. Soon I saw that some of these sardines were as big as mackerel!

"Usa two hands! Usa two hands!" the boss yelled at me above the din of the machinery. There were knives at the end of the conveyor belt that cut off the heads and tails of the fish. The fish then dropped into a bucket. These were collected and counted at the end of the day. If you had more than a certain number you got extra pay. I only got the eighty-nine cents an hour which was the minimum.

One time my trough was empty. The foreman was supposed to fill it. That was done by pulling down on a handle that was attached to a shaft above and over to one side of us. I was the only one at the trough. If it happened that we ran out of fish we were to call him as soon as possible so we could keep on working.

I looked around furtively to see if anyone would call him. Everyone was busy with their heads down.

"Fish!" I said out loud. No one heard me.

Then I ventured a little louder.

"*FISH!*" That time I was sure the foreman would hear me. Nothing.

The fish were in a huge tank filled with water. The tank was located on a balcony just above us. The foreman would pull the handle down, opening a chute and the fish would fall into the trough. Then he would push the handle back. I'd seen him do it and it looked easy.

I somehow figured that other workers like me just pulled the handle themselves when their troughs got empty. Well, I was a kid who weighed all of one hundred and ten pounds but I was sure I could pull that handle. I reached up, but couldn't quite grab it. I tried again without results, so I jumped up and got a good hold on the handle. The trapdoor opened and about a hundred fish tumbled down all over me. They were in my hair, my boots, every place! They were overflowing the trough!

It would have felt like this was the longest day of my life, except for one thing—that eighty-nine cents an hour!

I worked there for a few weeks. The first time I took the bus home I wondered if people would walk away from me; if the seagulls would pick me out of a crowd. I sat on a bench and noticed the woman next to me didn't move, so I got closer. She didn't seem to realize I was a fish canner. As a matter of fact, Heddy Lamar, that famous movie star, worked in the film, "Cannery Row" which was filmed right in Pacific Grove.

Bill's pay finally came through and he got his orders to leave the day after Christmas for O.C.S. at Fargo, North Dakota.

Christmas Day he had charge of quarters, which meant he didn't get the Christmas dinner President Roosevelt promised. I ate by myself at a Fisherman's Wharf restaurant.

The next few days we spent having a mini-vacation in San Francisco, and then we boarded a train with an upper berth courtesy of Uncle Sam. We slept so well that the first thing we heard was, "Last call for breakfast!" We staggered through the train to the dining car. The seats were all made up. People were all awake and reading their newspapers.

Later we changed trains so Bill could continue on to North Dakota and I could go back to Brooklyn.

That's the way it was—the long hours of hard work, the bittersweet meetings and partings during the war years. I wouldn't change it for a million dollars.

❖ Colrain Memories ❖
by Louise Bowen O'Brien, Colrain, Massachusetts

I met G. William Pitt when I was librarian at the Griswold Memorial Library in Colrain, Massachusetts. He was a short, rotund man with a bald head and a cheerful manner. He invited me to a meeting of his newly established Colrain Historical Society which met at his home near the library.

During my first visit to his home, he led me to a large room furnished with heavy, dark wood furniture including an imposing four poster bed. The bed was carved all over with intricate designs and figures. Bill proudly presented it as a bed slept in by Queen Elizabeth I of England. While he was on tour in England with a theatrical company, he had arranged to have it sent back to his home in the states.

To create its first display space, the Society cleaned the Old Methodist church on the common and displayed artifacts there. Townspeople and friends donated or loaned articles and keepsakes for display. A few years later the church building was sold. We had to move everything to the outbuildings by the Pitt house.

One item is a unique flag believed to be the original flag made by farm families on Catamount Hill in Colrain. It is thought to have been preserved since the War of 1812. Descendents of hill families kept it until recently when Florence Davenport Reynolds presented it to the society. It has a large white star in the center of a blue field and is made of materials one might have found in the surrounding farm homes. It was the first United States flag to be flown over a public school. That little log school on Catamount Hill is now being restored. A monument on the hill marks its location.

Since the society has grown, we have worked to have the Arthur A. Smith covered bridge placed on the National Registry of Historic Places.

That required two years of accumulating research, essays, and pictures. Many townspeople donated funds to repair the bridge when it was declared unsafe. Their names will be on a memorial plaque mounted on the bridge when the restoration is complete.

Some years after I met him, Bill died of a heart attack. He willed his home, its furnishings and property to Colrain for the Colrain Historical Society. He told me that he intended to give it to us. Today it is the G. William Pitt House on Main Street in Colrain. We rent it to a caretaker and it is open to the public on special occasions.

I believe that Bill Pitt's spirit lives on in his beloved home. I can imagine him chuckling as he points out one of his favorite paintings to a visitor, or perhaps he plays an old hymn on his grand piano.

May the Colrain Historical Society always keep alive Bill's dream of preserving Colrain.

❖ Bikes & D.O. Paul's Store ❖
by Joseph A. Parzych, Gill, Massachusetts

When I was 12 years old, I thought I was the only boy in school who didn't have a bike— maybe the only one in the country. I found one for sale—$25, the man said, and not a cent less. WW II was on and there were no bikes in the stores. All I had was $5. When Ma asked me why I was looking so glum, I told her of my problem, never expecting she could help me. But she gave me $20 out of her stash. I never forgot that. With my own set of wheels, I now could join the guys who hung around D.O. Paul's general store in Gill, Massachusetts. It felt good having a bike, to be one of them.

D.O. was tolerant of the kids who came to the store. He and his wife, Edna, were childless, but had raised a couple of boys whose mother had died. Those boys had gone off somewhere by the time we arrived on the scene and few people knew of their existence.

Mr. Paul's first name was Dorilla, but everyone called him D.O. Kids sometimes called him Dorilla the Gorilla, though not to his face. He was anything but a gorilla—slight of build, weighing about 125 pounds with his overcoat on, and not much over 5 feet tall. He had a mild manner—except when it came to politics. Herbert Hoover was his man—Roosevelt, he hated with a passion. But kids he tolerated, and maybe even liked, though it was hard to tell.

D.O. stocked canned goods, ice cream and soda, and other convenience store items. Best of all he had penny candy—a whole row of clear glass jars filled with candy. The decorative square jars had glass covers that fit snugly. But they couldn't contain that wonderful aroma of penny candy.

When a kid came in with a few pennies to buy candy, the transaction would take forever.

"How much are the root beer barrels?"

"Two for a penny."

"How much for the green gummy leaves?"

"Six for a penny."

The buyer would ask the prices of one candy after another—chocolate babies, Maryjanes, licorice, orange sections, butterscotch drops, bubble gum and red hots, then ask D.O. to repeat the prices, over and over.

D.O. would stand peering through his owlish glasses with infinite patience, repeating the prices, until the pennies clutched in a sweaty paw would be exchanged for the little brown bag filled with delicious treasures.

D.O. lost an eye somehow—no one ever wanted to ask—and it was sometimes disconcerting to have one eye fixed on you while the other one wandered about a bit. I could never figure out which eye was real and which was glass.

Each summer, D.O. closed the store for a month and took to the road in his big Buick to travel the country. The loss of an eye didn't keep him from driving long after the vision in his remaining eye dimmed considerably. Though his cross country trips finally ended, he continued to terrorize local motorists on his occasional forays into Turners Falls or Greenfield, Massachusetts.

He drove looking at the tree tops to gauge the center of the road, giving way to an oncoming car at the last minute when it got close enough for him to make out a moving shape. When folks in town spotted his approaching car straddling the center of the road, they'd pulled over to give him wide berth in passing.

In his younger days, D.O. chauffeured a limousine in Washington D.C. and he liked to reminisce about the time he chauffeured the Ambassador of China around the Capitol. He'd driven a Washington dignitary (perhaps the Ambassador) to Kitty Hawke, North Carolina, to witness Wilbur and Orville Wright's historic first flight of a gasoline-engine powered airplane on December 17, 1903.

D.O.'s life span included both that first flight and the first man landing on the moon. But nothing was as remarkable in our eyes as the fact that he'd never had an accident driving his Buick, even when he was too blind to read the gas pumps at his store when filling a customer's tank.

D.O. had left the excitement of Washington, D.C. when his father died. His entrepreneurial father left him the store in Gill and Ford automobile agency along with a fair number of investment securities.

Even during the Depression, D.O. prospered from the combined income of his store, auto repair shop, WPA salary, truck rental, and a rental property, in addition to income from his father's investments. When income tax was first voted in, only those earning more than $5,000 needed to file. That was when many wage earners grossed little more than $500 a year through the depression years.

Because he'd earned far more than the minimum, D.O. went to the Federal Revenue Department to file. The government agent looked over his income statement, and then tossed it in the waste basket, D.O. said.

He didn't file again until the federal government got serious about collecting taxes after WW II. Despite his more than comfortable income, D.O. and his wife, Edna, lived modestly in a small apartment over the store. His only extravagance was his annual migration out West, and trading for a new Buick every couple of years to avoid buying new tires.

Though D.O. prospered under the Roosevelt Democrats, he was a staunch Republican and railed on about Roosevelt, his good eye flashing. "No wonder the country's going to hell— Roosevelt greased the skids," he'd announce, waving his arms and raising his voice, face reddening and spittle flying.

Despite his loathing of Roosevelt, D.O. wasn't averse to allowing some of the Roosevelt grease cross his palm. When the Work Progress Administration (WPA) under Roosevelt began building roads, D.O. got a job as WPA foreman and put his Ford dump truck to work on WPA projects, as well. And if the workmen knew what was good for them, D.O.'s store was the place to cash their pay check, do their grocery shopping, buy their gasoline, insure their car and, for God's sake, try to remember not to say anything good about Roosevelt. Since D.O. was also the tax assessor, few people took issue with him on any subject figuring it was best to keep on his good side at all times. He never once scolded a kid for running a bike over the hose that lay across the approach to the gas pumps, sounding a bell inside the store and annoying his wife, Edna, no end. He would gaze out the window and tune out her sputtering.

D.O. died in 1971. His life span included both the Wright's first flight at Kitty Hawk and the first manned flights into space. Suzie and Phil Maddern run the store, now—penny candy and all. I brought my kids to the Gill Store when D.O. ran it, and now my son brings his. There's no alarm hose to signal a gas customer; environmental regulations ended gasoline sales, but kids on bikes still hang around the store and Suzie still carries on the tradition of patience, especially when dealing with kids buying penny candy.

❖ The Wedding ❖
by Charlotte Potter, Turners Falls, Massachusetts

My cousin Lois had lived with us while we were in Machias, Maine. She and my husband worked for the Maine Extension Service. When she was planning her wedding she asked our son Noel to be ring bearer.

We proceeded to buy him a white suit which made him look really "spiffy." It was quite plain, just shorts and a little shirt. Noel was four years old at the time. Since I was pregnant with Nedine, it was not considered proper for me to be part of the wedding party.

Everything went well until rehearsal when Noel and the flower girl were supposed to walk down the aisle together. The flower girl was anything but tactful and informed everyone that Noel was "too little" for her to walk with. Fortunately, Noel was easy going and proceeded to ignore her remarks.

In one picture, Noel is in his spiffy white suit doing what he did best—eating. I have a feeling he had his eyes on the refreshment table even before the ceremony began. He couldn't wait to get all his goodies after the wedding ceremony was over.

By the way, a potentially awkward situation was solved by having the flower girl march down the aisle by herself while Noel followed along behind her.

❖ The Cousins ❖
by Charlotte Robinson, Turners Falls, Massachusetts

Once, when I was eight or nine, we were visiting my mother's sister, Aunt Bessie, at her home in Hopkinton, New Hampshire. We were probably just about to leave for our home in Stoneham, Massachusetts. It seemed to me that every visit, the time of departure meant that someone would locate a camera for the mandatory "leaving the farm" pictures.

The routine was always the same—someone in charge would arrange the people in the picture in a 'well-balanced' arrangement. The three in the back row of one photo are my only maternal cousins. There had been an older son, but he died when he was twelve. Those three remaining were always arranged by height so that the oldest was always in the middle, the one with the uncontrolled mass of hair and the youngest were on either side. Then we were arranged by age. In this photo we seem to be a bit misplaced as my sister Priscilla's head erases the youngest cousin's chin.

I was always in the middle, but my brother Ross Jr. and Priscilla switched sides depending on the mood of the arranger.

The youngest cousin, though a girl, was like a substitute son to Uncle Ira when it came to farm work. She could toss a fork of hay nearly as easily as he did. She could layer hay in the wagon so the load didn't become top heavy. The oldest cousin, who was named after my grandmother, helped with the indoor work of cooking, cleaning, washing and generally assisting Aunt Bessie who was handicapped. The cousin with the unruly hair, being "sickly" could always be found napping or reading a book.

Aunt Bessie's handicap came from an accident when she was thrown from a carriage. The horse shied when a car horn blasted too close to it. As a result of that overturned horse-drawn cart, many of the bones in Aunt Bessie hips and leg were rearranged. There were many doctors in the Concord, New Hampshire area who could have put her back together again (like Humpty Dumpty), but Aunt Bessie always said that she had been through enough pain from the accident. She actually chose not to go through more pain to get all of her bones straightened. So the rest of her life she shuffled around the house with two canes while telling everyone else what needed to be done.

Priscilla and I are wearing our beautiful (but too big) "hand-me-down" coats in this photo. We seemed to gather "grown-out-of" clothing: suits, jackets, hats and long white stockings. In the picture, Priscilla and I and the flappers in the nation's big cities were all in high fashion wearing dropped waist dresses as Ma, even though she was an excellent seamstress, didn't alter our clothes except to take up hems (which to our desires were always left too long).

When Uncle Ira and his brother Fred were in high school, their father told them that he couldn't afford to send both boys to college. Fred chose to go to college and Uncle Ira inherited the farm which encompassed almost all of Putney Hill. Fred graduated from college, married and had a good life. The three sisters sold their house lots on Putney Hill for outrageous sums of money. Uncle Ira managed the farm.

I don't remember the name of the dog which appeared in many of the photos. The sun was always in our eyes which accounts for the hangdog expressions on our faces. I don't know why we weren't wearing hats. Maybe it was because the older cousins just grabbed their coats when summoned for another picture. Our hats were probably in the car. We would certainly wear hats in the car because the car had such thin walls that the wind blew right in as we proceeded home at a rate of thirty-five miles per hour.

❖ Fun & Games in Turners Falls, Massachusetts ❖
by Juliana Sivik Samoriski, Shelburne, Massachusetts

During my childhood, we had what are quite rare today—empty lots of land. Although they were private property, owners didn't seem to mind the neighborhood kids playing on them. For no reason, at any given time, a group of us could gather spontaneously. Seasonal games were played regardless of the number who made themselves available.

In early fall there was a short lull in the gatherings because everyone was busy adjusting to the new school year. It was not long before the "gang" congregated in the field to play kick the can, releavo, hide n' seek, giant steps, red light and if someone had a few pieces of chalk from school, we played follow the arrow around Grove Street, Chestnut, Maple, Prospect, Park and Central Streets. These were pretty much daylight games.

Shortly after school opened, the clocks were turned back and that meant an eight o'clock curfew. The factory whistle blew loud and clear and our games were over. It was time to go home, or else!

In late fall we played tag football. I was usually able to get a cloth bag from a ten pound bag of sugar. We stuffed the bag with fallen leaves for a football. It needed additional leaves often and after a while this football got quite hard. I know as I was once hit over the head with it because I pushed an opponent a little too hard.

Once the snow fell, out came the skis, "rips," sleds, toboggans and skates. We shared what we had. When Thanksgiving vacation started on Wednesday at noon, my friend Mary and I checked the frog pond on the Rys' property to see if it was frozen. Invariably it was and our skating season began. Daytime skating took place at the frog pond. For evening skating we went to the "baby swimming pool" on First Street near Unity Park. This was complete with a heated shack and a nicely flooded skating rink.

All types of skiing were done on our own Hillside Avenue hill, though to look at the hill today it looks so small! The street was blocked off for skiing by the town. There were several streets blocked off throughout the town which meant that cars could go around cautiously. Of course, these hills made for the best skiing in Turners Falls. Unity Park hill was also filled. We slid down the small school hills on salvaged pieces of cardboard and automobile number plates. The number plate was the fastest down hills and of course we all preferred using one when we could.

During the winter season, homework took a back seat to winter sports. Often times I found myself fumbling before our class geography recitation because I had not done my homework. I often wondered if the teacher knew I was with the noise making crowd on the nearby hill!!

When Spring arrived, the neighborhood gang took to the surrounding empty lots again. Someone was usually able to come up with a bat and a ball. If we were lucky we shared a baseball glove or two. Baseball season began! And so did the noise! Once in a while we were told to cut down on the arguing and the noise. Sometimes we were even told to leave a lot, but that wasn't often. The adults would sometimes come out and watch us and even play ball with us.

It seems we always thought of something to do. Sometimes it was a good thing, and sometimes not so good! When it became dark and it was still before curfew, we would play "ring the doorbell." One of us was chosen to stick a pin in a doorbell so it would ring continuously. Then we'd all run and hide and watch the reaction of the person answering the bell. Sometimes we got caught if we played the game too often and that was bad news!

Another game we played was pea shooting. We bought a pea shooter which was a hollow tube through which you could blow dried peas. We could spend a whole evening trying to break a streetlight bulb with a pea. This took a good part of the evening. These last two "games" were usually followed by police cruisers combing our streets. That meant it was time to go home quickly. No doubt the powers that be knew the culprits.

Spring brought daylight savings time and a nine o'clock curfew. One whole extra hour to play! *Whoopee!*

Soon school was over and summer had begun. With the roads being tarred and the weather so hot, the neighborhood kids made their way to the swimming hole we called "The Birches" on the Connecticut River. There was a very steep, sandy hill you had to go down to get there, so we bounced down. Returning from there I remember moving slowly and being completely exhausted.

The water was very deep, but we could all swim. Pollution did not enter our minds at all, though the river was brown after a rainstorm. I remember swimming a distance out from the shore when I saw a large dead fish floating downstream. I vividly remember picking up the fish and throwing it out of my way. We had a makeshift diving board and between swimming and diving the summers slipped away fast.

We had clothes we wore only to church and clothes that were only for school and clothes that were only for play.

Sunday was a quiet family day. We went to church, had dinner and went visiting. Saturday afternoon was generally movie day at the Shea Theater. For only ten cents we saw Paramount News (sometimes "The March of Time"), a serial like Rin Tin Tin, Tom Mix, The Lone Ranger, maybe a comedy starring Laurel and Hardy, The Three Stooges, The Marx Brothers, to name a few. Plus we saw a feature presentation and sometimes a double feature. Oh, how we cheered when Mr. Shea announced the coming attractions at his theater! Monday he had a five o'clock special movie for children. It cost five cents. A comedy and news with a full-length movie. Tuesday afternoon and evening was known as "theater dish day" meaning every adult received a dish eventually making up a twelve piece set of dishes. The Shea was the central point for town entertainment.

We did not have a television when I was a child. We played children's card game and board games. The new popular game back then was Monopoly (TM). To this day, I believe repeatedly playing this game helped me a great deal in mathematics and in later years helped me understand real estate.

Thoughts of those years gone by bring pleasant memories of people and places in Turners Falls. I still smile over each memory.

❖ The Cat ❖
by Doris Shirtcliff, Greenfield, Massachusetts

He was a fifteen pound altered male cat—gray and white short hair. "Just another cat," you say? Wrong! From a humble beginning, he rose to aristocracy. Not only his physique, but his mental prowess was responsible for that.

Several years ago, he was one of a litter of six born to a barn cat. He was a small, round, fat thing. He was wild and skittish—afraid of any noise and unfamiliar thing and quick to back up and hiss and scamper away. No wonder! He was taken from a familiar background—the sweet smell of milk and hay, the playful antics of his siblings and the warm, watchful eye of his mother.

Moving to a residential area near downtown made him strictly a house cat. However, his mistress soon learned that this demanding four-legged creature could raise havoc with an apartment. He didn't want to be alone all day. He wanted out and shortly became acquainted with the back porch and yard. From there he ventured across the street to sit on someone else's porch. Rather than call to him and take a chance on him being hit by a car, it was better to cross the street and pick him up and he had no objection to this. He quickly associated this action with his evening meal and began to arrive home and wait for his mistress about that time.

There was an adventurous time in his young life when he assumed the role of an alley cat. He ventured out at night after supper and returned very late. Even on cold winter nights he didn't seem to be wet or cold. He smelled of fish and french fries and other greasy food. We think he slept near the hot air vent of a local fast food restaurant.

He was never a lap cat, but wanted the comfort of sleeping in someone's bed or in the best chair of the house. He loved the members of the household, but a stranger could not get close. Perhaps this was the reason for his survival.

Four years later he moved to a rural area. This is when he truly became a "Cat" with a capital "C." New sights and sounds caught his attention. He pounced on every crawling, hopping thing and promptly deposited them on the back steps. He walked atop stone walls like the lord of the manor. His pink paw pads became black and tough as leather. His body became a mass of well-developed muscles, all working in unison when he slinked along the edge of a meadow. Stalking through the tall grass, he could manage a loud, long *"Meeeooowww"* with a guttural tone. This meant he was clutching something in his mouth. He would emerge proudly, head held high and tail pointing straight up. We were never too happy with the gifts he brought us from there. If his mistress went away for a week, he paid her no attention on her return. He was punishing her in his own feline manner. However, he had been known to wander off for a week at a time, causing everyone concern, only to nonchalantly appear smelling of warm milk and hay, expecting to be loved and welcomed—and he usually was.

When a snowstorm was expected, his green eyes flashed and he got a little crazy. He raced across the top of the divan, jumped from armchair to coffee table and acted like a kitten again. He ended these capers with a twisting jump and would throw his hip against the wall making a dull thud.

For all his size and bravado, he melted when confronted with his female companion. She was a small tiger cat that shared the house with him. She was a small, fun loving feminine kitty. He tried to teach her to hunt, but only had moderate success. He usually had to help her finish off her prey, but stayed his distance until she needed help. He wouldn't eat from the same dish if she got there first. He sat patiently, letting her have her fill and then took his turn like a true gentleman.

Milk was his favorite food, but it had unpleasant consequences, so it was rationed. He knew I would give him some and as I didn't see him often, I didn't feel guilt about it. He rubbed against my leg, usually causing me to stumble. I scolded him and he sat aside staring me down. He squinted at me and I understood what he was thinking: "Well, are you going to give me some of that milk or be an old witch?"

Epilogue:

The cat died one January day. He was found dead in the garage with no sign of injury at all. He was just stretched out, full length, as though asleep. He was buried in the garden in a wooden box with a blue towel for a liner. We still miss him! However, we feel better knowing he has a job. He helps the daisies and daffodils grow.

❖ Aniwa ❖
by Norah (Noreen) J. Torrey, Greenfield, Massachusetts

In the summer of 1928 our whole family took off for a vacation on the Isle of Man, which is a small island located between England and Ireland. I think it has only two claims to fame: that it is the home of the famous Manx cats, which have no tails, and that it is also the site of the T.T. races which are motorcycle races well-known throughout Britain. It is, in addition, a very beautiful little island with lovely glens and beaches.

As my English grandfather's family expanded to nine children, it became too expensive to stay in hotels during their vacations, so he had a large, three-story house built outside the little village of Kirk Michael where all of them could be accommodated in comfort. The house was called "Aniwa" and our whole family—including numerous cousins and their families—has happy memories of vacations spent there.

The first holiday at Aniwa of which I have any memory was when I was five years old. I think the reason I remember that visit so clearly is because of two incidents that took place during the visit. The first one was actually on the boat going over from England.

We had recently returned from India, where my father was a missionary with the Church of England. I was the third of four children with an older brother and sister and a much younger sister who was an infant at the time. The journey across took about four hours and was often quite stormy. Walking up the gangway to the boat, holding my mother's hand, I happened to look down at the narrow strip of water between the boat and the dock. Down there, bobbing around on the choppy water, was a trunk. I could see quite clearly the initials "L-W" on it. My maiden name was Lea-Wilson with a hyphen, so I knew it was our trunk. I tugged on my mother's hand and said urgently, "Mummy, Mummy, our trunk fell in the water!"

Of course my mother didn't for a minute believe me. She maintains that I often used to invent stories, so it's quite understandable that my claiming our baggage was in the water would seem a little far-fetched. She was probably feeling a bit harassed trying to get us all safely aboard, so she just said briskly, "Don't talk such nonsense, darling, come along now." I tugged on her arm again, trying to convince her. "It did! It did!" I kept saying. I remember the feeling of frustration when she wouldn't believe me. However, there was nothing more that I could do. I finally gave up and we walked on to the boat and started the trip across to the island.

Oh, how sweet was my triumph a few hours later! At the end of the voyage, all the passengers assembled on the upper deck. Their names were then called out alphabetically so that they could claim their baggage. When the "L's" were called out and we were not among them, my parents were not too worried as we would quite often be listed under the "W's." However, the "W's" came up and we were still not called. Finally all the passengers had been accounted for and we were still standing there. At that moment an official came up to us and said that the captain would like to speak to my parents in his office. Of course I was not allowed to accompany them and had to stay with my older sister and brother, but I knew exactly what was being said in the captain's cabin! Most of the contents of the trunk, which they had managed to retrieve, had been ruined by sea water. Although we were reimbursed for our losses through the ship's insurance, the money meant nothing to me. I was much too busy basking in my moment of triumph, while graciously accepting my father's admiring comments and—sweetest of all—my mother's abject apologies.

The second memorable incident which occurred during that holiday did not have quite such a happy outcome—at least for me—although I have long since come to terms with it.

In addition to our own family, there were several of our cousins and their families staying in the house. One of my father's unmarried sisters, Aunt Norah (for whom I was named) and an adult family friend, who also happened to be named Norah, were included in the party. My parents decided, very sensibly, that having three Norahs in the house was too confusing and decided to make some changes.

There were two living rooms in the house one for grown-ups and one for children. I remember vividly the day my mother came into the children's room with the news that the grown-ups had been talking it over and had decided to change the names of two of the Norahs. Aunt Norah was to stay the same, the adult friend was to be called "Nona" and I was to be "Noreen". My siblings and cousins immediately started to tease me, repeating "Hello, Noreen! Hello, Noreen!" over and over until my tears began to flow.

Since I was only five years old, it seemed rather traumatic at the time—almost like suddenly losing my identity—but the name stuck and has stayed with me for the rest of my life. Although I still have to sign my checks and carry out any other official business transactions as "Norah," all my family and friends know me as "Noreen."

Years later it almost caused a crisis when I was getting married because my American husband-to-be wanted me to use the name "Norah" during the marriage ceremony. I think he was worried that we might not end up properly married if I said, "I, Noreen, take thee, John!" However, in the end we compromised and I said "Noreen" during the ceremony, but signed the register afterwards with my official name, "Norah."

Many years later in 1956, after spending seven years in California, my husband and I travelled to England on the Queen Mary with our three small daughters. This was my first visit home since our marriage. An uncle and aunt were living in Aniwa at the time, so I decided to take the girls over for a visit while my husband was attending some meetings.

They all loved Aniwa! The two older ones, who were five and six, can still clearly remember the visit. (My oldest daughter was just reminding me that she first learned to ride a bicycle at Aniwa.) My uncle and aunt had had central heating installed and had made many other changes which had turned their home into a very comfortable home for their retirement years.

My husband and I subsequently had two more daughters but the house had been sold by the time we returned to Britain, so they were never able to see Aniwa except in pictures. It remains, however, a vivid memory of my growing up years and our five daughters loved hearing stories about life on the Isle of Man.

One of the stories they always enjoyed was about my namesake, Aunt Norah. We youngsters would be sitting happily installed in front of a roaring fire in the children's room—our noses buried in books—while the wind and rain were lashing at the windows. At this point, Aunt Norah would come bouncing in and exclaim with great enthusiasm,

"Take me to the sea!" We would all groan loudly. Finally, with much reluctance, we would drag ourselves up to put on raincoats for the long trek to the beach. I should say, in her defense, that we usually ended up having a wonderful time in spite of the rain as she was one of our favorite aunts. We would all arrive home, soaking wet, but rosy-cheeked and laughing.

Aniwa remained in my family for many years but, after my uncle's death, it was turned into a nursing home for a while and then subsequently sold to a private owner.

The Isle of Man holds many memories for me and my siblings, but perhaps those two events that took place there in 1928 had the most profound impact on me. My family's lack of belief in me and my triumphant vindication, rapidly followed by the ignominious loss of my name, made for a very memorable vacation for a five-year-old.

Now about to enter my seventy-eighth year, and enjoying the privilege of spending my remaining years in this beautiful town of Greenfield,

Massachusetts, I often look back with love and nostalgia to that big house on a far-away island in the middle of the Irish Sea.

❖ The Wedding ❖
by Leona Robert, Turners Falls, Massachusetts

A wedding can be the occasion of excitement, preparation, happiness, a wee bit of sadness, humor and anxiety. Such was the case on May 30, 1981, when our granddaughter Phyllis was to be married. She was the oldest of Theresa and David's three daughters.

Phyllis wanted her reception to be held in her parents' backyard which was a lovely spot. There was to be no caterer; only her mother's cooking qualified for the event. So each night after work for days in advance, Theresa prepared dozens of dishes lasagna, casseroles, baked beans, meats desserts, and more. All were stored in their freezer and the freezers of many neighbors. Tables and chairs were borrowed from the church; tents were rented and set up as protection from rain or the heat (which soared to 100 degrees that day).

The day finally arrived. After much hustle and bustle everything was ready. All were dressed; the neighbors' ovens were turned on and filled with dishes to heat while we attended the service. Off we went to church.

Everything was going so smoothly. The bridesmaids and ushers looked their best and the bride was just beautiful walking down the aisle on her father's arm.

About midway through the ceremony, a huge spider could be seen hanging from its web on the ceiling and lowering itself down directly behind the minister. All eyes were on that spider and many, trying to suppress giggles, hoped it would not land on the minister.

The church had no fans and was becoming very uncomfortable. Suddenly, Kristen (one of the bridesmaids) fainted, falling hard to the floor. The ceremony came to a halt as the wedding party gathered around her. Some tried to fan her; others went for cold water to cool her. Finally, she was helped to a seat in the front row where she remained. The ceremony resumed and the "knot was tied." Leafy, a neighbor, had his camera and snapped a great shot of the bride bending over the prostrate bridesmaid.

After we returned from the church, neighbors paraded in from everywhere carrying hot dishes of food. They were a terrific group of friends.

The remainder of the day went on without further problems. Poor Kristen, however, had to refrain from much of the merriment that followed.

It was a wedding we will always remember.

❖ Back Home to the Farm for Christmas ❖
by Ellen C. Tosi, Northfield, Massachusetts

One snowy day, early in December, many years ago, my father hitched Jenny, our frisky horse, up to the sleigh. Soon we left our farm and were on our way to town traveling across the frozen Connecticut River to my grandparent's house, Crane Cottage in Northfield, Massachusetts. What an exciting day it was in spite of the fact that my mother was going to the hospital so close to Christmas Day.

My brothers were going to be staying with my father on the farm and my little baby sister was going to a friend of Mother's. I was the lucky one to be going to Grandmother's huge boarding house full of hiding places and long hallways to race through. Best of all, there was a lady who lived there who had two little girls a little older than me. They played games with me, especially hide-and-seek, in Grandmother's big house. This was a special treat for me, as there were no little girls to play with on my family's farm.

There was also an elderly lady who taught German at the girls' private school across the street. She taught me how to make six-pointed stars: bright red ones, yellow, green and all out of bright, shiny paper so I could hang them on my Christmas tree when I got home.

About halfway through my visit, I came down with a cold. Grandma put me to bed and started trying her old fashioned remedies on me. A mustard paste was applied to my chest (I hoped I could avoid that!). There was Vicks Vaporub to breathe and to be rubbed on my throat. She lavished me with her homemade chicken soup garnished with little wisps of grated cheese floating on top. There was the freshly squeezed orange juice, as well as delicious custards and store-bought ice cream. On the farm, ice cream was made only in the summer and only the old-fashioned way in a crank freezer with heavy cream from our Guernsey cows. In winter, the cream was made into butter in the big wooden churn. Store-bought ice cream was a special delight in winter.

Before bedtime, I was soothed with a quick, warm bath. Grandma scented it with fragrant crystals and bubbles unlike my bath at home where I washed in a tub in front of the old Crawford stove. Before saying goodnight, Grandma would tuck a lovely, little lavender sachet into my hand. I felt wonderfully spoiled and I loved it!

While I was sick, my older brother came over from the farm one afternoon and entertained me. He could think of more funny things to make me laugh! Like how the little cat, Buster, tried to walk, but was so fat that just as he was starting to walk forward, his gears shifted and he was going backwards! We laughed so hard and I could see it was getting to Grandma. After he left, she said she was glad he was gone. It was fun for me, but Grandma hadn't had children around for years and didn't appreciate his humor.

Finally, I began to feel better and the novelty of being at Grandma's began to wear thin. It had been so much fun at first.

Christmas morning finally came and Grandma woke me to say Santa Claus had come the night before while I was asleep. She said he left me a string stocking filled to overflowing with candy and toys. It hung on the bedpost at the foot of my bed. I could see an orange in the toe of the stocking and goodies all the way up to the top. I knew Grandma wanted me to be excited, but suddenly I wanted to be home to see the Christmas tree I knew my father and brothers had brought down from the woods. It would be hemlock, tall enough to touch the ceiling in the parlor. Its flat side, which hemlocks always seem to have, would be against the wall. More than just seeing the tree, I wanted to hang my stars in its branches.

I was never happier when my father telephoned that Christmas morning and told me he was coming to take me home.

After breakfast I stood before the window where I could see way down the road, and I watched for our horses. When he came in sight, I rushed out onto the porch to hear the sleigh bells, *our sleigh bells*, jingling down the road.

I will never forget how excited I was when my father drove into Grandma's yard with Jenny prancing like one of Santa's reindeer.

When we got back to the farm, I dashed in to find Mother checking on the Christmas goose in the old Crawford stove.

I made a beeline for the parlor to hang my stars on the Christmas tree and there it was, a hemlock, tall enough to touch the ceiling with lots of branches just right for my bright, shiny stars.

I knew then, the only place I wanted to be for Christmas time was home.

❖ Fond Memories of My Father ❖
by Priscilla Tromblay, Turners Falls, Massachusetts

As I remember my father, he was a large man. Six foot two and over two hundred pounds. He always seemed twice as large to me, as I was very small and the youngest.

Dad was born in Chesterfield, Massachusetts in 1876 and was named Charles Austin. He was one of seven sons of Austin Amos and Ellen Marie. In 1889, his parents bought one hundred and eight acres of farm land in Westhampton, Massachusetts. This is where my father grew up.

His family home was good sized: five bedrooms, four on the second floor and one bedroom and six other rooms on the first floor. The first floor consisted of a front parlor that was used only for church visitors, a living room, a dining room with a large table that would seat twenty, china closet, buffet and twenty ladder back chairs. Grama had re-caned many of the seats.

There were two kitchens. One was a full kitchen in the main house and on the other side towards the barn was what was called a "summer kitchen." Between these two rooms was a sink that went through the wall with a pump in both rooms. In the cellar there was a spring where food that was used daily could be kept cool. It was a great house and I remember when all the family was there for the holidays, all the cousins had a great time together. Grama would let us run all through the house except for the front parlor.

Grama was a heavy-set woman and Grampa was a tall, thin man with snow white hair and a goatee. Grampa would get after us if we got in his barn or apple trees. We would run and hide behind Grama. Of course he knew where we were, but he'd pretend that he could not find us. What fun we would have!

Grampa had four milk cows and three horses. A pair of dapple grays did the farm work, pulling the hay wagon and getting the logs down off the mountain to the sawmill for lumber and firewood. The other horse was a shiny black mare with white markings on her face and four hooves. Her name was Dolly. Dolly pulled the hay rake and the carriage for going to church or visiting. Dolly was also used to pull the wagon when my grandparents were going to Northampton to sell vegetables. When they went to town, Grama would do shopping for the staple foods and household goods that she might need. After Gramp sold the vegetables, he would pick up Grama and they would go home by way of Cummington, Massachusetts. In Cummington there was a feed store where they could get the oats and dry corn for the farm animals.

Shopping in town was a big day for them. While at the feed store, Grama would buy some feedbags. Some had pretty prints on them and some had just the writing. Grama would turn the pretty ones into aprons, dish towels, and kitchen curtains. The ones with writing she would bleach and lay out in the sun to help the bleaching. The scraps were always saved and went into quilt tops. Grama made quilts for all her grandchildren. I wonder where they went.

My father went to a one-room schoolhouse at the top of Perry Hill. The boys all worked with Gramp after school. During the summer months, they would work for other farmers in town and in the fall, they would pick apples at Fiske Orchard. The orchard was where Regional High School in

Westhampton is today. One of my father's first jobs off the family farm was on the Smith Ferry that crossed the Connecticut River in Northampton. Later, he became a fireman and then he became an engineer. He held that job for thirty-two years.

When he married my mother they lived in Springfield, Massachusetts. Dad had three sons—two that I called my older brothers because Dad had been married twice. My mother and father had one son and two daughters. I was the youngest. My brother Charles and sister Dorothy stayed in Westhampton with Grama and Grampa when I was born. At the time, Infantile Paralysis was affecting people and my brother came down with it. When we were all back home, Dad was the one who took care of me and I became "Daddy's girl."

Dad and I spent lots of time together when he was not on the road. I would go with him to the garage when the car needed to be serviced or to the barber shop when he needed a haircut. I remember one time when I was in second or third grade, I went to the "X" in Springfield to meet him at the trolley stop where I thought he would get off. A man spoke to me and asked what I was doing there. I became scared and ran all the way home. When I told my father he said if anyone asked me again I should just say I was waiting for my father. He also told me not to go by myself again until I was older. I never did.

We had only one car as my mother did not drive. She was what was called a "homemaker." Dad would take us anywhere we wanted to go when he was home. In the winter and summer time we made many trips to Forest Park. Sometimes Mother would pack a lunch and we would play while they read the paper or just listen to the band that was playing in the park. During summer vacation we would stay in Westhampton. At this time both my Grama and Grampa had passed away and Dad had made a summer place out of the barn. We stayed until school started in September.

Dad loved to plant and we always had a big garden. When he got home, if we had kept the weeds out from between the plants and all the rows were weed-free, he would take us to Pine Lake Island. This was a freshwater lake and the water was ice cold no matter how hot the weather. We always had great summers.

When school started and we were back in Springfield, Dad would take us for car rides, never going the same way twice. He would tease us and say we were lost, but we always got back home. Sometimes in the spring when we were still in school, we would sit on the front porch and wait for the ice cream truck. Dad would get us all a cone even one for the dog! He would hold it for the dog until the last bite!

I was in my first year of high school when my uncle came to school to tell me my mother needed me at home because my father had died. It was the eighteenth of December and a sad Christmas for us all. I am so glad to have so many fond memories.

❖ Dear Enzo... ❖
by Robert Viarengo, Heath, Massachusetts

In the fourth month of your mother's pregnancy, I began rebuilding the stone wall on our home's eastern boundary. Starting out, only a lonely broken line marked the area, but as I probed and dug it turned out that a treasure trove lay below: a dump for the glacial stones wrested from the soil by the people who lived here in Heath, Massachusetts over two hundred years ago. With the passing decades those stones had sunk beneath the surface. Slowly I exposed them again.

I needed a broad selection of stones as I blended what I found: boulders and slate, lumps and slabs. I might try eight or nine pieces in order to find one that would nestle into the curves of its neighbor. Bulges and irregular edges are hidden within. Only straight faces of rock see the sunlight. The smooth, rectangular shape of the wall that the eye beholds, like the banter passing between casual friends, masks the complexity of the hidden interior.

Spring comes late—and grudgingly—here in Heath, but by late April it arrives. Snowdrifts which covered the wall on the day of your birth are gone now, leaving only traces of dirty, white snow nestled in the shade of the stones. By noon, sunlight melted the night's frost. I brought out my pry bar, gloves, kneepads and finished the work. The wall is not really straight. It is wider in some places than others, as I left some of the larger stones in the beds they had chosen over the decades. It is solid, though, and should withstand the forces of nature for generations to come.

Now, Enzo, you are two. The towering maples are in full leaf, their canopy creating a dappled play of light and shadow on the sturdy stone wall. A gentle breeze rustles softly over the spreading branches. I watch you walk confidently on the top of the wall, each footstep planted carefully on the larger stones. The sun backlights your light blond hair and a smile of pleasure crosses your lips as you contemplate this new found adventure.

In a few years, perhaps, we will stand here together, under the shade of these old sugar maples surveying this wall and speak of the bond of love between us. Perhaps someday you'll visit here as an old man with your own grandson. The sunlight will be warm, bathing the different hued stones of the wall in delicate colors. In spring, he will see a background of flowers; in winter, the sparkling snow; in summer shimmering shadow-shapes will play across the stones; in fall he will see the orange and red leaves of the maples towering over my wall, carpeting it with color as they drop to the ground.

Tell him that this wall was my gift to you, conceived and created as you were being formed. Tell him of your joyful walk when you were two. Tell him that he is loved as I love you.

Enzo, I hope this wall and this place will welcome all the future generations of our family.

With caring and affection,
Your Nonno

❖ Asolo, Italy: 1909-1915 ❖
by Hélène Walker, Ashfield, Massachusetts

Winters in Asolo held a few gorgeous days, but were basically dreary. At least they were short.

The lighted evergreen is a northern symbol of the birth of Christ. In Italy, Christmas was a day of reverence and candles in church. Parties and the giving of gifts erupted at New Year's and Midwinter Carnival. We did, however, have a Christmas tree and gave away presents at Christmas to those that needed them.

Our celebration was simple with a few people and no frills. Old and young people made up the peasant family who washed our laundry. A son of the patriarch, or his niece Carlotta, picked up our laundry every week or two with their mules to carry it. They had been invited to our Christmas party, but lived too far out in the countryside to brave the weather. Mother planned to send their few gifts by driver and I asked if I could go with Rosina and Gigi, our carriage horse and driver. Mother said yes.

It was a cold night with stars here and there between scudding clouds. Snow streaked along the road in patches, glancing on banks and in ditches and gullies. It was a secret night, traveling to the clip clop of hooves and sibilant leather against leather. The carriage wheels ground suddenly over pebbles. The driver shushed companionably to his horse through the dark.

I savored this independent adventure like a present received for no reason at all except the delightful reason that I was to give rather than receive. Under the blankets at my feet were half a dozen tagged parcels nicely wrapped and ready for delivery.

The farm was several miles away on a well known road. In the daytime you could see the road ran between vineyards and olive trees. Wild things bloomed on the banks in spring and hazel nuts fell there in autumn. In summer, it was a long, hot promenade, the farm always appearing to be around a further corner where at least there would be a cup of spring water. Even the thought of spring water in the heat of summer was not as excellent as this cold night, though. The air was in my face and I had a feeling that some part of my past was falling away.

I wished the night might go on and on, but soon the drive was over. We turned into a courtyard between groups of stone buildings. A house, a hayloft and cow barns appeared barely darker than the night. There was no light in the house at all.

"Too cold in the house," Gigi said. "They will be in the stable."

One window gleamed in the courtyard.

"Will they *all* be in the stable?" I asked.

"Probably." Gigi said as he pulled the carriage over, dismounted and reached up to help me.

"You knock," I said.

I was a bit timid thinking of the stir I would cause. He knocked, and in time a crack opened and there was some talk. Then Beppi, the son who drove to town with our fresh laundry came out.

"Signorina! You are here at this hour!" he said.

"I bought a few Christmas presents for some of the children. May I come in?" I asked.

"Si, si, certamente. You will find us as we are, but you are most certainly welcome."

The men helped me with the packages and Beppi walked me around to meet his people.

The smell of the animals, the must of the feed, the offal, the weight of the hot and used up air were like a blanket thrown over me. As we entered, I could not breathe and the one lantern was so dim I could barely see. As my eyes adjusted, I saw the old grandmother, the first to salute me and fuss. I shook hands politely, the way a well brought up girl might do meeting guests in the drawing room. Carlotta, beautiful as a Bellini Madonna with small angels around her, was curtseying awkwardly. People were coming out of corners, big and little faces that I didn't really remember or know. Their clothes were rumpled and stuck with hay from where they'd been laying, some even sleeping. There were gentle murmurs from the cows. The mule stood up at the sound of many soft voices in unusual commotion at such an hour. The newest baby slept in a hay crib, rosy and tousled. I was urged to lean over and see how he slept in comfort like the infant Jesus had.

I turned to hand out the packages as people squeezed to look. There were so few packages for so many and I was amazed I had come with so little. I felt a queer tightening at so much kindly fuss for the tiniest offering of presents. Nothing like what my sister and I would receive the next day.

"Will you have some warm milk right from the cow?" someone asked.

"No, no thank you. It is late and they will wonder at home. This is the envelope with my parents' best wishes to you all," I said handing over a Christmas bonus.

Someone stroked my coat admiringly. I was glad Gigi had gone outside and I was alone a few minutes with these warm souls in their haven.

They thanked me as though the gift I bought had been precious and rare. They crowded to the door standing dimly lit against the dark night. Again I caught my breath—not just from the cold, but from a sudden thrust within me. I had not just been quiet all the way out, but edgy, too. I was quiet driving back, but for different reasons. There was nothing about the farm people that I had not enjoyed, but now I knew there was much more about them that I had not known.

Fifty years later, the Prelate at St. Bartholomew's Church in New York preached a Christmas Eve sermon. I was there with my youngest son. Had I told him this story now renewed in my mind? I was surprised that the priest, an educator, told so little of the truth as he described the birth of Christ as filthy, unwholesome, some of the same thoughts that passed through me as I entered the peasant's stable so many years before.

Didn't this priest remember the times in our human past when there were no imaginable comforts? Those were the times when family had been the base of our safety and felicity.

Local Color #3

❖ Pieces of My Past ❖
by Allan D. Adie, Gill, Massachusetts

Our bathtub was copper. It was made of copper strips riveted together to form its shape. The toilet was also copper. It was made of copper sheets wrapped to form the stool. This copper was never polished. The stool of the toilet, where you sat, was framed in wood. It was covered with a wooden lid about an inch thick and twenty inches square. The lid was kept down when not in use. On each side of the toilet was a wooden shelf and the stool was enclosed in wood. Our family used newspaper or pages from the Sears Roebuck catalog cut to five-inch squares for toilet paper. I'm not sure what other people used.

❖ ❖ ❖

Clothes were washed in what was called a "set tub." It was made of what we called "earthenware" and consisted of two tubs separated down the middle. Each compartment was about eighteen inches square with the top compartment a little larger than the bottom. One compartment was filled with hot water. My mother washed the clothes in the hot water tub by scrubbing them on a scrubbing board and applying bar soap. The soap was Kirkman's Borax. It was a brown bar soap, four inches by two by almost two inches thick. P&G was also a popular bar soap for clothes, but it was white in color.

The soapy clothes would be put into the second tub, which was filled with cold water. The clothes would be rinsed in that tub, and then squeezed as dry as possible by hand. Finally, the clothes were hung out in the backyard on the clothesline to dry.

❖ ❖ ❖

When I was a boy I broke my wrist during outside play. A boy stepped on my wrist while I lay on the ground. It hurt very much, so I went to the doctor. He had a fluoroscope light that helped him see my bones. The bones needed to be reset and the doctor encouraged me to take ether, but I refused. The doctor, and another doctor called in to help, began to pull on my wrist. I screamed, "Give me ether! I'll take ether!" It was too late. They'd already set the bones, but it hurt like the devil.

They put two thin, finely polished, pieces of wood called a "splint" on the top and bottom of my wrist to cover the area that broke. The splint was about a foot long and wider than my arm. Several long strips of adhesive tape held the splint together.

Everything was going fine until I went back for a check-up a week later. The doctor unwrapped my wrist, checked for swelling, and then re-taped it. After the doctor's visit my mother said I could go to the movies, so I did. In the movie theater my wrist began to hurt. The pain continued for several days, so my mother brought me back to the doctor. He couldn't figure out why I was in such pain. The pain was so bad I felt like killing myself. The doctor wanted to cut off my thumb, but my mother refused. I don't remember taking any pain pills, but after eight weeks the pain stopped. When the splint finally came off I had "dropsy" of the wrist: I couldn't hold anything like a spoon or fork. (In retrospect I learned the radial nerve had probably been damaged.)

My mother's favorite saint was Saint Theresa of the Little Flower. My mother had a paper rose with a stiff wire stem and inside that rose there was a small picture of Saint Theresa. After a few weeks passed and we saw no improvement in my hand, my mother took that paper rose and rubbed it over my hand and wrist. I don't remember if she said prayers, but within hours I could hold things and my wrist was normal. It was a miracle!

❖ School Traumas❖
by Edna Baublis, Athol, Massachusetts

No bragging, but I was always a good student. I never, never, ever brought home a "D." My father's job was to earn a living; my mother's, to keep house, and mine was to do well in school.

I remember once, in second grade, we were reading Peter Rabbit. It was my turn to read the paragraph where Peter was in the watering can and sneezed, "ah choo." Miss Parmenter did not like the way I read "ah choo," and I had to stay after school and read that section to her again. Still, I was unable to read it to her satisfaction. My homework was to go home and practice that word.

Now, I ask you, how many ways can you say "ah choo?" I tried "AH choo," "ah CHOO," "ah choo," "AH CHOO." I was ready.

Next day at school, it was my turn to read again. "All right, Edna. Read," said Miss Parmenter. So I read about Peter Rabbit and the dumb watering can! Still she didn't like it. She looked at me, marched me down the aisle, and demoted me from high second group in as much time as it took her to switch my desk from one row to the other. The demotion lasted one day because Ed-vard (French pronunciation), whom she promoted to high second, couldn't make it.

I wasn't going to tell my parents because I knew they would be disappointed, but my friend Ruthie raced home to tell my mother. I can still see the expression on her face.

Things went along well until seventh grade math—my least favorite subject. Mr. Hastings (you notice, I have never forgotten his name, either) gave us a list of math terms to memorize. Because math was my least enjoyable subject, I always put it off until the end of homework studies and sort of skipped over it.

Next day, we had to give the definitions. I was asked, "What's the shortest distance between two points?" I blanked out. For the life of me, I could not remember. And then this hand waved in the air, and "Teacher! Teacher!" accompanied the arm waving semaphore. It was Norman. Teacher called on him and he answered, "The shortest distance between two points is a straight line." Which, as everyone knows, is correct.

My mouth hung open. Norman was not the brightest one in the class. He never knew the right answers. I had to stand by my desk and recite, "The shortest distance between two points is a straight line," ten times. For my reward, I received my first and only "D" on my report card.

I have never forgotten Norman and I have never forgotten that the shortest distance between two points is a straight line. If I should ever appear on one of those current millionaire shows, I hope that that would be one of the questions. I wouldn't need a lifeline and I know what my final answer would be.

❖ The Baby Carriage ❖
by Rosalie Bolton, Greenfield, Massachusetts

What a special honor it was to push the baby carriage! I'm talking about the one made of wicker. The carriage that was renewed every few seasons with a coat of soft gray paint. The body of the carriage was set high on a strong metal base with four large wooden wheels and thick rubber tires. It was the mode of transportation that was loaned out to cousins, friends, neighbors and the friends of all these people.

"Could I borrow your old carriage for two nights? My sister is coming and I don't have a crib." One person we hardly knew sent us this note! Of course we lent the carriage, but I didn't like the word "old" in reference to it.

That carriage had a bounce to it as it rolled along the sidewalk. I might have even run with it, to the delight of the child inside. It could hold a small baby and a two year old, and a loaf of bread or other groceries or schoolbooks. It was larger than some of the newer carriages. The hood was trimmed with a large rim. None of the newer models had that decoration. The large top kept out the sun and the wind. A baby could be out on the porch in cool weather, kept warm with blankets, made to feel secure. The carriage was built so that I could stand next to it and talk to my friends, put my hands on the side of the carriage and rock the baby to sleep. There was a strong brake on the bottom frame, which would stop the carriage fast. It was sturdy, heavy and wouldn't tip over easily.

Yes! It was a huge, hulk of a carriage! I could trace the handiwork of the wicker woven in and under and out. I didn't know that it was willow. It wasn't in the latest vogue, not like that new, thin, imitation-leather hood and metal body that some people were using at that time. It didn't have a hood that folded down, just a large, plain, rounded, old-fashioned wicker hood.

At ten years old I told my mother, "Here I am, riding the baby in this old thing! It doesn't even have a hood that folds down. It doesn't have a little window in the side. It's big. Why don't you line it with pretty, flowered cloth instead of this plain, tan pongee, or whatever it is, tacked inside there?"

My mother laughed at my ten-year-old advice and said, "It serves the purpose."

I'd forget about seeing modern carriages when I rode my baby sister in our old carriage after school. It was my job. My friends wanted to walk with me. No, they couldn't take the handle. I was in charge. Yes, I was the envy of others.

When grown-ups weren't looking, and baby wasn't in the carriage, I'd push the empty buggy, then go into a run and put my feet up on the wheelbase and have a fun ride down the street.

Inside the carriage, under the mattress, was a compartment with a sliding door where I could hide things: an extra rattle, a bottle, a dime tied in the corner of a clean handkerchief. What a secret place!

One Saturday afternoon when I was at the ten-cent movie, the fast moving comedy showed a man being chased through the city streets by policemen on foot. The man was running, pushing a baby carriage like the one I wheeled. When the police caught up with him after a rapid chase, the blankets were torn off the carriage. Inside there was no baby. The carriage was full of liquor! It was Prohibition!

Years later, when I was of driving age, I saw a similar carriage. It was on a farmhouse porch on a country road in Montague. When I asked my mother what had become of our well-used baby buggy, she said she had given it away to a family in Montague. I'd seen our carriage. There it was, still in use!

That carriage was a warm bed, with a hood, which seemed to envelop the baby, keep it warm and provide safe haven. Yes, it did indeed serve its purpose.

❖ Who Remembers "The Gables"? ❖
by Estelle Cade, Turners Falls, Massachusetts

As traffic whizzes along Route 5 in South Deerfield, Massachusetts, with people headed for work or school, to the butterfly house or Yankee Candle—or even perhaps an auction at the Douglas Auction Galleries—I wonder how many, if any, recall the days when the auction gallery building was called "The Gables" and was a popular roller skating rink.

In the 1940s there wasn't much in the way of entertainment except for bowling and the local movie theaters (which were always filled to capacity). The roller rink was a place to go with your friends, meet new people and have a great time, all for about fifty cents.

On Saturday or Sunday nights, the fellows with cars would gather up a group of friends and head for South Deerfield. Entering the rink, we'd be greeted by the sound of music from the speaker system, pay our fifty cents and be issued a pair of white shoe skates (black for the fellows, of course). I always held my breath hoping there would be a pair small enough to fit me decently so I wouldn't have to spend the evening falling over my own feet! (I think I got the kiddie size).

We'd sit to lace up the skates and then the moment of truth, as we gingerly made our way to the edge of the floor and let go of the handrail. Once you let go, you were on your own! It was mesmerizing to see everyone going around the rink, all going the same way. Some brave souls were more in the middle, actually attempting some dance steps. Others, who were new to this sport, were trying to skate in a walk pattern, never leaving the very outside edge and falling frequently (at which point you devoutly prayed that no one would run over you as you tried to scramble to your feet. Scrambling quickly with skates on is like riding a bike in ski boots—not easily done).

The evening was well organized by the owner. First, everyone went out and skated around the best they could, or as excellently as they could depending on skill level. This was fun, as you could greet your own friends and exchange a word or two with individuals you'd seen and chatted with other evenings and still have time to practice a few turns of your own. (Girls frequently skated together because it was wartime and male friends were in short supply.) You might have attempted a few fancy steps, turns, spins and even managed to talk a bit.

When "Men Only" was called, girls would sit and watch, sipping on a cold "tonic." Can't you picture the amount of "showing off" that went on by the men to the admiration of the watching girls?

"Ladies Only" was a time for us girls to get in our bit of showing off—turning neat corners, skating backwards and turning quickly, always hoping you wouldn't fall and look like an idiot! Sometimes during "All Skate" the call would be "Gentleman's Choice" and the race would be on, as suddenly, some male or another, would skate up behind you to partner-skate. This could be quite exciting, as everyone was going at a rapid pace and the trick was not to get your skate wheels caught as your partner came up alongside you. As I write this I am struck again, by what a good time this was!

The Gables floor was made of beautiful maple, "cornered" at the corners for proper turning radius. The people were friendly and just having fun. The music, I'm sure, was records, but I wonder if sometimes it wasn't live music by Roger "Red Socks" Johnson, who was a fixture at the Gables Restaurant organ for many years.

The Gables roller rink was a place to go to "see and be seen." The girls dressed in neat blouses and full skirts that flew out when they spun. The boys wore nice slacks and shirts. I'm so glad we were young before the grunge look arrived!

The evenings spent roller-skating were always fun and each week we looked forward to the question "Want to go to The Gables Sunday night?"

So if any of you reading this travel Route 5 fairly often, take a quick look at the auction gallery. You might hear a whisper of "roller-skating music" wafting out. As you pass, remember that inside that building is one of the most beautiful maple floors in the Valley, on which, perhaps, your mother and dad, or your grandparents (depending on your age), spent many happy hours whirling around. In fact they might have met there—on roller skates!

❖ A Dog Names Captain ❖
by Guy Carey, Jr., Warwick, Massachusetts

Much has been written about how people care about their dogs. As I revived these memories of Captain, it came to me that his story was more about how a dog cared about his people.

I do not believe that we could have ever guessed how much a part of the family Cap was destined to become. Cap was the name chosen for Captain by us children, so he would have a nickname like us. He didn't seem to be anything special the day Dad brought him home, just a strange looking dog. He was a couple of months old and had a strange looking head. He was large for a pup. Some kind of big hound fathered Cap, but his mother was a Saint Bernard. Cap had the Saint Bernard head, but not their long hair.

Nothing in Cap's actions distinguished him from any other pup at first, except when he saw us fighting. When one of us boys would lose our tempers and start fighting, Cap would come bounding into the fray and drag us apart. If we insisted on continuing, he always seemed to know the aggressor and would clamp onto an arm and wouldn't let go until you stopped. This really endeared him to mother, because when Cap was around, there were fewer split lips and bloody noses among her four boys.

About a year after he became part of our family, Cap bounded into our bedroom one night and tried to roll us out of bed. No matter what we did, we could not stop him. This woke father who smelled smoke and ran to the kitchen to find a fire in the oven. Dad had a habit of putting the wood mother needed to cook breakfast with in the oven the night before. That was what was burning. After Dad had put out the fire, Cap curled up in his usual spot and went back to sleep, ignoring all our praise.

Cap walked to school with my brothers and sister and waited there to walk them back home again. At that time, Cap was almost full-grown and must have weighed over one hundred pounds. When some parents saw Cap dragging a kid away from an angry tussle, as he did with us at home, they were so upset about it that school officials informed us that Cap would not be allowed on school grounds anymore.

Cap always begged to go hunting with us. He was a silent hunter on the trail, so he really wasn't much use to us unless we were close by when he treed something. At times he would come back dragging game he caught himself. As intelligent as he acted about most things, he never understood how dangerous porcupines could be. Time after time he would come home loaded with quills. Some of us boys still carry scars from the scratches we got trying to hold Cap long enough for Dad or Uncle Leon to pull quills from his mouth and head. Dad finally made a kind of stantion out of an old dung fork. That invention enabled us to hold Cap's head pinned down to get the quills out. After he found out he couldn't get free of the stantion, he gave up fighting us when we had to remove quills.

Cap came home once with a nasty looking cut on his front leg. The cut was so bad that Dad decided that we should chain him up for a while to give it time to heal. A couple of days later, Billy, a boy from the neighborhood, was walking by and started into the yard. Cap gave a strange growl and ran so fast and hard at Billy that he broke his chain. Billy stood frozen in his tracks and Cap knocked him to the ground. After I pulled Cap off, Billy went running out of the yard yelling, "He didn't bite me! He didn't bite me!" I had never seen Cap act ugly before and even if he had only pinned Billy to the ground I was afraid this might mean we would have to put Cap down.

When I told my father what had happened, he and I went to see if Billy was all right. His mother said that Billy had been more scared than hurt. Dad said, "I don't know what caused this, but I guess it means we have to get rid of old Cap."

"Please don't blame Cap!" Billy said. "Last week, while hunting, I mistook Cap for a deer and shot at him."

"Well that explains the cut on his leg; still, this could make him dangerous. Billy, why don't you come to the house and see Cap. If we can get him to accept you, we might not have to put him away."

At the house Cap growled furiously when Billy first came into the yard, but my father talked to him soothingly while holding Billy close. In the beginning, I didn't think it was going to work, but after a few stressful moments, Billy and Cap were playing together. Cap seemed to understand how important it was to forgive him.

A couple of weeks after that incident, our cow had a calf that my father decided to raise for veal. The calf was a couple of weeks old when Cap came charging into our bedroom one night and started rolling us out of bed. When he acted that way, we knew there was trouble somewhere. Everyone, fearing a fire, flew out of bed.

Downstairs, Cap ran for the door begging to go out. That's when we heard a commotion in the barn. The calf was racing around its stall having a fit. Dad said it looked as if the calf had milk fever. Despite doctoring the calf all night, it died the next day. I think it was after that incident that we began to realize how special Cap had become to the family.

One deer season, my brother shot at a deer in our lower field. He was certain it was a clean shot, but the deer bolted into the woods. Though he searched until near dark, he wasn't able to find it. Cap, because of the incident when he was shot for a deer, was kept chained days during deer season, but let loose at night.

When Uncle Leon came in from town the next day, he said, "I just saw the darndest thing down in the lower field, come look!"

We went down to the lower field, and there was Cap dragging that deer across the field a foot or two at a time.

One winter during a terrible blizzard, the women who lived above us on the hill became stuck in the snow a couple of times trying to make it up the hill to their house. They decided it was safer to leave their car by our house and walk home. When they left, Cap followed them. They were back in a few minutes saying Cap would not allow them to go any farther than the four corners above the house.

"If Cap wouldn't let you go, I better have a look," Dad said.

Taking a light, and going back with Cap and the women, Dad found electric wires down in the road. Cap had protected them from blundering into a live wire that they might not have seen. Dad helped the women around the wires and came home beaming about how he picked the smartest dog in the litter when he brought Cap home.

There were many incidents like these during the nine years or so that we had Cap. Even after over fifty years without him, at family gatherings someone usually has a Cap story or two. When my grandchildren were young they would ask over and over for the stories about Cap.

Though we had always tried to be very careful about getting all the quills out of Cap, his nasty habit of getting into porcupines finally undid him.

Cap had been with us almost ten years when some kind of infection caused his head to swell. The local vet figured that quills had gotten an infection into his bloodstream. We tried many different remedies, but Cap became so weak and ill, it became evident that it would be kinder to put him down. Nobody in the family felt able to shoot him, so Billy's father offered to do it for us.

Though most of us put up a good front that day, I do not believe that there was a dry eye in the house that night after we reached our beds.

❖ The Hurricane ❖
by Mary Ciechomski, Turners Falls, Massachusetts

During my high school years, I was fortunate enough to have secured a job doing housework for a Mount Holyoke College professor. Mrs. Matthias, a widow, had three boys.

Everyday after school, I would take the school bus up to South Hadley Center, Massachusetts to my job. I also worked on Saturday mornings from 9:00 a.m. to 12:00 noon. For this effort, I received a grand total of $3.00 a week or 50 cents for three hours a day. It was hard work, but I considered myself lucky to have a job as my family needed the money.

Each Monday, I would do the washing for the family of four. There were no automatic washers then, and I handled all the laundry in a wringer machine with a set tub for rinsing. There were also no clothes dryers at that time, so I had to hang all the laundry on an outside clothesline.

Tuesdays were for folding clothes and ironing, which most likely carried into Wednesdays. Thursdays were usually spent on baking, and so on with my various tasks culminating on Saturdays with general house cleaning. After all this, I would collect my $3.00, which I promptly brought home to my mother. Most days, except for the rare ones when I could beg my brother for his bike, I would walk home. It was a mere two miles, but in winter, when it was freezing, it felt more like ten.

It was in the fall of my junior year on what started out as a beautiful, fall, day in October. It was a Tuesday, and, as usual, I took to my normal task of picking the clothes off the line, then folding or sprinkling the ones that need ironing.

During the early part of the afternoon, it started getting dark with all indications of rain. By the time I had begun ironing, rain had started coming down in torrents, accompanied by very strong winds. I turned on the lights, because it had turned so dark, and continued ironing, glimpsing frequently out the window at the driving rain. There was no television at that time, and I was not in the habit of turning on the radio, so I was unaware that I was witnessing a hurricane. Some time between 4:00 and 5:00 p.m., the electricity went off and, of course, I had to put the ironing away.

Shortly before 5:00, (I normally worked until 5:30), Mrs. Matthias arrived home and told me that she would drive me home. What a treat! We ran through the rain and got into her car and proceeded down the street in the pelting rain. The ride home should have taken no more than five minutes. About one-half mile down the road, we were stopped in traffic as a great, giant tree had fallen across the road, right in front of the Tissue Mills, completely blocking the road. No one could get by. Just by luck, a bus was also standing in the stalled traffic and Mrs. Matthias gave me a dime and told me to get on the bus. She felt that, eventually, the tree would be cleared and I could get home. I was surprised to see one of my friends on the bus. Winnie B. had a similar job to mine, working after school for a professor. Her boss had given her a dime to take the bus home, too.

After sitting there for about one-half hour, the bus driver said that he did not think the tree was going to be removed soon and he thought he would detour over Morgan Street and then down Granby Road (Route 202) to possibly get us home. He turned the bus around and off we went.

All went well on Morgan Street and then we were on Route 202 when, lo and behold, there was another giant tree blocking any further progress. After sitting there for another half-hour or so, Winnie said, "I am going to walk home". I said, "Well, we might as well". Off the bus we went and started walking. We reached Winnie's house and after saying "So long," I kept on walking for another mile until I reached my home.

By this time, about 7:30 p.m., the rain had stopped and I was very glad to be home. In the meantime, my Mom had noticed that the rain was slowing down and had sent my oldest brother to pick me up in his little car. He found the first fallen tree on College Street had been cleared enough to allow traffic through and when he got to Mrs. Matthias' house, she told him that she had put me on the bus. No one seemed to know where I was. My Mom was so glad to finally see me and I, too, was relieved to get home. That was the hurricane of 1938.

❖ Ice Cream, Anyone? ❖
by Margaret M. "Pat" Currie, Turners Falls, Massachusetts

When I was growing up in Greenfield, Massachusetts in the 1930s, ice cream was a way of life and there were plenty of places in town to get it. For instance, at the lower end of Main Street was McCann's, a small store where you could get a pint of ice cream for fifteen cents, or a regular-sized ice cream sandwich for a nickel—the larger size was a dime.

In the next block, right on the corner was the Chocolate Shop. It was a drugstore, but it had a counter and tables. You could get cones and sundaes or ice cream sodas there.

The Olympia Fruit Company was next door to that. As named, it had fruits and vegetables in front. Way in the back was a counter and a couple of booths. I always thought it was a sort of "hangout." Girls who worked downtown were the usual crowd and they were allowed to smoke there! It was said that you could leave your half-smoked cigarette there and pick it up at your next break. Of course, this was the thirties!

On the next corner of the same block was a great place with round tables and wire chairs and the best sundaes—especially hot fudge!! There was also the Five & Dime, which also served meals and ice cream.

Now when you came across Chapman Street, there was the "Vic," a movie theater and the adjoining small shop where you could get a cone or candy for the movies and sometimes a soda or sundae after.

Going further up the street was Liggett's Drug Store, the largest place of all. It had a long counter covered with sandwiches, pies, etc. You could also have sundaes or double dip ice cream sodas. Naturally, they also sold drugs and remedies. Two other drugstores (one on each side of Main Street) also had counters, but they catered to "old folks."

The other two theaters in town were next to and connected to stores or drugstores. The Garden, the largest movie house in town in the 1930s, had a few booths for ice cream, sundaes, milk shakes or ice cream sodas. Next to The Lowler was Skinner's Drug Store. It had a soda fountain. I always dreamed of getting a job there! I thought it would be so great to make drinks and sundaes for people!

The best place for me was Rita's on Federal Street. It was a popular place for high schoolers. You could get a nickel coke or ten or fifteen cent sundae. For twenty-five cents they'd add hot fudge, marshmallow (my favorite!) or whipped cream and pecans. Those were the days, don't you agree?

❖ My Story ❖
by Robert A. Desilets, Gill, Massachusetts

In 1924 we lived in Trois-Rivières, a city situated between Montrèal and Quebèc, Canada. In the spring, my father disappeared. He had gone to the United States and returned three months later. He went to visit his cousin who was a carpenter and building inspector. No one knows why he made the journey, but at our age we didn't ask questions. My father was the type who worked very little—a week here and there with a break in between. It wasn't easy to raise a family on that kind of income, but we managed somehow.

Then came the summer of 1926. There was a rumor that we would be moving to the States. Why? We were well enough off—not rich, of course, but comfortable and at home. We weren't starving or persecuted or evicted from our house. We lived in a beautiful, single house with a fenced-in yard. There was enough space for a garden in summer and ice-skating in winter. We had a parlor, a large kitchen and a large bedroom on the bottom floor. On the second floor were two bedrooms with two beds in each room, six girls in one and six boys in the other. Two of the twelve children were employed. The eldest made $10.00 per week and the other a meager $8.00. I worked Friday afternoon and Saturday morning doing delivery service at an open market, with the aid of a small wagon or sled in the winter. There was enough money coming in to pay for food and our $25.00 per month rent. During the summer, my brother and I would fetch two cows from a pasture two miles away and lead them to a stable near by to be milked. This was in the afternoon after school. The next morning we would return them to the pasture. We made a few dollars each week doing that job. Thus, in the summer of 1927, we wondered why were moving and where we would get the money for the move. How would we get to the States? We had no car. A plane would be ridiculous. A ship would be unnecessary. Maybe we would go by train?

My father decided to make a visit to his brother-in-law's to ask for the much-needed funds. My father managed to get $300.00 from him, but how far would that go? Passports alone cost $10.00 each times 14 people. My father managed to rent a large truck and a driver to move us all. One day it happened and we were all going to move to the United States. It was Monday October 23. We loaded the truck with all our furniture (five beds, a few bureaus, chairs, tables, clothes, and record player). That night we slept at the house for the last time. We slept on the floor or wherever we could, to wait for the next morning and our big move.

The next morning, October 24, we embarked on our journey south at 5:00 a.m. There were fourteen of us plus the driver. My mother had made tons of sandwiches for the trip. We drove 100 miles west to Montreal to obtain our passports. We were amazed by the size and height of the buildings, the city traffic and the people.

At 2 p.m. we left Montreal and reached Swanson, Vermont by 7 p.m. We stopped there and dined on more sandwiches. After dinner we started off again and traveled until dawn. When we got out of the truck that next morning, we marveled at the beauty of the mountains around us. They were covered in color, as it was foliage season. At 3 p.m. on October 25, we arrived at our destination—Leominster, Massachusetts. After thirty-four hours of traveling we had finally arrived. All fourteen of us crawled out of the truck to begin a new life. We entered a brand new, beautiful five-room home.

Few people were there to greet us at our new home. There were no city officials or a parade to meet us, but here we were! All fourteen of us were now in a strange, new land with a strange, new language and new atmosphere. By the time the first bills were paid for our arrival, there wasn't a spare penny left over. The second week, my eldest sister found a job at a local shirt shop for $8.00 per week. My oldest brother got a job at a meat market for $12.00 per week. Father got a job as a carpenter for two weeks and then he got sick.

Soon it was time to go to school. Eight of us kids attended the parochial school three blocks away. In Canada, I had been in the seventh grade, but here I was placed in the fifth grade. In 1931, I graduated and went on to attend high school until 1935. After school hours, I managed to find work at a store for two hours a day and made 50 cents per day. In the spring of 1934, my mother decided to return to Canada to repay her debt. I accompanied her on the trip by train from Fitchburg to Montrèal to Trois-Rivières. It would be one of the last times back to my native land.

Looking back, though our move seemed unnecessary it certainly happened for a reason. If my mother hadn't moved us down to the United States, I never would have had the opportunities that I've had. I wouldn't have met the people I know, become the father and grandfather I am, or do the things I've done in my life. Over the years I thank God continuously for the events that have taken place in my life which have all led up to this point—living with my son and his wife in Franklin County and helping them develop a new Catholic school.

As a young boy riding in the back of a pick-up truck across the border from Canada, I never dreamed of the multitude of blessings and gifts that were to await me in the U.S. I'm convinced that God had a plan in mind for my family and me and that's an endless revelation to me.

❖ Childhood and Leisure ❖
by Elisabeth R. Donaj, Greenfield, Massachusetts

Happiness is my memory of days in my childhood. Seeing myself as early as a non-walking babe crawling up the long flight of stairs only to sit down and "walk" on my backside from step to step downward and all the while making singing noises. I already remember feeling delight in such activity.

We lived in a country schoolhouse, as mother and father were both teachers. The house was set on a large piece of land. There was much land around and a yard in which to play. A colorful parrot, white sheep and lambs, and a dog belonged to the family, which made me think we were rich! Yes, we were rich in as much as our lifestyle was "tuned in" and "comfortable," and our experiences of nature around us gave us pleasure. Later in life, those experiences provided an insight into the beautiful world around us, which grew into an understanding we needed to appreciate life's value.

Both parents read tales and stories to my smaller brother and me. We played games and father was the inventor of games. He could lead people on with impromptu fun things to do. We laughed a lot and learned many basic values in these "togetherness activities."

We walked a lot to enjoy and see "nature's faces." We picked wild berries often and picked nuts for winter. I believed those activities were "just for fun."

Later I was allowed to ride horses and then a bicycle. With such possibilities I began to grow independent, enjoy freedom, learn responsibility.

These years of growing up changed in my sixth year. My family moved to the city where my father had grown up and received his education. We moved so my brother and I might receive an education. I began school at six years old.

My parents were strict in holding me to schoolwork. Work was serious, but playing time for outdoor and indoor activities was always given. My favorite things were visits to museums and then at vacation time visiting the country or the seashore. As children we learned to swim at an early age and spent long afternoons in the water.

Three times a week I was sent for extracurricular light athletic exercise. Through our church I began singing in the choir. My father was the organist, which made me proud.

Reading and talking about books was encouraged and we received books as gifts on certain occasions.

My parents had a large circle of friends and we mixed freely with their children.

In retrospect I had a healthy childhood. There was reasonable balance between serious preparations for life and leisure time, which we filled with opportunities to learn more creatively and grow.

❖ Myrtle's Gun Shy ❖
by Vera Farris, Northfield, Massachusetts

Proverbially, a bird in the hand may be worth two in the bush, but to Walter, with the advent of October 20, it posed a slumber-disturbing problem. It is the season when birddogs and zealous hunters take to the woods in feverish search for feathered prey.

Over a month ago, while fishing for trout in his favorite haunt, Walter startled a partridge, which quickly disappeared into the brush.

A second visit to the woodsy dell brought the partridge out again. This time it grumbled its defiance at the trespasser from a safe distance before it flew away.

Sufficiently warmed up to this game of hide-and-go-seek, Walter made repeated trips to the vicinity and called out soothing and reassuring phrases to the bird. He affectionately dubbed it "Myrtle."

After a short period of deliberation, Myrtle must have realized that this man, known enemy of the bird, was an exception to the rule. She consented to become fast friends and after some cajoling, even came forward to eat out of Walter's hand and pose for pictures when unbelievers doubted Walter's prowess as a bird charmer.

The uncanny way Myrtle had of recognizing Walter's car was astonishing! A tap of a stick on the country road and his voice was all she needed to come on the run. She seemed to enjoy walking in her mincing manner at his side and made clicking noises in response to his many questions. To tease her, Walter broke into a run, and Myrtle fluttered to his ankles with a sharp cry and nipped at him to impede his progress. She was often ruffled at this childish sport and turned her back on Walter and nibbled at leaves, unmindful of his fumbling apologies. When playtime was over she was bid a fond and safe good-bye, after which she took to the deeper woods.

All the while Walter guarded the secret of Myrtle's hideaway with more painstaking caution and anxiety than an H-bomb scientist. His immediate family was allowed to accompany him and view the friendship only after each promised to never reveal the hiding place. Myrtle never resigned herself to the added interlopers and peevishly and loudly reprimanded Walter for bringing them.

It was such fun…but would these actions bring about the possible early demise of his friend, grieves Walter? Would the bravado of this game, little bird make him a better target to the sporting instinct of man and his big guns?

Walter, a keen and enthusiastic hunter, hung up his own guns that bird season and in the immortal words of somebody or other, and with plenty of revision, cried: "Hunters! Spare the bird!"

❖ A Trip to a Wilmington, Vermont Square Dance ❖
by Edith J. Fisher, Leyden, Massachusetts

When I was about eighteen, my future husband and I and a few friends decided to go to a square dance in Wilmington, Vermont. It was the middle of winter and a blizzard was blowing. It was COLD! We were traveling in an unheated Model "T" or "A." I can't remember which. Of course we were all bundled up.

When we got to the dance hall, there was no heat! Everyone was dancing in coats and boots. The band had their coats on, too!

We decided to leave after about an hour or so. When we got back to Guilford, Vermont, my future husband and I had to walk about a mile to his house—uphill!

I can't remember being so cold! When one is young one does some stupid things!

❖ Our First T.V. ❖
by William R. Fitzgerald, Ashfield, Massachusetts

It was the mid-fifties; we had just bought the farm and had lots of expenses like machinery, seed and fertilizer. There was no room for luxuries from one very, ordinary salary and very little farm income.

It seems nearly impossible now, that a family could get along without a television set then. They were just becoming popular and our kids came home from school telling about the programs, who had a set and who didn't. It seemed like this T.V. subject came up every evening at dinner.

That scenario reminded me of the Orphan Annie and Jack Armstrong, "The All-American Boy," programs that came on the radio early every evening in the 1930s when I was a kid. We didn't have a radio back then after moving to our "un-electrified" farm in rural Conway, Massachusetts. The kids who had radios in town discussed these programs every day and the teacher brought up news items she had heard on the radio. I was silent during these discussions, which was out of character for me. When my folks finally bought a battery radio we kids were ecstatic! We were equal with the townies!

It was my wife Marian who came up with a great idea. I had been saying that cider apples were high that year and we should shake those old Baldwin trees that dotted our farm. They were the survivors from a once profitable enterprise that almost every farm once had. She suggested we all pitch in and let the ciders (cider apples) we sold pay for the T.V.

Every afternoon after that, I hurried home from work and we, as a family, enthusiastically picked up apples before chores. Even the littlest one got the spirit. Soon we had enough to load onto Charlie Ward's truck. Then all we had to do was wait for the check to come in. For a while, every afternoon when the school bus arrived, the question was "Did the check come?" After the check came, the question was "Did the T.V. man come?"

Collecting apples was an exercise in how well we could pull together as a family, as well as a valuable economic lesson. We put the T.V. in the other room so we wouldn't have a distraction at dinner and our dinner discussions were not always necessarily about T.V. every night.

❖ Christmas with Uncle Frank & Aunt Ruby ❖
by Margaret "Peg" Folgmann, Shelburne Falls, Massachusetts

For years, at least it seemed that way as a child, our family enjoyed the annual Christmas party held at the old Town Hall on Creamery Road in South Ashfield, Massachusetts. Real lit candles on the real tree. The tree was large and selected especially for safety as well as for beauty. For reasons I did not understand at the time, and still don't, these wonderful gatherings came to a halt. My Uncle Frank said, "We'll have a Christmas gathering of our own at our home." And so we began gathering at Christmas at the farmhouse where Uncle Frank and his family lived in Conway, Massachusetts.

We usually got together just before Christmas Day. The parlor was opened up, dusted off and the woodstove made ready to provide warmth. We kids were expected to provide some sort of entertainment, although Irene and Grandma were the only really talented ones among us. It did not matter though, because all was in fun.

Grandma always sang, "Star of the East," beautifully. Irene fascinated us with "Dizzy Fingers" on the piano. We were all so very proud of her. She led us in song as we stood around the piano. The men folk usually had a few choice poems to recite and stories to tell. They also enjoyed card games. One year our party was held on Sunday. Grandma felt that it was sinful to play cards on the Sabbath. Suddenly she realized what was taking place and reminded those engaged in card playing that it was Sunday, (As though they didn't already know!). Grandma scolded some, but the men folk kept right on playing pitch, hearts, poker or whatever for a while.

Some of the young children brought along a special toy. We played well together and had so much fun! One year my brother brought his cork gun. It was safe. The cork was on a string attached to the gun. Furthermore, we were taught at a very young age that we must *NEVER* aim a gun at anything or anyone unless we intended to destroy it. My brother loved his gun. He was known to take it to bed long after the newness wore off.

One Christmas during the Depression, we were reminded by our mother that there was very little money to buy presents. She said that some of our cousins had much less than we had. Our mother explained why she planned to buy little gifts for them and not for us. She showed us these gifts and we knew how happy our cousins would be. Most toys were of the wind-up variety costing no more than 35-40 cents each. They were sturdy little metal toys. We didn't seem to resent her plan. Vicariously, there was a lesson to be learned.

Soon after we arrived at the farm, we were directed to the festive sideboard set with the very best Aunt Ruby had to offer. The food was super! On our way to the dining room, we had a preview of what was to come as far as deserts and bread were concerned. You see there was a good-sized butry (pantry) that opened from the kitchen and another door that opened from the dining room. There were long broad shelves along each side of the pantry…what a sight! No one could make the variety of homemade candy that Aunt Ruby did. Such temptation! No one snitched a thing that we knew of. There were pies and cakes all set to go. In the background there was a high mound of popcorn balls stacked perfectly.

First came the main meal. Some people brought dishes, which made preparations of the meal easier for Aunt Ruby. We didn't dare NOT eat because we knew the desserts to follow. Grandma would say grace. Of course the longer variety took precedence on this special occasion. All were appreciative of this grand annual get together. Aunt Ruby's dark brown eyes, broad smile and a special manner made her the perfect hostess. Grandpa sat there taking in everything, rarely uttering a word. He made his home with Uncle Frank and Aunt Ruby. In those days there were wood boxes to fill and a variety of other chores to be done, offering Grandpa a real purpose in life. Uncle Frank and Aunt Ruby had two sons younger than we were. Grandpa was the oldest family member present and the youngest was baby Richard.

Sometime during the gathering, we were all directed to the porch where we lined up for a snapshot to be taken by my mother. She had a Brownie Kodak box camera given to her at age sixteen. We are thankful for the many pictures she took over the years. This explains why she does not appear in the pictures.

My sister and Aunt were always asked to stand together. They were referred to as "the twins." My grandmother and mother gave birth to babies on the same date. It was Grandma's last child and my mother's first.

The Christmas tree stood in the parlor with gifts for the children. A second tree stood in the kitchen between the two north windows. This tree was small, but held ornaments including cookies and other edibles. The lower branches were stripped of cookies as the dog found them easy to reach. No one seemed to mind. To this day, one of the families puts up a "Charlie Brown" tree each year in memory.

Coming down through the years, thoroughly fixed in my mind, are the poems that were regularly recited at these Christmas gatherings so long ago. Now, I share them with my grandchildren and great grandchildren.

After Gramps died on November 14, 1933, the family Christmas gatherings as we knew them years ago came to an end, but memories linger on. We are now the "old folks" in the family gatherings.

❖ When Rover Saved the Day❖
by Jane L. Gilbert, Turners Falls, Massachusetts

My parents always had Newfoundland dogs at our Bernardston, Massachusetts home from the time I was a little girl. Strangers who didn't know the dogs were often frightened of them because of their size, but those dogs were really just gentle giants. They used to follow me around to keep me out of trouble. They were my playmates and guardians.

When I was old enough to start elementary school, the boy next door used to meet me at the corner of his street. We would then walk to school together as it was a short distance down the street.

The street corner where I met the boy was within sight of my home and Rover could usually be found stretched out on our steps enjoying the sunshine. One day, my friend was a little bit late, so I was standing on the corner by myself. An old car with two men in it stopped and one of them said he wanted to give me a ride to school. When I told them they were going the wrong way, one of them got out of the car and started coming towards me. Rover must have been watching what was going on, because when the man came out of the car towards me, Rover gave a loud

WOOF! and started pell mell toward the man.

I never saw a man run so fast as he did when he heard Rover bark and saw him rushing towards him. The man leaped into the old car and sped away as fast as he could make it go. For all I know he is still fleeing!

I bet he never tried a caper like that again for fear a dog like Rover might be around!

❖ Halloween Capers ❖
by Dorothy G. Hmieleski, South Deerfield, Massachusetts

The celebration of Halloween sixty years ago was somewhat different than today. Children in those days did not go "trick-or-treating." Occasionally, children dressed up or made Jack-o-lanterns, but practical jokes were more the order of the day!

One of the favorite jokes in Montague Center, Massachusetts where I grew up was one that was repeated year after year. Someone placed a large sign on the schoolhouse, which read, "FOR SALE—See Jessie L. Wheeler." Jessie taught seventh grade at the school for many, many years.

The school was often the focus of Halloween jokes. One year, an old horse buggy mysteriously appeared ensconced on the roof of the little porch that graced the school. Another time, the bicycle racks were carried from the schoolyard and left to rest on the front porch of Mabel Lincoln's home. Miss Lincoln gave piano lessons to many of the town's young people. However, somehow or other, she discovered who the perpetrators of the deed were, and enlisted them to repaint her porch floor to cover up the scratches their prank had left behind.

❖ Playing Paper Dolls ❖
by Irmarie Jones, Greenfield, Massachusetts

When cold winds blew outside, my sister, Maydee, and I preferred sitting on the floor, huddled next to the radiator where it was warm "playing" paper dolls.

In the summertime, when it was hot and sticky and we didn't feel like running around, what did we find to do? Play paper dolls.

But, it didn't begin with us. Judging from the large supply we inherited from our mother and her sister, Lilly, paper dolls must have been an important part of their young lives in the late 1890's. They, too, spent hours and hours at what was to become our favorite pastime. Once in a while we were allowed to play with their paper dolls—chubby little girls with elegant dresses that reached to the ground. Large hats with bows and flowers completed each outfit. Dolly Darling's winter school dress had long puffed sleeves and fur trim at the end of her floor-length skirt.

Besides entire figures, some of those old dolls were merely heads and shoulders on which costumes could be hung. There were dogs, cats and bears with clothes. One outfit even had a dog playing a drum. All those fragile pieces of paper were once so full of life.

For girls like me growing up in the 1930s, paper dolls were an important part of our lives. Each Sunday we grabbed the funny papers to find out what new paper dolls had been printed that we could cut out. Each week several comics would print their leading young women characters wearing discreet slips that came below their knees. These figures would be accompanied by at least one dress, maybe a hat.

Tillie the Toiler, Toots and Casper and Flapper Fanny were the comics that were sure to have a paper doll. Once in a while it would be Casper and then we would be disappointed, because we liked to draw clothes for the women. Sometimes Flapper Fanny's little sister would be printed and we enjoyed making little girl's clothes for her.

I can't remember how we decided who would have what doll, but Maydee and I each collected a large supply. Each doll had its own envelope, with an extensive homemade wardrobe.

It was in the five and ten cent stores (when they really were five and ten cents stores!) that we found paper doll treasures. A book of several dolls and dozens of outfits cost one dime. They reflected the films and celebrities of the day.

Quintuplet paper dolls were all the rage when the Dionne quintuplets were born. There were also Shirley Temple paper dolls. We could outfit the beloved child movie star in dresses and coats from her films.

My favorites were "Little Women," from the film with Katherine Hepburn as Jo, and Frances Dee as Meg, Jean Parker as Beth and Joan Bennett as Amy.

Because movies inspired most of the dolls, you could also find Jane Withers, Judy Garland and Deanna Durbin paper dolls. Jane was always the mean little girl in Shirley Temple films. In recent years she has been Josephine, the lady plumber, on the Comet(TM) advertisements on television.

Deanna Durbin was a girl with a remarkable voice. Judy Garland needs no introduction. Later, "Gone with the Wind" paper dolls were an especially big hit.

Jeanette McDonald was my sister's favorite. Jeanette, who? A beautiful soprano with red hair, Miss McDonald and Nelson Eddy starred in several 1930s films and sang of their mutual love. We saw every one of those films more than once.

I remember one book we bought was a complete wedding party that included the parents of the bridal couple, the ring bearer and the flower girl. There were honeymoon clothes for the bride and bridegroom. As my sister says now, "Weren't we all dreaming of a big, beautiful wedding when we were little girls?"

Cutting out paper dolls and the clothes really took a lot of time. For the especially intricate cutting, like ruffles and pleats, mother would let us borrow her embroidery scissors. You had to be sure to cut out the tabs for holding the clothes on the dolls. Paper dolls on newsprint were much more fragile and if we found one we liked, we would paste it on light cardboard before cutting, to make sure it would last.

One problem was the tabs on the clothes. If we kept folding them over to hold the clothes on the dolls, eventually the tabs fell off and we had to try to put them back on with plastic tape. The newspaper tabs were especially delicate. Some of the dresses for the bought dolls were double, with fronts and backs and a slit at the top so we could the dresses over the head of the doll.

In those days, there was no such thing as jeans or slacks and only occasionally, shorts. The dolls wore dresses for almost every occasion, even sports.

My sister, my friend, Pat Ryan, and I would spend hours making up stories and putting our paper dolls through all kinds of adventures. A tabletop became an apartment and we would outline, with chalk, the rooms where a great deal of "activity" would take place.

But, for the three of us, the greatest joy of paper dolls was drawing new clothes for them. We made ball gowns, glamorous robes, stunning sports dresses, fancy coats and outrageous hats. At a time when debutantes at their coming-out parties smiled from the society section of the Sunday papers, why couldn't we put ourselves in their places with paper dolls? It was a great way to live in a fantasy world.

Actually, by the time we were twelve years old, we had become quite good at fashion design and I even won a national contest, sponsored by a children's magazine, for designing a child's dress. The prize was one dollar. I'm sure that one reason we stayed with paper dolls through junior high was because of the fashion designing.

Most of my durable paper dolls from the stores have survived and amazingly, one of the newspaper dolls is still around creating a real nostalgia collection for my sister and me. "Little Women" has disappeared, but I still have the quintuplets, Flapper Fanny, the wedding dolls and many more.

Maybe there was a deep, dark philosophical reason for us to play with paper dolls…The Depression had hit our family income and there were scant toys…perhaps we dreamed of becoming fashion designers…or, as I said, there was the fantasy aspect of being someone glamorous. But, no, it was none of those reasons. Playing paper dolls was just plain fun.

I'm planning to buy a book of paper dolls for my granddaughter for her fourth birthday.

❖ Reflections ❖
by Jean Kozlowski, Northfield, Massachusetts

Being a teenager during World War Two taught me that even in bad times, good things could happen.

On December 7, 1941 while I was finishing my homework, I heard on the radio the grim announcement of the Japanese attack on Pearl Harbor. Little did any of us realize how this event would affect our lives.

My dad, a World War I veteran, was so concerned about the news that as a family we listened to H.B. Kaltenborn, the radio commentator, every evening until the war ended.

During this time, the city of Portland, Maine where I lived, was ill-equipped to deal with the number of sailors who were part of the Atlantic fleet anchored in the harbor. In addition, shipyards in South Portland were filled with people who worked around the clock to produce ships for the war effort. The usual bright lights of the city were gone as blackouts were enforced.

Gas and food rationing were everyday realities. My mother would travel to Commercial Street to buy heart, liver or tripe for us to eat. Recipes for these delectables were shared with women who stood in the ration lines. I often smelled those sweetmeats cooking slowly in an iron skillet on the back of the stove. Mother would ask us how we liked her recipes. We agreed the hearts were quite tasty.

At school, Elizabeth Ring, my history teacher declared that every Friday our class would study the war including where the troops were, each campaign and what was happening. We all looked forward to Fridays. It was truly American History.

I recall my classmate, Connie Baker, explaining to the class her cousin's internment in a German prison camp. She talked of the lack of food, terrible cold and inhuman treatment. His release meant he was sent to a sanitarium in the U.S. to recover.

There were other troubling reports. At the movies, the news would be flashed before the main feature. A furnace with the remains of children's shoes and clothing were shown. I sat frozen in my seat as I realized children's lives had been snuffed out. In my sheltered life I had little comprehension of such horrors.

One day my dad announced that a German submarine had washed up on shore at Cape Elizabeth. On a sunny day, if I watched the Western Promenade, I could see the faint outline of the U.S. Atlantic fleet in the distance. The harbor was well mined. It reminded me that the Germans were nearer to the U.S. than we realized.

One summer we stayed at our camp on Sebago Lake. We started a Victory Garden. My mother canned and we even had a root cellar. All of us worked together to plant, to care for and to harvest this garden. I was recruited to weed and to water. I learned about pests that invaded our patch, like potato bugs, cutworms and beetles. It was fun to watch our seeds mature into edible plants.

During our stay at the lake, my father needed the car for work. Because of gas rationing, he seldom came to the lake. We were able to borrow a Shetland pony, named Lady. We kept her at our neighbor's barn. I learned to harness her to a wagon, feed and groom her as well as ride her. She was a sturdy, twenty-year-old pony, almost a horse in size, but a very stubborn one. We rode by wagon to the store to make our purchases. Once we attended a ball game at Panther Pond. Lady would go very slowly from the barn, but on the return she tore through the main street much to the amazement of the town's people.

When the war ended in August 1945, I heard the church bell tolling across the lake. It rang continually, so I harnessed Lady and my brother and I rode to the church to help ring the bell again and again.

The pealing bell meant new life was to begin. Freedom had won out. At last American boys would no longer have to give their lives for their country.

The war taught me that life goes on, small things matter and that our country was a great one that could pull together for a common cause.

❖ Twenty Minutes a Day ❖
by Elisabeth Leete, Ashfield, Massachusetts

"You have such good posture," Sally (seventy-seven years old) said standing erect on the steps of Elmer's, the landmark country store in Ashfield, Massachusetts. "How do you do it?"

"Simple," I (seventy-one) replied. "It's my big green ball, my exercise bench, my weights, my rubber band, my jump rope and my abs."

Sally asked about my exercise routine.

It all started years ago when I decided that I didn't want to have osteoporosis and that my daily walks were not sufficient. I also hoped getting fit would make me want to stop smoking. I haven't stopped smoking, but I don't have osteoporosis. Pushing a heavy wheelbarrow filled with large logs doesn't hurt my back. Stacking wood is boring, but a cinch. I easily bend down to lift things from the floor or stretch my arms to reach upper shelves in my kitchen, remembering to flex my muscles. I smile condescendingly when men offer to carry my bags or my cello ("too heavy for you!"). My stomach isn't exactly flat, but what the hell, I am not looking for romance. And I like to think that my mind is as agile, or maybe more so, than when I was 60 or even 55 years old.

The very day I came to the decision to take better care of my body, I found a card at the bank in Shelburne Falls, Massachusetts that said, "One to One Fitness." Just what I needed. I went to see Gayle Olson the author of the card.

"Let's start with quads," beautiful, gentle and limber Gayle said.
"Quads?"
"Quadriceps, the muscle in front of your thighs."

My vocabulary was expanding, but when I tried to squeeze my left leg behind my back holding the foot with my left hand, my leg came up only half way. There was work to do.

My routine divides itself among the rooms of my house. The living room is for jumping rope—eighty jumps is my record so far—preceded by quad stretches and calf stretches against a closet in the kitchen. I could jump rope outside, but I am a little shy because of the neighbors. This exercise is followed, in the kitchen, by the Right Angle Stretch. Bending forward at the hips, I reach the table with straight arms and stretch my hips and spine until my body forms a right angle. This is also called Table Pose. Some days I am more in the mood for jumping jacks than jump ropes. I do them in the hallway, looking at the sky through a small skylight.

I play with the big green ball in the bedroom. The king size bed near me gives me a feeling of security when I sit on the ball, lifting one arm and the opposite leg ("Good for brain neurons," Guru Gayle explained). Mustering a little enthusiasm, I do ten knee-ups: I lie on the ball on my stomach, then throw myself forward, pulling my knees all the way to the top of the ball if possible. I confess this is hard.

I had to get rid of a chair in the guestroom to make room for my exercise bench. It's not decorative, but my guests can sit on it to pull up their socks, or lay some of their clothes on it. Sitting on the bench, I lift fifty pounds with my legs twenty times (trying to remember to exhale when the effort is greater). Then, on my stomach, I lift thirty-five pounds ten times with the back of my legs, grunting a little. I also lift two ten-pound weights with my arms, lying on my back. This list is not complete, but it gives you an idea. After that, I go to the kitchen to stretch my shoulders and my chest.

In my room, before playing with the big green ball, I use the rubber band to stretch my arms and back ("Excellent for your posture!" Gayle said) and strengthen my hamstrings—the muscles behind the thighs—and my biceps.

The last set of exercise is "abs" or abdominals, which I now practice on my bed—softer than the rug. I bicycle, lift my legs, bounce left and right. But I do have to lie on the floor to do the bridge pose and the shoulder stand ("Circulation!").

Besides thinking I am probably crazy, you must begin to wonder if I spend my whole life standing on my head and jumping around. Relax: I do one set of exercises every day and that takes me twenty minutes, not counting my almost daily walk and "salutations to the sun," a yoga pose I choose to do at night, saluting the moon and stars.

❖ Lafayette, I Am Where? ❖
by Warren LeMon, Turners Falls, Massachusetts

In June 1960 I completed my French course at the Army Language School in Monterey, California. I was one of two students in our class of twenty-one who had been assigned directly to Paris. After a month's leave at home in Arlington, Virginia, I reported to Fort Dix, New Jersey to wait for travel to Europe.

I sat there for three weeks doing nothing.

One day my name was called. I stood in a long line. When my turn came, a sergeant searched through his file cards. Finally he looked up.

"Germany. Bad Kreuznach. Aircraft maintenance detachment."

"What about my French schooling?"

"What about it? If you get across the border, you'll be way ahead of your buddies, speaking the language."

The next dawn I joined a shivering band of soldiers headed for Europe. After my interview I had gone to the European processing supervisor. I showed him my diploma and my school orders.

Local Color 225

"Look out now. I think we screwed up. How about if we cancel your orders and start all over again next week? We'll make a fresh start."

I cannot repeat the language I used in reacting to his suggestion. He let me simmer down, which was accommodating since he was a senior master sergeant and I was a mere buck.

"Tell you what, troop. When you get to Frankfurt, since you're determined to fly, here's a note for Ryan in personnel. He knows me OK. Happy landings."

My note read: "Ryan, this guy should go to Paris. Sincerely, Casey."

On the flight line, our individual records were consolidated into a hefty packet and given to the ranking sergeant for delivery to Frankfurt. About fifty yards away, a group of Hispanic troops clustered near another plane. Somebody said they were short-timers heading to Puerto Rico for discharge.

Our voyage to Frankfurt was placid. I held onto my skimpy note with its homely message. On the bus from the airport to the processing center the custodian called out:

"I'm tired of carrying these files. When I call out your name, sound off and grab your records."

"Santiago, Jesus…Diaz, Romero…Torillo, Alcalde…Say, what the hell's going on? Did we drop everybody over the Atlantic?"

"Whyn't you call out somebody's name what's here?" one soldier said.

The custodian went through the entire stack. Not one person whose name was called was in our group. He held the records of those soldiers heading to Puerto Rico for discharge. And it then dawned on us that all our records were flying high over the Caribbean.

To be blunt, in English, French and Spanish we were screwed.

I showed my note to Ryan. I told him that my orders were erroneous and my records were missing.

"But I do have this note for you."

As though it were the Magna Carta, I handed him the scrap I kept in my wallet. He read it twice, looked at me, smiled, and finally said:

"How's old Casey doing? Does he like that New Jersey beer?"

I stared at him in disbelief.

"Relax…we'll have you on your way to Paris in a day or two. It won't go anywhere."

❖ In Memory of Nellie Doran ❖
by Janice Howard Lepore, Greenfield, Massachusetts

Now that I have been a grandmother for over twenty three years and currently "substitute for mom" to my granddaughters after school several days a week, it is only natural to remember my grandmother. In reflecting on my journey through life, I find that my growing up years in the Midwest are colored with memories of my Grandma Nellie, but I don't remember her words. Some scenes I remember are her peeling potatoes, doing dishes, sprinkling Monday's wash and rolling it up neatly in a big basket, picking up after us or finishing up our half done chores.

Even though I now know she had been rather tall, I only remember her as old, round shouldered, in cotton print dresses with a bib apron sashed around her middle. Her hair was pushed back from her face into a roll at the back of her neck. It is so sad to remember her trudging around day in and day out in old, broken down, black shoes, doing housework, or lugging water to the grove of trees she helped plant. The seedlings were courtesy of the federal government, but after they were planted were not accompanied by even a threat of rain.

Grandma Nellie and her two babies had come to South Dakota to homestead with her parents and brothers around 1905. She came after her husband, Patrick Howard, had been killed in Iowa while training horses. I don't recall anyone talking about my grandfather or his family.

When I was eighteen, Grandma and I went to Iowa to visit relatives, but there were only a couple families still living. There were no families with the Howard name and due to a fire in Walnut City many years before, there were no records to search, either.

Grandma Nellie kept in touch with relatives Celia and Nell Curran in Emerson, Nebraska. Their sister, Bessie Solberg and daughter Betty would come to visit from Sioux City, Iowa on occasion. They were generous with their store-bought clothes, jewelry, and hats, latest hair accessories and piano sheet music, which I have to this day. My sister and I proudly wore the Sunday dresses Mom fashioned from their hand-me-downs.

Grandma Nellie never had a room of her own, let alone a house. These were the Dust Bowl years on the prairie. She took her daughter with her from place to place, caring for families—usually mother and baby situations. I don't know if she was referred to as a "midwife" or "nurse," but she was always needed by someone. She stayed with one family for many years after the mother committed suicide when the eighth child was born.

Her only son, my father, was on his own earning a living at twelve, having finished sixth grade. Years later, he returned to try to save the homestead in Sanborn County, but his granddad died and another dream withered with the economic depression.

Four generations—Grandma Nellie, her bed-ridden mother, Mary Jane Holland Doran, her son, his wife and three babies—relocated to a more desolate farm further off a traveled route. Grandma's brother Bill lived with us off and on. Her uncle Dan Holland, from Wisconsin, visited often. He eventually bequeathed her some land with more rocks than soil, which is still known as "Grandma's Place" even though no one ever lived there.

We kids had many carefree days never realizing the poverty and struggle that surrounded us. The prairie fires, cattle stampedes, wild horses we were cautioned to stay away from when Dad was breaking them, blizzards, wind, dirt, were all just a part of life. I remember the peace and comfort Grandma gave us kids when our five-year-old sister and Mom's parents were killed in a car accident one hot, windy August day. There was so much commotion and confusion with people coming and going. Children in those days were meant to be seen and not heard.

Eventually we moved to a farm closer to town so we kids could all go to Catholic school, instead of walking two miles to the one-room schoolhouse that I had enjoyed for three years.

Grandma Nellie was busy ironing clothes with a heavy flat black iron that was heated on the stove one November day when I found my two year old sister unable to move in her crib. My sister was diagnosed with polio and we were quarantined on the farm for school vacation. Even though Grandma shared a room with us kids where ever we lived, I don't remember her telling stories or singing. She did have a big Bible that she let us look at often. I also remember her cleaning and filling the smelly kerosene lamps that were stored in our room.

On my twelfth birthday, Grandma gave me a wooden box of stationery and cologne. I was crushed to find the cologne had frozen and burst the following morning, but I treasured the hinged wooden box through the years and gave it to my eldest granddaughter on her twelfth birthday.

I didn't understand at the time, but Grandma went away for a rest, supposedly. My interest in writing blossomed and I used the stationary to write her heaven knows what. She always made me feel as though my letters were her salvation as she missed being needed and didn't like living with strangers. Her daughter Marie needed surgery about this time, so she came home to care for her and her family. In her later years, Grandma finally did have a room of her own with peace and quiet.

I regret not knowing her in my adult years, as I left home at eighteen with the same vague naïve dream that I am sure Grandma Nellie had when she left home to marry in 1900. She had a hard life, but was not one to complain. Unfortunately I didn't inherit her patience, but I think she did teach me to be a good listener. My life story is a prime example of how important it is for children to have a consistent caring person, besides their parents, in their formative years.

Grandma enjoyed playing bingo at the November church bazaar and usually won several turkeys for the holiday meals. I remember how everyone enjoyed going to midnight Mass Christmas Eve after the traditional supper of oyster stew and Santa's quick stop, which we were never fast enough to witness.

I will always remember Grandma Nellie as one of those "Dear Hearts and Gentle People" described in her favorite song which I was privileged to play many, many times for her on the piano. I remember her smile and wish I could recall her voice.

Born November 24, 1881 in Nebraska to John and Mary Jane Holland Doran, Grandma was always known as Nellie even though she was christened Ellen Theresa Doran. She was big sister to Frank, Charles, Matt, William and Agnes who died at a very young age. Grandma died February 26, 1968 and was buried on the 29th in St. Wilfred's Cemetery,

Woonsocket, South Dakota with her parents and several of her siblings.

❖ Trabili ❖
by Phyllis Loomis, Ashfield, Massachusetts

I can still see and feel Trabili's little hand as her tiny fingers played with the loose skin on the back of my old, weather-beaten hands. I was a fifty-seven-year-old white woman living with a Swazi family on their homestead in the most northwest corner of Swaziland, South Africa. The year was 1978. I was midway into two years as an American Peace Corps Volunteer.

Each afternoon, Trabili met me at our gate and together we walked across the well-swept, dung-polished yard of our homestead. We always stopped before my rondovel (house) to look at ourselves in the dime store mirrors that hung on the door.

Each evening before sunset, I took those mirrors inside and then re-hung them the next morning. Mirrors were not a common thing in Swaziland. Most people had never seen one. Mine drew visitors from far away. Everyone worried about the spirits of the dead returning at night to look at themselves and perhaps to help themselves to my treasures.

Trabili at two would see herself in the mirrors: a tiny Swazi child in bare feet and a dress, no jewels, no tattoos. Only a plastic net onion bag on her head as a hat or mask, or on her arms as a sleeve or on her leg pulled as high as her short leg would allow. She would make faces at the mirror-child that magically made faces back at her.

I would see Trabili with a thin, gray haired woman in a wraparound skirt, sweatshirt and good, strong, hiking boots looking older than fifty-seven years. We would see us together. We always looked at those "strangers" and practiced our language lessons. Trabili was my greatest teacher. We learned siSwazi together laughing at each other's new vocabulary as we taught new words to one another. Then we would walk to my bathroom-sized home. A bed, card table, bookcase and two-burner camp stove nearly filled my floor space. There was only one chair at the table and a rod stretched across one corner of the room to hold my few clothes.

We sat on the bed to look at Trabili's only book. It was an ever-growing book of photographs of David Toshimi Loomis, my first and only grandchild, who was born two months after I left home. He was about a year younger than Trabili.

Together, Trabili and I sat and talked of that far-off child. As the young Swazi child on my lap lovingly played with my very real hand, I realized, with surprise, that though I was so white and she so beautifully, ebony black, that at that moment she was all mine.

❖ A Snowbird Story ❖
by Lorraine Madden, Greenfield, Massachusetts

It was time to leave for Florida for the winter months, as we did each year. We had missed going the previous year because of medical reasons and had rented our place through a rental agency, temporarily, to an elderly widow.

One day, during the season we rented, we received a note that said the tenant was in an automobile accident and was in the hospital, but was recuperating nicely.

A month later we received a letter from the agency saying that the tenant had died suddenly and the house was closed up. Her son had come to visit her and found her dead. We had no further information.

The next year, after the last leg of driving for twelve hours, we arrived at the house in Holiday, Florida around ten p.m. We unpacked the car and my husband suggested we get some rest and finish in the morning. I kept hesitating and sat in the living room. Again he called and said to get some sleep after that long drive.

I walked to the bedroom door and said I didn't really want to sleep in that bed.

"Suppose the woman had died there?" I said and returned to the living room.

It wasn't much later when I heard light snoring and thought, "How can he go to sleep not knowing?"

I sat up as long as I could and then decided to sleep on the couch until I found out what the woman had died from and where she had died.

The next day I cleaned and washed everything in sight. I even called a company to come and clean the rugs. I rubbed and scrubbed and the next night, again, I slept on the couch.

The next day while we were having coffee in the morning, my next-door neighbor, Edith, dropped in to join us. She was one to keep track of everyone in the area and knew what each was doing—our friendly watchdog!

I asked her if she knew what our former tenant had died from and felt relieved, more or less, when she said it was a heart attack. Her son had come to visit her and found her dead. At least it wasn't some bad disease!

My next question was "Do you know which bed she died in?"

"Oh," said Edith. "She didn't die in the bedroom, she died on the couch in the living room."

❖ When Greenfield Was a Seaport ❖
by Eileen Marguet, Greenfield, Massachusetts

In 1634 a Dutchman, Adrian Block, was sailing through Long Island Sound on his way to Manhattan. One of his ships caught fire and he was forced to land around Saybrook, Connecticut. He discovered the Connecticut River and began to study the area and possibilities for navigation.

He made several maps of the terrain further up, and claimed the place, "New Netherlands." It wasn't long before the English took the same route and renamed it "New England." The native Indians had been traveling up and down what they called "The Long River" for five hundred years before it was 'discovered.' There were many skirmishes between these groups before it became a safe route.

By the end of the seventeenth century, the Cheapside section of Greenfield, Massachusetts had all the importance of a small seaport. Situated on the Connecticut River, just above Deerfield, it was the head of river navigation. It became the point of exchange for all heavy merchandise. Several stores were erected, although small and modest.

In 1795 traders began to appear. Joseph Swan was the first. He had three hundred bushels of Turks Island salt to exchange for flaxseed. Willard Wait had copper. He moved from the upper part of Greenfield to Cheapside and became a partner to Cephas Hoyt.

As the small settlements increased up the river, flatboats were built which could be pushed up the swift current using poles. In 1749 a schooner was built at Cheapside and in 1755 a man-of-war named "Oliver Cromwell," which carried twenty-four guns, was built there. These boats required much patience, skill and muscle.

After the Revolutionary War, the population increased and necessities for the people required quicker and less expensive transportation to and from the markets. In 1792 a canal was built around South Hadley and one around Turners Falls. Great things were expected from these improvements.

The advent of the steamboat brought many more changes. In 1828 a steamer was built in New York for the Connecticut River Company called the "Barnet," which reached Hartford and started for Barnet, Vermont. She towed a large barge loaded with people who waved to the inhabitants on shore. She arrived at Cheapside on December 2 and was greeted with cheers from hundreds of people and fifteen guns from the Old Deerfield cannon.

Businesses of many kinds were prospering. John Williams opened a store just below the bridge and had all sorts of goods to exchange for staves, headings and hoop poles. Cephas Hoyt hung out a sign showing a white horse painted on a black background and called his place "White Horse Inn."

In 1800, John Williams, Jr. established a packinghouse for beef and pork. The Abercrombies bought a boat called "Voyer" which cost $185.00. They later changed its name to "Free Trade" and made three trips to Hartford during the season. The freights downward were composed of ash plank, brooms, cider brandy, fire boxes, boxes of hats, cranberries, poles, scythes, rake and fork handles, leather, limes, axes and great quantities of wood. The up freight consisted of English and West Indian gods, corn, flour and cotton. The cost of down freight was $2.25 per ton to $2.50 per ton and up freight was twice that amount.

In 1839, the Abercrombies bought the "Donner" and made four trips that season. In 1835, Allen and Root bought the steamer "Greenfield" which was run by Captain T.W. Dewey. They also had a line of boats consolidated under the name of Stockbridge, Allen, Root & Company.

It was in May 1841 that Greenfield and Cheapside were vying with each other for the county seat. Reasons were given to the legislature to have it in Cheapside. Mr. Griswold said, "It is the territorial and traveling center of the entire county. It is the head of boat navigation for this part of the country. It has been a great outlet for the produce of the farmers."

Some noted that there were fewer inhabitants in Cheapside and only a few habitable houses. Two gentlemen stood ready to build two taverns in whichever location was decided upon.

Then Samuel E. Fields added his affidavit declaring that there was more business done in Cheapside in one day than there was in Greenfield in one week. The long struggle between the two towns ended with Greenfield being in possession of Cheapside.

Although the glory of Cheapside proper departed with the change of transportation from the river to the railroad, the great industrial work that was brought here was more than had ever been known in this area.

❖ Ma's "Watchdog" ❖
by Marjorie Naida, Gill, Massachusetts

After my father, TaTa, died in 1980, we knew Ma was lonely, but she insisted she was keeping busy all the time. During the next several years she would say she wanted to buy a HUGE watchdog to guard the house. He would stay in the backyard and bark to keep strangers away, she'd say.

We made weekly trips to Springfield for shopping excursions and doing chores around Ma's house. Well, imagine our surprise when on such a Saturday we were greeted at the door by Ma's new guard dog,

Mickey. He was an adorable one-year-old black poodle. He weighed all of five pounds! Amid kisses, barking and faces being licked, Ma excitedly told us how she acquired him. He was listed for sale in the classified section of the Springfield newspaper. She had no means of transportation to Chicopee where the breeder lived, so the breeder brought him to Ma's house so she could check him over. It was mutual love at first sight! We laughed all day long about the HUGE watchdog that was going to protect the property.

This small bundle of energy was devoted to Ma and brought her thirteen years of love and companionship. He cuddled in her lap when she rested and he followed her wherever she went.

Ma had a hemorrhagic stroke five years ago. During her recovery she would call out for Mickey. The nurses asked who Mickey was and when they realized he was her pet, they told us to bring him up to Rehab for a visit. When we did so, Ma was happy and relaxed to know Mickey was all right. Ma improved and we brought her up to Gill along with Mickey to be part of our household. They were a happy addition to our lives.

Several months ago Ma died and Mickey was as depressed and lonely as the rest of us. We still have him with us and he is fourteen years old now. Ma had a blanket remnant he slept on and another one to cover him. Now I'm treating Mickey the same as she did and I smile when I think of the companionship and pleasure the little dog provided her.

I often asked Ma if she was lonely when she lived alone and she would say, "How can I be, when I have Mickey to keep me company?"

Her HUGE watchdog now weighs a hefty eight pounds and is protecting our home.

It makes me happy to know how much Ma loved Mickey and that the feeling was mutual. He was the best watchdog she could ever have had.

❖ Little Church on Christian Hill ❖
by Louise Bowen O'Brien, Colrain, Massachusetts

In the winter of 1915, Marshall Looman and his twin sister Margaret made their first visit to the Christian Hill Baptist Church. Tucked in a large wicker clothesbasket, they rode in the sleigh drawn by a farm horse over Colrain's rough hilly roads to the little church where their parents were active members.

All the families on the hill attended the little one room church for Sunday services and to socialize with their neighbors.

Today the little white wooden church still stands on the hill. The wagon shed is gone, but the church building remains the same. There is no central heat, only an ancient black woodstove located at the back of the church. There is no electricity, only kerosene oil lamps suspended from the ceiling. A wooden pulpit stands in the center of the raised floor at the front of the church. An antique organ is nearby. Rows of wooden seats fill the small room. Plain glass windows let in light. At Easter Sunday sunrise service, it is an inspiration to see the sun shine through the east window.

In 1997 the church celebrated its two hundredth anniversary. In memory of the old church's history, members of the new church held services there.

Through the years, services have been held at the old church on special occasions. The Christmas Eve service has become a tradition with guests from neighboring towns crowding the little building to join in the caroling. The little organ wheezes and candles flicker in the drafts, but there is a feeling of goodwill and the spirit of Christmas.

At eighty-five, Marshall is the oldest member of the church. As he says, "I've belonged to this church since my first trip here in a clothes basket."

Note: Marshal Looman died February 2001.

❖ Immunity, Love & Learning in a Red Brick Schoolhouse ❖
by Joseph A. Parzych, Gill, Massachusetts

A red brick schoolhouse once sat at the crossroads of a dirt road and one of the only two tarred roads in the town of Gill. The best thing about our school was our teacher, Miss Pogoda. She made suggestions instead of rules.

"You boys look so nice," she said one day, "I wonder if we could start school each Monday with a clean shirt."

Boys were apt to wear the same shirt to school, week after week, until the sleeves took on the sheen of leather. From that day on, the boys came to school on Monday with clean shirts. Pants were another story. Most boys had but one pair of school pants. They were changed with the seasons, but she let that go. Girls were no problem because they usually wore clean dresses and did not get them dirty the way the boys were inclined to do. Often, the girls had but one good dress. It was washed on the weekend and worn, week after week, for the entire year.

Miss Pogoda allowed the boys to come to school barefooted. In the fall everyone wore shoes on the first day of school. After that, boys vied to see who was toughest in braving the cold the longest. She said the custom of going barefoot could continue as long as the boys washed their feet before coming into the schoolhouse. Since there was no plumbing at the school, we washed our feet in a nearby brook. It would have been good if we'd drawn our drinking water from the brook.

Miss Pogoda rewarded boys by choosing among the best behaved to fetch water from an old bachelor's dilapidated house diagonally across from the school, never thinking the water was anything but pure. Run off from both roof and yard drained down into the bachelor's well in the cellar. A school committee member had the water tested. It was highly polluted. From then on, we carried water from a farm, a little farther away.

The farm water ran by gravity through a lead pipe a fair distance from a spring high up in a cow pasture dotted with meadow muffins. Since the family who lived there were fine upstanding people, I doubt the school committee would have risked insulting them by having the water tested.

We carried water in a galvanized pail. Everyone lined up in a back hall to drink from the pail using the same dipper. Kids dipped only the amount they could drink. In our strict code of sanitation, only the empty dipper could be returned to the water pail. Each person had to drink all they'd dipped out, since there was nowhere to discard the water remaining in the dipper.

If an epidemic struck, our drinking water arrangement served to keep the duration short. Once someone came down with a contagious disease, the whole school came down with it shortly thereafter. The epidemic didn't get dragged out as it did in other schools where contagion wasn't spread as expediently.

Barring rare epidemics, the school body remained remarkably healthy. Perfect attendance was common. Perhaps the constant exposure to a variety of germs served to build immunity, putting us on the cutting edge of inoculation. The school doctor put our little vaccination program in jeopardy by recommending that each student bring an individual drinking glass.

On a shelf by the water pail, we lined up an assortment of glasses and jelly jars, each labeled with the student's name on a piece of adhesive tape. The jars gathered dust while we continued lining up to take turns drinking from the dipper.

Miss Pogoda never learned of our arrangement because she never drank from the pail. Other than drinking tea from a small thermos bottle, a sip or two of soup was the only thing we ever saw her eat or drink. The soup was part of our Hot Soup Program—one can of Campbell's Alphabet Vegetable Soup to 4 cans of water heated on a hot plate.

At about a quarter to twelve, our teacher sent a couple of girls into the back hall to prepare the soup. Soon the delicious aroma of vegetable soup drifted into the classroom. I don't know why it was always alphabet soup. Perhaps the school committee felt it would be more educational. Maybe they were right, because we often tried to arrange letters to spell out words in a game of edible scrabble limited to very short words. Though the soup was thin enough to rival soups served in the Nazi concentration camps, it was hot and a welcome addition to the jam or mustard sandwiches we brought from home.

The girls preparing the soup gave Miss Pogoda a generous portion of vegetables and letters. Not completely selfless, they took turns finishing off Miss Pogoda's uneaten portion out of sight in the back room where they washed the dishes.

Miss Pogoda was barely out of her teens and not yet graduated from college. She taught at our school as an intern in place of college classes as part of a special Depression program. She handled all eight grades alone, with outdated textbooks that were in tatters and supplies all but non-existent. But when Gill students graduated to Turners High School, they often did better than students who'd attended the much nicer, better equipped Montague schools.

Miss Pogoda needed to report to Fitchburg State College from time to time and always brought back school supplies.

"I'm leaving you on your honor to behave," she'd say before departing the school Friday noon. We sat in utter silence doing our schoolwork until the end of the school day, then left and locked the door behind us. Only then did we speak.

The school committee heard rumors that Miss Pogoda was leaving the entire school body unsupervised for half a day at a time. Suspecting mayhem, they decided to investigate. We spotted them parking their car some distance away. We signaled each other with a nod of the head and watched out of the corners of our eyes as the school committee members crept up to listen at the window. The schoolroom was as still as a cloistered convent. The school committee members raised up their heads to peek inside. They saw a room full of silent kids bent over their work. They turned and walked back to their car looking disappointed.

Soon after that, the school committee sent Miss Pogoda a problem student from another school. He was no problem for her. She was petite with brown hair, sparkling eyes, and a warm smile which had a benevolent power over the most unruly child.

The red brick schoolhouse in West Gill is long gone but the happy memories of those days with our beloved teacher will remain with me forever.

Note: Blanche Pogoda married Andrew Seremeth and later resumed teaching in Bernardston. She lives in Greenfield, Massachusetts.

❖ The USS Montague AKA-98 ❖
Submitted by Nicholas Prokowich, MM2/c, Turners Falls, Massachusetts

There was a ship named the USS Montague that served in both World War II and the Korean War. I believe I am the only one in this area that served aboard her. The ship was actually named for a county in Texas where we'll have our next reunion in 2001. These are my memories of my journey on her from the States to the Mediterranean Sea, then to Japan and finally Korea for military duty.

I entered the Navy the fifth of October 1948 with Jim Mathews. We went from Greenfield to Springfield then to the Great Lakes Naval Station in Illinois by train. Upon our arrival, we were examined, had our hair cut and were issued our Navy gear. We were assigned to camp (Moffett), Company 389. We started boot camp training, had a break for Christmas and then returned to finish boot camp. After the first of the year we went Main Side and were assigned to Machinist Mate School.

After the completion of our service school requirements we enjoyed a ten-day leave and then reported to Little Creek, Virginia. Both Jim and I traveled there and were assigned our ships after a short wait. He was assigned to the USS Catamount LSD-17 and I, the USS Montague AKA-98 (AKA stands for Amphibious Cargo Attack vessel). Thinking Jim had put the guys up to play a game with me I said, "Come on and give me the right ship." To my surprise, it was the right ship! I came aboard her on the 27th of May 1949.

I was assigned to the Engine Room, 'M' Division, third Section, and made trips to Guantanamo Bay, Cuba. We went to Port au Prince, Haiti and later to the Vieques Island. I remember that we anchored off shore there and the crew had a swimming party all day. When we left , we went to Willemstad, Curacao for a short stay and then headed to Boston,

Massachusetts. This was for the weekend and then we headed back to Norfolk, Virginia.

The story really begins here, on our trip to the Mediterranean and on to Korea. (The story does not end there for me, as we retuned to the States after being away for over a year and we were allowed to fly a pennant—one foot for every man aboard ship—which ended up being 345 feet in length and held up by weather balloons.)

We arrived in San Diego, California to go into dry dock for upkeep. After that we loaded with cement bags for cargo and headed for the Philippines. The cement was for the construction of an airfield. We did spend some time in Manila and then off to Japan.

Besides a trip to Korea, we did go to Hong Kong for ten days. The ship's engineering crew had three basketball games with the Chinese Athletic Club, winning one, losing one and the last one got called due to rain. The games were played on an outdoor court under the lights at night. We returned to Japan and went to the Northern Island of Japan with the Navy Seals for training.

After Japan we left for Pearl Harbor. Coming into the channel we saw the sunken ships and memorial for the crew of the USS Arizona, which had been bombed during the attack and sunk. We had a crewmember aboard our ship that was on the Arizona when it was attacked and sunk. His name was Don McDonald MM1/c who told us he was blown into the water by the bombing and didn't know how he got there.

When we arrived at our pier in Hawaii we were greeted by a band and hula dancers. We stayed three days then back to San Diego.

We anchored at North Island for a while and then were assigned to Long Beach, California. This is where I was transferred to San Diego Naval Station for discharge. I was there just a few days when I recognized the voice of my friend Jim Mathews. He was also there to be discharged. I had not seen him since Japan. Our ships had been in landings together and in port together, but trying to see each other was something else.

We finally did get discharged the 25th of September 1952. We traveled together to Massachusetts by car across the country, the same way my mother and sister had traveled to California for my discharge. We took the southern route to Texas and then upward to Massachusetts. We both returned to work at the Millers Falls Tool Company where we had worked before we enlisted in the Navy.

So many things about my service were memorable to me: coming aboard the USS Montague as a Fireman Machinist Mate, getting the machine shop aboard ship, making third class Petty Officer and being put in charge of the watch list, doing qualification of personnel to stand engine room watch, making second class petty officer, being assigned to stand Chief watch underway, being in charge of the Engine room, being able to lite-off main engines (preparing the ship ready to leave) and securing them.

Serving aboard the USS Montague was a great pleasure and to live in Montague, Massachusetts could not have been any better.

❖ Gardening ❖
by Leona Robert, Turners Falls, Massachusetts

My husband Phil took great pride in his garden. Each row was straight as an arrow, having been carefully laid out, the distance between each row measured exactly. He enjoyed tilling the soil, planting the seeds and just watching them grow under his tender loving care. Then came harvest time and sitting back to review the fruits of his labor.

In 1958 he suffered a severe heart attack and was unable to return to work. Eventually, working at his own pace, he could continue gardening. Since we had an extra large lot with plenty of unused space, brother-in-law Charlie suggested raising more. He would help with the work and they could sell the surplus vegetables at the restaurant where he was a chef, sharing the profits. Among other things, they planted Bermuda onions, which seemed to like that soil and grew to be extra large.

That same summer, our granddaughter, Ginger from San Diego, came to Massachusetts to spend part of the summer with us. She was about eleven years old then. During her stay, Phil ended up in the hospital with another heart attack.

One morning Ginger decide she would stay home while I went to work, fix us lunch, and then go back to the office with me for the afternoon. As I drove into the yard at noon, I noticed a lot of onion tops overflowing the trash barrel near the back of the garage and thought Charlie must have come up for some vegetables. Ginger never mentioned anyone having been there as we prepared lunch. As I headed for the refrigerator I asked, "Did you have any company this morning?"

"No," she replied.

At that point I opened the refrigerator door and nearly went into shock. All I could see were beautiful, big Bermuda onions, all peeled! There must have been a bushel of them. Food had been removed to make room and every shelf was pile high. There wasn't even room for a toothpick!

"I was walking in the garden," Ginger said. "And saw the onions were ripe, so I thought I'd help Grandpa and take care of them."

I stopped at the hospital and told Phil what happened. He was a very patient, easygoing person and just said, "It's done now so there's nothing you can do."

That night I had to face Charlie and was dreading his reaction.

After work I packed the onions in containers and drove to his house. I told him the story. If it had been one of the local kids he would have blown his stack, but to my amazement he roared with laughter.

"That's about what you'd expect from a city kid! What do they know about gardening!" he said.

In fact, many years later when Ginger was getting married, a bridal shower was held for her. The last gift to be opened, a beautifully wrapped box tied with a pretty ribbon and bow, was from her Uncle Charlie and Aunt Ina. The gift was protected with much soft tissue paper which Ginger removed carefully, trying not to break anything underneath that might be fragile. At last the gift was revealed—a nice, large Bermuda onion!

❖ The Picture as Posed ❖
by Charlotte Robinson, Turners Falls, Massachusetts

We three younger children had never been professionally posed as far as I can remember. We were so far removed from the older brothers that I have no idea if they had ever been posed or not. I have no inkling of the reason that sprouted the idea of a photographic adventure. Perhaps a grandparent requested a posed picture—we had only two grandmothers.

In the photo are Charlotte G. Thompson, Priscilla E. Thompson and Roscoe L. Thompson, Jr. smiling a practiced grin. We may look happy, but those are really forced smiles. We each had chosen a toy from a rather large assortment of thin tin toys. When holding a toy, children didn't move their hands enough to spoil the photo.

Looking closely, one might see glistening in my eyes. The last evidence of the tears that flowed when Ross decided he liked my choice of toy better than his own choice. This is now called "favoritism" but then it was called "Give it to him!" I was then allowed to either keep his disdained toy or make another choice from the box. I did keep his and hugged that tin Dodge to prove to him that I was happier with it. Ross, of course, found less to like about his gas truck. The wicked games we played against brothers and sisters to destroy their morale are the same now as then—except that we didn't have access to guns!

Crossing legs at the ankle was in vogue then as well as today. Then it was another stunt to keep the feet from pressuring the floor and turning the chair at just the wrong time.

Note the cotton stockings. I swear that there was only one size ever made. Therefore they were always too short or too long. Some had a kind of panty top. Some had to be attached to garter belts.

Even with the shortest garters the stockings were still too long. The panty type had to be constantly hiked up at the hips to avoid an accident. If too long, the result was the ever-present ripples of extra stocking at the ankles. Crossing the feet at the ankles also produced a better view of these ripples, which acted like a magnet to draw the eyes of everyone to this area.

The dutch-boy-uni-sex haircuts were as endemic then as the mushroom cut that today, boys everywhere, just have to have. The short hair also means that summer is on the way. Or maybe, just because of the ever-present lice with their multimillion eggs.

Our best go-to-Church dresses hung straight down from the shoulders. We had no sash or belt to help emphasize our shapes. The cap sleeves on the dresses and rolled up sleeves on Ross were other evidences that warmer weather was on the way.

In this photo my shoulders are hunched up. I still hunch my shoulders in pictures unless someone pushes them down where they belong.

❖ The Grocery Store: Circa 1939❖
by Juliana Sivik Samoriski, Shelburne, Massachusetts

When I was growing up, I sometimes felt my peers envied me because I could have all the cookies and gum I wanted. Why? My father was a merchant; at least that is how his occupation was listed. He owned the store under the name of The Liberty Cask Market on the corner of Third and "L" Streets in Turners Falls, Massachusetts. It was across from Shea's Garage, Jackson's Gas Station and Stotz's Store. There was a stoplight at the corner because the traffic was heavy on Third Street with trucks, buses (going to Boston, New York and Springfield), and many automobiles. The streetcar or trolley tracks were intact, but unused due to the introduction of buses.

The store entrance was from "L" Street. Steps and a porch lead customers into the inside of the store where an appetizing supply of cookies in cookie cases appeared in full view.

To the left of the cookie cases were a couple of bunches of bananas hanging from the ceiling. I often remember seeing a huge, hairy spider fall to the floor while I was cutting bananas from the stock. I proclaimed the area off limits, to me, for weeks.

The deli meats were on the left of the store entrance in an enclosed glass case. Sandwich meats were sliced to order. Krakow's Boiled Ham was twenty-five cents a pound. Bologna was ten cents a pound. Next to the case was a huge counter where a side of beef could be seen. Beef was cut to order in the form of roasts, steaks, and stew meat, plus hamburg was ground in full view of the customer. They also pointed to the cut of meat they wanted.

Kerosene by the quart could be purchased in the back of the store from a small kerosene drum. What a Board of Health nightmare that would be today!

Canned goods and dry goods were on shelves on the opposite side of the store. Cans of string beans, corn, peas, kidney beans and the like cost ten cents per can on the average. Scott's Toilet Paper was a nickel a roll. Paper towels and Kleenex tissues were unheard of during those years. A long pole pincher "gizmo" was used to pluck cans from the high shelves.

Wonder Bread(TM) was eight cents a loaf and was located in a bakery display in the middle of the small market. Milk was ten cents a quart. Sugar was sold in two-pound and five-pound bags. Sugar was purchased in fifty-pound bags and was weighed in individual bags in the store. Fruits and vegetables were strictly seasonal with the exception of bananas. Bananas were imported from South America and delivered from Springfield, Massachusetts by Martinelli Brothers who also sold lettuce wholesale.

My father enlisted family members as store helpers. This arrangement caused much frustration for him. One brother, when sent on an errand, would disappear until store closing time. As a result, I remember that when I was about age eight my father began to regularly send me to the bank with a paper bag. My instructions were to go straight to the bank and stop for no one. I was to give the bag to the lady at the bank. I could not see over the teller's counter, so I reached up on tiptoes and placed the bag on the counter. Upon my bank arrival, the teller would smile at me, take the bag and make a telephone call. Years later I learned that I was making my father's weekly bank deposits. I received a nickel for my services.

Butcher knives were sharpened weekly by hand on a grindstone located in the store cellar. Someone would turn the wheel, as it rolled through water, while my father sharpened the knives. Turning the wheel was hard work, so when knife-sharpening time arrived, everyone scattered. The slowest one got the "wheel."

Telephones were a rarity in those days. There was a crank telephone in the store. That is to say, there was a crank on the side of the telephone that you'd crank to alert the operator that you wanted to make a call. Then you'd give the number you wanted to call to the operator. If there were a problem in the store, my father would just pick up the telephone, turn the crank and tell the operator to call the police. The problem immediately "vanished."

The National Cash Register in my father's store was opened by a turn of a crank too. The crank was turned and a loud bell sounded and the cash register drawer opened. The register only showed the sale price of an item. Change was figured out mentally. Mistakes were seldom made because groceries were often charged. That is, people placed their bill "on the books" and paid up weekly. On the back of the credit slips was a neat poem I have remembered through the years. It read:

You need your money—and—

I need mine.

If we both get ours, it will surely be fine.

But if you get yours—and—

Keep mine, too,

What in the world am I going to do?

THINK IT OVER!

Some people paid their bill weekly, some monthly and some not at all. One person paid his grocery bill long after my father retired. Another person paid several months after my father died.

Each year, at the same time in the spring, the gypsies went through Turners Falls and stopped at the tree belt in front of the store. My father gave them sandwich meat, bread, and other food he had put aside expecting their arrival. He was known as a kind, generous man. My mother had a deep fear of the gypsies and when they arrived she "yanked" me into the house and did everything short of boarding up the windows. I could only get a short glimpse of the gypsies.

Store hours were 6 a.m. to 6 p.m., Monday through Friday. Saturday 6 a.m. to 10 p.m. Closed Sunday. There was no last minute dash to the store for forgotten eggs, milk or whatever because there was delivery service regardless of order size. Milk and bread was delivered to the store before 6 a.m. It was left outside and theft was minimal.

My father retired before the height of World War Two because of the forthcoming food rationing. Food rationing stamps were a storekeeper's nightmare. Perhaps more important to his retirement decision was that his family store helpers were in military service.

Gradually, in Turners Falls, the independent grocery store faded into history opening the gates to a new concept—the Supermarket!

❖ Moving ❖
by Doris Shirtcliff, Greenfield, Massachusetts

We were a family of movers. Just about every two years my father would decide it was time to travel on. Come spring he would find a reason this should be done. A new place would be easier to heat in winter, or he wanted space for a small garden. To his way of thinking, he always found a better place.

Going to see a new house was always a big happening. My bedroom was usually the smallest room in the house and I made girlish plans about curtains and wall decorations. What difference did it make if I didn't care for the rest of the house? We'd move again anyway in a couple of years!

Of course, moving meant changing schools, but this was no big deal. You took transfer papers and cards to the new principal. She escorted you to a class, introduced you to the teacher and left you on your own. After three days I had it made. It is easier for kids to make friends and remember names than it is for adults. Kids look for friendship first. Changing schools was not traumatic. It was a bit different, but fun.

My mother never complained about this moving around. I think she helped plan it! She had one priority—move the stove first and get it connected up at the new place right away. That in itself was a big job. The hot water tank had to be emptied. All sorts of pipes in the back of the stove and the copper coils on the inside had to be dismantled and reassembled at the new house.

Moving day was always a Saturday and always hectic. The old creaking truck with high sideboards backed up to the front door. Amid much disorganization, shouting and damnation, beds, mattresses, springs, boxes and crates were loaded onto the truck. Then the truck would wobble off only to return hours later for another load.

Moving was not the slick operation it is today. We didn't hire any professionals. We had three regulars my father recruited. There was Ollie, Joe and Bill.

Ollie was a two hundred pound bachelor glad to make a few extra bucks on a Saturday. Joe was a sometime bookkeeper, car salesman and various other things. He was always glad to get away from his wife on any day.

Bill was a plumber. He was always good natured and reassuring. Chewing on an unlit cigar, he managed to sing and whistle in between lifting and tugging, but swore softly when pipes broke or didn't fit.

After the stove was connected and the beds set up, my mother always managed a sizeable meal for all of us. It was a celebration! We had moved again!

Local Color #4

❖ The Civilian Conservation Corps ❖
by Allan D. Adie, Gill, Massachusetts

The CCC, or Civilian Conservation Corps, was made into law in 1933 under the urging of President Franklin D. Roosevelt. It is perhaps first remembered as made up of young men. Ninety five percent of these young men came from the cities to live in camps made up of tents or wooden barracks many miles from their homes. Workers from camps like these all across America built small bridges and dams across brooks, carved trails through the woods or cleared forest areas for public parks. About August 20, 1935, I came to Turners Falls, Massachusetts, about 100 miles west of my Boston home. I had spent my twentieth birthday at Camp Devens in Ayers, Massachusetts.

I wonder how many people remember or even think of how important the CCC camp on Millers Falls Road in Turners Falls was to Franklin County's trees? We were a gypsy moth camp. This moth had been introduced to America from Europe and fed on the foliage of trees. The only moths we city boys knew were the ones that ate holes in clothing.

All CCC camps, I believe, had two sets of supervisors: USA Army or Navy Reserve Officers and Trained Forest Rangers. The officers had charge of the camp and the rangers were in charge when we went out to work in the woods. In our camp, the officers and rangers worked together if a problem arose.

The foresters told us that if the gypsy moths were not destroyed and continued to eat the foliage of a tree for two consecutive years, the tree would die. Pine trees were not affected even though they could be infested with many clusters of gypsy moth eggs.

In the winter, we would leave about seven in the morning. We were taken to the woods in canvas-covered trucks that had benches inside on either side. The only way we got out of work was if the temperatures dropped to below zero.

Gypsy moth eggs hung in clusters fastened mostly to the bottoms of tree branches. The clusters were protected by a light tan covering, about the size of a dime. Our job was to paint these clusters with creosote so the eggs wouldn't hatch. Remember, this was 1935. One group would carry a fifteen foot wooden or bamboo pole with about an inch wide paintbrush fastened to it. You would dip the brush into a small pail about six inches deep and eight inches in diameter filled with creosote. With the creosote-covered brush we could cover all the clusters we could reach. The pail had a cover slanted towards the middle and had an opening in the middle. This special cover prevented the creosote from falling out when we tripped and fell on our way to our destination. Falling was very easy when we were learning to use snowshoes!

While some worked from the ground, other CCCers would climb. Trees that had branches low enough to reach from the ground were climbed by young men. Fastened to their waist was a special belt. A metal container, 4 inches by 2 inches and 6 inches tall, filled with creosote, was hitched to this belt. This container had a screw type cap with a brush inside the can. With this simple equipment, a man could hold onto a branch as he twisted and turned to creosote the eggs. Some trees didn't have branches except near the top. Clusters on these branches had to be reached by other climbers having the same equipment and using spurs like the utility workers would use to climb telephone poles years ago. Climbing could be dangerous especially if the trees had some snow on them.

This creosote operation occurred in the fall and winter. The degree of infestation limited what we were able to accomplish in one day. If we weren't too far away we would come back to camp for dinner.

Even extreme cold didn't kill the eggs, so after the snow melted there were still plenty of clusters on the bottom trunk of the tree and we would creosote those, too.

In the spring, everyone carried strips of burlap about a foot wide and four feet long. We would wrap this around a tree and tie it in the middle with some thin rope and then fold the top half over the bottom half. When any remaining eggs hatched, the larvae would climb up the tree only to be stopped at the burlap. They would be squashed periodically until all the eggs had hatched.

I wonder how many autumn tourists Franklin County would have if the Civilian Conservation Corps hadn't eliminated the infestation of the Gypsy moths many years ago?

❖ Through the Eyes of a Child❖
by Joanne Balzarini, Bernardston, Massachusetts

When I was young and the air raid whistle sounded, it was frightening. My mother was a nurse and had special assignments out of town. My dad was an air raid warden and my brother a junior warden. They wore white vests and metal helmets. Their job was to watch for foreign airplanes or other foreign activity from the street.

I was quite young and could not stay alone. My grandmother lived with us and took care of the home front. We lived in a suburb of Boston where all windows were hung with dark, double-lined shades that had to be drawn at night. With World War II on it was law. Lights if seen by an enemy aircraft would indicate a city with many people living there and the capital, Boston, nearby. Grammie even covered the light that came from the radio dial. There was no TV then.

Thankfully, enemy planes never flew over. A big "Thank You" to the veterans that helped keep us safe!

❖ Learning to Drive ❖
by Edna Baublis, Athol, Massachusetts

I learned to drive in a 1930 Pontiac Sedan that was as big as the Titanic. It was navy blue with black fenders, spare tires in the fenders, running board, and a big black trunk on the back. It was literally a trunk—it could be removed.

I had started to learn to drive when I graduated from high school, but then war broke out and rationing was in. If you think that my father would use his precious gas rationing coupons to teach me to drive, think again. I could wait and I did.

The Pontiac was manual transmission as I think most of the cars in those days were. The gearshift was in an "H" position—reverse, upper left, then down to low, up to the upper right hand corner for second, and then smoothly down to the lower right, for high or third. You had to coordinate your left and right feet on the clutch and the gas pedal. Looked easy when I watched my father.

On the appointed day, we were off. We drove down South Athol Road, in Athol, Massachusetts, which was not too well traveled. He pulled over to the side of the road, explained the mechanics of driving to me and then told me to get out and go around. So I opened the car door and went around the back and then sat in the driver's seat.

Eyes on the road, feet on the clutch and gas, I shifted into low and the fun began. We jerked and jerked and jerked. I think I got whiplash.

Ordered by my father to pull over, I jerked to the side of the road.

"Get out," he said. He slid over to the driver's seat and I raced around the back of the car to the passenger seat. Again he, not quite so patiently this time, demonstrated to me the procedure. Feet, clutch, gas. He did it so smoothly.

"Get out," he said again. And I did so in reverse this time—from passenger to driver's seat.

"OK, go," he said. Jerk, jerk again. It took me longer to drive the car smoothly than it did to learn the Italian swear words that my father said. I didn't even know he knew those words!

After a while, I succeeded in going forward, still jerking, but once I got started it was OK. Now I had to learn to go backwards. I pulled up and went backwards. Soooo smoothly! If only I could go backwards all the time.

The day of my first lesson was not a happy one. My father could not understand why I could not drive forward smoothly—I was reasonably intelligent. Easy for him to say. When he bought his first car in the 20s, they handed him his keys, his car and his license.

When we got home, my mother did not have to ask how the day went. She just looked at us and knew. My father was muttering under his breath in Italian and I was teary eyed. I didn't think he would ever take me out again, but he did and eventually I learned to drive.

The next bugaboo was turning on a hill. I still don't understand why I had to learn to turn around in the roadway on a hill. It was on Exchange Street hill that they took us for our license test, and that is where my father took me to learn. I'm sure the hill looked as high as Mount Everest to me that day. I told my father that when I got my license I would go miles out of my way before I would turn around on a road on a hill. A grunt was his response. After many tears, I mastered the stupid turning around on a hill and I have never, ever used that bit of expertise since.

Then my father told me the next step would be backing into a parking space. He measured out the space and I practiced and practiced and practiced. I finally got that down to his satisfaction—and to this day I'm darned good at it.

Finally the big day came. I took the written test, went out for the road test and came home with a pink slip. I passed!

❖ The Necklace ❖
by Rosalie Bolton, Greenfield, Massachusetts

The woman sat there, in the back seat of the parked car. The door was open on that hot summer day. She seemed to be surrounded by color.

My friend and I stood on the sidewalk and watched, enthralled as the woman in the car deftly slid beads onto a twisted, strong cord. The woman in her pretty, cotton dress talked to us as she worked. She wanted to know our names, how we liked school and in which house on that street we lived. She looked up at us a few times as we talked about school, but she never stopped sliding the beads onto the cord one after another until she reached the ends of the string, tied a clasp quickly, and then held the necklace up with a flourish for us to admire. All this in a few minutes! We stood there on the sidewalk in Turners Falls, Massachusetts amazed at her speed and marveling at her creations.

From time to time her husband returned to the car and placed six or seven strands of beads across his forearm—over his white shirtsleeve—and then went from house to house selling the unusual ornaments. Such soft, pretty colors of pale blue, lime green and pink!

These were not ordinary beads the woman told us.

"They are made from paper," she said.

"From paper?"

She explained to us that the wet paper was dyed in different colors, rolled into little balls and shaped into small rosettes. She offered to let us put a few imitation roses on the needle, but we declined. We were too bashful or too "country-fied." We did want to help her, but we were afraid that we wouldn't do it right.

As we stood at the car, we could see her husband talking to people at their door. He was holding the beads near a woman's face and, I thought, telling her how nice they would look on her if she bought them. My friend told me later that she had the same thought.

In the years of the Depression, door-to-door salesmen were a daily occurrence. Yet, on this day, we had a special treat. We had never seen a combination like this. These two people, this duo, a woman in a car working in that hot summer afternoon heat and her husband walking up onto shady porches, often even sitting on a porch rail, to show his wares.

My friend and I talked about these two people and their roles in bead making and selling. To us this work seemed ideal, especially the woman's part as she worked in the car wearing a pretty dress and shoes with high heels.

When we got home, we saw our mothers in faded housedresses and old aprons; my friend's mother was feeding chickens; my mother had just adjusted the meat grinder to the kitchen table and was about to grind leftover roast to make hash.

The other woman was sitting in a car, wearing a pretty dress, stringing rose shaped beads to sell .

Now that was something for two ten-year-olds to think about!

❖ The General Store ❖
by Estelle Cade, Turners Falls, Massachusetts

"She needs something for her feet—the mud outside is terrible," was probably the conversation between my mother and father on one of our visits to my grandfather in South Ashfield, Massachusetts in the 1930s. So off we went, my dad and myself, up the hill to the South Ashfield Store.

Accustomed to Filene's revolving doors in Boston, (Of which I was quite afraid! I once got my foot caught, to my great embarrassment and my mother's great annoyance!), you can imagine my surprise when we opened the old fashioned door to this store, and a friendly little bell jingled to announce our arrival.

We stepped in, and there I stood, totally amazed by what greeted my eyes. To my right was the long counter where purchases were paid for. The cost of items purchased were added up in pencil on the brown bag they would be packed in. There was also a large roll of butcher paper for wrapping meat items and a cone of white string for tying up packages. Part of this counter was taken up with a glass case full of "penny candy"—candy sticks, "Boston Baked Beans," licorice whips, Walnettos, Mary Janes, other goodies and of course gum! My eyes studied this case carefully.

There was also a cutting board with a glass dome covering a wheel of delicious sharp cheese that New Englanders called "rat cheese." It was cut and sold by the chunk. In our family that was *THE* accompaniment to a warm slice of my mother's real apple pie. No cheese today has the proper "bite."

Shelves along the sides held such things as assorted groceries, canned vegetables and fruits, Fels Naptha(TM) soap, Lava(TM) hand soap, stove blacking, laundry bluing, dish towels, work gloves, heavy socks, "Tucks" chewing tobacco, cigarettes of course, pipes and pipe tobacco (remember the joke of calling the store to ask if they had Prince Albert in a can and saying "Well, let him out!"), red bandana handkerchiefs and other necessities of country life in the 1930s. There was a Coats and Clark's thread cabinet where ladies could find just the right color thread, as well as packets of needles and boxes of straight pins.

Hanging up over my head, were rubber boots, kerosene lanterns, assorted graniteware pans and other items I could only guess at. The store also had barrels of molasses (you would fill your own jug), as well as kerosene barrels in the basement.

Up front were those tempting, slanted-glass containers of cookies, Nabisco(TM) of course—ginger snaps, wafers, fig newtons and on shelves nearby, boxes of saltines and the New England staple— "Cream lunch crackers." These were so tasty crumbled into chowder or eaten as "crackers and milk," for a Sunday night supper.

The final fascination was the South Ashfield Post Office—a real U.S. Post Office—housed in a little room in the very back of the store. Mr. Mekeel would go there and become Postmaster, then he could give you your mail, sell you stamps or give you a money order. I was most intrigued by the rows of little doors with numbers on them. Years later, when we actually became residents of South Ashfield, we had our own little door— #52, I believe it was.

There was so much to see, to absorb and yes, I did get a pair of rubber boots—so cute with buckles in front and just my size, amazingly enough. I can still recall my dad and Mr. Mekeel making very sure that I had just the right ones for me. It seemed so funny to be trying on boots with all those things hanging over my head, and a customer or two coming in and greeting my dad with "Hello there, Charles—up for the weekend? This your oldest? How's Uncle Will (my grandfather) gettin' on?" When we left, I was given a lollipop and had another chance to jingle the cheerful little bell as we went out the door.

I've shopped in many stores since then, but I've never forgotten my first experience shopping with my dad in a real country general store.

❖ The Henderson Ice Company ❖
by Guy Carey, Jr., Warwick, Massachusetts

I remember when the Henderson ice trucks used to come around our neighborhood peddling ice for our iceboxes. This was a great treat for us kids if the driver was friendly, or at least in a good mood, when he came.

Some of the houses in the neighborhood had cards with numbers like 25, 35, 45 and 50 on each side of the card. People placed these cards in their windows. The number that was at the top would tell the iceman how many pounds of ice they needed for their iceboxes. The iceman would take an appropriate piece of ice from inside the truck with his ice tongs. Then he would hang it on the scale at the back of his truck and brush the sawdust from the ice. If the cube of ice was a little too large, he would take an ice pick and chop slivers of ice off until it was near the right weight. Putting on a large leather apron that fit over his shoulders and using his ice tongs, he would carry the ice into the house on his shoulders and place it into the icebox. The fun part for us children was when we could grab the pieces of ice he had cut off, run inside and rinse them in the water pail, then eat them. Back then, that ice was tantamount to the ice cream children get today from ice cream trucks that come around.

This was in the early and middle thirties and as more and more of our town obtained electricity, people started installing refrigerators. Seeing the iceman became a rare occasion.

During World War II, as more of our men went off to serve their country, many jobs became available for those of us who were too young to go to war. One winter during our February school vacation, I got a job at the Henderson Ice Company cutting ice. I was quite excited about being part of the company that was such a joyous part of my childhood. The excitement soon dimmed as I quickly received a cold and brutal awakening regarding the realities of cutting ice. There was little that was pleasurable about working on the cold ice all day, especially with a foreman who seemed to be looking right at you every time you tried to take a little break.

In the center of the pond a channel was cut about eight to ten feet wide that narrowed down to about three feet wide where it reached the icehouse. There was about twenty inches of ice where we worked cutting the floats of ice free. Early in the morning we would cut kerfs in the ice using a saw rig designed especially for cutting ice. This was a rig similar to the one used to cut cordwood into stove lengths, except it was built so the circular blade could be lowered into the ice. After starting the motor and lowering the blade into the ice, we would drag the rig along the ice cutting a kerf about sixteen inches deep. Dragging this back and forth across the pond, we would cut a kerf in the ice every couple of feet. After finishing cutting about twenty or so lines in one direction, we would make cuts across them every couple of feet in the other direction. This created a checkerboard pattern on the ice similar to the cuts one would make in a pan of fudge. Before we could float ice to the icehouse, we would have to free the channel of the ice that had formed overnight. After the channel was de-iced, we used hand ice saws and sawed four blocks back from the open water every fifteen blocks along the checkerboard. Then two of us would take bars that had flat sharpened heads and start chipping towards each other along the line that was four blocks back from the water line. With a little practice, we got so we could break away a sixty-cube float in very little time. It became a game to see who could do it the fastest. After the sixty-cube float broke free of the ice, it was poled out to the middle and down the channel. There were three bridges on the channel and, as the floats reached them, men on the bridges with heavy bars split the float into individual cubes of ice. In the channel by the icehouse there was a chute with an escalating chain that carried the cubes of ice up to a long slide. The slide was adjusted up or down to the height of the ice that was already piled in the icehouse. The slide carried the cubes down to the men who swung it into the icehouse doors. Most days there were two or more doors of the icehouse were worked at the same time. That way if the first swingman missed a cube, it was picked up by the swingman at the second door. The men inside the icehouse stacked the ice in layers with ice tongs and covered each layer with sawdust to insulate it.

There was a heated room at the end of the icehouse. A big woodstove was kept burning there all day. This was our break and lunch room. We were allowed so little time for breaks and lunch I sometimes wondered why they wasted all that wood. It was not long before I found out why they kept the fire burning all through the workday.

We found it was easier to jump on the floats after we broke them free and poled them down the channel using our pike poles, than it had been to guide them from the edge of the ice. So, as soon as we broke a float free, one of us would jump onto the float and pole it down the channel until we reached the first bridge.

One afternoon, just as I went to jump on a float, somebody gave the float a hard push with his pike pole. I missed the float and landed in the water. Dressed in heavy boots and clothes, I panicked as I went under the water. When I sputtered to the surface, almost everyone who had a pike pole was there ready to pull me out. As they dragged me back onto the ice the foreman came over yelling, "Who was the stupid idiot who fell in?" Seeing it was me he said, "I knew we were going to have trouble using a damn bunch of kids. Get your butt down by the stove and strip and get your clothes dry. I expect you back here in an hour."

With chattering teeth and pant legs that were already forming ice, I stumbled to the warming room and stripped off my clothes. As I was hanging them above the stove, one of the Henderson owners came in. He said, "It is only a couple of hours before quitting time, so you stay here until then. I will take care of the foreman."

I was glad I didn't have to go back on the ice because some of my clothes were still damp when I put them on to go home.

The day of that swim was the next to last day of our winter school vacation. My mother insisted that I should have some enjoyment on my vacation and should not go back to work again. Though I put up a big fuss so I would look brave, inside I was happy that this became the end of my employment at the Henderson Ice Company.

❖ Girl Scout Camp ❖
by Mary Ciechomski, Turners Falls, Massachusetts

I remember the week I spent at Girl Scout camp when I was twelve years old. I enjoyed Girl Scouts and attended every meeting held at my grammar school, but I knew my folks could never afford to send me to camp. The summer I was twelve, I was overjoyed to learn that I had been awarded a campership for a week at Camp Lewis Perkins in South Hadley Center. My bubble of joy was quickly deflated, when I realized that I did not having the clothing to attend such a camp. That obstacle was overcome when Mrs. Ryan, a local civic leader, showed up with a box full of Girl Scout middies and bloomers and I was soon off to camp.

I cannot remember just how I got there, the camp being about six miles away, but I arrived one Saturday afternoon. We were assigned to a tent (one tent for six girls) and were told to get into our swimsuits and go down to the lake to test our swimming ability. I had never undressed in front of girls my age and was quite shy doing so. I waited until all the girls had left the tent! That was my first recollection of camp, but I soon overcame my shyness and had a wonderful week at camp.

The days flew by with the various activities and making new friends, one whose name I have never forgotten: Lizzalotta Zangengast. I wonder what she is doing today?

The next Saturday finally arrived and after breakfast, we went back to our tent to pack up and say our good-byes. Parents and friends picked up the girls one by one, and I kept wondering how I was getting home, as our family had no car.

It was close to noon and most of the campers had departed when I heard what I thought was a truck coming up the hill. Soon it came into sight, and indeed, it was a bakery truck—Wronski's Bakery. My poor mother had gone crazy trying to think of some way to get me home and when the baker came to the house on his regular Saturday call, Mom prevailed upon him to pick me up. What an ending to a great week of camping—returning home in the baker's truck!

❖ Corn Stalk ❖
by Genevieve Clark, Northfield, Massachusetts

She was probably born in early May, on the mountainside above my home—a tiny, spotted, whitetail deer. For a couple of months, all went well. The fawn stayed quietly in a hidden spot, while her mother browsed. As the fawn grew she was not far from her mother's side. Then something drastic happened, and the fawn was left alone. Perhaps it was a pack of coyotes or a poacher, but the fawn's mother was gone.

A part-time farmer living on a dead-end road by the woods was fixing fences one day when he discovered the fawn, weak but alive. After getting permission from the proper authority, he and his family nursed the fawn back to health. They were not to keep the deer in an enclosed pen, or treat her too much as a pet, so that eventually she could return to the wild. Nevertheless, the deer learned to recognize the sounds of the children returning from school each day, and she would go to meet them. She was soon named Cornstalk, as her coat was the color of dry cornstalks in the fall.

The deer grew and, despite being left on her own, she became almost tame. In the fall, during hunting season, the family was allowed to lock her in the barn. Afterwards, day after day, the farmer would walk off into the woods and fields, the deer following. Little by little, Cornstalk stayed in the woods longer and longer, spending less and less time at the farm. Eventually, she was on her own.

It was during this time that some of my family went for a walk up the hill and around the fields. How excited my young granddaughter was to have a deer walk up to her! Also, Cornstalk would sometimes appear at other homes where children lived, possibly drawn by their voices. It was a thrill for them all, but I think Cornstalk was meant for an even bigger role.

At Linden Hill School on South Mountain Road in Northfield, Massachusetts, a ten-year-old boy was struggling to find a place for himself. His parents were divorced and his father had been remarried to a girl in Peru, South America where he worked and lived. The boy Joey, as I shall call him, had spent vacations in Peru, but found it difficult to fit in. Joey was an All-American, apple pie type of boy—curly red hair, light freckled skin, and blue eyes. His new stepbrothers were dark-haired and olive-skinned. Language was also a barrier for the young American.

Here in the states when Joey went home from school, it was to his mother who lived in New Jersey. His young mother was busy finding a new way of life—free and single. His grandmother tried, but she was tired. She loved Joey, but had already raised her own family. Joey's feelings of not being wanted were strong. He was often filled with anger and frustration. As his teacher, I was often the target of that anger. Another woman telling him what to do! My heart felt for him, but try as we all did, there was only so much the school could do.

One day, late that fall, we were in the midst of a lesson when we heard a commotion in the room next door. Cornstalk had come to visit. All of the boys were thrilled to see her, but she soon bounded off into the woods behind the classroom building. Occasionally, after that, she visited the athletic fields when the boys were playing, or watched them from the edge of the woods.

One day we were again surprised as the boys were working in the classroom. There was Cornstalk looking in at the window! It was obvious that she liked the children, so quietly I let my three or four students go outside where they touched the friendly animal, but it was the sight of Joey and the deer that I will never forget.

When his turn came to pet the deer, Joey quietly and silently wrapped his arms around Cornstalk's neck. She turned and nuzzled his face. When he twisted around and looked at me, his face had a look of pure bliss. I don't think I have ever seen anything like his expression and smile—wide and happy and full of love. Heaven obviously was not far away.

I don't know how Joey's life went after he left the school, but I often wonder if he thinks of that brief time with Cornstalk. Perhaps that moment showed Joey how to open his heart to others. I somehow hope that moment in time holds as great a memory for him as it does for me.

I do know that Cornstalk had at least one baby, a little buck. What happened to her after that is only a matter of speculation. Once, out walking by myself, a deer up in the field stared at me for a few minutes then tentatively walked towards me. I stood quietly waiting. As she drew nearer she suddenly stopped, stared and then dashed away, her flag upright. I had no doubt it was Cornstalk, but nature had taken her back. She truly had returned to the wild.

❖ The Boat Train ❖
by Margaret M. "Pat" Currie, Turners Falls, Massachusetts

One night at supper time, my dad broached the subject to my mother and me of going on a boat train the following Sunday.

"What's a boat train?" was my first question.

My dad explained that the B&M railroad was exploring a new idea. A train would take you from Greenfield to Boston's North Station, and then you'd be transported to a ship at Rowe Warf, which would sail out into Boston Harbor. Today, I suppose, that kind of service would be called "Rail & Sail."

My mom and I thought it sounded great! Then my dad said I could take a friend. I chose my friend Mary.

We left early on Sunday morning. Mary and I exchanged ideas on what it would be like.

When we arrived at Gardner, Massachusetts and saw the huge chair that advertised the city's furniture industry, we realized we were about half way to Boston.

When we finally arrived at Boston's North Station, Dad bought us each a treat before we boarded a bus to take us to the ocean.

When we saw the ship we thought it looked like an ocean liner! After boarding we were told that there was something for everyone. We learned that we could go to a section where there would be board games and another section where there was music for dancing. There was also a snack bar. If we wanted to, we could just stroll the deck outside.

My parents went to a section where people could gather in groups or enjoy playing bridge or whist or other card games.

Mary and I decided to first stroll along the outside deck. Some people were enjoying sitting in deck chairs. We kept looking over the side of the boat for sea life, hoping to see a whale or a shark. I don't remember how far out we went, but we had a great day and were looking forward to doing it again when we realized the boat had turned around and we were already back at the dock.

As the train headed back to Greenfield, Mary and I fell asleep. It must have been the sea air!

❖ Gratitude ❖
by Elisabeth R. Donaj, Greenfield, Massachusetts

A family reunion takes place each summer on June 9, the birthday of my maternal forefather Johann Jager of Neukirchen, Schleswig-Holstein,

Germany. This celebration was instituted by clan members long ago and began on the 100th birthday of the man from whom we all derived.

In 1938 came my turn to participate in the celebration with my new husband Josef Jodokus Buhr. We had gotten married on the day prior to this special event. On the big day, my husband could meet and get acquainted with the entire family as the newest member.

It had been a dreadful summer, especially for the agriculturists among them, because the land was parched by a long drought. They were hard hit and downhearted. The men sought solace in each other. They went on an inspection tour to view damage to the crops.

After their return, we all gathered around and began to pray together for survival—that is, for rain.

Windows were thrown wide open, yet the atmosphere was still stifling. Suddenly, we sensed a breeze coming up, heard a wind starting with a swishing sound and then blowing strong. Before we could believe our luck, drops fell onto the hot earth, sending up its new scent. The air was scented in its own wonderful, promising way. The miracle happened. The heavens opened up, sent their blessings—finally—and rain came.

Our men stepped outside, bared their heads, and expressed their endless gratitude in deep felt prayer. Our spirits soared in those touching moments! Now was time to be filled with true gratitude.Beethoven must have felt a similar gratitude when he created his great works of music in which he praised the wonders of earth and all living souls. I do believe gratitude is the most wonderful emotion we humans are capable of, and it is the most restoring power for our hearts.

❖ The Picture ❖
by Rena Finch, Northfield, Massachusetts

The picture hung on a wall in the corner of our living room. It was a small ink sketch that depicted a row of high-gabled, medieval style houses set on a bank of a river. There was a stone wall directly below the houses and trees hanging over the bank on the opposite side. The skyline was made more impressive because of the spires of a cathedral and what almost appeared to be a castle towering over the buildings. The artist had identified his scene as Tubingen, which was the small town in Germany where I was born.

I don't really remember this part of the town. My recollections were more of country lanes where my brother and I used to run and play, but I do remember a large Lutheran church whose interior stone façade made it seem cold and stern. Maybe that's why the sunny, simple churches of New England appeal to me.

I don't remember the University for which the town was famous, but I do remember my mother and father coming home in their doctors' uniforms after a day at the University hospital.

I grew up fantasizing over this small picture. We had arrived in the States in 1939 and, in my mind, the scene in the picture came to represent a beautiful, tranquil remembrance of my younger years. So when I went back to Germany fifty years after leaving, finding this spot in my birthplace became almost an obsession for me.

When my husband and I drove into Tubingen, the first thing I noticed was that it had grown into a large city. When we found the old market square in the center of the old section, I was thrilled to see the old burgher houses with window boxes overflowing with flowers and a magnificent fountain in the square. This was the Germany I wanted to remember.

After leaving the square, we drove around in circles trying to find the spot which had become engraved in my mind as the romantic scene of my childhood. When we finally found the river, we left the car and set out on foot to find the bridge from which the scene in the picture could be seen. And, suddenly, there it was. We were standing on the bridge and the scene unfolded before us. The old houses still lined the riverbank and the branches of the trees still swept into the water. But the buildings near the bridge were very modern, with the headquarters of a newspaper on one side and other commercial buildings on the other. Throngs of people were rushing back and forth, taking away the tranquility I had always associated with this setting. Somehow, it just did not seem the same, and I felt let down somehow.

They say you can't go back, and maybe that's true, but the picture now hangs in my living room and when I look at it, I still like to think of it as a picturesque, romantic scene from my childhood.

❖ An Apple Pie Story ❖
by Edith J. Fisher, Leyden, Massachusetts

Years ago I used to make apple pies for my husband every week because apple pie was his favorite dessert.

One Saturday, he stayed at the neighbors too long "at the cider barrel." When he came home, he dropped a bushel of apples on the kitchen floor, and said, "Maybe I can have an apple pie once in a while."

I never said a word. Come Monday he had an apple pie for breakfast, lunch, dinner, supper, in his lunch box, as a snack and before he went to bed. He had his regular meals, but for snacks and dessert he had apple pie.

Neither one of us said a word all week long about it. The following Sunday I gave him apple pie as usual.

All he said was "You can start making something different if you want to." Then things got back to normal.

❖ Getting Juiced Up ❖
by William R. Fitzgerald, Ashfield, Massachusetts

With the news of the airliners hitting the buildings, and thoughts of their hitting some of our atomic generating plants, I got to thinking that the plan was to hit symbols. They had previously tried to blow up the Twin Towers in New York, but they hit upon a better way to get the job done. We have a tendency to take our amenities, like electricity for granted, except of course when the monthly bill has to be paid.

When we moved to the farm in 1929, we had to make the change from having electricity to doing without. It must have been especially tough on my mother because she wasn't all that enthusiastic about moving into the boonies of Conway, Massachusetts from what used to be modern, civilized Holyoke, Massachusetts. She was used to electric lights, a copper, Easy washing machine, an electric iron and plenty of hot water. She even had had steam heat where radiators used to sing and hiss on a cold morning, versus a kitchen wood range and a Glenwood chunk stove to heat a whole, uninsulated, Colonial house.

In the evenings, we all gathered around with our backs to the kitchen table where an Aladdin lamp gave enough light to read by. Mom sat with her feet on the oven bumper with the oven door open. It was also necessary to do your homework at the kitchen table where there was no goofing off.

At bedtime, you knew your way to bed in the dark and there was no reading in bed. I don't even remember the use of candles. They were too dangerous. We did have candles on the Christmas tree and on Christmas Day we lit them, but we never left them unattended and were aware of the danger.

We used lanterns in the barn and got the hay down before dark. Lanterns were unthinkable in the haymow. The cows were milked by hand and we had ice cut in the winter to cool the milk. The ice was stored under sawdust in the icehouse. It would take about a hundred pounds of ice to cool forty quart cans of milk. Plus we had an icebox in the house that would take a quarter of that. Kids weren't allowed to hang on the door while they made up their mind. Soda was only for birthdays and the Fourth of July.

The water was heated by the woodstove in the kitchen and stored in a thirty-gallon tank behind the stove. On washday (Monday, of course) Mom had to get that stove going early with a kettle and copper boiler on top. That was OK in winter, but that kitchen got mighty hot in summer. Early on my parents bought a gasoline-powered Kenmore wringer washer with a kick-starter like a motorcycle. The guys had to gas it up and bring it into the kitchen. It was put next to the set tubs and the exhaust hitched to a long pipe to carry the carbon monoxide outside.

Freezers were unheard of, so we butchered a hog in the fall and had all the hams and bacons smoked so they would keep. We even had our own smokehouse for a while. We had a hog washer that was an all-in-one tank that would hold a pig with a firebox underneath to scald those dead hogs to get the hair off their skin. I say we did. The hired man was told to clean up after the deed was done, and he threw a pail of cold water into that hot cast-iron vat and it promptly snapped. I can imagine what a great antique planter it would have made.

The fresh loins had to be consumed unless it was cold enough for them to freeze by hanging them in the attic. I'm sure that's where "eating high on the hog" came from. All the lard was put into crocks in the cellar to be used for frying and baking. The scraps were ground into sausage, mixed with spices and salt, packed into homemade cotton bags and dipped into hot lard to seal them off. Must be Dad didn't like salt pork, so we were never subjected to that horrible stuff. The beef was butchered in a cold snap in December and hung in the attic where it promptly froze. Someone went up occasionally with a meat saw and sawed off a hunk. By spring, about all that was left were the legs and these were cut up and canned.

During the late thirties the farmers organized to form a rural electrification cooperative. The government under the REA (Rural Electrification Act) would loan money to the rural cooperative to set the poles and wire and the Co-op would bargain with the power companies for the electricity. That woke up the electric companies and they stopped dragging their feet. They promptly signed up the larger farmers on a run that wasn't too long and broke up the cooperative. (Farmers have been famous for shooting themselves in the foot even to this day.)

Under government pressure, the electric companies continued to work down through the easiest to serve and each line had a guaranteed minimum monthly charge. The three farmers on Poland Road had to agree on a minimum of eleven dollars a month total. We put in lights and over the first few years a milk cooler, milking machine, refrigerator and yes, a washer. We soon used up our guarantee.

The electricians that wired those old colonial, post-and-beam houses had to drill through oak and chestnut timbers by hand using a bit brace. It took quite a while for Newell Morton and his helper to wire our house and barn. I remember the fall Thursday night that the electricity was turned on.

I had been peddling the *Greenfield Shopping News* in downtown Conway and came up the hill to home after dark. The house seemed to sparkle, it was so bright. In retrospect we probably only had forty watt bulbs. My little brothers kept running around switching lights on and off and my folks kept ordering them to stop, albeit with a trace of a smile on their faces.

It was not until the late fifties that the last of the single farms on a long road got wired. The Stroheker farm halfway up Ashfield Mountain, off Route 112, was among the last. The wires ended at the foot and top of the mountain. Those last few farms that were hooked up pretty much ended the ice cutting on Ashfield Lake.

Some farms had a Delco System in which they had a generator, batteries and an undependable gasoline engine. This was a thirty-two volt system and so whatever appliances they had were unusable when the new one-ten volt juice came by. Those Delcos were pretty expensive, but they enriched a few electricians quite handsomely.

During the 1938 hurricane, we were milking and going about our usual evening chores. We knew that there was quite a rain and windstorm going on, but we didn't have electricity at that time yet so it wasn't missed. We didn't know the enormity of the storm until the next morning.

It is almost impossible to think of all the things in our homes and daily lives that depend on electricity today. A brief power outage reminds us of how dependent we all are on "Reddy Kilowatt," which is an anachronism. As a matter of fact, so am I.

❖ Coon Hunting ❖
by Margaret "Peg" Folgmann, Shelburne Falls, Massachusetts

Young fellows looked forward to going coon hunting with my father. Back in the 1930s, it was a way of life in the country. It was a test of endurance, a super experience few boys could even imagine. It was a hunt involving a dog and a gun. The wail of the dog as he picked up the scent was music to the hunters' ears…the chase was on!

The dog and the coon made better time through the woods than the men and boys who were slowed up by underbrush, swamps, cliffs and ravines. Other threats were old cellar holes and rotted water well covers. My father knew the whereabouts of these hazardous areas, and warned those who had joined the hunt.

Often, young as he was, my brother would go along. I also went enough to know what it was all about. Tramping through the woods was fun. Once in a great while, if the person ahead let a branch go without warning, you were switched and it hurt. We were cautious, though, but sometimes the underbrush would get away from your grasp. We learned to walk a little distance apart to avoid injury. My father was always in the lead. He was a strong, sturdy man. Clear, crisp, fall nights were best as pelts were in their prime then. They were durable and worth more money.

The raccoon, being a nocturnal animal, meant that coon hunting was a night activity. After chores were done and supper was over, the large flashlight was supplied with good batteries. Then the gun and ammunition were readied. Incidentally, the gun was always ready, as it was unloaded and cleaned after each hunt. The gun was not loaded until reaching the treed raccoon, so that there was no fear of the gun going off if one accidentally stumbled. The barn lantern globe was cleaned and lit to light the way of the hunter in the lead.

This was a profitable hunt. Any additional income during the Depression years helped a great deal. Not only did this animal provide a valuable pelt, popular at the time as fur coats worn by both men and women, but also it provided delicious meat for the table, often served with a prune dressing. The dried out fat produced coon's oil used to rub onto a congested chest, plagued by a mean respiratory infection. They were healthy animals and carried no harmful diseases then.

It was not difficult to tell when a raccoon was treed. The barking did not waiver. As the hunters came closer to the treed animal and dog, the excitement multiplied. The lead hunter approached the tree and directed the flashlight toward the raccoon, easily targeted and dropped. The hunters behind stayed back a distance, so as not to disturb the dog at the terminal point of the hunt.

Having a good, accurate, calibrated compass, the stars in the sky and a good general sense of direction, the men, boys and dog made the trip back to the car and home. Incidentally, this could be many miles from home. Returning at ten, eleven or midnight was usual.

I remember one particular evening in the early 1930s when my father made a phone call to a lad named Stewie to invite him to go hunting. Stewie lived in the village and came home from college on weekends. It wouldn't take him long to get to our house on his bike as we only lived a distance of about three miles from his home.

The hunt continued on into the night. It was very late when the coon was finally treed. The men were late getting home. For Stewie to go home at that late hour could disturb a sleeping family. My father suggested that he get into bed with my brother in the room at the head of the stairs. Half asleep and exhausted, Stewie accepted the offer. He fell into bed and dropped off to sleep immediately.

In the morning, I opened my eyes, face to face with this young man. He didn't get into my brother's bed—he got into mine! I carefully got out of bed. Stewie never knew. That is, not until he was told at a later date. All through the years, whenever we met, Stewie reminded me of his mistake. A big smile would come over his face and, as I grew older and less and less intimidated by this true story, I, too, found it equally amusing.

❖ The Farm ❖
by Katherine L. Forster, Orange, Massachusetts

My earliest recollections of "The Farm" in Orange, Massachusetts are from stories told to me by my father, Albert, who was born during the Civil War. He walked from town to Uncle Sam Rice's farm known as the "Rice Farm" to play croquet and help with the chores. In the summer he enjoyed a swim at North Pond, now Lake Mattawa in Orange. In wintertime he cut ice on the farm's own pond and helped store it in the sawdust in the icehouse for summertime use. Whatever season, there were fun activities and get-togethers at "The Farm." Work and play were more interesting when shared by friends and neighbors.

Even after the "Rice Farm" became the "Leavitt Farm" in 1895, it still served as a place for family, friends and neighbors to gather for shared fun such as hikes, horseshoes, or picnics, and work including haying, animal care or general repairs.

In January 1926, my sweetheart, Clifford, purchased "The Farm." It included a 16-room farmhouse, a horse barn, a cow barn, and a pigsty, along with a sugarhouse, chicken house and corncrib. After a two-week honeymoon, my love and I moved into what I thought to be a palatial house with the neatest Home Comfort stove I had ever seen! This stove not only had an ample cooking surface and oven, but on the side was a large holding tank in which to heat water.

We started our "Forster Farm" with our wedding gifts of Dinah, the horse, and Daisy, the cow. As the years passed, our farmland produced a variety of fruits and vegetables to amply feed not only our family and friends, but also to sell our milk to customers and local grocery stores. The dairy herd increased to a high of thirty-five cows, so we were able to deliver milk to customers all over Orange. We even delivered half-pint glass bottles of milk to the town elementary schools. Deliveries at first were made by horse and wagon and then later with an old Chevy sedan.

When our son and daughter were old enough, they took part in such activities as haying, mucking out the barn, garden planting, weeding, harvesting, woodcutting and washing those glass milk bottles. With many other youngsters in the neighborhood, they managed to provide entertainment for themselves and the entire neighborhood by putting on circuses, complete with a merry-go-round. The merry-go-round consisted of a piano stool and it did present a bit of a liability hazard, because if it was spun too fast and too hard, the passenger could end up on the ground. Our 86-year-old neighbor experienced such a fate and we were glad that his sense of humor was not injured in the fall. Other activities in the neighborhood included picnics, swimming in the old water hole, hiking and camping along with the ever-popular games of croquet and horseshoes.

Hard times struck this idyllic farm life as it did the whole country during the Depression. During that time, we had plenty of food from farm animals and vegetable gardens, but income from milk sales was scarce because folks couldn't pay. My husband continued to deliver milk and never complained that the money wasn't forthcoming.

The hurricane of 1938 damaged the roof of our cow barn so it needed to be replaced. Also, in 1941 the government passed legislation requiring the pasteurization of milk, which for us would mean the purchase of expensive equipment that we couldn't afford. Our son and daughter were nearing college age, thus we decided to sell our cows and go out of the dairy business. It was a very sad time, but the loss of the cattle did not mean our home and land lost its title of "The Farm."

With the birth of our second daughter in 1944, a new era for "The Farm" began to unfold. Big brother went into the Navy, for World War II was in full swing. Big sister helped with the baby while finishing high school. While our oldest children were in college, "The Farm" was a great place for college-mates to come during class breaks for good hearty home cooking, rest and relaxation. The old piano, drum set and cornet were played for some rollicking sing-a-longs. I even got a chance to take part in a college psychology course, when my son-in-law gladly let me write his papers while he ironed my clothes.

My older children were both married in 1951 and started their families within the next two years. Thus another generation came to "The Farm" to play and grow up enjoying country activities. Dogs and cats were the only animals by that time, but the grandchildren made their own entertainment. The hen house became a playhouse and the attic loft was a special secret place to play. They made up and produced their own plays for adult viewing. Many imaginary trips were taken in the old '29 Model A Ford, farm truck. "Camp Wow," a woodland cabin, built by my son-in-law near a brook, provided us with camping experience right on our own land.

Now that my ninety-fifth birthday is here, I can look back on these wonderful memories of fun times with my husband, children, son-in-law, daughter-in-law, grandchildren, and now great grandchildren and smile. Plus, I remember the years shared with wonderful neighbors and many friends brought to "The Farm" by family members.

My youngest daughter, who never left "The Farm," plans to protect our acres by placing a conservation restriction on the land. We wish to share with future generations the pleasure of walking in the quiet woods, playing lawn games, bird-watching, sing-a-longs by the campfire or just sitting in a lawn swing and watching the beautiful scenery that God has so graciously loaned to us over the years.

❖ A Dog's Tale ❖
by Henry Gabriel, Northfield, Massachusetts

I don't recall the name of this dog. For the sake of this tale, let's call him Dennis. Dennis was, or maybe is, a beagle of common everyday beagles. (I hope he can't hear me, sorry Dennis). He belonged to one of my neighbors on Old Street in Randolph, Massacusetts.

Seemed like Dennis was the type of dog who wanted to be part of the gang. Whenever the neighborhood kids were off to the ballpark or schoolyard, Dennis was on their heels. Dennis' claim to fame happened one day after a snowstorm. I was out in the driveway shoveling snow after work one day.

I must have been really focused on my snow shoveling. At one point I looked up. I think that was my mistake. Trying to be friendly, I said "Hi" to Dennis. I don't know what it was, it must have been the way I said it, but Dennis started to bark.

He would not stop barking no matter what I said. Maybe it was the way I said it. Maybe it was me shoveling the snow. Perhaps he liked the snow just where it was.

It was funny, the way we pursued this problem, looking back. Talking to him was no good—he continued to bark. I tried throwing a shovel of snow at him. I do believe he could read my mind. Before I could heave the snow, he was off. At one point we were going back and forth. It was like one of those toys—the type that has two objects controlled by one string.

I was not going to give up. This went on for fifteen minutes. Finally, my neighbor came to his door and called, "Bad dog, get in here."

That's what he said, but I can't say what I said.

❖ Pud: A Cat's Tale ❖
As told to Jane L. Gilbert, Turners Falls, Massachusetts

My name is Pud. I'm a cat. I was born on a farm out in the country. I loved to be out in the cattle stalls at milking time when the herdsmen would fill low pans for us cats who were standing around waiting for the warm milk. After the milking was over and the cows were out in the pasture, we could relax a little and not have to watch out for the cows' clumsy feet coming our way.

One day, towards the end of the summer, the farmer came along and picked me up on his way to his loaded truck, which was waiting outside the barn. On the seat was a cardboard box for me so I wouldn't fall on the floor when the truck went around corners. Off we went. We drove for a while until the truck finally stopped in front of a neat little house with a pretty green lawn and paved walk leading to the front door.

The farmer scooped me out of the box and headed straight up to the door. The lady of the house opened the door and invited us into the house. After she and the farmer settled down he handed me to the lady and she petted and cuddled me (Little did I realize then that I was going to live with her and never see the farm again.). She kept me and was good to me. She gave me delicacies to eat and bought me some kitty shampoos to make my coat shine and stay clean.

So we lived together happily and I grew and grew and grew! We were happy together until one day she wasn't there any more. The lady's daughter came everyday and left a supply of food and water. Now I was lord of the manor, but it got kind of lonesome. I explored the house carefully hoping to find something exciting, but every day became just like the day before.

One day the daughter of the lady was busy moving things and picking up odds and ends, while I lay on a high window ledge sunning myself. I saw a car pull into the driveway and a young couple got out and started up the walk to the door. As they neared the house, the lady pointed at me and turned to the man beside her. About that time something told me I had to disappear for a while, so I found a little nook that was just right for my disappearing act.

In a while the lady's daughter began to call me, so I crept out of my den. I peered around one corner and saw all my belongings stacked by the door. My fears had come true! I was being given away to the younger couple!

Then I heard the young woman call me by name, "Pud! Pud!" That was it! I was going to another home. The new man of the house, the young husband, lifted me into his arms and followed his young wife out to the car. Once there, he deposited me in her lap and as soon as my belongings were packed in the trunk, my new "father" started the car and away we went.

I was a little uneasy as we rode along, but my new "mother" tried to soothe me as her gentle hands held me. The trip wasn't very long and soon we arrived at my new home. As soon as all my belongings were carried into the house, my new "dad" gathered me in his arms and carried me into the house followed by his wife.

Later in my life with this wonderful couple, when "dad" got ill, I spent my time trying to comfort him. I stayed on his bed most of the time until he went to the hospital.

❖ Heaven Continues to Open Up ❖
by Suzanne Gluck-Sosis, Greenfield, Massachusetts

It is now five years since we moved into "Heaven" here in Greenfield, Massachusetts and astounding miracles continue to happen.

We now have a sixth grandchild, Luke, born to my son's wife in April 2001. My husband Phil and I no longer drive to Vermont to see them or to New Rochelle, New York to see his son, Richard, and his family. The reason is that Phil's struggle with Parkinson's disease increased, making it more difficult to navigate or take long car drives. However, his spirits are high and he expresses happiness at being alive in this idyllic woodland setting.

The year we moved here we learned about a program where people examine what caused a person to commit the crime they did, what harm it caused and the loss of trust the community suffered. The program tries to deal with wrong-doers without putting them in jail. It is based on a process used in the aboriginal community in the Yukon Territory.

We also became members of our community's organic foods co-op. I serve there as a volunteer two hours a week in the herb department. I've learned to experiment with herbs not previously known to me.

We also discovered conscious communications skills that help you know what you want to say when you don't agree with an important person in your life (your child, partner, boss, friend) and yet to keep connected with that other person in a respectful caring way. You learn to create win-win situations. This is quite a feat in a world that, I feel, up until now has honored winning, power-over, domination, competition and control. I now co-teach a basic class of skills that are necessary and amazing to learn in a world that I feel cries out for a transformation in the way we treat others and ourselves.

❖ The New School Teacher ❖
by Dorothy G. Hmieleski, South Deerfield, Massachusetts

(The schoolteacher depicted here is my aunt, Clara Tanner O'Toole, who taught in a one-room schoolhouse in Sheffield, Massachusetts in the early 1900s)

The new schoolteacher stepped off the train at the Sheffield station and looked around. It was bitterly cold and windy. The ground was covered with snow. The superintendent had come to meet her with his horse and sleigh. He helped her into the sleigh. Fortunately for the teacher, he had brought his wife's fur coat with him. He wrapped the coat around the teacher and transported her to the house where she was to board. The next morning, school began.

Her school was a one-room schoolhouse and in the corner stood a large wood stove. As the new teacher was wondering what she would do about that, an eighth-grade boy approached her and announced that he would take care of the stove and he proceeded to build a fire. The new teacher was happy to delegate that chore to him!

The children continued to arrive. There was one little girl in the first grade and fourteen other children in various grades, including a girl who had finished eighth grade, but couldn't go to high school because it was too far for her to travel.

During the course of the day the new teacher opened one of the desk drawers and found that it was full of all sorts of items from tops to jacks which the former teacher had taken away from students. The new teacher put all the objects on top of her desk and said, "These do not belong to me. Please come and take them so that I can use the desk drawer."

The children came forward happily and claimed their possessions. From that time on the teacher had no trouble with her students.

Once a week the class had music. The teacher brought the students to the house where she boarded because there was a piano there. The new teacher did not sing very much, but she did play the piano.

❖ That's the Way It Was ❖
by Leona Jarvi, Athol, Massachusetts

I was born in Keene, New Hampshire on Marlboro Street. The house where I was born is still standing there. My grandparents owned the house in which all of us lived, including my cousin.

There was a little house on the property where my mom and dad lived. All five of us grandchildren lived in the "Big House" with Grandma and Grandpa. Our bedrooms were upstairs. We had kerosene lamps for light, a water pump in the sink. The outhouse was in the shed. Boy! Was it cold to hike out there in the wintertime! We had slop jars under the beds for use at night. The iron stove (with a deep well at the end for hot water) used both wood and coal. I used to walk with my grandfather alongside of the railroad track, after the coal train passed by. We had gunny sacks with us to pick up the coal that had fallen from the trains to fuel our stove.

I remember the large washtub that Grandma put in front of the stove while she ladled water from the reservoir into it for our baths. The boys were chased upstairs, while my sister and I were being bathed. The boys used to try and sneak down the stairs and peak into the kitchen. Grandma was wise to them and let out one of her famous war whoops. They skidaddled back into their rooms. After we had our baths, Grandma would add a little more hot water to the tub and the boys got to take their baths, while we left the room.

Rocks were kept on the back of the stove in the wintertime. They went into the foot of our beds for warmth. We would warm up our nighties at the stove and then run like the devil to get under our wool blankets.

Dad raised a garden, Grandpa picked mushrooms and berries, and Grandma picked dandelions and berries in season. Often times, this is what we lived on. I remember very little meat on the table.

When I was four my parent's divorced and our grandparents lost the house which changed our lives considerably. We left with our dad to live in Detroit, Michigan.

Jumping ahead. When I turned six years old, we returned to New Hampshire with our grandma who was living on a farm with a gentleman friend of hers. We loved the farm.

There was electricity in the house, although kerosene lamps were still used. A water pump in the iron sink and a woodstove for heat and cooking were available. I can still remember the smell of homemade bread coming from the stove. The outhouse was in the backroom. It was a little bit warmer in the winter than the one back in Keene.

There were two washtubs now, one for washing clothes with a scrubbing board and the other for rinsing. These tubs set on a frame with a hand wringer between them. My sister and I took turns wringing the clothes that fell into the rinse water. Then they had to be wrung out again and tossed into an apple basket to be hung out to dry.

I loved to play in the barn with the calves. One calf was special. She had a white diamond-shape on her forehead. I watched her growing into a heifer. One time I thought I would ride her like a horse. I tied a long rope onto myself and around the neck of the calf as I sat on her back. She then took off out of the barn and jumped all around, knocking me to the ground and dragging me all over the barnyard. My screams brought my grandmother to my rescue. She managed to grab hold of the calf. I had scrapes up one side and down the other. Grandma was a good doctor, though. She had a remedy for everything. Needless to say I never went riding again. That rope was at least nine feet long according to my grandmother, when she was telling the story to her friends. They sure had a good laugh. I ended up laughing with them. Grandma had a way to make you laugh at yourself when things happened.

One time her humor backfired, though. I came down with the chicken pox. My face was all covered with blisters and I was uncomfortable, so after I had eaten an orange, she cut some big teeth out of the peelings and put them in my mouth. She was roaring with laughter and handed me a mirror. What I saw in the mirror was a monster. I screamed blue murder. She had a hard time convincing me that it was OK—that it was just me.

Then, there was the time that the men had loaded a truck with manure to haul up to the garden. Grandma rode with them. We were told to stay in the yard. Well! We decided we wanted to take a ride in back, so we snuck in behind the manure. The garden was about a mile or so up the road. When we got there, we expected them to stop the truck and we would hop out. They just kept on moving and dumping the truck at the same time. We ended up sliding out with the manure. We were half buried in it. You better believe we were screaming. Grandma and the men folk were laughing so hard that we also began to laugh. While still laughing, Grandma took us down to where there was a brook at the bottom of the pasture. We cleaned up there the best we could. Later a tub bath helped, as did leaving our clothes outdoors.

We sure knew how to get into mischief on the farm. One of my brothers thought it would be funny if he left the barn door open after the cows and heifers were in their stalls and the bull was admitted into the barnyard at the watering trough. Well! That bull made a beeline for the door and was on a rampage pacing back and forth behind the cows. We scampered out of there. You couldn't see us for the dust! The bull quieted down in a while. Several months later there was a new calf born. My grandma found a job for my brother on another farm. Farmers like to plan for any new arrivals.

We left the farm before the calf was born, but I did witness the birth of another calf. On that particular day, when I was playing with the calves, one of the cows was left in the barn waiting to deliver. She started to make a lot of noise. When I looked over to see what she was doing I saw some hoofs and a nose coming out from under her tail, which is just where my grandma told me a calf would come out. I ran in to tell my grandma, but I said a calf was coming out. She told me, "Well chase her back." I finally managed to get her to understand what I was talking about. She went out and gave off with one of her war whoops to get one of the men from the pasture. The calf was already born when we got back to the barn.

We left the farm to be with our mother in Massachusetts. A couple of years later I went with my grandma back to the farm for the summer. The first thing I did was to run out to the pasture to see if the calf with the diamond-shape on her forehead was still living there—of course I knew that now she'd be a cow. I sat on the fence and looked them over and sure enough, there she was! I called to my grandma, but by the time she got to me that cow had left the herd and came strolling over to me. I really believe she knew me.

And that's the way it was!

❖ Living with a Limited Amount of Water ❖
by Irmarie Jones, Greenfield, Massachusetts

Across the country dire warnings are being sounded about water shortages as many communities struggle to supply this vital resource to their residents.

While living in a rural area for several years, I learned how precious water really is.

Having grown up in a city, I had always taken water for granted. It was always available at the twist of the faucet anytime for a drink, for washing dishes or for a shower.

In August 1960, my husband and I bought a farm in the hills of Western Massachusetts. The quaint farmhouse, almost 200 years old, had water piped in by "gravity feed" from a "never fail" spring. The spring water flowed into a shallow well in the shaded woods on the hill behind out house and from there, was piped into the house.

There were three faucets in the kitchen—one for regular hot and cold water and one directly from the spring for drinking water. I will have to admit that the drinking water, cool no matter what time of year, was the best water I ever tasted.

But, working out the logistics of our other water supply for the hot and cold faucets in the kitchen and bathroom was another story. In the second-floor shed, over the kitchen, was a large wooden storage tank, lined completely with metal sheeting. A pipe ran into the tank from the spring to keep it full of water, and pipes went from the tank to the two sinks. An overflow pipe carried the excess underground and into our brook.

The first day we moved into the house, we turned on the faucet to let the water fill the storage tank. It came with a rush. The next morning I went into the kitchen to get breakfast.

"Come quickly," I shrieked.

The kitchen floor was floating in water. There were holes in the tank's metal lining and the water had leaked out.

As I mopped the floor, we drained all the water out of the tank. We plugged in a long extension cord with a high-wattage light bulb on the end of it and dropped it into the tank to dry it out. This took time—a day or two. Then my husband patched the seams of the metal liner with a black, tar-like substance used by roofers. Of course, we had to keep the light on to dry the tar.

That meant that for several days the only water we had for cooking, bathing and washing came from the faucet directly from the spring. The ice-cold water had to be heated for sponge baths and washing dishes.

In a few days we turned on the water again. After two or three more leaking nights, our patching system finally worked. However, once in a while pieces of tar would float in the water, sometimes blocking the overflow pipe, making the water spill over the sides of the tank, down into the kitchen again. We had to remove the tar pieces. Bits of tar found their way into the other pipes. I would turn on the faucet to do dishes. No water. The pipe was stopped-up and we finally had to take long pieces of wire to clean it out. Finally the problem was solved. Then, late in that first fall, the water began to taste strange. We climbed the hill and looked into the shallow well where the spring water collected. A chipmunk had fallen in and was drowned. Once that animal was removed, we let the water run a long time to get rid of the foul water. And my husband built a new, tighter cover for the well.

Of course, there was always the difficulty of frozen pipes in the winter. We learned the hard way, when we got up one morning and found no water…again. On the bitter nights, if we remembered to keep the drinking water faucet running, just a trickle, there was no freeze-up. But, forget to turn it on and frozen pipes confronted us in the morning.

In order to have hot water, we had to keep a fire in the wood-burning stove we had acquired when we bought the house. It was connected to the hot water tank. City bred and used to central heating, I never did a very good job of building a fire. Usually it was just as easy to heat water on the electric stove on the other side of the room for doing dishes and to fill a bucket for a sponge bath.

The next summer offered the test on whether our spring was "never fail." It was true. There was always water, but it did run slower. Sometimes if I were doing a wash, the water from the holding tank would diminish to a trickle. Then I would have to wait for an hour or two for the tank to fill in order to get any kind of pressure or flow at all. After struggling for a couple years with a wringer washer, we bought an automatic washer, which was wonderful. But it seemed to take forever to fill each wash and rinse load.

We had long since disciplined ourselves during the simple task of brushing out teeth. We wet the brush, turned off the water, brushed our teeth, turned the water back on, rinsed our brush and rinsed our mouths. No heavy rush of water going down the drain as we brushed our teeth. That was wasteful.

Not a lack of warm water, but lack of adequate water limited most of our summer baths to sponge baths. Really, all you need is a big bucket of water, set in the tub to get clean. After soaping up, we'd pick up the bucket to shoulder height and pour it out to rinse off.

Once we had cows, the spring water was also piped to the barn and it provided drinking water for the animals all year long.

If we pastured the herd near the house, where there was no water in the pasture for them to drink, we set a huge galvanized tub in the field. We ran a hose from the kitchen faucet to the tub. When I saw the cows coming toward the tub, I would stop whatever I was doing—scrubbing vegetables, doing a handwash—and connect the hose, turn on the faucet and the cows would have a drink, as a trickle ran into the tub.

After six years we sold the farm and moved to a house in town. When we turned on the faucet, the water gushed out. I don't think there was anyone who paid a water bill more happily than I. However, even today, almost forty years later, I can still remember the taste of that wonderful spring water.

❖ Josie ❖
by Jean Kozlowski, Northfield, Massachusetts

With World War II in full swing, ration stamps were a precious commodity for purchasing some foods. Therefore, my mother bought her eggs and butter from the farms outside the city. The farmers were more than willing to sell their eggs to customers who came to their place rather than sell them in the stores.

Jim's place was located on a dirt road. The farm was in need of repairs and paint, but it was wartime and those chores would have to wait. In the driveway a few guinea hens scuttled out of our way. In a large pen were several geese that honked upon our arrival.

As soon as my mother purchased her dozen eggs, she glanced at the geese.

"Nice looking ones," she commented.

"Yep," the owner answered. "They are pets."

My brother, who was only five years old, wanted to pat one. The owner called one by name, Josie. Dutifully, Josie stuck her bill through the fence while my brother, David, fed her a carrot. My mother eyed the goose thoughtfully.

"How much to buy Josie?" she asked.

The owner looked astonished, but named a fair price.

"Sold," said my mother as she opened her pocketbook. "David will love Josie."

I remained skeptical, as a goose of that size would not make a very good pet. David drew back inquiringly, glancing at my mother.

"Of course you'll like her. She's such a darling!" Mother said.

I could not agree, but since I had no say, I helped squeeze Josie into a cardboard box. Her head and neck were well above the edge of the box, but her feet were hobbled so she would not take off.

David looked on dubiously, as we loaded her into the car. I had the honor of holding the box with her in the back seat. The owner waved to us enthusiastically as we moved down the driveway.

As we sped away, my mother mentioned the fact that Thanksgiving was only three weeks away. I groaned inwardly, as I realized I was holding our Thanksgiving dinner.

"Josie can live in our garage," she explained. "You can take her out each day for her outings."

"Outings!" I replied. "What outings?"

"Of course she has to be let outside and we must feed her—fatten her up a bit."

David clapped his hands and turned in his seat to pat Josie.

On the following days, I tied a rope to one of Josie's legs, carried her to our backyard, and exercised her. I felt very self-conscious, as one does not usually walk a goose on a rope, especially in the city in one's own backyard!

My neighbor, Mr. Stedly, watched me from his kitchen window. Soon he trotted out to ask me what I was doing.

"Meet Josie, Mr. Stedly. She's ours. Yes, that's right. She's David's pet," I said.

"I betcha she's not," he said and winked at me. "If I know your mother, she has something else in mind."

"What?" I asked rather pertly.

"A nice roasted goose would taste pretty good for Thanksgiving."

I sighed. "Probably you are right, but for now I have to exercise her and we need to fatten her up."

Josie turned to me and quacked. Then she continued chewing a few blades of grass, not realizing what fate held in store for her.

David, in the meantime, fed Josie innumerable times during the day. Even at his young age, he was eager to have a roasted goose for Thanksgiving.

Every day that I walked her, Mr. Stedly came out to view Josie. "She's looking pretty good," he'd say.

I couldn't wait for my job to be completed. Of course, Josie eventually was no longer a walking goose but a fine roasted one ready for our feast.

By Thanksgiving, twelve guests gathered and were none the wiser as to how we procured a goose in such difficult times. David and I had been sworn to secrecy.

After Thanksgiving, Mr. Stedly yelled across his fence," Why aren't you walking Josie anymore?"

I shrugged my shoulders and smiled knowingly.

"Have a good Thanksgiving?" he asked.

"Very good," I answered.

"Never saw anything I enjoyed more than that goose strutting in your yard," he replied.

I smiled back, happy my responsibility was over.

❖ My First Cello Lesson ❖
by Elisabeth Leete, Ashfield, Massachusetts

I was nine years old. My father had just died. I don't remember exactly how I felt, but my little girl's heart must have been bleeding. My mother, a musician, decided I needed music so my heart would heal.

I do not remember the details of my first cello lesson, but it must have been important because, sixty-two years later, I am playing again.

I shall try to re-create some of the details of my first cello lesson.

We are still living in the parsonage on Rue de Saint-Jean in Geneva, Switzerland, but not for long. The new minister and his young wife will be moving in soon. My beloved Swiss German nanny, Rösi, is still living with us, but not for long. We do not need her anymore.

It must be Saturday morning. In mourning, I wear a plaid black and white skirt, a gray sweater, white knee-long socks and comfortable, but worn, brown shoes. For a while I'll be carrying my three-quarter (or was it half size?) cello, then Rösi will take over the burden. It's going to be a long walk—three miles at least, I think—from the parsonage to Number 250, perhaps 366, Boulevard de la Coulouvreniere. We walk down steep Rampe de Saint-Jean, take a shortcut on an unpaved path on the right, turn left on Boulevard Georges-Favon…and suddenly we are passing a small chocolate factory on the left. Chocolate, pale brown, dark brown and white is oozing out of big blue machines and the fragrances delight my nostrils and comfort my wounded nine-year-old soul. I am not sure who is carrying the cello, where or how. Under the left arm? With the right hand holding it like a suitcase? I have to stop. We go inside and Rösi buys me a small chocolate bar I'll be savoring the rest of the walk.

At 250—or was it 366—Boulevard de la Coulouvrenière, we walk into a respectable six-story apartment building, take the heavy old-fashioned elevator to the fourth floor, ring the bell over the golden sign that says "Montandon." Mademoiselle Montandon opens the door. She may be about thirty years old (how can I tell?), she is tall, has curly brown hair and the trace of a mustache over her smile. She leads us to a comfortable living room, invites Rösi to sit in a soft, yellow armchair. I am a little apprehensive.

What happened next?

"I am going to show you how to unpack your cello," Mademoiselle Montandon says, "and how to rub the bow with rosin. Now sit down. Sit at the edge of the chair with the cello between your knees. Relax your shoulders. I'll show you how to play open strings, just copy me."

And here I was making awkward, loveable sounds as Rösi smiled from her big yellow chair.

The cello routine continued, every Saturday morning I think.

My father had died. Rösi left. My mother, my two older sisters, my mother's old black Steinway piano and I moved to a small apartment. My sisters were taking piano and violin lessons and, from time to time, dressed in our identical mourning clothes, we played easy Haydn trios. My gifted mother harmonized "Jesus, Joy of Man's Desiring" for the three instruments.

At age twenty-three I immigrated to the United States with a full-size cello. I played for a few years until career, marriage and motherhood interfered. I sold my cello.

Many, many years later, I own a new cello. I have a wonderful, young teacher at the top of a hill and I play Bach.

❖ Memories of When I Was Ten ❖
by Janice Howard Lepore, Greenfield, Massachusetts

It seems my memories are as erratic as the black and white movies my grandmother took us to on occasion. (The film was projected on the side of a large building and everyone watched, sprawled on the ground. I suppose it was forerunner to outdoor theaters with their individual speakers.) I do recall, however, how I enjoyed the rope swing, with a board seat, held up by a couple spindly tree branches. By New England standards, the few trees I remember being clustered together would not qualify as any kind of a shelter from the sun. Fortunately for us kids—actually only about five of us at any one time—the trees were far enough from the house and other farm buildings to be an oasis, especially if we had company--us and /or our folks. We enjoyed ourselves!!! It might have been difficult for an onlooker to discern since we were talented at bickering to the point that the youngest, five-year-old Irene, would chastise us from time to time. She was the only one with golden curls surrounding her freckled face. We all had more than our share of freckles, which made for many non-humorous comments and a few tears.

I don't recall toys in the sense of today's abundance or the need for them. We shared whatever we had and spent many hours making mud pies in our makeshift orange crate kitchen under the trees. Just to be free from chores and left to our imaginations was joyous. Life was carefree. Time was as vast as the sky. Our parents were busy before the sun came up and the day ended with the darkness in the era of the kerosene lamp.

We wore "Sunday" clothes to church and changed upon returning home. Sundays were special in that Dad didn't go to the fields, cousins came to visit, and we got to listen to radio programming in the evening.

The dirt, wind, outhouse, clothesline and chickens were part of the landscape. The other farm animals were associated with responsibility. The dog was trained to fetch the cows. The cats were barn-bred and of interest, but not really pets.

The one-room schoolhouse with potbellied stove was an inspiration, even though the teachers were demanding. The teachers never stayed more than one year. I assumed it was because the older boys played so many tricks—like putting snakes in the outhouse or creatures in the drinking water pail. It was more likely that it was the work involved in taking care of the building, especially during the winter, and the fact that women couldn't teach in those days if they got married. We looked forward to hiking off to school with our metal lunch pails. I'm sure it was the social aspect that fascinated us, not the learning.

I remember summer being long, lazy and hot to the point the earth was a series of cracks—no particular size or shape. The windmill would whir with the blades flashing in the sun to no avail, and the men would haul water from somewhere.

One time it rained unusually hard and a nearby lake overflowed with big useless carp. We kids proudly hauled them home in a wagon only to haul them back a few hours later. If they weren't dead when we picked them up, they sure were by the time we hauled them back.

I don't recall anyone talking to us kids in detail about death. It seemed we absorbed our insights from listening to adults. I do remember our adeptness at getting Grandma to finish our chores, therefore keeping us out of trouble with our parents many a time.

Today, a perky five-year-old chirping, "Grandma, rise and shine, it's morning time," often shatters my predawn reveries. Ironically she will never know how much joy she has brought to our retirement years, but I can hope that she will remember a happy healthy youth.

❖ Winter Squash ❖
by Phyllis Loomis, Ashfield, Massachusetts
(A thank you note to two young friends who remembered me.)

What a great old friend is winter squash.
Planted in the spring,
always off to a slow start.
Runs all over the garden
then
blossoms in mid summer.
Just before the frosts of fall
its fruits are big and scattered

far beyond its starter roots.
Squash keeps well in cool, dark places,
lasts 'til spring,
holds its bright orange color
and
brightens many a gray winter table.

It makes friends with fruits and vegetables, meats and fish.
Shows up as a canapé, a soup, a main dish,
a bread, a helper in salad
and takes prizes under the name of pumpkin pie.

Squash is a simple edible,
belonging on a working woman's table.
No trouble to bake,
it mixes well with most leftovers,
forms its own serving dish,
making life easy for the clean-up crew.

Now and then by happy chance
it combines with something creating a dish fit for a queen.
That happened the day it married ginger, lime and coconut
in the form of soup.
I ate that dish this noon.
Still swooning
I thank you girls, for the introduction.

❖ The Radio ❖
by Lorraine Madden, Greenfield, Massachusetts

It was 1935 when I began to work for RCA in Harrison, New Jersey assembling radio tubes.

I worked in a very large room and we sat on long benches at small welding machines operated with a foot pedal.

In assembling the tubes, a small, white, coated filament was placed in the center and the two tails welded to a grid. If the filament chipped while welding it was returned and marked against you. After five rejects, you would be called into the office and spoken to.

After the tube was assembled, it was placed on a tray in front and an inspector would occasionally walk by and inspect the tubes. In the beginning, I chipped my filaments until I learned to ease up on the foot pedal.

We each had a quota to have at the end of the day. At first I found it very difficult to keep up, and I would work through my lunch hour and still not have the amount due. Those wonderful, understanding girls alongside of me would each assemble tubes for me and place them on my tray until I was able to meet my day's quota.

There was no air conditioning and I would place wet paper towels on my lap when I felt too warm.

RCA also had a swimming pool available in the building, which was a pleasure to use before or after work.

Music would play on the radio while we quietly worked and I recall one day when the popular song of that time was "I'm in the Mood for Love." As it played, we would sing along and sway to the tune as we continued to work.

Now when I hear that tune, it brings back the many happy memories I have of RCA and the many friends I made while working there.

The RCA building is no longer there. It was replaced with a shopping plaza.

❖ Soft Shell Crabs ❖
by Eileen Marguet, Greenfield, Massachusetts

Having dinner at my mother's home in Brooklyn, I remarked about how delicious the fish was.

"It's crabmeat," my mother said. "You can get it at the fish store on your way home. Just ask for three soft-shell crabs."

That sounded easy. At that time in my life I was not an expert, but how could I go wrong with crabmeat?

The fish store packed my crabmeat in a neat little cardboard container with a metal handle. I brought the box home and put it on the kitchen table. I started to open it and left it for a few minutes to hang up my coat.

As I walked back to the kitchen to examine the crabmeat, I was horrified to see three live crabs walking around—one on the table and the two others on the floor. I screamed bloody murder! My mother didn't prepare me to face these wild animals!

Frantically, I threw my coat over two on the floor. The third crab was meandering on a chair. Screaming, I found out, didn't provide a solution. I remember my mother saying something about boiling water. I captured the third crab and scooped him into a pot and covered him quickly.

I called my mother and she must have given me some instructions about how to handle the other two. Whatever she told me to do I must have managed to do. I can still see those poor creatures trying to swim in the boiling water!

To this day whenever I eat crabmeat, which I love, I try to convince myself it came from somewhere else, not like the crabs I had to kill to eat.

❖ The Player Piano ❖
by Marjorie Naida, Gill, Massachusetts

While rummaging in the basement for tag sale items, I came across a pile of old, forgotten sheet music. As I read my name, Marjorie Frances Reilly, on the colorful covers, I sat on the stairs, closed my eyes and imagined the sounds of our player piano filling the air. I smiled as I recalled the music.

Ma and my dad, TaTa, moved into the Russell Block on Deerfield Street in Franklin County shortly after they married in 1924. The apartment was cozy and warm compared to the farmhouse Ma grew up in. A black woodstove warmed the kitchen, but the other rooms were always chilly. The outhouse was especially cold in winter! Times were tough, but my parents worked hard and managed to pay their bills. Ma worked for Dr. and Mrs. O'Brien as a cook and housekeeper. TaTa was a farmhand in Deerfield, Massachusetts. Eventually, they saved enough money to buy a new velour parlor set and a Koehler player piano from a grieving gentleman. Sadly, this gentleman's wife had passed on before they were ever able to enjoy the furniture. Ma had often commented on buying a piano, since neither she nor TaTa could ever play it, however, they enjoyed listening to the player piano rolls. She took several lessons before they had to put the piano into storage and moved to Bellows Falls, Vermont.

TaTa worked construction building a new bridge in Bellows Falls, while Ma helped prepare meals at the boarding house where they resided. When the bridge was finished it was time to look for new employment. Jobs were scarce, but TaTa was able to find employment in Springfield, Massachusetts. He was hired to drive trucks for the Arthur Fogarty Company. The Fogarty Company delivered produce to the Great Atlantic and Pacific Tea Company (known as the A & P). TaTa worked many long and hard hours; he drove trucks for Fogarty until his retirement.

The furniture finally came out of storage and Ma lovingly polished and cared for the piano.

I was born in 1930, and grew up listening to the happy sounds of the player piano. I can still hear the "plinkety plink" and "plunkity plunk" of the piano roll tunes. Because money was scarce, Ma never took another piano lesson.

In 1940, we lived on Leslie Street in Springfield. As luck would have it, a neighbor, Mrs. O'Brien, gave piano lessons. After I begged and begged, my parents agreed to let me take lessons. The lessons were fifty cents an hour and I promised to practice faithfully. They were pleased that I was interested.

As I practiced simple scales and chords, my parents would grin at my progress. It was fun to get a new lesson to learn. After several months, the thrill was gone!!! As I stared at Mrs. O'Brien's bejeweled fingers moving gracefully over the keys, with her wrists held high, I wondered, "Could I ever play as wonderfully as she?" I began to daydream and wish I were outside playing with my friends. The weather was too nice to be inside. Lessons weren't as much fun as I thought. I enjoyed popular music, however, Mrs. O'Brien would choose slow, classical pieces for me to learn. One hour of lessons seemed like two. Remember the old saying, "Be careful what you wish for, you might just get it?" Many times I was told to "start all over and play with more feeling."

"Have you been practicing?" Mrs. O'Brien asked.

"Yes," I would reply, feeling guilty.

One unforgettable day, Mrs. O'Brien's doorbell rang. As she went downstairs to answer the door, I was told to "continue playing" until she returned. On impulse, I skipped two pages of lessons! Just as I was finishing the piece, Mrs. O'Brien returned. With raised eyebrows she asked, "Did you play the whole piece through?"

"Yes," I fibbed.

"Did you make your First Communion?" she asked.

"Yes," I replied, nodding my head.

"Then you know it is a sin to tell a lie, don't you?"

Shamefully, I agreed as my face turned beet red. Being an obedient child, I was ashamed and mortified. That day I learned a good life lesson, "Dishonesty doesn't pay."

Mrs. O'Brien made me play the whole song all over again and I did it with a lot more feeling! I loved music and wondered why the lessons seemed like such a chore. Ma made sure I practiced, but my heart was not in it.

Playing piano rolls was a lot more fun. The roles hooked onto a cylinder, which rotated when you pumped the foot pedals. With various levers, you could play slow or fast, loud or soft. Words were printed on the rolls and a person could sing along.

In 1945, after moving four times, my parents purchased a new home. No more rentals! Each time we moved, the movers always handled the beautiful piano with care. Through narrow doorways and winding stairs, the piano was never scratched or damaged and retained its beauty.

I convinced my parents that I played the piano well enough and I wanted to discontinue my lessons. Since our new home was a distance from Mrs. O'Brien's, my parents agreed. Lessons were over, hooray!!!!!

I began to purchase sheet music from Woolworth's. A clerk would play the latest hits for customers at their request. It was fun deciding which songs to buy. I have to admit, I sounded pretty good when I played them. Perhaps I had been given the wrong type of music to hold my interest, but I did learn a lot in spite of myself. Many happy hours were spent with friends playing the piano and letting them play the rolls.

The piano had been in our various living rooms for over thirty-five years, when Ma decided to redecorate. The piano was moved to the basement and replaced with shelves and a mirror to hold knick-knacks. I was married by then and still played the piano whenever we came to visit my parents. One unfortunate day, the basement was flooded and the piano was damaged. It was moved out of the house and never replaced.

I never purchased a piano, nor have I played for years. I didn't like to practice, but I grew up loving music and that piano.

I think I will take better care of those sheets of music I found. They bring back happy memories of the piano that Ma and TaTa so wisely purchased when they were newlyweds.

❖ Castle in Wales❖
by Louise Bowen O'Brien, Colrain, Massachusetts

While traveling with a tour group, we spent one night at a castle in Wales. Ruthin Castle had been restored as an unusual hotel. Smooth, green lawns and beautiful rose gardens greeted visitors. The roses were so lovely that I took time to walk among them for a few minutes at sunset. The blue delphiniums, the red and blush pink roses and the fragrance of lavender sweet peas made the garden a joy to visit.

After a bountiful meal, we gathered in the great hall for a social hour. Tapestries, old portraits and exotic urns decorated the walls. Easy chairs and lounges were arranged in a group where, after-dinner coffee was served.

A beautiful grand piano had a place of honor at one side of the room. Someone suggested that we have a sing along, but no one was proficient at the instrument. My best effort was to pick out America, which is also God Save the King, with one finger.

I asked the young owner of the castle to play for us so we could sing. He was gracious and an expert at the piano. Like most Welsh people he loved music and was happy to entertain us.

Later we sat admiring the great hall with its stone walls, and a great suit of armor placed on the first landing of the stone stairs that led to the upper story. One person remarked that the armor was large enough to hide a man inside. Another said a ghost might be lurking there. I said that I would like to see a ghost once to prove there was such a thing.

"Oh no!" my friend exclaimed. "Don't say that! One might appear!"

At that moment a big black bat flew down the stone stairway, glided past the suit of armor and headed straight for our group. It circled us and headed back the way it had come.

My friend clutched my arm and cried, "See, I told you!"

"But it's a bat," someone exclaimed.

"Of course it was a bat," one of the men said. "Bats live in old buildings."

"But it was odd it flew around us, wasn't it," someone else said.

"Odd things happen in old castles," explained another man. "When I was shaving, the mirror fell off the wall. I didn't touch it. It just dropped off the wall."

After a little more discussion someone reminded us of the early start next morning. With one mind, we rose and started up the impressive stairs to reach our rooms. I noticed that we stayed together. There were no stragglers that night.

I never returned, but sometimes I wonder if there is a ghost in Ruthin Castle.

❖ Working on the Railroad ❖
by Joseph A. Parzych, Gill, Massachusetts

The Greenfield, Massachusetts Railroad Station once stood at the end of Miles Street where the Energy Park is now. Wide porches reaching out to the train tracks gave the appearance of a mother hen sheltering her brood with widespread wings. The station sat between rail tracks headed North- South and East-West.

During WWII the railroads were desperate for help. Someone told me, "If you want a good paying job, just walk in to the Division Engineer's office and ask for a job."

I was scared, but broke. So, in I went, without knocking. The Division engineer, Mr. Wilkens, sat behind a big desk with stacks of papers strewn about, barking orders into a candlestick telephone. My heart began pounding a hole in my chest. I couldn't decide whether to turn around and leave, or wait until he hung up and threw me out.

"What can I do for you?" he growled.

"I'm looking for a job," I blurted out.

His manner seemed to soften. "We can sure use some help," Wilkens said. "Go down to the section gang shanty and tell the foreman I hired you. If anyone asks you, tell 'em you're 18."

He didn't tell me where the shanty was, but when I left the office, I saw a man wearing a striped railroad cap standing on the station platform. He pointed out the shanty to me. I couldn't wait to get a railroad cap.

The foreman asked for my name and social security number and wrote it down in his time book. There was no question of age. If I remember right, his name was Casey.

It was the best job I'd ever had. Though the pay was more than

I'd ever earned before, I think I'd have worked for nothing just to be part of the excitement of working on the railroad and being involved in such critical work.

Next day, the men in the gang taught me how to swing the long-snouted hammer designed to clear the rails when driving spikes, how to space the rails to an exact width and other essentials of the job. They were a rough, hard-drinking bunch, but they treated me all right. They called each other "gandy dancers." The name came from the little dance the section men did when tamping down crushed stone when laying railroad ties. Our gang generally maintained tracks in the vicinity of the railroad station.

Prior to a train's arrival, passengers arrived by taxi, car, or on foot. Some came with family or friends to bid farewell; others came alone. Waiting passengers soon filled row upon row of wooden benches in the high ceilinged station waiting room. Curved iron armrests kept people from crowding too close or stretching out to sleep.

When a train pulled in at the station, a great hub-bub arose with a lot of hurrying back and forth. This was the era of the steam train. Steam locomotives have a lot of character. Steam hissed out of various ports as the train sat in the station hissing and panting like a huge beast. The enormous steam cylinders and connecting rods that drove the massive iron wheels were all out in the open. The train engineer wore a striped railroad cap, denim coat and pants, leather gloves with gauntlets and a red kerchief around his neck. He climbed down from the locomotive carrying a big oil can. He directed the long nosed spout at various exposed parts of the steam engine and pumped a judicious squirt of oil onto slide valves, connecting rods and other moving parts.

"Using too much of the expensive oil is wasteful," a railroad man told me, "and too little will let the parts run dry and wear excessively."

Occasionally, the engineer would entrust the oiling to the fireman staring out of two holes in a face blackened from stoking the coal-fired engine.

The conductor, the commander of a train, carried himself with a fair amount of dignity in his dark blue, nearly black uniform and a distinctive cap with the words "Conductor", above the visor. He set a footstool on the platform under the train stairs and offered a hand to help ladies step down.

Passengers came in waves. The sleepy station, deserted and quiet, suddenly came to life when a train, or sometimes two on either side, pulled in. The station doors burst open and throngs of people surged in to grab a seat at the counter like a game of musical chairs. This was no time to be polite if you wanted a quick bite to eat. The lunch counter later offered more complete meals for passengers who had a longer wait in the quiet time between trains.

Baggage men pulled high-wheeled wagons to transfer boxes, bags and trunks to and from the baggage car. There was an air of urgency about working on the railroad. Everyone took pride in performing their job. They knew just what to do and they did it with little or no supervision.

Passenger trains were one of the chief means of travel. Freight trains were essential for factories to receive raw materials and ship finished goods. Just about all factories had rail sidings. Store goods also came by rail. Troop trains moving servicemen and railcars bearing tanks and big guns gave me a sense of being part of the war effort.

As soon as arriving passengers got off a train, departing passengers began to board. When the time drew near the scheduled time of departure, the conductor hustled stragglers along, helping little old ladies on and a few young ones, too, if they happened to be shapely and good looking.

Soon the conductor announced "Alla Boardt!" The engineer rang a big, brass bell, "ding- ding-ding", warning folks to keep clear of the train. Then he gave two sharp little toots of the whistle. The conductor picked up the step stool, grabbed the handrail and swung himself aboard the moving train. He climbed the stairs and dropped a steel platform with a bang, to cover the stairs. The train went on its merry way, huffing and chuffing, faster and faster, then a farewell blast of the train whistle as it clickety-clacked on out of sight.

With the train gone, calm and quiet descended on the station. The baggage men leisurely wheeled the baggage wagons to the baggage room to stack away the freight. The lunchroom lost its urgency, and counter help relaxed after the big rush. A brassy blonde waitress often bantered with railroad workers. They liked to tease me, and egged her on to show me her butterfly tattoo. One evening when we were working late clearing snow and the station was quiet, the waitress raised her skirt to show me the butterfly on her inner thigh. I wasn't exactly sure what she wanted to show me and I didn't dare look. The men howled when my face got red. Later, I wished I'd taken a peek.

Working on the tracks was a dangerous job. Dropping a rail could smash toes or break a leg. Sometimes a train bore down on a different track than expected, catching trackmen unaware, especially after working long hours with little or no sleep.

One day, when we needed to repair a track out of town, the section gang got out a little platform car they called a "put-put". A "one-lunger" single cylinder engine sat underneath the platform. A steel wheel, at right angles to the face of the flywheel, drove the car. The center of the flywheel had a depression; that position was neutral. Moving the wheel out from the center was slow speed. Moving the drive wheel out to the edge of the flywheel made the car go much faster. Moving the drive wheel all the way across the flywheel in the opposite direction made it go in reverse as fast in that direction as the other.

Before placing the car on the track, someone sang out, "Remember Calaboosa!" It sounded like a battle cry. The foreman stopped and went back to get a long bamboo pole, with wires attached, and hooked it onto the telephone wires that ran along the track. One of the men explained that he was calling to make sure it was safe to travel. He went on to tell me how Calaboosa, a track inspector, and his helper had gone out with a "put-put" to inspect the track. They'd inspected tracks for years and knew the train schedules so well they seldom checked.

On this day a "special," an unscheduled train, came up behind them just out of town. The helper jumped off, but Calaboosa tried to outrun the train. The train ran over the car, killing Calaboosa..

The put-put really didn't attain any great speed, but it seemed to rocket along as I hung on, sitting in the open with the wind blowing in my face and the track going by at a furious pace just a few feet below. I looked back from time to time to see if a train was gaining on us.

When it snowed, the section gangs' job was to keep the rail switches clear of snow and ice. If a switch didn't close all the way, it could cause a train to derail. After clearing the ice and snow away, we lit kerosene smudge pots to keep the rail switches from freezing. If it snowed all night, we worked all night, then worked the next day, too. The first eight hours pay was straight time, the next eight was time-and-a-half, the next eight double-time, then back to straight time the next day. The railroad lunch counter closed about ten o'clock but Smitty's Diner never closed.

Smitty's sold a delicious bowl of beef stew and a big chunk of crusty bread for 40 cents. That big bowl of hearty beef stew kept my stomach quiet all night. It felt good to have a pocket full of folding money; to eat out instead of carrying a lunch bucket; to work all night with the section gang and be accepted as a man doing a man's job even though I was only sixteen.

When it looked like the snow was letting up and we might not work all night, the gang took Casey to the Polish Club for a few drinks during supper break. While they were getting him mellow, my job was to get a good fire going in the railroad shanty. If the shanty was warm and cozy, Casey would soon doze off and snore through the night.

Some men occasionally checked the smudge pots and switches while the others curled up on benches to catch a snooze— at overtime pay. I stoked the pot-bellied stove through the night between snatches of sleep. At about two clock in the morning a train came thundering by, making a horrendous noise, shaking the shanty as though the train was going to take the shanty with it. Someone stirred to say, "There goes the bootlegger." (That train, the Montrealer, got named "boot legger" during prohibition when people took it to Canada to bring back whiskey).

The train roared off into the night and quiet descended on the shanty. The foreman's snoring continued, uninterrupted. The next morning, Casey was hung over and grouchy. The crew took him out for breakfast and a cup of Irish coffee.

My first paycheck was for more than a months pay as a store clerk. But I never did buy that striped railroad hat. I worked school vacations until World War II veterans began coming home to reclaim their jobs.

Often when I see a train go by or hear a train whistle blow, that old railroad feeling stirs in me. Someday, I'm going to buy myself that railroad cap.

❖ Spring Fling ❖
by Dorothy M. Persons, Northfield, Massachusetts

In spring, the garden, birds and wild flowers need checking out to make sure all made it through the winter successfully. An April day, with the blue skies of October, and the softest of summertime breezes, is sure to lure me out of my house, and so it has happened.

Now that the crocuses are finished for this year, the daffodils are trumpeting for my attention. I admire them appreciatively, remarking on the pleasant contrast of their sun-yellow petals against the new yellow-green spring grasses. Their blue-green leaves cool down the composition nicely.

On to the rhubarb, which is curling frantically in the race to be the first fruit of the garden. It will have to hurry, because the asparagus doesn't have to go through those contortions to attract my notice. No signs of it as yet, but I know it will show up soon, though never soon enough for me, and it's all mine! My daughter hates it! (Some people have no taste.)

Since I have my trusty binoculars at hand, or rather around my neck, I take a trip into what we call our "back forty." (Yards, that is!) I check out the yellow lady slippers. I planted them years ago in a wet spot in the later-to-come shade of a honeysuckle bush. Yes! There they are there! One, two three—twelve sprouts. There should be twelve blossoms this year. How smart of me to think of protecting them from the occasional marauding deer with that circle of tall metal fence.

The leek bed is faring well. Are those mandrake seedlings? They must have been carried by birds to be this far from my big bed farther up. And the hepaticas are still as blue as ever, though they only started blooming a couple of weeks ago.

A fleeting motion catches my eye in a clump of brush. I spot a junco, which should have left for the north last week. I wonder if he's planning to nest here this year? Ma and Pa cardinal hover nearby. He sings—and what's that? A white-throated sparrow sings my favorite of bird songs. I hear it only infrequently now, because of my increasing deafness. One step and a mourning dove, almost under my feet, takes off with a clatter.

As I stand drinking all this in, a pileated woodpecker lights on a stump and casually eyes me as he proceeds to knock out a meal. Totally ignored, I dare not move, lest he be deprived of sustenance. Oh, what a day to be alive!

❖ A Magic Spring ❖
by Marilyn M. Pinson, Bernardston, Massachusetts

I was raised by parents who were in the entertainment business during the "Big Band" era. We moved each spring and fall to wherever the band was booked, resulting in a variety of summer vacation homes.

Early one spring morning in 1936, I was awakened by very loud, unfamiliar music. Peering out the window of our summer cottage, I was astonished to see a huge circus tent had been erected in the meadow overnight! What great mysteries were to be found inside?

Birds, startled by the shrill whistles of the steam calliope, flew away in all directions, followed by the scampering of small woodland animals seeking new apartments, I am sure.

After a quick breakfast, and filled with excitement, out I went to peek into the open tent flap. In the center ring was a stage. The stage was lit by a rotating color wheel, which focused on dancers costumed in sequins and rhinestones performing their routines. Overhead, a trapeze artist left me breathless as he daringly swung from bar to bar!

To the left of this scene, tumbling acrobats bounced and jumped on teeterboards, tossing each other high up in the air. They held me spellbound in quiet fascination.

As I looked around further, I spied a table with a large crystal ball, behind which sat "Lady Mahann" the famous mind reader! Her long, bright flowing robes and matching turban complimented her jet-black hair and piercing dark eyes—all adding to the mysterious aura around her.

I timidly went forth as she motioned to me, although I was shaking inside. She was absolutely charming. She put me at ease and welcomed me to visit often during the circus' temporary stay.

During all this, the circus band rehearsed new tunes. The calliope whistled and steamed; the dancers twirled and the acrobats somersaulted; the trapeze artist flew back and forth, while a twelve-year-old girl was entranced in their magical world!

❖ A Childhood in Turners Falls❖
by Francis R. Pleasant, Erving, Massachusetts

I was born and raised in the village of Turners Falls in the town of Montague, Massachusetts. Several of my friends from Fourth, L and Fifth streets, and I spent all of our time together. Every once in a while, the police chief, Walter Casey, would see us on the street and remark that he had picked up a "drunk" in front of some hotel, the Moultenbrey Hotel, for example. He'd remark that some change fell out of his pocket on the tree belt. We would hurry to the scene and paw through the grass picking up several pennies. This was a goldmine, as we could buy an ice cream cone at Sabato's Store for three cents or a double scoop for five cents.

One Halloween evening, I was in a playful mood and dumped over a rubbish barrel on the Avenue. I looked up and Chief Casey was coming down the street. I promptly ran down the Fourth Street alley (Chief Casey weighed over 300 pounds and I knew he didn't have a chance to catch me). Several weeks later Chief Casey told us he had, again, picked up a "drunk" in front of the Grand Trunk Hotel this time, and change would be in the tree belt. (We'd find out later he was just dropping the change for us to recover). When we got to the Grand Trunk, and I was down on my hands and knees looking for the money, I got a kick in the rear that made my eyes water. I turned around and there stood the chief.

"Pleasant," he said. "Remember when you tipped over the rubbish barrel and ran down the alley? You thought I couldn't catch you, but I just did!

I attended St. Anne's Parochial School as a child and lived there, as my father was custodian of the church. Monday was a special day, for the Shea Theater had an "after-school special:" a movie, a cartoon and a serial, which was the kind of movie that would end with Tarzan hanging over a pit full of gators so you would have to come back the next week to see how he got out of there. The movie was five cents. My friends and I always had the nickel for the show, but sometimes we didn't have the five cents for popcorn.

We would cut through the alley behind Trudel's Pharmacy and since he kept his returnable bottles in cases in the alley, we would each take a bottle. We would then run over to Greisback's Grocery (the VFW is there now) and get the nickel return to pay for our popcorn.

One day there was a sign in Trudel's window: "Closed next week for Vacation." Oh, oh! No popcorn!

That week we cut through the alley as usual and, although the store was closed, there were three soda bottles sitting by the back door. He must have known all along what we were doing. God bless him!

Growing up in downtown Turners Falls, Unity Park was my universe. My friends and I would go down each morning to play ball. If you needed a bat or glove, Matt Care in the field house would give you whatever you didn't have. At noon the whistle blew over the fire station on Third Street and you hurried home for lunch and then back to the park.

Halfway up the hill, at the eastern end of the park, was an old Austrian canon. When World War II came along, one of my favorite pastimes was to sit on this cannon and pretend to shoot over the bandstand at an imaginary enemy over the Connecticut River in Gill. We saved foil from our gum wrappers and we picked milkweed to stuff life jackets for the Navy. All metal went up to the high school for recycling. Then came the time when the U.S. Army came and took our cannon to be melted down. When the cannon came off the hill, the officer stated that when the war was over, the cannon would be replaced.

O.K., let's advance thirty-two years. It was 1976. Our country was to celebrate its two hundredth anniversary. I was named to head a committee for a town of Montague celebration. No budget was available, but I had an excellent and enthusiastic committee to work with.

I remembered the promise made to us kids during the war and wrote to the Defense Department, but to no avail. I then heard that Senator Kennedy was coming to Greenfield, Massachusetts for a fund raising affair. There was my contact!

I bought the $100 ticket and got to talk with the Senator. I mentioned to him "If we could leave three and one half billion dollars worth of military equipment on the beaches of Viet Nam, the U.S. Army could give the Town of Montague back a cannon."

Senator Kennedy must have taken my request to heart, and I was notified that I could pick up a cannon in Letterkenney Army Depot, Chambersburg, Pennsylvania.

Again I contacted Senator Kennedy and he arranged the National Guard to go there with me to claim it. The Montague selectmen designated the spot to place it and it remains there to this day. My only regret is that regardless of my personal cost to retrieve the cannon, I was never able to complete the job as I had intended. I wanted a plaque in front of the Howitzer that read:

> *May this cannon and all the cannons of the world,*
> *"Rest in Peace"*

❖ Christmas 2001 Perspective ❖
by Marjorie Reid, Greenfield, Massachusetts

On September 11, 2001, my husband, Bob, and I were on our way back from our morning walk in the woods near our Greenfield, Massachusetts home with the dogs. Our daughter, Liza, came out of her house when she saw us.

"There's been a terrible accident in New York City," she said. "A plane has flown into one of the World Trade Center towers."

We hurried home to turn on our TV in time to see another plane crash into the second tower. We watched in horror and disbelief as bodies fell from the tower, injured people ran screaming down the street and police and firefighters disappeared in the rubble of the collapsed buildings. We heard that the Pentagon had also been hit and that another plane had crashed in Pennsylvania. We learned that it was not an accident at all, and tears streamed down our cheeks.

After a while I said to Bob, "I can't bear anymore. I'm going out to pick peaches."

"I'll help you," he said. He needed a respite, too. He carried the ladder and I brought a basket.

We have a little peach tree in our field that our children gave me for Mother's Day a while back. The first year mice girdled it and we thought we had lost it. The second year, mice girdled it again and we thought it would surely die. The third year, a septic tank worker backed his truck into it and bruised it badly, but this year—overcoming all odds—it was full of peaches. Because the summer had been dry, the peaches were small, but exceptionally sweet and flavorful.

Bob picked the fruit and handed them to me and I put them in the basket. It was a beautiful day. The sky was a brilliant blue and the peaches looked golden in the sunshine. It was hard to believe that such unspeakable tragedy was unfolding less than two hundred miles from us.

I tried to watch more news in the afternoon, but it was too much, and so I made peach jam.

At Christmas, almost three months later, we opened a jar of our peach jam and as we did, we realized it was more than preserved fruit and busy work. It was for us, a symbol of healing, hope and eternal goodness.

❖ Mother's Apron ❖
by Leona Robert, Turners Falls, Massachusetts

One article can serve so many purposes. Recently, I was picturing my mother wearing a wide, half apron, tied around her waist. She would reach down, pull up a corner to wipe her sweaty face, wipe her hands or perhaps wipe the dirty face or nose of one of her brood.

Her apron might serve as a potholder when removing loaves of bread, pies or other food from the oven or from the top of the wood-burning stove.

If she went to the hen house, she would gather up two corners of the apron so it could serve as a basket. She would pick up eggs and gently place them in her apron to be used later for making cakes, cookies and more.

Roaming through the garden, she again gathered the corners of her apron and filled it with whatever vegetables were ripe: peas, green beans, or tomatoes. Sitting under the shade tree in the yard, with the help of some of us kids, peas were shelled or beans snapped, all into the trusty apron. Later these vegetables would be taken into the house and prepared for dinner or canned for meals in the coming winter months.

I can see my mother standing on the steps outside, without a sweater, the apron pulled up around her bare arms, which were folded in front of her.

On washday, many aprons were hung on the clothesline to dry. I wonder how many she had? There must have been a drawer full!

❖ A Night to Remember ❖
by Charlotte Robinson, Turners Falls, Massachusetts

One night in March 2001, as I was sitting quietly in my living room about nine o'clock at night, there came a knock on the back door and my son David, daughter-in-law Gail and granddaughter Amanda burst in all covered with wet, sticky snow which fell off them and onto my rug.

"What are you doing up so late?" loudly giggled Amanda.

"Get dressed! Get your coat on!" from David.

"You'll be safe. We'll look after you." from Gail.

"But I'm all ready to go to bed." from me.

Several minutes later—stuffed with hats, boots, jacket, scarf, gloves—I was being led to a streetlight shining through the gusty, thick and wet snowstorm. Arriving at the streetlight we all stopped. Looking up into the light I could see myriad snowflakes dancing up and down and here and there and everywhere.

The three visitors were laughing, crying out and jumping crazily. The snow was about six inches deep already. The plow hadn't been by, so the walking was very treacherous and I kept my eyes on my feet. Occasionally, I could see the full moon shining as the clouds jumped into new positions.

Suddenly, Amanda stopped right in front of me.

"Grandma, you are not playing right! You are supposed to let the flakes fall on your tongue. We came here under the light so we can see the flakes coming down and onto our tongues."

Then from David: "When we were little you made us go outside a hundred times to swallow the snowflakes—and sometimes we were even in our pajamas!"

From Gail: "I don't remember even having snow when I was little. Now I'm having as much fun as Amanda and Dave and Grandma."

Soon we all followed Amanda into the backyard—all singing and sometimes falling into the soft snow and then purposely falling again. Amanda led us into my snowplow alleys—throwing soft snowballs—shaking the trees to let snow fall on us—making angels on our backs! (Of course, I had to have help from all of the others getting back on my feet again.)

I thought of the lack of snowstorms for the last several years. Only the vicious ice storms. Thought of the millions of children who never had the chance to let snowflakes fall on their tongues.

The trees and branches, heavy with this snow, made little caves for us to crawl into and investigate. Each of us had a turn to lead the rest into the blackness. Just a little scary if you are such a little girl.

Several memories came to brilliant life for me. Once, as a kid, I awoke to a heavy snowstorm. I dressed quickly and went out to greet that snow. There was a rope swing hanging just inches higher than the snow. I heard a loud "crack" as I swung followed by a fast descent for me, the swing and the big branch it was tied to. I went all of the way to the ground—but the heavy branch just spread out on top of the snow. I crawled out of my nest like a baby bird. I was not hurt—just surprised.

"You know that spruce branches are very brittle," from my mother.

I thought of previous winters and the skating rink I made each winter in the backyard and of many neighborhood children (and adults) who had fun on it. And how icy my hands got as I sprinkled the rink each night. The gliding at Unity Park where I could watch the cold children from the warmth of the car. We sometimes went to Highland Pond in Greenfield for the ice-skating where there was always a hot fire in the shed. Making the huge piles of snow for fanny sliding. When I was little, our family had to help shovel the long driveway so my father could drive to his train. And how wet we got as kids from trying to slide or ski.

The memories I have of when I was a little child, when my children were little, and now when Amanda is still little are all mixed up together.

Son and family have departed. I am soaking wet and shivering. My toes are frozen from the snow that fell into my pull-on boots and turned to ice. My fingers are senseless. It was hard pulling off my soaking wet gloves. My hat had become stiff and my ears are still lifeless.

I mentally review the activities of the evening and I will fall asleep thinking beautiful thoughts.

As I crawl into bed I am content. All's right in my world. I am a kid again.

❖ The Past Revisited ❖
by Juliana Sivik Samoriski, Shelburne, Massachusetts

My twelve-year-old grandson called one day and asked me to name utilities we have now that we did not have when I was a child. He asked for ten and said it was for a school project. In just a short time I had filled his request. My list included a refrigerator, electric oven and range, microwave oven, garbage disposal, automatic washing machine and dryer.

Following his phone call, my thoughts dwelled upon my experiences with some of the utilities we used. Our ringer washing machine came to mind first. One day, to be of help to my mother, I placed a garment between the rubber rollers to press water out of it. Suddenly, my hand and arm went through the ringer up to my elbow. My mother quickly programmed the roller part of the machine to release and reverse. My arm was saved, but what a frightful experience!

We washed clothes and hung them on an outside clothesline to dry, summer or winter. In the winter, the clothes were brought into the house frozen stiff to thaw and dry. What a waste! It was explained to me that they were hung outside for the smell of freshness.

As more thoughts danced around in my mind, I envisioned the big black kitchen woodstove. It was always burning wood with a kettle of water on the top. On Saturday, a pot of beans was in the oven all day. Saturday night was pork and beans night in New England. It seemed the whole neighborhood smelled of baked beans and molasses.

Ah, but the utility that kept my reflective mood the longest was the icebox in our kitchen corner next to the sink counter. It had a top that swung open upward and a latched door at the bottom for food. The top area was lined with metal and housed a solid block of ice. How often the kitchen floor was flooded! Neglected, melted ice would overflow in the water pan on the bottom of the icebox.

If the ice could communicate what unique stories it could tell. Just how did it get into peoples' homes in the first place? Each week on a given day, my mother would place a red card in the front window. It was one foot by one foot, with numbers on each side reading ten, twenty, thirty and forty. The number appearing on the top would specify the number of pounds of ice needed for the week. This card was for Davis' iceman who had a truck full of ice tucked in hay for home delivery. He would clean off a cake of ice, chip it to size with his ice pick, pick it up with ice tongs and carry it over his shoulder (which was padded with rubber) and place it in the ice box. During summer, small chips of ice were available to us children who gathered around the truck.

The ice was delivered from Davis' icehouse near the Red Bridge at the bottom of Ferry Road in Turners Falls, Massachusetts. (Davis' icehouse and the Red Bridge have been since torn down). When Davis' cut ice on the Connecticut River during the winter months, this indicated the river was safe for winter fun. The word was "Davis is cutting ice!!" Out came the skates, and soon we were skating around Barton Cove. Fishermen cut holes into the ice and sat on inverted pails and fished for hours. Small iceboats were built to glide on the river. My brother and his friends built an iceboat in our cellar and found it was too large to move out of the cellar without dismantling it. Needless to say, none of his friends became engineers.

A few times while in high school, a member of our group would drive his father's car to school. Shortly after school was out, we would all pile into his car and drive toward the icehouse. Once there, we would drive on the iced river, go very fast, "jam" on the brakes and do "wheelies" near the narrows. As I remember, we would hear the ice crack, but that did not deter the excitement and fun.

After a few such trips, the driver of the car could not take his father's car to school anymore. I wonder why?

Today we have luxurious electric or gas ranges, automatic washing machines and home dryers plus deluxe refrigerators. The ice cutting and winter sports on the Connecticut River are nostalgia.

I was pleased my grandson called because his request took me down memory lane for a while and brought forth a few private smiles.

❖ Just Passing By ❖
by Doris Shirtcliff, Greenfield, Massachusetts

Going, going, gone—those men you used to see weekly or monthly: the baker, the milkman, the iceman, the gas man (who collected the quarters from our gas meter), the Jewel tea man and the Fuller Brush man are all gone. They dropped off gradually—swallowed up by planned development and progress. Only one remains constant today—the mailman.

My first recollection of a peddler was a character we called "The Banana Man." He came by every week or so in his high, horse-drawn, bright yellow wagon. The bed in the back was layered with hay to make a soft place for the load of bananas. The wagon creaked when it moved.

The shaggy horse was old and slow, and the dark-skinned man mumbled softly to the horse in a foreign language. I suppose he was telling the animal stop, go or hold. Or perhaps he was cursing the noisy gang of kids that followed him! I don't know!

His method of advertising was simple. The horse had a bell attached to his harness and when he plodded along, it tinkled softly. Every few yards the man would yell, "Banana-a-a-a-s!" in a low-pitched voice. We could hear him coming from across the street at the top of the hill.

We didn't know his name and if we asked he would drop one eyelid and stare at us. We ran and screamed. My father solved the problem and nonchalantly said, "Oh, call him Mike." So we stood by the side of the road and shrieked, "Hi Mike! Hi Mike!"

His answer was a stare and a low call, "Banana-a-a-s! Banana-a-a-s!"

❖ Tamie ❖
by Margaret D. Smolen, Bernardston, Massachusetts

When I was a child of about four or five, we used to have a few chickens, a rooster, a cat and a dog. I loved my dog and cat, but somehow I became very attached to one of the hens. I called her "Tamie."

She was a Rhode Island Red and very beautiful. I would feed her out of my hand and carry her around the yard for hours at a time. This went on for several years. Each year we would get new chickens and thin out the old ones by eating them one at a time. However, my father always saved out Tamie each year and we did not have her for dinner.

Tamie grew old eventually. Despite the best care I could give her, one day Tamie died. I don't remember how old she was.

My father made a small box for her and we buried her in the backyard.

❖ Remembering Mr. Lyman ❖
by Helen Carey Tatro, Baldwinville, Massachusetts

I received a calendar for the year 2000 with old-time pictures of the Mount Grace area. The month of August had a picture of the Warwick Store with Mr. and Mrs. Edward Lyman standing on the porch. The picture brought back memories of when I lived in Warwick, Massachusetts as a young girl.

Whenever my mom needed something from the store she would send one of us children up to get it. She always said, "Tell Mr. Lyman to put it on the slip." Many times I did this errand for my mother never knowing what "Put it on the slip" meant.

I remember Saturday nights when Ma and Pa would go to Orange for groceries (and sometimes a movie). My brothers and sisters and I would ride up to Lyman's store with them, each of us with a penny. Pa would go inside and do some business with Mr. Lyman and leave. It dawned on me after a while, that Pa was paying the weekly slip. We kids would stay there and agonize over how we would spend our penny. There was a long, glass case filled with penny candy. Mr. Lyman waited patiently while we talked, pushed and changed our minds many times.

Mr. Lyman had many wonderful things in his store that all the kids found interesting. One of the things was a big-wheeled coffee grinder. It was tied or chained so you could not push the wheel around. I do not believe it was still being used then—at least I never saw it.

A week or so before Valentines Day, Mr. Lyman had one counter covered with valentines in the corner of the store. Beautiful, paper, lace and standup cards and a box of penny cards. I spent a great deal of time going over and over those cards. Mr. Lyman never seemed to grow impatient with me, even though, looking back now, I believe that he and I both knew I wasn't able to buy any.

I remember going into the store in the spring just to listen, when the baby chicks came into the Post Office that was in the store. The whole store would be filled with their "peep, peep, peep."

When we would go home for lunch from school, we would often see Mr. Lyman out on the porch with his gray, store coat on. He would put peanuts in his pocket and the squirrels would come from the park and go into his pockets for the peanuts. He often signaled us to wait and watch. One time on the way home for lunch I saw a family sitting on the porch steps—a man, a woman and a couple of children. They were there for some time that day. Later, the story was told that they were gypsies and the little girl wet her pants on the step. I am sure Mr. Lyman gave them food. I never heard anything else about the gypsy family.

Mr. Lyman's mother was elderly and lived with them in the house next to the store. I remember that a friend and I picked mayflowers and took them to Mr. Lyman's mother. She was confined to bed upstairs. Mrs. Lyman had us go up to her bedroom and visit. I remember she was very old and we had problems knowing what to say. Mrs. Lyman was very gracious and thanked us for coming.

Mr. Lyman was a gentleman always. He and Mrs. Lyman would take short walks on Sundays (when the store was closed). They would walk around the center of town arm in arm. He wore a dress hat and whenever he met another person he would tip his hat. He would tip his hat not only for adults, but also for kids—even if we were on bicycles.

I believe I left Warwick before Mr. Lyman closed the store for good. No one I have discussed this with knew where they went when they retired and left Warwick. I think this is sad because the Lymans were such a big part of the Warwick of their time.

Recently, I discovered the Lyman gravesite at the Warwick Cemetery with a stone for Mr. Lyman and his wife Nellie. I plan to leave memorial flowers there remembering Mr. Lyman from now on when I make my visits to the Carey family plot.

❖ A Bottle Full of Memories ❖
by Lynne Warrin, Northfield, Massachusetts

The Victorian perfume bottle sat uncertainly on the shelf built into the closet door. The yellow buttercups painted on each side of the vessel were clear, crisp and seemed "pickable" to the child who looked at it in wonder each time she went to her grandmother's house. Around the lip of the bottle was gold paint that bled up into the stopper topped by three tiny flowers and a knob of gold. A single pale yellow butterfly adorned one corner. No one knew who first owned this lovely confection, but as great grandfather's business had been china painting, it was always thought to be one of the pieces remaining. No one really cared about it. If they had, it wouldn't have been put on the shelf on the door.

One day the child swung the door open too abruptly and the china perfume bottle crashed to the floor in pieces. She was inconsolable. Grandmother told her not to cry because it was just an old bottle. Grandfather scooped up the pieces and put them on the kitchen counter. He looked sad as he began to patiently assemble the shards. With tender care, he fitted the rough edges together. A wide smile slowly covered his craggy face and he told the child that there were only three large pieces and no small ones. The bottle could be restored with a little glue. He promised it would be as good as new and that it could be hers when he no longer wanted it on the shelf.

I sit here now, sixty years later, with the perfume bottle on the desk next to my computer. The glue has held but, of course, it has discolored and makes a fine, tan line all through the crack. From a distance, the bottle is beautiful as ever. From one direction, the crack is totally unnoticeable, but I know the entire base is cracked—not unlike life, I think. We all start out as beautiful bottles, a wonder to behold. As time goes on, however, we tip over and become held together with the glue of life.

But in spite of our seams, we are still beautiful to behold.

Local Color #5

❖ A Clerk in a Grocery Store ❖
by Allan D. Adie, Gill, Massachusetts

In 1933, when I was 18 years old, I worked as a clerk in a small grocery store on Washington Street in Roslindale, which is a section of Boston, Massachusetts.

As clerk, I would stand behind a counter and the customer would tell you what they wanted. You would then go and get the item and put it on the counter. If the customer had several items, they would read them off so you wouldn't be making a lot of trips back and forth. When you had all the products needed on the counter, you would take a brown paper bag, similar to what we have today, and mark in pencil the price of each item on it and add them up. If two bags were needed, you made certain you put some of the items in the priced bag. The people could check if the either the prices or total were wrong. If a mistake was made, the customer would bring back the bag. In those days, as it was a so-called neighborhood store; people shopped almost every day so they could carry everything home.

Ninety-five percent of the customers were women back then. Children would come in for one or two things—usually a loaf of bread or penny candy, like a Tootsie Roll. Men would usually come in for cigarettes, cigars, or tobacco for their pipes. You didn't have much trouble with young men trying to buy cigarettes. Actually, they usually just picked up cigarette butts from the ground and smoked them. They didn't have any money and had never heard of any disease one could get from discarded cigarettes. Perhaps women smoked, but if they bought a pack it was assumed it was for a male family member.

Some customers were allowed to charge during the week and would pay when their husband was paid at work. The only food sold for cats was a can of mackerel or a can of pink salmon. Each cost ten cents.

Dogs had Ken-L-Ration in a can. Of course, every one would let their dog have the pleasure of eating meat bones. Wonder how they survived?

We didn't sell meat or fish. Milk was in a glass bottle with the cream staying in the neck of it. One just asked for a bottle of milk. We may have had more cereals, but Corn Flakes and Wheaties were the popular cold cereals. Regular Quaker Oats was the number one hot cereal. These and some other products that weren't very heavy were on the high, top shelf. I used a large pair of tongs at the end of a long wooden pole to reach those items. I would hold the pole and reach the tongs up, put them around the box, close the tongs, and bring the box down to me.

Winter potatoes from Maine came in 100-pound burlap bags, which we would dump on the floor in the back room. They were sold by the peck (15 pounds) or ½ a peck (7½ pounds). They would be scooped up by a device I have never seen since. It consisted of several metal rods about an inch apart fastened to a handle which held the potatoes and allowed the dirt to fall through. The potatoes would be dumped into paper bags. In the spring, the potatoes would come from Virginia in large, wooden barrels. The cover was burlap, which hung over the edges and was tied down by rope. The skins on these potatoes were much thinner and cleaner than the Maine ones. To weigh these potatoes, and other food, we had a scale which was fastened to a wall and hung down. The weighing trough looked like the bottom half of a football made of polished metal, only longer and deeper and held by three chains to a round scale that had numbers on it. A large, metal piece, like the hand of a clock, would move to the numbers when food was placed into the metal trough.

I believe newer models are still being used.

I had only been working a few days when a lady ordered a peck of spinach. I grabbed a bag and pushed the spinach into it. When put on the scale it weighed three and a half pounds, so I jammed more spinach in the bag. Result 4 pounds. I went to get a couple more bags when the manager told me with a smile that a peck of spinach was only 3 pounds!

Most of the homes back then were called three-deckers because the roof was flat and they were three stories high with an apartment on each floor. These apartments were heated by what was called a coal stove located in the kitchen. I remember my grandmother getting up early in the morning to light a fire because it would go out during the night.

The four sides inside the front of the stove were lined with a special heat-resistant lining. My grandmother would crumple up some old newspaper, put what we called kindling wood on top, then some nut coal, sprinkle some kerosene on it, put back most of the covers on the stove, light a match to it (I know what you are thinking), and put back the other cover.

Not many homes, especially three-deckers at this time, had furnaces. The grocery store where I worked sold nut coal in strong, paper bags that contained 25 pounds. Now, because I am a country boy instead of a city slicker, what we called "kindling wood" was slab wood cut up into small pieces. This wood was also contained in a strong paper bag about a foot round and 2½ feet tall. The bags weren't very heavy. I had a cart in which I would load bags of coal and wood to take to a customer's home. The most coal I could carry on my shoulder was 75 pounds or three bags. I would just about make it to the third floor apartment. No one ever thought about giving tips and I never expected one. It was part of my job. I can't remember how much pay I made. My father had died when I was two years old and, like everyone who worked in those Depression days, I gave all my pay for my family's benefit.

My boss was an Irishman, as were many store managers in those days. The store name was J. T. O'CONNOR, of which there were several in the Boston area. MIKE O'KEEFE stores had several in the same territory, plus there was another company, whose name I haven't been able to remember, that had several stores. In time, these three companies combined and became FIRST NATIONAL STORES. The first chain of grocery stores, I believe.

❖ Memory Lane ❖
by Edna Baublis, Athol, Massachusetts

Last week I took a stroll down Memory Lane. I am still smiling inside at the memories.

My high school class, Athol High in Athol, Massachusetts, is celebrating its 60th year out of high school and I had some business to attend to in my old high school. After the new high school was built, the old high school became the junior high, then the middle school, and now it houses some social service agencies and the Head Start Program.

I walked up the outside steps, opened the door, and was transported back to a simpler time. I walked up the stone steps, grooved and scraped by the thousands of young feet that walked, ran, or skipped up the stairs.

The sign on the door said for all visitors to report to the office (that hadn't changed), which I did. Today the office is divided into four small offices. I stated my business and was told Mrs. Graziano's office was Room 206.

I sauntered up the steps—with not quite the energy I once had—same old brown tiles on the stairs, but with the addition of a chair seat for the handicapped. I thought to myself, 'ummm, Room 206—where I had Miss Armstrong for US History.' When I entered the room, I almost saw Miss Armstrong standing in the front of the room trying to impress us with the importance of history.

At the end of my dealings, I looked into Room 205—where I had taken shorthand and bookkeeping—and remembered how Miss Ramsay made me work on a trial balance for three weeks before she would tell me that I was adding 9 and 4 wrong and that is why I could not balance. She would not let us use the over and under method.

I peeked into the library then walked to the end of the corridor. There was Room 201, French with Mr. Berard and Room 202, Latin with Miss Ellsworth. I peeked into the teachers' lounge—looked like the same old furniture.

There was an alcove that had lockers in it. Because it was such a cramped place, either all boys or all girls had lockers in the alcove when I was a student there. Heaven forbid that both sexes were in that cramped space. What if a boy accidentally bumped into a girl!! No. It was better to separate the sexes.

Now the alcove is a little sitting area for youngsters. The lockers have been removed and child-sized chairs have been placed in the area.

Downstairs, I peeked into Room 105, Mr. O'Brien's classroom where he taught commercial geography. Then to Room 103, English with Mr. Ellis and Room 108 Senior English where every Friday several of the students would have to stand on the stage and give an oral report. Or we had to recite what we had memorized the previous week—you know, Shakespeare, Longfellow, or whatever was on the agenda for that term. Oh, the quaking voices! There were always snickers from someone in class.

Then I looked into the gym and into Rooms 101 and 102 where commercial students learned typing on big Underwood or Royal typewriters. Mine was an Underwood—and at the end of the line of my typing the bell would "ting" and my left hand would go up to return the carriage.

First we had to do our exercises, though—asdf,;lkj—and Miss Streeter would bang the ruler on the desk to keep us in rhythm. When we changed a typewriter ribbon, she would check our hands, and if she spotted ink on our hands, she would give us an "F" for that day's work. I prided myself on being able to change a ribbon without getting ink on my hands.

Perhaps we didn't have the amenities that the schools now have, but we did have cooking, sewing classes, woodshop and sciences. And we had gym—or rather we shared a gym. A tarpaulin net was pulled across the gym floor separating the boys from the girls. Believe me, there was nothing sexy about our blue, bloomer gym suits.

Looking back, I enjoyed my high school years and I'm sure that I shall hear some of the same stories on Saturday—sixty years after graduation. Perhaps the little peccadilloes will even become much bigger and more daring, but for a few hours we will be transported back to very naïve 16 and 17-year-olds—we'll shed a tear for those who have gone and wish well to those whom we may not see again. Nostalgia reigns!

EPILOGUE

Saturday, October 13, 2001, dawned clear and the sun shone brightly. It was a perfect day for a reunion.

At eleven a.m. I said good-bye to my husband and said I would see him later at my reunion and please try to be there by 12:30 p.m. I patted him on the head and off I went.

The tables were set with white tablecloths and flowers were in the center of each table. White vases with green carnations and green and silver balloons were ballasted by the bases. We had bought green napkins to use with the white tablecloths. The room looked festive.

I felt a little nervous! Even though we had received reservations for 60 people, and reservations were made for 55 (because we knew that there were always some who would not show) there was still that moment before the countdown.

We need not have worried! They started to arrive at noon and soon they were coming in bunches. Screams from the women—"Oh, you look so good"—and then corner huddles with old friends. (Did you ever notice that when a group gets into a room the voices get louder and louder and higher and higher?) Well, that's what happened.

Some came under their own power, some supported by their wives or husbands, a few with canes, and one in a wheelchair. No matter. They came and for a few moments we were giggly 17- and 18-year-olds.

School nicknames were used—names that probably were not heard since high school days. It was amusing to hear "Hey, Skinny" shouted across the room and a very successful, portly, white-haired man turn and say, "Sonny—how the hell are you?"

After dinner and a short business meeting, the necrology report was read. The list is getting longer and longer and many an eye had a tear in it. We have reached "that age."

And then, a few brave souls got up and sang our class song! They really got a big hand!!

Soon those with some distance to travel started to pack up and leave. "Have to get home before it gets dark. I don't like to drive at night," was heard being said by more than one person.

With a touch of sadness we said good-bye to our friends—at our age we don't have enemies—and amid shouts of "See you in two years," we all went off commenting on what a nice time we had.

❖ It's Freezing Out There! ❖
by Rosalie Bolton, Greenfield, Massachusetts

In winter, after school, when my mother sent me to the yard to take the wash from the line, I hurried. The air was cold and windy. "Raw," my mother called it. "Raw, New England weather."

"Chills the bones," my grandfather said. "It's good for you. You're young. It won't hurt you."

The snow-covered, wooden clothespins with little heads on them looked like birds on a wire, clinging, refusing to get off when I shook the fluffy snow from the clothes. I had to push back and forth on the pin to loosen its hold on the rope line. Sometimes I pulled so hard that the clothespins split in two and pieces of wood flew past me to the snowy ground. My brother had shoveled the snow from under the clothesline so that I did not have to stand knee deep in the shiny crust. The clothes, frozen stiff, were like cardboard cutouts, people without heads, hands, or feet.

I laughed at my grandfather's underwear, that long, swinging, creaking union suit. I hit the frozen garment with my fist to see it swing back and forth. Then I hit it again. I tried to bend those sleeves—so rigid! The woolen legs of the underwear would not crack or twist. It was a white scarecrow hanging on the line. I pulled the clothespins off the shoulder parts of the union suit and placed that frozen garment on top of the wicker basket. It stayed defiant, straight across the top of the basket. I slapped the towels down their centers to soften them so that I could fold them over once. The muslin sheets bent after I persuaded them with a whack. When I tried to fold the clothes, I heard them snap and I saw little ice particles fall off where I had creased the cloth.

I called for someone to shut the door. "It's freezing out there!" I made an announcement as I clumped across the yellow and green linoleum floor with my overshoes unfastened, noisy, flapping against each other. I wore them like the older girls—Anna and Jo my neighbors—wore theirs.

"Why, on earth, don't you buckle your overshoes? It's dangerous. You'll trip," my grandfather said.

My hands were cold, puffy, and red. I held them over the black iron stove, hot with the coal fire, and rubbed them. I wanted my brothers and sisters to see and hear about all the work I had done. I wanted to make a show of it.

"That's a big help," my mother thanked me.

My mother reached for the rack hanging on the wall near the stove; the wooden rack with the six long fingers squeezed together. She pulled the "fingers" away from their clutch. She held and spread their long rods to hold the clothes to dry. Once I put my wet school book there to dry, page by page. My brother brought a larger wooden rack in from the shed, opened it out and stood it on the floor near the stove to hold the heavier materials. The stiff clothes, so arrogant and brazen out of doors, lost their frost. They softened, went limp, and became meek before they dried. As the clothes and I warmed up I realized when I brought in the wash, I brought in the smell of the outdoors for a while.

My mother dried the inside of the Easy Copper Washer with the wringer on top. She wiped the three large cups that went up and down, up and down to clean the clothes. I picked up the big, round cover of the washer and walked by my brother holding it like a shield.

My sister and I set the table in the dining room. The stew of carrots, potatoes, and lamb was on the stove. The lamb was left over from Sunday's roast. There was homemade bread and fluffy, tapioca pudding for supper. Monday was over . . . school and washday.

❖ The Magical Surprise ❖
by Estelle Cade, Turners Falls, Massachusetts

Going with our parents for a Sunday dinner and visit with Dad's aunt and uncle was never a bore or a chore for me and my younger sister, Carole. The lovely, white, Dutch Colonial home in Newtonville, Massachusetts was a welcoming place, and Aunt Annie and Uncle "Wingie" (their last name was Wing), childless themselves, always greeted us with open arms.

The built-in bookcase, beside the living room fireplace, held one shelf of books that were just for us to have. They were old-fashioned books, but fun for us to read. In the front hall, one of the doors in the mahogany sideboard could be opened by us to retrieve some puzzles that were kept there. I still remember those "Little Rascal" puzzles. We put them together at every visit, not minding at all that we'd done them many times before. Children of our generation did not require something new every minute, but were quite content with the familiar.

Down cellar (warm and spotlessly clean), where Uncle had his workbench and where he and my dad smoked—pipe and cigarettes respectively (no smoking in the house!)—and chatted companionably, my uncle had hung a small swing so Carole and I would have a place to play on winter afternoons.

One day, however, when we arrived for our visit, the adults seemed unusually eager for us to go downstairs and swing, so down we went, obedient children that we were! As we came down the stairs, what did we see against the near wall, but a dollhouse—a most wonderful dollhouse that left us wide-eyed and amazed. Where had it come from? Our uncle had built it three rooms high, two rooms across, with an attic at the top. It was as tall as I was, at about seven years old, and was an imaginative child's dream. Aunt Annie had furnished it to perfection with a mix of antique dollhouse furniture and modern pieces, all 1" to 1' scale.

Many years have passed now, and I've forgotten some of the wonderful details, but I do recall the kitchen—white, 1930's style, with a bonnet-top refrigerator (the Frigidaire brand, electric refrigerator, with the motor on top), white sink on legs, cabinets, and a kitchen table and chairs, which she'd dressed up with a tiny checked tablecloth and napkins, and the bathroom with currently "in-style" pedestal sink, "built-in" tub, and modern toilet. In the parlor was a bookcase holding miniature books that could actually be read (one was a bible); a dining room with table, chairs, and glass-front china cabinet stocked with miniature dishes; a child's room, complete with old-fashioned crib, and a master bedroom with a four-poster bed. The attic held a mixture of items that any attic should hold! It's impossible now to recall the plethora of delightful objects that this loving couple had included in this incredible gift, but I've never forgotten the hours of pleasure it gave to two little girls, and how dearly we loved the givers.

To this day, I love all things miniature. A few years ago I was able to fulfill a childhood dream when I saw "Queen Mary's Dollhouse" in London. As incredible a piece of art as that house is, it is the memory of my own magical surprise, and my dear aunt and uncle, that is still the most precious to me.

❖ The Fire ❖
by Guy Carey, Jr., Warwick, Massachusetts

In 1943 I was sitting on what used to be the front lawn of my home at the foot of Mount Grace in Warwick, Massachusetts, my body wracking with inconsolable sobs because of my torn and ruined life. I was certain that even if I survived the day, I surely would live with a heart forever broken.

The night before had been extremely warm and I had escaped from the heat of my bedroom to the open front porch. I vaguely recall my father, uncle and older sister leaving for work in the morning. My dad and uncle left long before the morning light. The sun was in the sky when I heard the piercing screams of my sister as she came running from her room next to the kitchen yelling, "FIRE! FIRE!"

Mother rushed from the back of the house and called to me, "Bud! Run upstairs and get the rest of the children out of the house then go to the neighbors for help!"

I ran upstairs and roused my brothers and ran and alerted the neighbors. As I ran back to the house, it was plain to see there was no saving it.

The house was of the old style with the shed and barn connected directly to the house. The fire had started in a chimney between the barn and the house. Mother had already driven our Model A out of the barn and freed the animals. Now she was frantically trying to pull her Frigidaire out of the kitchen. Flames poured out of the windows and through part of the roof and forced her to give up her quest.

My brothers and sisters all huddled out by the road. Some stared wide eyed, others cried softly, as they tried to cope with their rude awakening. The neighbors came running to help, but when the old fire truck finally arrived on the scene, it was clear to all that there was no way of saving anything.

The women of the neighborhood took control. Some consoled Mother and others gathered up us kids. We had escaped with only what we had worn to bed. One of my brothers had only a blanket to cover his nakedness. The neighborhood women took us to their homes and gave us clothing.

After being given some clothes and seeing that everyone was being cared for, I ran back to the house. I arrived just in time to see what was left of it crash down and fall into the cellar hole. That's when my loss really hit me. I had won a trip to scout camp for two weeks and had been excitedly counting the days until my departure. A couple of days before the fire, one of Mother's friends gave me some real Boy Scout uniforms and two semaphore flags. The suits were a little big, but my mother was in the process of altering them. My excitement about the trip and the uniforms was partly what had made going to sleep so hard that night.

I lay on the lawn completely involved with my personal sorrow: the flags and uniforms had burned in the fire that was probably going to end any chance of my going to camp. What had been a dream come true, a really impossible dream for a boy with nine siblings in a family that was still suffering from the Great Depression, was lost.

I was lying there, inflicted with the pain of my thoughts, when I spotted my father coming across the field. Someone must have gone to where he worked in the woods and brought him home. My first thoughts were, "Dad can help!" He will understand my loss and know what to do. As I watched him cross the field, it seemed as if he became older and more stooped over with each step. By the time he reached my side, he was as white as the ashes of the fire still burning in the cellar hole.

He placed a hand on my shoulder. My grief brought such a look of fear to his eyes that it shocked me to silence. He stood by me on the lawn quietly, trying to form words that did not seem to want to come. Finally, in a shaky voice, he asked, "How many in the family did we lose?"

"Nobody, Dad. Nobody was even hurt," I answered.

The fear left his eyes and his shoulders squared.

"Thank God for that," he said. "Anything else we had is of little consequence."

It has been over fifty years since that fire and my father's words "Thank God for that." That day and those words have stayed with me as a tool to use when dealing with any of the crises that happen to plague my life.

❖ My First Car ❖
by Mary Ciechomski, Turners Falls, Massachusetts

When I married Steve in 1946 he owned a '40 Chevrolet. I was so proud to have a car to get around in. During my years before marriage, our family never owned a car. We depended a lot on walking or the trolley and later the bus. I really felt like a "Big Shot" to be the owner of a car.

My husband used the car to get to work at the Springfield Armory from our home in South Hadley, Massachusetts and so I had no transportation during the day. I scheduled my shopping and errands for when the car was available.

The children came, and grew, and they had to have dentist and doctor visits. I would take my husband to work so that I could have the car. This necessitated getting everyone up at six a.m. and driving to Springfield, Massachusetts at 6:30 a.m. with four youngsters in the car. We'd repeat that trip around 3 p.m. to bring my husband home from work.

When the Armory closed in 1966, my husband secured a salesman's position and was given a company car to drive. What joy! I had a car exclusively to myself!

The children were growing up, too, and one by one they obtained cars for themselves. I can recall that at one time there were four cars in the driveway leading to our one car garage. We bought the lot next to our property and made a parking lot there for the excess cars.

Today it seems that every home has at least two cars and a garage for at least two or three cars. Most children, my grandchildren especially, seem to have a car waiting for them when they get their driving permit around age sixteen. I wonder what kids would do if they had no "wheels" or had to drive an hour in the morning and another hour in the afternoon just so that they could have a car for the day?

❖ Gramma's Kitchen ❖
by Genevieve Clark, Northfield, Massachusetts

When I was a girl of about eleven years old, in the summer of 1937, our family lived for a few months in a small house not far from my father's parents in the small Berkshire town of Florida, Massachusetts. By then, my grandmother, a long-time asthmatic, was finding it more difficult to keep up with everyday chores around the house. Why, I don't know, but I became the designated grandchild to help out.

Several times a week, I would enter her house through the squeaky screen door. Knocking was done out of politeness, as the door itself gave ample warning of someone entering. No doubt Gramma was aware of me arriving anyway, as she usually sat in her chair by the window facing the road. Her binoculars were always in place on a nearby table. Gramma, in spite of her physical limitations, kept a firm hold on her place as matriarch of the family.

To greet me, as I entered by that kitchen door, were the aromas that tended to fill grandmothers' homes in those days. The kitchen itself was ever fascinating to me. In the center of the room a sturdy, rectangular worktable held sway. Its well-scoured, maple top, covered with a variety of stains, cut marks, and worn areas betrayed the countless number of fresh berry pies, biscuits, cakes, and breads that had been created there for her family of six boys and a girl.

    Sometimes when I entered I would find my grandmother busy at the blue-painted, pine, Hoosier cabinet. The cabinet stood regally as a self-appointed guardian over the rest of the kitchen. It was tall, at least to me, and had a built-in flour sifter capable of holding a twenty-five pound sack of flour. A roll-down cover hid the top shelves, but was seldom used. A narrow work surface could be widened by another foot when pulled out. Its shelves held an amazing assortment of cooking needs. Jars of dried beans, split peas, cornmeal, and graham flour; crocks of nuts and raisins; jugs of honey, maple syrup, and molasses covered the lower shelves. Above them sat the ever tantalizing spice boxes with their stashes of brown, curly cinnamon sticks, and little egg-shaped nutmegs. Cans of ginger, cloves, dry mustard, and other spices, each with their own nose-tickling smell, sat alongside them. On hooks arranged along the edge of the shelf, hung the nutmeg grater, a pastry blender, an eggbeater, several well used, wooden spoons, and the rolling pin. Often a coating of dusty flour from the built-in sifter covered the worktop. A black iron grinder, filled with fragrant coffee beans, was attached to the side of the cabinet. On the top of the cabinet was an interesting accumulation of unused kerosene lamps, unheeded cookbooks, and other forgotten articles.

    My eyes would follow each movement of the short, white-haired lady I called Gramma. How intently she bustled from table to cabinet and back. I was delighted when asked to fetch the butter and milk from the big, oak icebox. The icebox was located in an alcove adjoining the kitchen where it would stay colder. Its brass latches opened smoothly, and I lifted out the pitcher of sweet, cream-topped milk. Carrying it back to the table, I returned for the homemade butter. It was wrapped in waxed paper that covered the design left by the wooden butter mold. As I closed the heavy, icebox door, I could hear the slow drip, drip as the chunk of ice in the top melted slowly away.

After a quick trip to the pantry to get eggs from a hanging wire basket, the big, yellow and brown, earthenware bowl was soon filled with golden johnnycake batter ready for baking. I followed as Gramma entered the shelf-lined pantry. Here, pans of skimmed milk were slowly turning into the beginnings of cottage cheese, and baskets of early apples and new dug potatoes waited to be used. From a myriad of enamel pots, iron skillets, and baking tins stacked on the shelves, Gramma selected an oblong, tin pan, darkened with age and many uses. Soon the johnnycake was on its way to the oven.

The black iron range, trimmed with Nichol chrome, radiated its warmth throughout the kitchen. As Gramma lifted the lid and poked another stick of wood into the firebox, a shower of orangey-red sparks flew into the air. When the wood began to burn, it crackled and snapped as if protesting its fate. Opening the oven door, I could see a bean pot of baked beans bubbling away. Gramma pushed the pan of johnnycake into the hot, dark oven with them and shut the door.

As she retired to a chair to wait and rest, it was my turn to get busy. Under her watchful eye and with careful instruction, I carried dippers of hot water from the stove reservoir to the dishpan in the iron sink. After gathering up the dirty dishes, washing and rinsing them with more hot water, they were left to dry. The floor had to be swept of its telltale bits of flour and dust. Only then were my chores done.

If Gramma had happened to make a cake, my grandfather would often appear at clean-up time to assure me that it was his turn to "lick" the bowl! Usually we shared the treat, but those times of helping and silly fun gave me an insight into my grandparents that I otherwise would have missed.

After my grandfather passed away, I spent several months with my grandmother to keep her company. By then her strict, old-fashioned ways seemed unreasonable to me, but I've always been glad I had those precious days in Gramma's kitchen.

❖ Our Easter: 1942 ❖
by Elisabeth R. Donaj, Greenfield, Massachusetts

I can not forget.

We had just prepared to celebrate Palm Sunday in my home town of Lübeck, Germany. The annual ceremony was for young persons who had reached a point of maturity. They were to become confirmed members of their churches. Families had made preparations for that important event.

But it was wartime. Air attacks were the signs of war we had to live with. On that particular Palm Sunday, our beautiful city, the gothic queen of the famous Hanseatic League, became a target. Waves of bombers hit Lübeck all night long. Destruction was immeasurable; the loss of lives and property hit us all hard. The suffering was without end. Every person who had come away with their life had to make adjustments in ways unimaginable by all.

Then, Easter was upon us. Not for a minute in our splintered lives could we consciously direct our minds towards celebration. But a big surprise was offered my family that Easter morning. Out of another world, or so it seemed, appeared a courageous man. He was driving a team of strong horses pulling a flatbed wagon. He came to us and told us about how they had made their way with difficultly through the thickest of hindrances: high piles of rubble, miles of it, and over many rubber fire hoses.

He had come to fetch my mother, me and my scared, shivering, little daughters. He hauled us away from danger and hunger to be at his safe, country home for an Easter meal and to rest! Once there, that savior's family even staged an Easter egg hunt for the little ones. They never understood how special that loving gesture was to all of us.

The rescuer who had come for us had truly become our savior on that Easter day. His love for our mother, his aunt, had motivated his action. Prior to that event he had just been a dear relative and my mother's favorite nephew.

And so the world turned…

❖ Yellow Butterflies ❖
by Edith J. Fisher, Leyden, Massachusetts

Several years ago, a friend and I went to see a couple of friends in Halifax, Vermont. We went via the Green River Road, which is my favorite ride. It's beautiful along the river!

We must have gone about three-quarters of the way up from the Ten Mile Bridge when we hit a spot where some yellow butterflies were just hatching. There were thousands of them! I stopped the car. We were both awed by the sight. We just sat and watched. They were in the trees and in the air, flying everywhere. You can't imagine what a sight it was!

When we decided to move on, I was so afraid I'd run over some. We moved on.

❖ Montague, Memories ❖
by Alice Fisk, Greenfield, Massachusetts

My children asked one night about Montague Center, Massachusetts, not the old history, but through the last sixty years. I will try to remember what it was like in 1937 when I first moved there.

Though I was born in 1919 in Montague City, my family (railroad) moved often and I grew up in North Adams and Greenfield, Massachusetts. At eighteen I married Harry Fisk and on October 31, 1937, we moved to a small apartment in the Griesbach (next to the Grange Hall) house in Montague Center. That little four-room flat has housed many newly married couples.

The apartment was heated with an oil-burning kitchen stove, had a black slate sink, no sink in the bathroom. At that time a long porch served both upstairs apartments. Myron and Charlotte Griswold and two, then three small children lived in the other side. In the whole downstairs was the Dresser family: Bill, Marion and nine children.

Next door in the Loveland house was Mrs. Harrington, Louie's mother, and in a small side apartment was Mrs. Prentice, Mrs. Harrington's mother. Louie and Barbara Loveland and their sons, Donald, David and ??? (I can't remember the third son's name) lived in a small house in the back.

In the next small house was Harley Wiggins, a short, stout, ex-railroad man. Next was the brick house. Emma Griswold and her daughter and granddaughter lived upstairs. I do recall that that house had the bathtub in the kitchen. I do not recall who lived downstairs. The house at the corner of School Street was the Clapp house and I do not remember them. Across School Street was a big, old, store building and at the time either Roger Newton or Lee Sawin was running a grocery store there. It did not stay in business long. The store was demolished and Leonard Wonsey built a house.

Next up the street was Buckmaster's general store (the only store left. Now it's called the Minimart). It was really an old time store with a pot-bellied stove in the center (chairs around for the men to sit and talk). Along one side were barrels with beans, split peas, crackers, etc. There were cookies in boxes with isinglass tops and you could fill your own bags. There was an odd set-up between the store and the upstairs apartment. A tube went up thru the ceiling and when Mrs. Root (who owned the building) wanted to order something, she whistled into the tube and when she was answered, she placed her order. You could buy about anything there from kerosene to potatoes as well as winter underwear and boots and fresh meat and vegetables.

In one of the houses south of the store, there were beautiful parquet floors. A Mr. Hapgood had put them in. He also made inlaid furniture pieces. In the brick house on the corner was Mrs. Rockwell, who was a reporter for the Greenfield paper.

Beyond the intersection on the other corner was where Esther Coburn lived. She was the lady who painted the mural in the chapel of the Congregational Church. There was another house, built into the side of the hill, that was torn down later and a garage for equipment for the water department was built. Down the road on the opposite side there was a gas station. I believe it was run at that time by Lee Sawin.

Coming back north on Main Street and down into South Main Street, Clyde Hale had a feed store. He had a truck and made deliveries around town. I think his storage building is still there. On the east side of Main Street, the corner house was where Bill Dixon lived. He had a wholesale candy distribution business. Next to him in the big house was where the Cobbs lived. She was the widow of a doctor, and her son, Harold, lived with her. The next house was Arthur Fiske and the next one was

Mabel Lincoln. She was the piano teacher who taught generations of young Montague children (including mine).

There was a little lane next to her house that led down to the laundry. John Payne had run the laundry for many years. One of this services included washing the clothes and returning them wet to be dried and ironed at home. Charlie Ripley had a shop on this lane. He was the leader of the Sea Scout unit and helped many boys to build yachts. (My husband Harry's yacht seems to be the only one to be restored and is at the Historical Society in the Masonic building). Warren Welch lives there now.

In the brown corner house was where John Payne lived. The Masonic Temple was next and the caretaker lived in an apartment there. On the corner of Union Street was a market and butcher shop. Mr. Hoyle ran it at that time and some years later Albert Graves ran it.

Then beyond that was the Montague Inn. It was a long building, fronted with a veranda. At the end there was a small soda fountain. There was a dining room and many large groups met there. On the second floor there was a dance hall that featured a spring floor. At one time movies were shown for the children in town in this hall.

In the columned house was the family of Albert Clark. Mr. Clark was a farmer and had land in the meadows. He kept his work horses in his barn and every morning would hitch them up and go to work in his fields. He also was agent for the Grange insurance and had an office in his house. There was a building next door, a sort of English style with a second-story overhang. This building has since been torn down. Downstairs was Jim Manning's antique shop—mostly just secondhand furniture and odds and ends. There were outside stairs to the tenement upstairs.

The Misses Dean, who were both nearly 100 years old, lived in the next house. Their father had been a doctor. I interviewed one of them on her 100th birthday (I worked for the Springfield paper). When I asked her if she ever worked, she drew herself up and said, "Of course not, I am a lady!!" Later when I collected for some charity, she gave me a quarter and her housekeeper gave me a dollar.

The Post Office was in the next building. Lyman Wilder was postmaster at that time. He had handrails to help him get around as he was very lame. The mail still came in several times a day by train and Mr. Doolittle carried it back and forth. When we needed a ride to the train, he was always willing to give us a ride for a small tip. Later Mr. Webber carried the mail.

The next house was Isaac Newton's. He ran an auto agency on School Street. I believe he sold Buick cars. He also had a gas station on School Street. The house next to the church was the summer home of the Coffman family. Mrs. Coffman had been a Clark and her Grandfather Chenery had built the house and the family had always stayed there. Mr. Coffman was a lawyer in Washington, D.C.

Next was the Congregational Church. Outside it has not changed much over the years. The storage building is comparatively new.

So on to the side streets. Where the fire station is now was the Grange Hall. Across the street was Newton's garage and next to it was a blacksmith shop run by Walter Eddy and he still had an active business then. Later Ed Murphy bought it and ran it for a time. The only other house then was Pete O'Kula's.

The old, two-story, brick school was next to the school pond. All eight grades were there in the 10 rooms. There were no school lunches, but Mrs. Covey did serve cocoa and hot soup at noon. The school burned in 1945. Buckmaster's house was next to the school and there were two small houses across the street.

On Central Street across from the common was Luke Field's general store. They sold about everything. I bought a kerosene lamp there during the '38 hurricane. There was a gas pump in the front. To the left of that, was Etta Field's dry-goods store. It went out of business just about that time. Across the common was the Unitarian Church that still held occasional services. They sold it to the Grange in 1938 and it was renovated to the present Grange Hall.

Varney lived in the house next to the Grange and the big house on Central Street was "Mama" and Les Newton's. Mr. Newton was the ice man and ran a small farm. Mrs.Newton ran a boarding house and often had summer guests and served meals to many local folks. She raised many children besides her own and was very active in the community. In the little house next door, Lucy Fisk and her mother lived, and the Cutler's lived in the corner house. In the big, brick house across was the Lawrence family. Bartley's store was across on the corner. This was mostly groceries and meat, but there was also a gas pump in the front. The family lived in a tiny house beside the store, now torn down.

The other houses along Bridge Street are now about as they were then . . . Brown . . . Aubrey. Then across the bridge on the right were Owen Johnson's and Mrs. Gillette and Nellie Rist. There was a gas station across from the cemetery run by Cy (??) and then up at the corner of Swamp Road was Charlie Bardwell's. On the other side, there were several houses: Belado, Koch, Gunn, and in the brick house the Brice family. At the start of Greenfield Road was Martin's machine shop and Ray George's engraving business. Below that was Fiske's sawmill. Another house was on the left side and called the light house because it had many windows. It burned several years later. The little red house across the street was Grandma Lyman's.

We bought Shad Allen's shop on North Street in 1946. It was built by Ed Whitney in 1888 and had been used as a woodworking shop making croquet mallets, whippletrees, and broom handles. In the north end of the building was a blacksmith shop and the big double doors allow use for this. At that time there were only four houses on North Street: Merritt Richardson, the Loomis brothers, and Nellie Sadowski.

Up at the corner of Central Street was Luke Field and Chrisabel Burns. The Burns' were summer people. Along Central Street were Farwell's on the north side and across was Kate Hayden. Dr. Warren Thomas lived upstairs there and had two rooms for an office downstairs. Ruby Hemenway and her mother lived in the next house. Across in the big, pillared house was the Bartlet family. He had a dairy farm and at that time ('38) still drove his cows up Main Street to pasture every morning and home at sundown. Down a farm road beside the farm was a swimming hole in the Sawmill River.

Union Street is much the same in looks. The families have changed many times and the colors of the houses. I did forget to mention that on Union Street near Main, George Chapin had a coal and oil business.

Rollins Mill on lower Central Street was a summer home for the Connecticut family and next to it was a small dam that backed up a pond. It was fed by a canal behind Union Street. There was another gas station on what is now Route 63.

The trains still ran a local or two and we could (and did) go to Greenfield at 2:30 and return on the number 60 at 5:20. We often did this. Also, my folks lived at that time in North Adams, so we went there as well. The station was open for waiting, but you had to buy your ticket on the train. Next to the track there was a Potter Grain store.

The Grange was very active at that time with 100 or more at the meetings. The Masons also had a large membership and there was an Eastern Star group. The P.T.A. was busy as well with a large membership. There were active Boy and Girl Scouts and 4-H clubs later.

❖ A Ride is a Ride ❖
by William R. Fitzgerald, Ashfield, Massachusetts

Today it is unwise, and even illegal, to ride kids in the back of a truck, but not so sixty or seventy years ago. Of course there wasn't as much traffic on the roads, and it definitely went slower, and most of all when kids were told to sit down, they sat. During the early thirties there were many families who didn't have a car, much less a truck. Or, if they had a car it was "up on blocks" to save the tires until they could afford to run it again.

My father bought a farm in Conway, Massachusetts in the late 1920s, just before the economic storm clouds hit. He sold his business and home, taking a second mortgage. His plan was to let those second mortgage payments pay off his farm. Then the Depression hit, and all plans went awry. The bank foreclosed on the first mortgage on the business and said my father could take the business back, but he would have to assume the first mortgage that they held. But between the buyer's ineptness and the economic climate, all that remained was just a building. He opted to stay on the farm, but it must have been especially tough. Even under normal circumstances, it would have been hard.

His brother was out of work, as were most men in the cities, and hadn't registered his car. He used to hitch a ride on the milk truck from Willamansett, Massachusetts and work all week in Conway, taking home a big box of apples, potatoes, or milk and eggs. One less mouth to feed in the city and he came home with some groceries. My dad's five-year-old Studebaker was up on blocks, needing tires. I remember that the telephone company went up on their rates by twenty-five cents without notification and Dad called up and cancelled the phone. The cattle dealers did a number on this greenhorn from the city, trying to buy a few cows so he could ship milk for a couple of cents a quart.

After a few years Dad finally bought an old International Truck and it became our mode of transportation. We three kids, a hired man and as many as four foster kids rode in the body, with some old car seats. Three-foot sideboards broke the wind and some old blankets kept us more or less warm. We even went shopping at the Five & Dime in Greenfield, Massachusetts on a cold, Saturday night in December. I don't remember anyone *not* wanting to go because it was too cold.

One summer night Dad took us all the way to the Victoria Theater in Greenfield to see Bradley Kincaid, the cowboy singer we heard on WBZA Radio. We always listened to him and had in our mind a vision of a big, rugged cowboy in working garb. (The Marlboro Man(TM) was invented in kids' minds long before Marlboro cigarettes were). What we saw was a little, puny guy decked out in fancy—even gaudy—togs, with horn-rim glasses and a cowboy hat that seemed so big it could tip him over. He never sounded quite right again. In other words, he went down on our charts.

Dad had a way of rewarding us each year after haying was done. We all climbed into the back of the truck with a picnic lunch and went to Look Park, in Northampton, Massachusetts or Forest Park, in Springfield, Massachusetts for the day. What a treat that was in a day when many kids didn't get out of Conway before they went to high school!

Once we went all the way to Benson's Animal Farm in Nashua, New Hampshire. We took a half dozen neighborhood kids with us, too.

There was plenty of room in the truck. I recall the oldest girl sat down below the sideboards while all the rest of us shouted and waved at everyone in town. She was too embarrassed to be seen riding in a truck, but not embarrassed enough to stay home.

It didn't take great things to please us. I guess in life all things are relative.

❖ Bill Daniels ❖
by Margaret "Peg" Folgmann, Shelburne Falls, Massachusetts

Bill Daniels was known by all in our small town of Conway, Massachusetts, population less than 1,000 in the 1930s. Many individuals of prominence, who passed on years ago, have long since been forgotten. Bill will never be forgotten as long as there are folks alive who knew him.

Bill was born into this world to parents and a family of good character and living. Early in life, Bill married and was the father of two sons who grew up to be fine people. Bill took to the bottle and lost his wife and children; I'm not sure which came first. He became a hermit. He lived in a Cape Cod house just off Ashfield Road on Hickory Ridge Road. The house is still there on the right, before going across the bridge that goes over the South River.

My brother and I enjoyed visiting with Bill and did so often. Intoxicated or sober, he had many interesting stories to tell. I never remember Bill coming into our yard, but we went to him. Bill told stories about elephants and tigers on the hills around us. We never doubted for a minute that he saw them. We knew better, though.

It was fun, too, to pick blackberries Bill had at the back of his house. Bill would pick as droplets of perspiration ran down his bearded face, off his nose and chin and into the baskets of berries all spoken for by ladies in the village . . . we never told!

One of Bill's paying jobs was to clean out outhouses for folks. He had an old horse he harnessed up and attached to a stone boat, onto which he loaded full wooden tubs, replacing them with empty ones. Some of the sewage was spread on the ground in his berry patch . . . Miracle Grow!

Bill seldom washed or changed his clothes. He was all one color. He gave forth an aroma hard to forget. Bill liked children; he seemed to enjoy our company. We did manage to get into his house once in a while. We lived across the river in the Hemmingway place. Bill's house was also all one color. The odor was a combination from Bill, two mangy beagle dogs, a woodstove, and whatever kettle of food was on the stove for himself and his dogs.

One time, Bill shut his oven door not knowing that one of his dogs had climbed in to keep warm. We knew on a few occasions that Bill held illegal dog and cock fights in one of his sheds. We know now who, no doubt, reported the games and we were relieved.

Bill was a craftsman of sorts. He made beautiful hickory wood ax handles, known as helves at that time. He chose the lighter portion of the wood and used a template to cut out the handles. He would use a sharp drawshave, then a rasp and pieces of broken glass to bring about a smooth surface. His ax handles were the best. It was a pleasure to watch him craft them.

Bill could be seen every few days walking to the village for his groceries and booze. He walked with dispatch on his way to the village, but often staggered back home. The distance was close to three miles each way. He often talked to himself on his way home.

Bill received financial aid. Massachusetts prided itself, and rightfully so, on a wonderful plan to support those unable to do so. A 5% tax was added to the bill for meals at all restaurants. It was known as "Old Age Tax." No one seemed to object. Social Security did not come into being until 1935. Bill received a dollar a day. It seemed to be enough. At that time a man could earn a dollar for each cord of wood he cut. It was not difficult to cut a cord a day. No power tools then either.

Bill would cut enough wood to keep from freezing in winter, but never seemed to cut enough ahead so that it would have a chance to dry. We worried when we saw no smoke from his chimney some mornings.

When Harold and Edwina Fournier opened the local market in Conway, Bill traded there. He asked Harold for bones which he'd stew up for the dogs and himself. Harold never charged him for the bones. If the weather was bad or if Bill wasn't in a condition good enough for the trip home, Harold would drive him home, leaving his wife alone to tend the store. If someone came in requesting a certain cut of meat requiring handling a quarter or side of beef, it was too much for Edwina to lift. Eventually, Harold had to tell Bill that he could no longer leave the store to drive him home. Bill took offense. Poor Harold drove all the way back to the store with his car windows wide open in an attempt to clear the car of the awful stench. Rarely did folks pick up old Bill, but some did and were scolded severely by family members who found disagreeable, lingering odors in their vehicle.

One Fourth of July after dark, a few young fellows in town, including my father, had a plan for Bill. Nothing malicious intended, just helpful. They collected a full set of clothing, soap, and towels. Knowing that Bill wouldn't go willingly, they lured him into a vehicle and took him to the reservoir, undressed him, and literally scrubbed him from head to toes and put all clean clothes on him. All of this was not accomplished without a struggle, not only for Bill, but for the fellows doing the job as well. Bill hollered and yelled. The fellows were as gentle as possible and constantly reassured him that they were "doing it for his own good." Bill settled down when they told him that they were all going down to the Hotel for a bite to eat. No harm came of the incident.

One very cold winter day, on our way home from school, we saw Bill lying in the snow bank beside the road, not far from Hickory Ridge Road. It was snowing and he was partially covered. There he lay with his bran sack beside him. He was unable to get up. Surely when the plow made the next run, it would be difficult to see him. I stayed with Bill, and my brother Russ went home to get a sled. Bill groaned and grunted as he attempted to get up. He seemed somewhat disoriented. He was no doubt suffering from hypothermia. Russ returned with dispatch and we loaded Bill onto the sled. As he was pulled along, he had to be steadied as he was restless. It was mostly downhill. Soon we had him into his house and on his cot in the kitchen. It was a struggle. We started a fire and made sure that Bill was okay before leaving. The next day, Bill accused us of taking money from him. This was not so, but I'm not sure he was convinced. He had received his Old Age check, had stopped in for refreshments and no doubt someone might have taken advantage of him. Certainly we didn't.

Bill was getting along in years by that time, but he managed to get by on his own. He seemed to enjoy splitting wood, was often seen scything and kept brush trimmed and high grass cut around his place.

We wanted to get a photo of Bill, but felt that he would object. Our family had a Brownie box Kodak camera, but feared Bill's reaction to that much attention.

One day, years later, while at the Eldridge farm, I saw Bill walking up the road. Pretending that I was taking pictures of my son, I talked Bill into getting a photo of him sitting on the porch with Freddy. It worked. My son looked rather uneasy, but I got the job done. Bill's way of life didn't allow him to contribute much, but he was not a menace to society.

There was no one to rescue Bill years later when he fell in the snow and nearly froze to death. He had been drinking and walking was a problem. When Bill was found, he was transported to the hospital where he suffered severely from gangrene resulting in death.

We'll always remember old Bill.

❖ Spring❖
by Katherine L. Forster, Orange, Massachusetts

See the fields
Sparkling and white
Be of good cheer
Spring soon will be here
We have nothing to fear

I look at the scene
Fields so pure and white
And, tell myself
"No snow will be left
It will turn overnight
To a green that's just right."

The fields tell the story
If they're green or snowy
The sun shines bright
It's all just right
Spring's here—a beautiful sight.

❖ After My Phil ❖
by Suzanne Gluck-Sosis, Greenfield, Massachusetts

Phil and I were so fortunate to be in this house in Greenfield, Massachusetts for the final days of his life. Surrounded by evergreen trees, witness to all the chickadees, titmice, finches, cardinals, mourning doves, red-bellied woodpeckers, blue jays that came to our feeders or ground fed. We felt blessed, despite sensing that Phil was dying.

About one and a half months before Phil died a strikingly handsome bird appeared at the feeder in the middle window of our living room. We had never seen such an elegant creature! It reminded me of figures in Egyptian paintings with its sleek, brown head and glistening, black body.

Referring to Peterson's "Field Guide to Birds," we learned it was a cowbird, a smaller member of the blackbird family. It grew to be seven to eight inches long and the female was uniformly gray. Describing it to others, we heard stories about the bird, some of which were contradictory: that it was arrogant, put its eggs in other birds' nests, pushed newborns out of nests, was a companion to cows, was extremely hungry; that it was a gentle bird. What we saw was that it was a cheeky one! It filled the feeder with its body, puffed itself up, spread its wings, and chattered, keeping all the other birds, except its mate, away. He would puff himself up and "talk" to her and she would come right back with her own opinion. He was there every day, constant and steady. We wished we had a translator. When I told my daughter, Louisa, about the cowbird, she suggested that he was the bird of death coming to guard Phil and accompany him in his transition to the other side. Could that be possible?

One day, missing the view of other birds, I decided to remove the feeder, hoping the cowbirds would leave. A few days later, a male, rose-breasted grosbeak appeared, a rare visitor, and so the feeder was returned to its spot on the window. Almost immediately, the cowbird took back its place and the grosbeak was gone. It was no use; it seemed the cowbird was there to stay.

Four days before Phil was taken to the hospital for x-rays, another male cowbird joined the resident pair and they all stayed until Phil died at the hospital. Then I never saw them again. Perhaps they did come to accompany Phil on his journey.

Immediately after the cowbirds disappeared, a flock of black, shiny crows settled at the feeder in the backyard, raucously cawing, playing with a piece of wood on and around the railing in front of the house, congregating five at a time. One even squeezed itself onto the seed tray, which was no mean feat as he was huge. When I visited my friend, Lin, and told her about the crows, she pulled out her Medicine Card set and we looked up "crow." Its characteristic "keeper of the sacred law." Its cawing has to do with crying out against injustice and righting wrongs. It felt to me as if the crows were there to give me a message. This was to be my path now that Phil was gone.

❖ Field Days Revisited ❖
by Dorothy G. Hmieleski, South Deerfield, Massachusetts

As a child in elementary school, in Montague Center, Massachusetts, one of the events that I looked forward to greatly was the annual "field day" which was held on the baseball field across the street from the school. What I did not realize at the time was that I was participating in a tradition that began in the town of Montague in 1927 and lasted through 1958.

There were many good aspects to the event from a child's point of view. The field days were carefully orchestrated events that required much practice. Each class first began practicing the dance or exercise that was to be performed inside, but as soon as the weather turned warm in the spring, we went outside to practice. We were carefully lined up by height, boys on one side, girls on the other, then by class (first-graders in front), and then we marched down to the field. There the classes were positioned about the field and performed one at a time. What this meant was that many warm, sunny afternoons were spent practicing for field day rather than sitting in the classroom.

While there was no formal dress code for field day, the boys usually wore white shirts and often white pants as well, and the girls wore white or pastel-colored dresses. The clothes were enhanced by bright, crepe-paper decorations (hats, aprons, armbands, or other insignia) that were designed by the art teacher and made by the children in their classrooms.

Finally, when the field day itself arrived, the field would be surrounded by parents with younger sisters and brothers who watched the festivities and clapped and cheered after each performance. The afternoon ended with the distribution of a Dixie cup ice cream for each child.

❖ Liederkrantz Cheese
or Why Mrs. Furman Stopped Parking at the Loading Dock ❖
by Dick Hoyt, Winchendon, Massachusetts

My father's store, R. W. Hoyt Appliances and Propane Bottled Gas Company "Florence and Glenwood Ranges—Norge—Philco Appliances," used to be at 54 Bridge Street, Shelburne Falls, Massachusetts, two doors east of Baker's Pharmacy.

For a while, right after buying the business from Mr. Burnap in the 40s, Father kept the tanks of bottled gas next to the barn up in our backyard on Maple Street. As the business grew, he built a concrete loading platform out from the back of the store where the parking lot behind the bank and pharmacy are today. The platform was at the level of the body of the '49 red, ¾ ton Chevrolet pickup truck and the two-hundred-pound, full cylinders no longer had to be hoisted up from the ground and tossed into the truck. Father would back up to the loading platform, cup the cover of a cylinder in one hand, tilt it on its rounded base, and, pushing on the tank's shoulder in a circular motion, walk it to the back of the truck body where it was roped to the wooden sideboard, usually along with two or three other tanks.

Both the bottled gas cylinders and the various ranges and refrigerators were taken in and out of his shop via the loading platform in back of the store. He also had a steady repair business of these appliances. The front of the store was reserved for new models.

The pace of business was slower in the late '40s and early '50s. There was always time to visit. Father had good friends and enjoyed them. He had a Yankee sense of humor: quiet, and gentle. Guys my father had known since childhood were always coming into the back of the store to visit.

Then there was Mrs. Furman. She drove to town once or twice a week from her home on Route 2 east of town, in her old, huge, brown, Packard touring car. She invariably parked right in front of Father's loading platform when she saw the empty space. Father would come back from a delivery, see the touring car, swear a bit (he was not a heavy curser by habit), park the truck elsewhere, drop the bottled gas cylinders off the platform, and toss them into the back of the truck from the pavement, and wait for Mrs. Furman to move her car before backing the truck into its usual place.

Father avoided confrontations. It was against his nature to yell at anyone. It was beyond his imagination to think that someone would be so thoughtless as to park in front of that platform. But there are limits...

It had been a long day. It was August. He had just come back from North Heath, Massachusetts on a gas delivery and knew he had to turn around and head out for Ashfield right after loading up. (We didn't have a radio in the truck in those days.) There was probably a customer out of gas with a roast in the oven and most anxious about her dinner. And there was Mrs. Furman's touring car parked right in front of the loading dock with its owner nowhere in sight.

Oh yes, I forgot to mention: Father loved cheese. Not just any kind of cheese, though. It had to be strong, with an odor. And Liederkranz cheese met the criteria. It was soft, with a greenish/blue hue that smelled to me of rotten eggs. I couldn't stand to be anywhere near it. Father loved it. He even kept a chunk of it in a refrigerator right there in the shop for his lunch.

I don't know which one of Father's chums happened to be in the shop that day. It could have been his brother John, who owned C. W. Hawks Insurance down at the other end of Bridge Street. It might have been Lloyd Kratt, unless he was working on the B&M that day, or it could just have been Dick Gerry there in the shop. But Father had had enough of Mrs. Furman.

One of them sliced a thick slab of Liederkranz cheese from the block. Then the two of them crept out the back door of the shop, went to the front of the huge touring car, unlatched one side of the engine hood, and placed the slab of Liederkranz on the exhaust manifold next to the huge, straight, eight cylinder engine. They closed the hood, retreated back into the shop and waited.

A half hour later, Mrs. Furman returned from her shopping, got into her car, backed out of the parking lot, and drove away. I don't know how or when she discovered what had been done to her car. I can only imagine what that melted cheese on the hot manifold of her car smelled like as the car warmed up. Or how she figured out who was behind the smell. Or how, once discovered, she managed to rid the car of the odor of rotten cheese. All I do know for certain is that Father found that spot free for the rest of the time he owned the business.

❖ That's the Way It Was in the City ❖
by Leona Jarvi, Athol, Massachusetts

The Depression years are certainly a time to remember. I was born in 1929, two months before the stock market crashed. The first four years of my life were in Keene, New Hampshire. It was country living for us, which wasn't all that bad because Dad and Grandpa raised a vegetable garden and Grandma did the canning. Some farmers shared their meat for a small price. It was the city that was hard, especially Detroit, Michigan. Detroit relied on their industry. Plants and factories were closed down and bread lines were long.

When I was about four years old, Dad and Mom divorced. We went to Detroit with our dad in his 1929 Whippet. We lived in a duplex home on the East Side. The alley was our backyard. Dad worked in W.P.A. (Work Progess Administration), which was a work program for the unemployed, set up by President Roosevelt.

The alley was always busy with peddlers and their horse-drawn wagons, calling out their wares in a sing-song fashion. They could be heard way off in the distance. The rubbish men collected newspapers and rags, singing "Any rags today and newspapers?" We couldn't afford the paper and we had to wear our rags so we never had any to throw on the wagon.

Local Color 379

We used to go up and down the alley looking for edible fruit, also Wonderbread(TM) wrappers. Twelve wrappers taken into the store could get you a little mini-loaf of bread.

At Thanksgiving time, a charity group called the Oddfellows would drop off a turkey and a bag of little new potatoes the size of marbles. The Salvation Army was there for us at Christmas time with toys—dolls for the girls and trucks for the boys, blackboards for all of us. Dad bought what he could and Mom and Grandma sent gifts from New Hampshire and Maine.

We had a small icebox and Dad managed to save money for the ice man. He would put his card in the window for twenty-five pounds.

Coming off the Depression was a slow process. We were off welfare, but we were still among the poorest folks.

When we first arrived in Detroit, I was petrified. I never had seen any black folks before and I was scared of them because I didn't know any better. Where we lived, on Sherwood Avenue, there were mostly African-Americans, referred to in those days as colored or Negro. Those looking for trouble would call them worse names. There were a lot of fights amongst the black and white children because someone couldn't keep their tongue in check.

I learned very early in those days how to fight. Mostly because I had a sister two years older than I who was mildly retarded and other children teased her a lot. This instigated a fight.

I was about four years old when I fell off a boat my uncle was building and broke my arm. Dad took me to the Detroit Hospital. I was scared of all the people waiting with legs and arms all bandaged up. I jumped behind a door and a little colored boy was there hiding. He saw me and he screamed. Now! Here are two kids screaming. He had to be just as afraid of me as I was of him. My arm was put into a splint (they didn't use a cast in those days). I don't remember all of the healing time.

I was five when I went into kindergarten. My sister and I usually ran all the way home from Cooper School. There was so much in city living we were afraid of. We played in the alley and the field out back of our place. My sister and I had only one pair of skates between us, so we each wore one skate and pushed with the other foot to keep rolling. The skates were clamped onto our shoes using a skate key to tighten them on.

As the sun was going down, there was a lady who would show up once in a while to read stories to all of the kids in the neighborhood. We would look out into the alley and look for a little bonfire going with someone sitting around it, and we would know it was her. I don't remember the stories she read, but I do remember her. We also played Kick-the-Can in the alley; we played hop scotch and jump rope on the sidewalks.

Dad made a big deal out of Halloween, bobbing for apples and playing post office. We made our own costumes out of old rags and sheets and charcoal (from the cinders under our stove) to color our face. We went from door to door saying, "Please help the poor." Pennies were tossed into our cups. One time I got eight cents.

Sometime around 1935 we went back to Keene, New Hampshire, to our grandparents' for less than a year. We saw our mother once (she lived in Maine with her new husband).

My dad's sister came up from Detroit to bring us back. That's when we learned we had another sister, by my dad's first marriage. Dad had gone to Bloomington, Indiana, to get her.

By now I had become a tomboy. I found an old pair of pants and cut the legs off. By the time I ended up cutting, I ended up with a pair of shorts. Dad let me wear them so long as I didn't leave the yard. Girls didn't wear pants in those days, much less shorts!

Boys used to spit, so I picked up the habit. This didn't set right with Dad. He made me sit on the steps behind him. If I was to spit, it would be on this bald spot on the back of his head. Of course if I did he had his razor strop in his lap, which I would feel on my butt. I respected that strop, so I gave up spitting. Also, I didn't want to sit another day staring at that bald spot.

With food being scarce, I always looked out for myself. Often times I would sneak into the kitchen in the middle of the night. I'd put my hand into the bread bag and come up with a fistful of bread. One night I ended up screaming with my hand in pain. There was a mousetrap on it. The whole family was up. Dad was laughing. I saw nothing funny, but he thought the mice were getting into the bread. I guess it was a good laugh for all.

My dad was a drinking man, and when he decided to quit drinking, he turned very religious. He took us to all types of churches, from the Holy Rollers to the spiritual believers. I was baptized in a tabernacle with wooden benches and sawdust for the floor. The minister wore a white dress with a cape. All the children sat up on the stage with her. I had a white-caped dress with a blue print design on it. I thought I was the "Katz Pajamas" in this dress.

A Polish lady next door to us made a ruffled, black-and-white-striped dress for me to wear to her Catholic Church. I wasn't crazy about the hard, wooden board we had to kneel on. I told Dad I didn't want to go there again. That was okay, there were a lot more other churches he was getting us off to. I think he was getting out of hand with all this religion, because I remember hearing my aunt saying, "Roger, I think I would rather see you drunk than sober." This was after some heated words over all these churches and talk of religion all the time.

My sister and I were left alone one night. We were both under eleven years old. We were scared. Shadows were in the room and moving around; we were crying. My sister wouldn't wait alone while I ran a few doors down to get our aunt. She didn't want to go out either, so I just grabbed her hand and made her run with me down the alley. We must have looked like the devil was after us. Our aunt returned home with us and put on all of the lights in the front room. Nothing there but a sock and a shoe on the chair casting a shadow over the floor. She stayed with us until we went to sleep.

In the wintertime, we used to sneak up and down the alley onto the neighbors' back doorsteps and snitch the frozen cream on the top of the milk bottles that had been delivered during the night. Sometimes we were caught and chased away.

As the years slipped by, we adjusted to city life.

It was around 1939 when one day we heard a knock on the front door, which was hardly ever used. One of my brothers answered the door. We heard a lot of excitement and my brother called out, "It's Grandma." Well! We all went running. Grandma had bags full of things for us like crayons and coloring books. We introduced her to our sister from Indiana.

We didn't know it at the time, but Grandma was there to take us back East. It seems our sister was planning on getting married, so there wouldn't be anyone to look after us anymore. I became used to having another sister, so I knew I was going to miss her, as well as my dad. Grandma stayed a couple of weeks before we left.

There were a lot of tears the day we departed on the bus. We had a lot of mixed feelings saying goodbye to Dad and our sister. Yet, we were elated to think we were going to see our mother, who was now living in the town of Athol, Massachusetts, with her husband. It was a long trip with another viewing of Niagara Falls. We checked in at the Pequag Hotel in Athol the first night we arrived.

The next day we were all huddled in a corner while Grandma knocked on Mother's door. When Mother answered the door, we all popped out hollering, "Surprise" and surprised she was because Grandma never warned her that we were going to be there. She and my step-dad had only three rooms. We were surely crowded in until a larger place was found in this small town of Athol.

That was the end of living in the city with Dad. Now that's the way it was in the city.

❖ Radio ❖
by Irmarie Jones, Greenfield, Massachusetts

Actor and director Woody Allen had his "Radio Days," and I have had mine. I'll never forget what radio meant to me growing up in the 1930s in the depths of the Depression.

Who could resist "Jack Armstrong, the All American Boy," "Little Orphan Annie," or "Buck Rogers in the 25th Century?" Every weekday between 5:15 and 6:15 p.m. was the suspense-filled hour. My gang wouldn't miss it. No matter where we were playing, at 5:15 p.m., we'd rush into the house, crouch down on the floor, and listen to "Terry and the Pirates," with characters, of course, taken from the popular comic. The Dragon Lady sounded just the way she looked . . . sinister.

If I were home at 5:30 p.m., my younger sister, Maydee, and I would have our differences. She wanted to listen to "The Singing Lady," Irene Wicker, who told stories for Kellogg's. She had the wonderful talent of doing all the voices of the characters herself.

But, oh, I just had to turn on Jack Armstrong. I can still remember the words of the song that opened the program . . . "Wave the flags for Hudson High, boys, Show them how we stand. Ever shall our team be champions, Known throughout the land. Boola, boola. Boola, boola. Boola, boola. Boola, boo." Jack was supposed to be a student at Hudson High, but never seemed to go to school at all. Instead, he went on all kinds of exotic adventures around the world with his uncle and friends, Betty and Bob. I was glued to the set when that was on.

Then, at 5:45 p.m., "Little Orphan Annie." "Who's that little chatterbox, the one with pretty auburn locks? Cute little she, it's Little Orphan Annie," sang a man's voice, with organ accompaniment, to introduce the program. When Annie wasn't traveling around the world with Daddy Warbucks, she was home with Mr. and Mrs. Silo, solving a mystery. It's hard to believe, but all programs were live in those days. The actors read from scripts and the sound effects man was a very important person, creating the atmosphere. I was once told that to make the sound of rain, salt was shaken on a lettuce leaf close to the microphone.

On "Orphan Annie," usually something was given away to encourage the young listeners to buy Ovaltine. The secret decoder pins or special rings were yours for the Ovaltine seal from the top of the can. Our family could never afford that chocolate drink and that meant when the announcer gave out secret messages at the end of the program, I could never decode them.

Once an elderly neighbor gave me a seal. At that time the offer was a map of the town in which Annie lived with Mr. and Mrs. Silo. I came across that map recently in a box under the eaves. I suppose it is a campy collector's item now.

At 6 p.m. (news time on every station today) was "Buck Rogers in the 25th Century," my favorite. The show was introduced with a great roll that sounded like thunder. Buck, Dr. Heuer, and Wilma were always trying to escape the clutches of Killer Kane and Ardella. The amazing Rogers went to the moon, used disintegrator rays, and explored the planets. Their friend, young Willie, was once put into a state of suspended animation.

My sister and I would huddle around the radio to catch every word. Even our mother was interested. Little did we realize that the 25th century would be arriving in our lifetime.

On Sunday afternoons, my parents always listened to the New York Philharmonic, live, conducted by Arturo Toscanini. At first I found it very boring. Who wanted to listen to that dumb music? But, gradually, I came to enjoy it and began to recognize Schubert and Beethoven symphonies. That's when my love of classical music was born.

Sunday night brings especially warm memories: a game of Parcheesi after supper with our father and mother. Then, if we were washed and into our pajamas, my sister and I could stay up past normal bedtime to listen to Eddie Cantor. How well I remember the night Cantor introduced a new song, "Annie Doesn't Live Here Anymore," in that funny, high voice of his. In later years, there was Joe Penner . . . Joe who? . . . and Jack Benny. With those marvelous radio sound effects, you could hear Jack Benny walk down, down, down into his secret vault, hear the door creak.

Tuesday night was Fibber McGee & Molly and on Wednesday, Fred Allen. Just by their voices and the inflections, you could envision the characters of the loquacious Senator Claghorn, Mrs. Nussbaum, and the others Fred Allen visited every week in Allen's Alley.

All the characters on radio were as familiar and beloved as any you see on television today. And all of them are still living in my imagination.

❖ I Remember ❖
by Jean Kozlowski, Northfield, Massachusetts

Memorial Day always reminds me of my grandparents' visits to the cemeteries to pay tribute to those relatives who had died.

Grandma prepared, well before Memorial Day, by planting seeds and cuttings of geraniums that she grew in a sunny window in the upstairs bathroom. The geraniums were carefully transplanted into window boxes with sweet alyssum and greenery.

My grandfather's ancient Buick, with running boards supporting a trunk full of tools, was started up for the trips to North New Portland and Caratunk, Maine, and beyond. My grandma packed a picnic lunch of deviled eggs, cucumbers, cheese, homemade rolls, and her favorite molasses cookies. That, for me, was the best part of the trip.

The Buick puttered along the narrow roads, some merely dirt. The first cemetery was in North New Portland. My grandfather stood proudly on the ridge of stones representing five generations of Cottles. He scowled at his father's gravestone that had fallen during the winter. Quietly, they both set to work planting the large, red geraniums on the family plot.

Next was the obscure graveyard in what was known as Lexington. It was down a seldom used dirt road. About this time I was getting hungry, so Grandma told me as soon as we arrived she would spread out the blanket for us to picnic. My interests were not in the cemetery, but definitely on lunch.

The hushed silence of the place echoed everywhere. Not a soul in sight! I noticed very few plantings by the stones. I was told few relatives were alive now to attend to the graves. Flags fluttered in the breeze for those who had fought in wars.

I noticed my great-great-grandfather, John Nimmo's stone, with a three-leaf clover carved on each corner. He was an immigrant from Northern Ireland, my grandmother reminded me, and eventually arrived in Maine. His wife had been a teacher before she married him. The town, to honor the fact that she had been the first teacher, had erected a separate stone.

Caratunk was the next stop, to get my great Aunt Jessie. She traveled with us to the cemetery where her husband and son were buried. By this time I was bored and decided I needed another molasses cookie. Grandma had foreseen this and had carefully saved several cookies for our trip back.

By now most of the geraniums had been planted, grass clipped around the stones, and it was time to head back. I was reminded that I should remember where these plots were that belonged to the family. At ten years of age, contentedly chewing a cookie, I nodded my head that I would remember.

But roads and places change through the years and the next time I was to remember, I tried to find John Nimmo's grave. I searched many places. However, when I finally did find the right cemetery, my memory served me well as I said to myself, "I remember it was here." And so it was!

❖ Surprise at the Iron Bridge ❖
by Florence M. Lanfair, Turners Falls, Massachusetts

It was 1921 and I was nine years old. I lived in East Wilder, New Hampshire, just across the Connecticut River from Wilder, Vermont. We lived in a small settlement of six houses. We were a family of six: two parents, one brother, two sisters and me. I was the middle sister.

We had a very cold winter and the river froze over with thick ice. I remember when spring came, the ice in the river would begin to break up and we could hear it. There would be loud booming noises.

My sister and I used to walk to school. We crossed a large iron bridge, just above the dam. The dam made power for the International Paper Company mill. My dad and brother worked at that mill.

We were permitted to attend the Vermont school in Wilder, Vermont because it was much closer to our house and thus less walking for us.

One day as we approached the bridge, we saw a man with a movie camera on the shore. Out in the river, on a large cake of ice, was a lady floating down river. As we watched, the cake of ice went under the bridge and the lady was rescued just in time. She nearly went over the dam!

Later, we found out that they were making a movie. The lady we saw was Lillian Gish and the movie was called "Way Down East." My sister and I had a very exciting time. Years later I saw the movie.

❖ The Death of a Refrigerator ❖
by Elisabeth Leete, Ashfield, Massachusetts

He died peacefully, silently, at home, at age 32.

His demise took three days. One morning when I put my fingers on the frozen foods, they felt soft. I refused to worry. The next day the ice cubes had become water. I raised the thermostat to the coldest temperature, still hoping. But he still couldn't summon the strength to keep my food cold and fresh.

The next morning I cancelled all my activities, called an appliance store in Greenfield, Massachusetts, took measurements the best I could, called my daughter to ask for moral and driving support. She, being a wonderful daughter, obliged. I removed frozen foods, took them down to my freezer in the basement, sorted out the food too old to be saved, and drove to the dump.

Then came the sentimental work: the pictures.

Our house on Hawley Road in Ashfield, Massachusetts when my husband, Gurdon, and I, quite pregnant, bought it in the early autumn of 1964. The picture is tiny, and the house is a tiny white dot you can hardly see, drowned in pale orange trees and dark evergreens under a pale blue sky. We had bought the house and five acres of land for nine thousand dollars from a Polish carpenter who worked for J.C. Penney. It was the only house on the unpaved road except for Dan Howes' large house at the corner of Apple Valley and Hawley Roads, on the right side going towards Hawley. Then Dan begged us to buy his 70 acres on the same side for $2500 and we did. Little by little we sold much of our land. It was too much to take care of, and we needed income to pay for our daughter's education and our living expenses.

But I am losing track of Old Refrigerator and the pictures.

Here is Ted Howes the Patriarch, in a rocking chair at my neighbor Ellie's house, in Ashfield. He is wearing large boots, faded blue jeans, and a dark blue and white shirt. He looks straight ahead, his hands loosely crossed between his legs. His white hair and white beard are quite long and he looks straight ahead. You never really knew what he thought, but when you met him on the road as he drove his tractor or his old truck, you had to stop and chat about farming, obnoxious dogs, wild animals and nature, rain, snow, or shine.

On a black and white picture taken more than sixty years ago, my sisters and I stand smiling in front of a Swiss chalet, blissfully unaware that our father is close to death in a dark room in the chalet.

I am in the next one. I am in Sicily, seventy years of age, nonchalantly leaning against a wall in front of the blue sea and under a pale blue sky, holding a camera, my legs crossed, wearing white sandals, black pants, a blue shirt and a black cardigan. I look relaxed, but I am not relaxed at all, I won't tell you why . . . and now Lucy, my daughter, gratefully and humbly showing her summa cum laude diploma from UMASS nursing school. She wears a dark blue "Ashfield" sweatshirt and a thin crown of daisies against a bouquet of lilacs and a view of distant hills.

I am very fond of another picture of Ellie and me sitting on each side of her stone table back in Ashfield, probably in August. There is a bouquet of cosmos I had brought from my garden, and her sweatshirt matches the dark pink perfectly. It looks like a relaxed conversation. Ellie's head and neck are gently bent, in the same position as Norma's head and neck when she and I celebrated my birthday up the road at Teddy and Claire Pease's house. I wish I had a picture of Ted and Ruth Pease, Teddy's parents, to place on my new refrigerator. Next to the birthday party is a picture of Norma and I playing cello duets at the Art Bank in Shelburne Falls, Massachusetts. Enthusiastic amateurs that we are, we play in interesting places such as the hardware store and the pizzeria in Ashfield.

I have to mention the photograph of Bob and Marjorie Rosenthal, who live in Woodmere, Long Island. They were probably my husband's best friends, and Marjorie calls me every July 8 and every November 12 to commemorate Gurdon's birthday and death.

My new refrigerator arrived this morning. It was dragged from the road in snow and mud by two large, handsome, laconic black men in big boots who brought much dirt onto my kitchen floor, which I had to wash three times. Old Refrigerator was dragged on ice and mud onto a gray truck, and I couldn't help thinking of a body departing, silently, in a black hearse on a cold November day.

Soon, I will have to give a soul to my new refrigerator.

❖ Memories ❖
by Janice Howard LePore, Greenfield, Massachusetts

Branches of shrubbery danced
To the tune of the wind, whistling
Around the corner of the house.
A cold dreary day sunk
Into the shadows of the night.

The chill of the old farm house
Sneaked into her bones, but
The old woman continued to rock,
Staring across the barren field,
At a fading sunset on the horizon as
Her mind swirled with memories.

Siblings, school events, holiday parties,
Summer picnics, births and deaths,
Old friends, boys marching off to war,
Weeping wives consoling children.
Parents, stoic and proud, hearts fenced
In fear, their bodies a captive audience
With neighbors, flanking a corridor
Of fluttering flags, saluting the lost,
But not forgotten dead.

Time escaped the grasp of her frail
Fingers, but the solitude of the moment,
And the memories, warmed her heart.

❖ Memorials ❖
by Janice Howard Lepore, Greenfield, Massachusetts

It's a year later
An infinite period of time
To those who lost family and friends
On that infamous day in September.

Heroes were born in the dust and ashes
Pain and disbelief distorted the lines of diversity.
The vast cultures of America were challenged into
Confronting the vulnerability of our democracy.

Insidious veins of terrorism created doubt and fear
Ground Zero became a symbol of shattered dreams
Confusion and fear raged with the smoldering debris
Rancid smoke filled the lungs of selfless workers.

Today memorials of remembrance and sympathy
Seek justice and peace to the masses of heartbroken
Victims struggling to survive in a world of conflict,
Strength to families building futures with the knowledge
That life and liberty can never ever be taken for granted.

❖ A Gift was Given ❖
by Phyllis Loomis, Ashfield, Massachusetts

    A week ago, my car trunk was filled with half gallon cartons of fresh orange juice. They were a gift from an overflow in the grocery store. I just happened to be there at the right time. I took the trunkload to feed the hungry at the Greenfield, Massachusetts Community Meal, along with my hearty stew. There was much too much orange juice for the seventy hungry people to drink on the spot, and far too little to give everybody a bottle to take with them. I began giving orange juice to all my friends.

Yesterday in the parking lot of another grocery store, I opened my trunk to deposit my new groceries. Tucked deep in the back of the trunk was the last of the orange juice. A man, perhaps in his sixties, dressed in clothing that looked like he intended to take off when the warm weather returned, was coming around to the back of his battered pickup truck. He had just pulled in beside my car. I asked him if he could possibly use a half gallon or two of orange juice. He wanted the juice and gladly helped me pull it out of my trunk.

As he was putting two jugs into his truck bed, his short, round lady was getting out of her side of the truck. Her coat did not quite button in front. It was very cold that day. She held a small, white bundle of fur tightly against her chest over the open space.

When I asked if they could use just one more of the four remaining gallons, they consulted each other for a moment before agreeing that they could. He helped himself to another, and then closed my trunk. She meekly stepped directly in front of me, smiled broadly and stretched out both arms towards me softly saying, "This is for you."

I accepted her gift and thanked her as I looked down upon a lovely, soft, white teddy bear that obviously meant a great deal to her. I did not have a need for a teddy bear, but the gift was so warmly given I knew it was meant for me.

As I drove home with my new bear sitting in the front passenger seat, I kept thinking about its former owner and her partner because they suddenly seemed familiar. I had met them someplace not too long ago.

Ah, yes! I had recently served each of them some hearty stew.

❖ Memories of the Depression ❖
by Lorraine Madden, Greenfield, Massachusetts

My parents were hard-working people and when my father learned to be a baker, my parents bought a bakery store in Rosebank, Staten Island, New York.

Although we had a coldwater flat upstairs, as far back as I can remember we practically lived in a large room in the back of the store. My two sisters helped work in the store until they got married and left home. When my brother came of age, my father taught him the bakery business and he and my father did the baking. When I became thirteen years of age, I would help in the store after school and on weekends.

My mother employed a woman to help as the business flourished. Then in 1929 came the stock market crash. Newspapers had articles about unemployment. People that lost all their investments were jumping out of windows. The banks were having difficulty as people rushed to take out their savings.

In a short time, our bakery business felt the crash. Many of the customers were asking for credit as they bought the necessary food for the table. When they weren't able to pay their bills, they no longer came to shop and business got worse.

Finally, the day came when my parents were no longer able to pay their bills and credit was shut off. There were no more deliveries that necessitated our need to continue baking.

My parents spent sleepless nights, and one evening they sat down with my brother and me and admitted they were bankrupt. They could find no solution and decided to just leave everything behind and move away.

The decision was made, and one dark night, my parents and my brother moved our belongings and crept away at night to another state.

I was left behind for one more day to carry on so no one would know, especially the creditors.

I worked that day as usual with a small number of customers and that evening when it was dark I also left the premises leaving behind all the familiar things I grew up with in that large room.

As I placed the key in the lock for the last time, I paused with a feeling of sadness. I thought, "This is going to be a new phase in my life." I was just 18 years of age. Then the key turned and I took the bus to join my family.

❖ The Pencil Sharpener ❖
by Eileen Marguet, Greenfield, Massachusetts

Just as we were starting school in the fall, we each got a "pencil box." It was always blue, made of cardboard, and had a few pencils, a pen holder, some pen nibs, a small ruler, a soap eraser, and a pencil sharpener.

That sharpener got plenty of use. It turned a new pencil into a useful and necessary tool. We appreciated the newness of this arrangement.

There was just one thing that puzzled me. My family didn't lack for any of the essentials of learning, but my friend, Madeleine Kelley, had a mechanical pencil sharpener in her home. It was nailed to the wall and you inserted your pencil into a hole and turned the crank. Voila! You took the pencil out and there was a sharp point. I thought that was really nifty. Of course they had one in school, and perhaps in the public library, but none of my other friends had a pencil sharpener like that in their homes.

Years later when I was grown up and married, I bought what I thought was a sharpener like the one the Kelley's had. Somehow it was too flimsy or awkward.

We never had a satisfactory place to put it. Nailed to the woodwork, it was in the way. My husband wouldn't screw it into the desk because it would leave holes. We tried a few other sharpeners, but I would always end up using a pencil sharpener like the one in my pencil box.

Then another one came out. It was a cylinder, which took batteries. There was something unsatisfactory about that one, too. Either the batteries were the wrong number, or they were dead. I would have to resort to a little one that I bought for fifty cents.

Yesterday I had a carpenter doing some work here and he asked me for a pencil. The only ones I had were new and hadn't been sharpened. I knew Charlie could have sharpened one with a knife, but I reached into a drawer and found the small sharpener. In a few seconds there was a nice, sharp point.

They say, "The more things change, the more they remain the same." There are probably great sharpeners today, electric and manual, that cost several dollars, but they don't do any more than the one from my blue pencil box.

❖ Life on the Farm ❖
by Louise Bowen O'Brien, Colrain, Massachusetts

Back in 1920, when I was six years old, I lived on my grandfather's farm on the edge of Vermont. My two brothers and I ran wild, barefoot and happy. We explored all the buildings and delighted in climbing to the top of the barn. Up over the rafters we scrambled to the very top where we could peek through the slats of the cupola and see in the distance the top of Mount Greylock.

We loved the farm animals, especially the huge, black and white oxen that drew Grandpa's sled through the snow in March to gather sap from maple trees.

But we disliked the big red rooster. We thought he was mean to the hens. Whenever he "attacked" one of them, we would chase him away. Grandpa never said anything when he saw us chasing the rooster, but I did notice that he sort of grinned.

One pullet was our pet. She would follow us around and we could hold her and stroke her soft, brown feathers. We named her Petticoats. One day my little brother and I went to the south field to look for wild strawberries, and Petticoats followed us.

As we stooped looking for berries among the leaves, a shadow passed over our heads. Looking up, we saw a big, grey hawk hovering over the field. Before our startled eyes, it dropped out of the sky and landed on our little hen. Sharp talons pierced the poor bird's back. Before we could move, it had lifted our pet into the air and flown away with her. We screamed at it to drop her, but to no avail. With tears running down our cheeks, we went home without berries and without our pet.

Another time, Buddy and I went to a neighbor's house to bring home a quart of milk. It was quite a walk for young children, up to the main road and down the hill to the other farm. But we had gone there with our mother and assured her we could do it.

We picked up the tin pail of milk and thanked the elderly farm woman for the molasses cookies that she gave us to nibble on the way home. We were happy trudging up the hill swinging the pail between us.

We came to the top of the hill where the main road curved away toward the village. Our farm road led through some trees to the top of the field where our house was situated. We turned in that direction and came to a road through the trees, so we started down it.

We walked along and the trees grew thicker. We noticed that the road seemed rougher, but it must be our road. So we kept walking. Buddy got tired and began to complain because he didn't see our farm buildings, only more trees.

Finally when we were getting a little frightened, we came to a stop. A big tree had fallen right across the road.

Then I knew we were on the wrong road. We turned around and started back the way we had come. What seemed like a long time later, we met our mother coming to look for us. She explained that we had taken the old wood road, which was just before our farm road. She told us we were smart children to turn around when we found the fallen tree.

There were happy times on the farm, especially at Christmas. My grandfather would go into the woodlot and cut a big, beautiful spruce. His oxen would drag it home. Then Grandpa set it up in the living room and we had the fun of decorating it.

We made long chains of colored paper. Then we strung popcorn to drape over the branches. Mother showed us how to string cranberries to brighten the tree. She even hung a few bright oranges, piercing the skin with a darning needle and strong twine. This pleased and surprised us because we seldom had oranges. With a bountiful apple crop, Grandpa saw no need to buy store fruit. Last of all, our mother put on the lights. These were tiny candles held in little metal holders that clipped on the branches. It required great care so the flames would not ignite the tree. But how beautiful it was!

The best Christmas of my childhood was the year Santa Claus left me a little doll carriage, just right for my little Priscilla doll.

It was a different way of life, but oh, so dear in memory.

❖ Bedbugs & Root Beer ❖
by Joseph A. Parzych, Gill, Massachusetts

When my family moved to our farmhouse in Gill, Massachusetts we soon discovered that the bedrooms were infested with bedbugs. Bedbugs look like flat, brown lady bugs. After feeding on our scalps during the night, they'd swell with blood and turn a reddish, brown color. A substance they secreted numbed the skin so that their feeding didn't hurt us while they fed. The sores were small, but after the effects of their numbing secretion wore off the next morning, the sores itched and hurt. The loathsome bugs came back to feed, night after night. We hated those damned bedbugs and felt ashamed, fearing kids at school would find out we had an infestation of them and taunt us.

My mother would tear the beds apart and rub the crevices of the mattress with a rag soaked in kerosene. To get at bedbugs hiding in the coils of the bedsprings, she held a rag under the springs and poured kerosene onto the springs from the spout of a half gallon kerosene can. Bedbugs came running out. They'd fall to the floor and wave their legs for a few seconds before they died. She'd stamp them with her foot, giving a little grunt, as if to say, "There, you little bastards! Die!" even though they were dying or dead already. Sometimes their bellies popped with a little splotch of blood. I didn't feel sorry for the bedbugs, seeing it was my blood that made their bellies bulge.

Our beds stank of kerosene for weeks, and fumes stung our eyes until the kerosene evaporated. The treatment kept the bugs away for a while, but soon, more came out from under the wallpaper to chew spots on our scalps as we slept, making sores that never seemed to heal. We tore off the wallpaper, but they hid behind the plaster lathes where the horsehair plaster had fallen away, or between the cracks on walls covered with boards.

In the end it was the Raleigh man who saved us. He sold us some sort of insecticide. And by spraying every crack and crevice we could find, the hated bedbugs were, at long last, gone for good. "God Bless the Raleigh man," my mother said.

The Raleigh man came by the farm about once a month peddling patent medicines, household supplies, spices and miscellaneous extracts. The arrival of the Raleigh man was a little like Christmas morning. When he opened the back of the compartment on the back of his pickup to display his wares, we always looked with wonder at all the things we hadn't known we needed.

Ma was not supposed to have any money. Pa doled it out when she went into a store to shop and he'd have his hand out for the change when she got back to the car. But she'd short-change him, holding back a few coins so she'd have a stash of spending money. When she was short of cash, the Raleigh man took eggs in payment.

Ma always bought a squat, round, bottle of orange drink concentrate, root beer syrup, and a big bottle of vanilla. "This is good stuff," the Raleigh man said out of the corner of his mouth as he held the vanilla. "It's 80 proof."

Once, I told Ma we still had a small bottle nearly full of vanilla in the cupboard. She got red in the face and grinned. The Raleigh man grinned, too. Ma always bought the big bottle, but I never saw it in the cupboard. After the Raleigh Man left, she'd pack us a lunch with orange drink and tell us to go out into the woods for a picnic, or at least out behind the garage in the shade of the maple trees. When we got back she'd seem calm and rested, with a faint aroma of vanilla about her. Sometimes when we asked her to make root beer, she'd tell us she had to get the house clean and the barn chores done first. We'd hurry and work like mechanical men helping her get her work done. Then we'd get to help her make the root beer

It was an exciting time. First we'd round up all the bottles we could find. My job was to fill them with soapy water and a few pebbles, and shake the mixture until the bottles were scoured clean. When they were cleaned and rinsed, Ma filled them with a mixture of warm water, root beer flavoring, and yeast. We sealed them with a bottle capper that crimped metal caps on the bottles. The worst part was waiting for the fermenting yeast to give the root beer some fizz. It seemed to take forever. Sometimes Ma let me drink the root beer flat when I just couldn't wait another minute.

We really appreciated Ma buying root beer flavoring and taking the time to make that delicious treat when she had so much work to do. And best of all, we knew then that she loved us.

❖ Remembrance ❖
by Dorothy M. Persons, Northfield, Massachusetts

I remember an almost perfect day. It happened to me when I was about six years old, and to this day I can see the beautiful, blue sky with crowds of fair-weather clouds floating blissfully over my head. I say "almost perfect," for we had traveled to my aunt's house not too far from ours, but still an adventure in the old Studebaker touring car, open to four winds, rain or shine. If the car happened to suffer a flat tire, which it often did, one had to remove the tire from the rim in order to patch the hole in the inner tube. It may even have been the day we had such a hard time making the steep hill after rounding a sharp corner. The deep sand made the going as difficult as a foot or two of snow. I doubt if Dad's temper was well controlled!

The house was situated at the edge of a grove of huge pine trees. Trees so big no grass grew beneath, only a thick carpet of pine needles covered the ground. Of course, it was known as "The Pines"—what else? I was a bit scared to roam very deep into them. Close by was the site of an Indian massacre, and I had been informed of the presence of ghosts!

But the really perfect part of the day was the field or pasture just across the road, which divided pine trees from open land. It was absolutely knee-deep in blueberry bushes, underneath which grew huge, blue violets with very long stems. I picked and picked until I had a huge bunch to give my mother. Even today the scent comes back to me—fresh and sweet and cool.

Later in the summer we came back for the blueberries, of course. But the best time for me was in the spring.

❖ Stars in the Water of Star ❖
by Dorothy M. Persons, Northfield, Massachusetts
(Inspired by a sighting at Star Island, Isle of Shoals)

Star light, Star bright,
A million stars I saw tonight
Before the sun was set,
Stars in the waters of Star!

Scintillating, titillating points of light,
Stars in the water—not yet night,
Dancing, prancing, exploding with glee;
Nothing I ever expected to see!

A myriad of dancers cavorting
Airily on an ever changing floor.
A light-footed fairy troop glimpsed

For a second only. Each dancer
A star in a cascade of stars
To decorate our Island,
Our one and only Star.

Star light, Star bright,
A million stars I saw tonight
Before the sun was set.
Stars in the water of Star.

❖ The Ice Boat ❖
by Marjorie Reid, Greenfield, Massachusetts

I went to see my father yesterday. His room was in semi-darkness and he was lying in bed, curled up on his side.

"It's a beautiful day out," I announced brightly. "Don't you want me to open the blinds and let the sunshine in?"

"No," he said weakly, "they're fine." His pale, wax-like hands fluttered feebly on the blanket. I pulled a chair up close to his bed and leaned towards him. I always have to steel myself for these visits. It's hard for me to see him lying there with his eyes closed, as if he were just waiting for death.

"The pond is frozen and the children are skating," I said with forced cheer. "Did you ever skate when you were little?" There's so much I don't know about my father.

"Yes," he said.

"What was it like?" I asked, wanting more.

After a while, he said, "We had skates that you strapped onto your boots." His voice became stronger, and his eyes opened. I had almost forgotten what a bright blue they are. "And one winter I made an iceboat."

"An iceboat!" I exclaimed. "How old were you?"

"About ten," he said. "I used three skates. I put one on either end of a two-by-four. I put a crosspiece on the two-by-four, and put the third skate on the end of it. I borrowed a bed sheet from my mother for the sail, but she made me promise not to put any holes in it. I had to put thin strips of wood on either side of it so I could tack it to the mast without tearing it."

"How did you steer it?" I asked.

"With ropes," he smiled. "I lay on my belly on the cross-piece and steered it with ropes."

"Wasn't it scary?" I asked.

"No!" he exclaimed. "It was fun. The river had frozen solid, and I must have sailed down it for a couple of miles. I had to get off once, to take it over a bridge. I must have sailed for a couple of miles." He closed his eyes and his smile faded.

I got up and kissed him goodbye. His cheek was soft and cool. It was still hard for me to see him lying there helplessly, but for a little while we had shared the memory of a glorious winter day in Maine over 80 years ago, when he had raced with the wind down a frozen river on an iceboat he had made himself.

❖ The Brookside Maple ❖
by Theresa Richards, Orange, Massachusetts

A plain old maple tree lived on Brookside for years, just how long, I do not know. It was a strong and stately tree just outside my bedroom window. Traditionally it housed birds in spring. Many more birds took refuge from the rain there. In appreciation the birds sang many beautiful songs to the leaves, which bloomed their appreciation. As a human, I could only watch in wonder.

I truly loved that old maple. As I tried to sleep, especially when problems weighed heavy on my mind, the gentle maple waved back and forth; the leaves hummed a soothing noise, and soon I was asleep.

In the winter the tree had lost its dress and looked so cold as I looked out my window at the branches, so beautiful and delicate, reaching their arms and hands and fingers for the stars.

Once again trying to sleep, the branches danced as a beautiful ballerina executing her years of experience. And soon I started another day.

Over time the old tree was dropping its "hands and arms." One sad day we had it cut down. I still look out my bedroom window and when I have a very bad day and can't sleep, I remember the Brookside maple that gave me years of pleasure, and now resides in my memories.

❖ Memories and Gifts❖
by Leona Robert, Turners Falls, Massachusetts

Remember when the Grand Union Tea man, the Raleigh Man, the Fuller Brush man and others came knocking at the door? They would display a large variety of merchandise for sale.

There was also the Larkin Company. Individuals would contact relatives, friends and neighbors, showing their catalogue and taking orders. Spices, extracts, household products and more were available. In payment for one's work as a salesperson, one chose a premium. The value of the premium would be commensurate with the amount of the order.

My sister Myrtle was about fourteen years old when I was to be married in 1932. Not having any money to buy my husband and me a gift, she decided to take Larkin orders and gift us with her premium. As her premium she selected a set of dishes—service for six. The border was a very pretty floral design on a white background and a fine, gold line around the outer edge. We were so pleased with those dishes.

Everyone was still recovering from the Depression Era at that time. We had just that one set of dishes which we used daily. Over the years, and with small children, pieces were gradually broken until all that was left was a dinner plate and a platter. These I set aside as keepsakes.

Years later, after a meal at our house, two granddaughters were doing the dishes. I over heard the oldest, Phyllis, then married, tell her sister, "This is one thing I don't have—a nice, big platter."

I had to dispose of many possessions when I gave up my house and moved to smaller quarters. While sorting through my belongings I recalled the remark and gave Phyllis the platter. In 1999, she hosted the family Christmas dinner at her home in New Hampshire. The meat was served on that platter.

After I was married, my mother gave me a large, heavy, brown earthenware bowl. It had belonged to my Grandmother Howard. Around the outside rim, at the top of the bowl, is a raised border approximately two inches deep. It must hold at least four or five quarts. Mother said she remembered being invited to Sunday dinners at Grandma's after she and my father were married. They would be served delicious chicken and gravy, topped with homemade, golden brown, baking powder biscuits, from that bowl.

I gave the bowl to my granddaughter Beverly, in Maine. While visiting her, I've noticed her great great grandmother's old brown bowl filled with fruit in the middle of her dining room table.

I am sure the girls did not realize the pleasure it gave me seeing them use those old dishes I had received in 1932 and treasured for so long.

❖ The Book Bag ❖
by Charlotte Robinson, Turners Falls, Massachusetts

As I struggle into my knapsack, filled with heavy Greenfield Community College books, I think how fortunate we are, especially the young of today, to be using knapsacks to carry books, lunch, make-up, secrets, and perhaps some contraband. The bag with the two shoulder straps makes the wearer stand up straight, holds the shoulders back and the chin up. The only thing bad about the knapsack is that all of the pockets and other storage spaces open from the back. Anyone can get into these areas, which provide easy access to (perhaps) unfriendly persons behind.

I am very familiar with knapsacks, plain or with the metal frame that allows a sleeping bag and other items to be attached. I have been a hiker and backpacker most of my life, both primitive and campsite camping. Slipping arms into a forty-pound pack is a feat in itself—get one hand into a strap and that hand, holding the pack above the head allows the other arm to slip in easily.

When I was in fifth or sixth grade, in the late 1930s, some company designed a short duffle bag, about 15 inches square, of lightweight canvas. A long strap was inserted into the top hem and this actually closed the bag as the strap was slung over a shoulder. The strap was never slung across the chest. Every student just HAD to have one in their school colors. Mine was blue for Stoneham High School in Stoneham, Massachusetts. This was my first experience with fads. These bags held books, lunch (never heard of school hot lunches then), loose papers, etc., all of which ended up in a mashed jumble at the bottom of the bag, no matter how carefully it had been packed.

Almost everyone used the left shoulder to hitch up the strap, which put lefthanders at a disadvantage. The weight of the books caused a permanent list to the left and threw our entire body off center. Adults cautioned that it was dangerous to the spinal column. The bags could become lethal weapons, also, when you slung your bag into the backs of another's knees, causing an immediate loss of balance.

Those children who had square shoulders like I do, had no trouble keeping the straps in place. Those who had sloping shoulders were forever pulling the straps back up onto their shoulders again.

This fad continued for a couple of years and then faded as all fads eventually do. The bags were consigned to the bedpost as repositories for soiled clothes or pajamas.

❖ Memories of Play ❖
by Constance Sokoloski, Greenfield, Massachusetts

I remember the summers of long ago, when life was simpler and times were happier. People say that "the good old days" weren't the good old days, but they truly were. Things were slower-paced and people had time for one another, were kinder to one another, respected one another, and cared about one another.

As a child, I remember summer days in Turners Falls Massachusetts were filled with play and togetherness. There were so many children in our neighborhood; there was no lack of playmates. During the day we would go to the cement wading pool at Unity Park and enjoy the cold water and the sprinklers, along with many skinned knees as a bonus. The pool was crowded with children, laughter and squeals of happiness as they passed by sprinklers that shot out icy, cold water and gave instant goose bumps. What a joy!

After supper, many of the same children would come together to play games such as hide and seek, kick the can, relieve-o and giant steps. It was such fun. I don't think too many children today even know what any of these games are—what a shame! Children just enjoyed being with one another and playing together.

As it started to get dark, someone would decide it was time for a ghost story. Everyone would sit close together and some would hold hands to give each other a sense of security and safety. Sometimes the story was so scary, we would huddle a little closer and then the storyteller would make a sudden gesture and everyone would let out a scream and burst into laughter because they had been taken by surprise.

All too soon the day had come to an end. The nine o'clock fire department whistle blew, and everyone knew it was time to head for home, knowing that the next day held in store just as much fun, if not more, than the day that had just ended.

Ah! What I wouldn't give to relive one of those golden summer days of long ago. Thank God for memories.

❖ **Musings from the Senior Center News** ❖
by Virginia Taylor, Charlemont, Massachusetts

One Sunday night in January we had a wet snowstorm. Monday morning I woke up to a heavy coating of snow on all the trees and bushes.

Oddly enough, there appeared to be little, if any, on higher elevations such as Berkshire East ski area in Charlemont, Massachusetts which I could see from my kitchen window. Looking at the trees and bushes on my way to Shelburne Falls, Massachusetts with my driver that morning, we decided it couldn't possibly look any prettier if the sun were shining.

The following morning I looked out my living room window to see the sun shining and I could see the beautiful snow coating the trees on High Street. They were silhouetted against that gorgeous winter-blue sky and I realized it was indeed even more beautiful than the day before!

The snow does make it more difficult traveling and working outdoors, but it also does look stunningly, breathtakingly beautiful. We should take the time, now and then, just to glory in the wonder of the seasons.

❖ ❖ ❖

Did you lose your electric power during that severe wind storm in early February? I did but it didn't surprise me…never have I heard such winds, not even in the hurricane of '39. Pieces of ice and other unidentifiable objects kept hitting the building. I had to go look out my front door every so often, but I could never tell what might have hit the house.

Earlier I had filled the bathtub with water. I also filled juice jugs with drinking water, got out my long johns and other warm clothing, and blankets. I got my meds out and purse ready to grab at a moments' notice if needed, then went to bed to try and ignore the storm and sleep. It was a pleasant surprise to awaken to night-lights and blinking clocks the next morning. Hope that's the last storm of that nature for a long time.

❖ ❖ ❖

Back when I was a small girl, my mother used to brush and comb my hair into long ringlets. In the process, and not intentionally, she would pull it. Never very patient, I informed her that if she didn't stop pulling my hair I would cut it off. Needless to say, she still pulled it, though she tried not to. And, being the brat I was, I took some scissors and went out behind the woodshed, crawled in behind some boards leaning up against the back wall, and cut off what hair I could reach. Safe behind the woodshed I felt quite happy with what I'd done until nearly time for my father to come home from work. Finally I crawled into the kitchen and under the roll top desk in one corner of the kitchen and told my mother not to tell him what I had done. She solemnly vowed not to and we waited. Of course, all he had to do was look at me and he could have cried. He set me up on the desk and told me how much it hurt him and my mother to see me shorn of my pretty curls. I felt worse than if he had spanked me! Truth is, I missed them too, and never had natural curls again.

❖ ❖ ❖

When I was a kid growing up on a farm we had a small building next to the chicken run and the barn that we called the grain room. Whenever I opened the door and went inside I was met by the most wonderful smell. There were different kinds of grain there in big barrels for the different animals and the combination of the different grains was just the most heavenly, heady scent. Just thinking about that little room I can almost smell it! It was fun growing up there. (Sometimes we kids would squirt milk directly from the cow's udder to the waiting cat's mouth…but that's an entirely different story…)

❖ ❖ ❖

A while back, I made a comment here about squirting milk straight from the cow to the waiting cat's mouths. If memory serves me and my grandfather knew the cow gave a little less milk on those nights, he never said anything.

Thinking about that reminded me of the big water barrel that used to sit near the horse's stall. There was an old wives' tale I'd heard that if you pulled a hair from a horse's tail and put it in a tub of water, it would turn into a worm-like thing swimming around in the water! Of course I had to try that out. I remember standing nearby looking at the horse and its tail and hooves and wondering if he'd kick me or jump and knock me down if and when I got up the nerve to pluck that hair from his tail!

Neither of those things happened, though, and the hair joined the trout in the barrel, but nothing magical happened to the hair, so I decided "so much for that experiment!"

❖ ❖ ❖

When I was in high school and had to walk home after school, it meant a four mile walk which usually took about an hour. (And don't I wish I could still walk four miles!)

As I remember it, it didn't seem all that far. Some days I rode my bike and it didn't take as long then. But on a cold, blustery, snowy day the winds swept down along the railroad on Route 8A South in Charlemont, Massachusetts, blew right into my face and I had to lean into the winds sometimes to make any kind of headway. That stretch of road was the longest part of the way. My Grandma was sure I would get frostbite or chilblains or something worse because I refused to wear long-legged underwear, but my ski pants did the job nicely.

No parent in their right mind today would allow a child to walk that far alone. What a sad commentary.

❖ ❖ ❖

You know, it's really mind boggling when you think of all the advancements in travel just in my lifetime. From shank's mare, to horse and wagon, to trains, to cars, to planes, to walking on the moon and living in a space station—what more could there be?

Recently I was talking with someone and she said, "You know, I really think we had the best time to grow up in. Life was so much simpler then."

And I had to agree. No television to start hyping up Christmas before we've even had Halloween—makes everyone expect too much and then be disappointed when things don't live up to their expectations. I liked it better when life had a more leisurely pace.

❖ ❖ ❖

There used to be one special place back home in Charlemont, Massachusetts, where I grew up, where a bunch of yellow violets grew and blossomed every year. Nearby, a couple of beds of blue ones—big blue ones—grew as well.

Early in the spring there was one special place where I could find the sweet smelling Mayflowers, or arbutus. If I was lucky, they would be more pink than white. They had the sweetest smell.

There were also lovely wild blue gentians growing up the hill from our house. They were the loveliest things I think I ever saw and, as I look back on it, may be the reason why I've always favored the color blue.

We were given such a beautiful world to care for. Why haven't we done a better job?

Local Color Extras

❖ 2 Fer, 3 Fer ❖
by Edna Baublis, Athol, Massachusetts

I like to think of myself as a rather practical person. Usually when I buy anything, I comparison shop for the best price and quality. However, signs that say "2 for" or "3 for" or "4 for" get to me.

Never mind that the regular price of the merchandise is 26 cents a piece—when the sign says 4 for a dollar, I'm hooked!

I once bought ten one-pound boxes of salt because the sign said, "marked down to 10 cents a box." After I gave away five boxes of salt, I still had enough for a year.

"Big Y" Supermarket loves me! Buy one—get two free! I may have seven boxes left, but I say to my husband Joe, "Joe, it says get two free." I especially like to look at the receipt that tells me how much I've saved! My goal is to save more than I spend so that they will pay *me* money. My husband says, "In your dreams, kid."

My family has forbidden me to buy any more Spanish olives until we have used up the seven jars left on my shelves. When I look downcast, they always say that there will be another sale soon.

Back a few years ago, before the price of toilet paper went sky high, I accumulated 25 four-roll packs of the paper. When one of my sons wanted a package I grabbed it out of his arms and yelled, "No, not my toilet paper." The argument that I still had 24 packs left in the cellar fell on deaf ears. He had to buy his own.

I always have an extra one of something in my supply closet. I have on hand a new curling iron (why I bought it I don't know—I don't use one), a hair dryer, and an extra travel alarm clock. (How many of these do you need?) My granddaughter always tells her friends when she runs out of something that her Nonni will have one. "She always has everything."

Periodically, I vow to mend my ways. I won't buy anything until I've used up what's on my shelves, but then I go into a store. I see the sign, "SPECIAL—4 for $1.00"—and I'm off and running. Does anyone want a can of kidney beans?

❖ Orchard Days ❖
by Estelle Cade, Turners Falls, Massachusetts

"Apple pickers wanted--must be strong and willing to work"--that box ad in the Recorder the other day caught my eye and made me laugh.

It was September 1943 and a group of us—male and female—were being excused from high school classes at Sanderson Academy near my Ashfield, Massachusetts home. I was a freshman and we were going out to help harvest the apple crop. There was a war on, as the saying went, and help was scarce. We were still officially in school and had our usual homework assignments to complete each day. Mr. Yale, the VO-AG (vocational-agricutural) teacher, would make the rounds of all the farms and take daily attendance—No Hooky Playing Allowed! If it rained and we weren't picking, we were in our classrooms.

Dressed in my oldest slacks, long-sleeved shirt, sweater (it's cold in the orchards in the morning!), and my rattiest old saddle shoes, I was picked up at 6:30 a.m. and driven out to Apple Valley to Howes Brothers Orchards, I think.

The trees were filled with beautiful red apples waiting for energetic pickers like us! We were given canvas picking bags that went over our shoulders and fastened around our waists. (On some farms we used picking baskets.) The bags held about a bushel of apples and fastened in the front. We were shown how to open them when they were full and gently roll the apples into the waiting crates. This was the #1 crop of early Macs, so no bruising was allowed.

Up the ladders we went. The ten-foot picking ladders came to a point at the top. We plucked ripe fruit from the branches, filled our bags, then climbed down the ladder to empty them, then up to fill them again, and again, and again. At 7 a.m. those apples were COLD and wet with morning dew, but gloves were useless, of course.

We young women were not allowed to move our own ladders, so when all the apples within reach were picked, we'd call out and the hired man would come and move the ladders to another part of the tree or to another tree. About the time you'd begin to think you couldn't stand one more minute on those rungs (I used to hang by the heels of my shoes to relieve my arches), some wonderful person would yell, "Lunch break!"

How good it felt to sit down and relax on the grass chatting, eating and resting our feet. When break was over, it was back on the ladders until 3 p.m. or so, then home for a bath, supper, homework—and bed!

Once I worked in a packing house sorting apples. I stood on a box to pour the apples onto a sorting belt. I settled the best apples into the shipping boxes, covered them with blue paper and nailed on the slats that kept everything firmly in place. I became a very adept nailer of slats. It was hard physical labor—harder, it seemed, than the actual picking. Because of that, we girls became feminists at an early age! We discovered that the boys were being paid more than we were—fifty cents an hour to our forty cents. We decided this wouldn't do at all, and we went in a group to state our case to Mr. Yale. I do believe we got that raise!

At the end of apple season we received a certificate and a shoulder patch with the title "Victory Farm Volunteers," for our part in the War Effort. So when I read that farmers can't get pickers I recall how eagerly we 14-16 year olds picked apples for 40-50 cents per hour! Early Macs are still my favorite variety for the memories in each crisp bite.

❖ Getting My License ❖
by Mary Ciechomski, Turners Falls, Massachusetts

Getting your driver's license at age seventeen or eighteen was not a priority when I was young. My family, as well as many of my friends' families, didn't even own a car and used foot, trolley and later bus transportation.

So when Tony, one of my boyfriends, asked if I cared to learn to drive, I thought it would be fun, but never gave a thought to getting a license.

Tony would continually emphasize to "synchronize" the clutch and the gas pedal. I never had heard the word "synchronize" before. I enjoyed occasionally driving Tony's father's car, but never gave a thought to getting a driver's license until my brother Eugene went into the service and left his 1936 Plymouth at home. Graciously, he told me I could use it while he was in the Navy. I was thrilled until I found out that he had used all his gas rations up to August. This was only June and the tank was on empty.

I was working at Westover Air Force Base at the time and arranged to get hold of a gas ration stamp for five gallons. Fred, another brother who had a disability that kept him out of the service, suggested we push the car down our street to the gas station, where we put in five gallons of gas at 15 cents a gallon. Fred also was dying to learn to drive, and with my limited experience I proceeded to teach him to drive. At that time our street had not been accepted by the town as a legal road, so I felt it was perfectly all right to drive up and down the street teaching Fred to "synchronize" the clutch and the gas. After Fred had mastered the basics, we drove up the street and really did quite a bit of practice driving in the cemetery at the top of the hill. Oh the number of tombstones we almost took down! Finally, Fred and I had practiced enough and we both felt competent to try for our licenses.

We got the little book of questions from the Registry and spent hours memorizing the thirty-plus questions in that book. We both made an appointment at the Registry. On that important day we went down to the Registry, answered our three questions perfectly, and after a short test drive were issued our temporary licenses.

How proud we were to finally be able to drive on accepted town streets! I loved driving and always felt I was a good driver, with never a violation until sometime in my 72nd year. I was pulled over when driving through the University of Massachusetts campus. The officer said I was doing 40 mph in a 25-mph zone—IMAGINE!!

After observing my white hair and checking my license for any past violations, he issued me a warning and wished me a good day.

❖ Inflation ❖
by Elisabeth R. Donaj, Greenfield, Massachusetts

Sometime in the 1920s, an inflation hit my country, Germany. Suddenly the citizens were forced to handle money in a frantic manner. The reason was that prices for goods, the most needed stuff families depended on, rose and rose with great haste. Earnings had to be spent immediately if one did not want to suffer loss due to devaluation. Currency with established denominations were soon printed over in bold black print. Not that their values became better, on the contrary. For example, a normal five mark bill became ten times the value, some days later the notes were increased to one hundred times the original value. One had to run to get the most needed food stuffs before the prices would jump sky high.

I remember how nervous my parents had become. I could sense it as a child even though I did not understand it.

One day, out in the avenue after several wet days, I passed a puddle with a film of ice on it. On the rim, I spied a piece of paper that sat stuck in the ice. It looked to me like money. I took it out and thought, "Oh yes! This is the real thing!"

Suddenly the find delighted me. Boldly black numerals read "$1,000.00 marks." It didn't take me long to act. My childish ideas lead me to run into a grocer's store where mother never went to shop. (Most likely because the prices they charged were higher than the competitors.) My little friend had given me some exclusive candy with a yummy delightful taste at the time for her birthday. A sudden desire awakened in me to taste more of such. That's why I spent my rich find, from any normal mind's judgment, recklessly!

I gave the store owner my bill and asked for the most, best candy in the store. This alone should have made him realize that my childish mind was misguided. But he filled a bag right to the top and, with the friendliest gesture, handed it over to me.

Back in the street and alone, my conscience made me hesitate to go home. Instead I found some children playing. They had not been friends before, but as I offered them these rarely enjoyed candies, they sat down on their stoops to share my wealth. That went on for a lengthy time. Finally an urge needed to be taken care of and I needed to return home.

Of course, my mother had several questions, and she found out that I had been a very bad girl.

"We could have bought two loaves of bread for our table today for that money instead of wasting it foolishly. Shame on you."

❖ Inflation Caused a Turning Point ❖
by Elisabeth R. Donaj, Greenfield, Massachusetts

I once knew a man who had had the good fortune of having been on top of society's ladder. He had reached the zenith by becoming a successful business man and an owner of a manufacturing plant.

His only sister, who had received the same education as her brother, had gotten married and thereby left behind opportunities for professional endeavors in exchange for becoming a wife and mother of two children. Yet her situation did change drastically when she became a young widow. That was the time when her rich brother took on the responsibility to help her financially for her children's education. He also supported his sister and even provided a new place for them to live.

Then inflation came to Germany. The entire population plunged into devastation, without having been part of the cause, and yet having to meet this disaster that befell everyone.

When the widow and my family met and became neighbors, the inflation was long gone, but the suffering was still etched in our minds as dark memories.

One day my family witnessed a visitor that came to call on the widow. He was poorly dressed, disheveled looking, a bent down figure who evidently was to be her guest. I was still a child and watched this sad person and wondered if the widow would even share her day with him.

After the man visited, the widow came to our house to tell us that the man was her brother. She told us about his sad life.

He was the one who had helped her when her burdens were too heavy. Now, after the collapse of his fortune, how could she not try to help this soul with sympathy and not offer to quell his needs by giving him at least a warm meal from time to time?

He who once had a sound foundation on which he had built his life, who had suffered not only immense financial losses, but his self-worth, his pride, his joy of family and accomplishments as well.

His sister, the widow, spoke in deep sorrow.

"He is nothing but an angry man—one act in which he did express his defeat was by taking heaps of his worthless paper money and using it all as wallpaper in the rooms of his home!"

None of us shall be the judge. He lived his days in his self-created prison, where his soul did die long before his body gave up after long years of frailty.

To tell a story about "Rich Man, Poor Man" neither state should cause envy in any of us. We may learn from this:

> A man who has lost his spirits
> Has no longer the needed defenses
> To fight for his rights,
> Nor the strength to fight for his life!

❖ Night Flying ❖
by William R. Fitzgerald, Ashfield, Massachusetts

Some of my favorite war stories involve the effort to train a lot of pilots fast during World War II. This wasn't just a program to teach a bunch of young men to solo in a couple of weeks, but an effort to produce highly trained professional pilots to take millions of dollars' worth of hardware, and sometimes several men, into hell and back.

If they had not been in their early twenties or late teens, with the attitude of survivors, the military couldn't have pulled it off in less than a year. Conversely, that's why we have so many young men driving so recklessly. They think that they are going to live forever. They haven't been to enough funerals. Further, that's why so many Stearman primary trainers flew under the Cape Girardeau Bridge over the Mississippi River, sometimes six or seven at a time, and tried other wild feats of derring-do or insanity, depending on your point of view (and your age).

Night flying was the most hairy—particularly night landings. Landings are always the most difficult part of any phase of flying. Landings are a controlled collision with an immovable object. Unlike night driving, it's a whole different world at night in the air. You don't have street lights or headlights and your best source of orientation, the horizon, is sometimes kind of indistinct. The way to get the class to solo at night was to get about twenty to thirty planes, students, and instructors out there shooting landings. The procedure was to take off, fly about two or three miles, take two right turns, fly back parallel to the runway, take two more right turns and land. Immediately upon landing, the throttle was opened again to take off. This is called "shooting touch-and-go landings."

It got so crazy up there that the instructors got out as soon as they could and walked to operations with their fingers crossed.

One needed only to keep track of the white light shining dimly on the rear of the plane in front of you and follow it. If an occasional "Dilbert" somehow lost sight and zeroed in on a star or some distant light on the horizon, he would be lucky if he could find the field when we woke up to his predicament. And then he had to insert himself back into traffic. Talk about getting onto I-91 in Holyoke, Massachusetts during rush hour!

Everyone made those turns a little short and then the pattern became smaller and the planes closer together. Then everyone had to slow down, all the while knowing that under a certain speed the airplane wouldn't stay in the air. This brought on a spate of radio chatter, which the operator in the tower resented. He was supposed to be directing operations. The angrier and more officious he got, the wilder the yammering became.

The radio crackled with a call from Superman, who was five miles south of the field and requesting landing instructions. No answer, followed by the Green Hornet ordering the tower to give Superman landing instructions. Soon Superman would call again, ordering the tower to give him clearance. Still no answer. Then the comic would stick his mike out into the slipstream, producing a loud swishing roar and announce, "Superman on runway three five, request taxiing instructions." To fill the silence, Woody Woodpecker would laugh.

The current comedy playing at the post movie was about the adventures of Elmer Fudd. Soon Elmer came on air saying, "Wabbit Twacks, Wabbit Twacks, all I see up here is Wabbit Twacks. I'm going cwazy." Whereupon he got an answer, "This is Major Rock in the tower. Identify yourself, Mister." Silence for a moment, then Elmer answered, "I'm not that cwazy."

Tension was relieved, and with the Major in the tower no one wanted to cause the whole squadron to be restricted to post next weekend. The important business of night flying was resumed.

❖ The One-Room Schoolhouse, District No. 1 ❖
by Jane L. Gilbert, Turners Falls, Massachusetts

When I started school there were four school districts in different sections of my hometown of Bernardston, Massachusetts. One was in the north end for those children; one in the eastern section of town; one in the center of town and one on South Street. This South Street School was

District Number One which I attended. I never felt uneasy because the teacher, Miss Whithead, was next door neighbor to my grandparents, who lived next door to my family.

The first day of school was a busy day. Everyone needed to be in the right class, and books, pencils, and pens needed to be passed out. There seemed to be a large first grade, so the older students were in the "A" class and the rest were in the "B" class. The next order of the day was to send two of the older boys next door for a pail of water. We drank the water from that pail using tiny, thin paper cups. Those cups came flattened out in a large package.

The school day always began with reading a passage from the Bible. This was followed by a salute to our flag which hung above the blackboard. In good weather a large outdoor flag always flew from a tall flagpole in front of the school next to the street. Two older boys were responsible for raising the flag in the morning.

At the end of the day, the same two boys would lower the flag slowly, fold it carefully and bring it back to the classroom where it would be ready to raise again in the morning.

When the weather began to get cooler, a neighbor of the school always came in early and built a fire in the big square furnace on the north side of the classroom. In cold weather, you could see the flames jumping around through the isinglass insert in the door of the furnace.

When the holiday season drew near, our holiday preparations began. First we would write a play for Thanksgiving. We would then perform it for our doting parents. Then decorations for the Christmas tree would be made. Invariably a Christmas tree which had been set up by some mysterious person, would appear. Out would come the decorations we made—paper chains and ornaments—and we would decorate the tree. Finally came the drawing of names for gifts and we anxiously waited for Santa to arrive with a bag full of goodies that he passed out to willing hands.

And so the school year passed and before we knew it, it was time for the end of school picnic. The brother of Miss Whithead owned a piece of land just right for games. There was a brook that was just right for wading.

All too soon it was time to leave—another school year was over. We all went home to wait for summer to pass and school to begin again.

❖ Comet Teaches Me a Little Horse Sense ❖
by Jane L. Gilbert, Turners Falls, Massachusetts

It was a beautiful day in autumn when my horse, Comet, and I decided to make the most of it. The day was warm and the leaves were full of color when we turned up Fox Hill in Bernardston, Massachusetts. The road was a colorful carpet of autumn leaves as we ambled along enjoying the colors around us. The leaves were rich with color: red, gold, green, and warm browns. The colored leaves danced on the branches of the trees. Soon they would flutter to the ground.

We left the busy highway behind us when we turned up Fox Hill Road. We could hear the automobiles racing along the roads, traveling north to Brattleboro, Vermont. I thought how much beauty and peacefulness they were missing as we plodded along through the colorful forest.

As we neared the top of the hill we could see our farm house basking in the sun. We paused and looked back at the ribbon of color all around us and started for Old Coach Road, where stage coaches used to rattle their way to town. As we started down the old road, I was just thinking about the coaches when suddenly Comet came to a complete and sudden stop. Looking around I couldn't see anything that might upset her. That is until I turned towards West Mountain and there on the ground a few feet from us sat a stranger, all quills raised and ready to fire. In plain English it was a porcupine just waiting to open fire at the least motion. Fortunately, Comet knew to stand her ground. Finally the porcupine ambled across the road in front of us and up the bank on the other side of the road. Comet's horse sense had saved the day!

When it was safe to proceed, we resumed our trek down the trail and soon came to the road that would take us back home. A little way down the road we came to a house where a mother and son lived. I always stopped there when I was riding that way because the mother loved Comet and called her "Funny Baby" as she pet her. My horse seemed to like the attention, and every time I rode that way I stopped in for a short visit. It was a rather lonesome place to live and probably company was scarce.

Finally, I said a reluctant farewell to the mother and son and headed home. It was getting on towards feeding time and Dad's little bay mare would be calling for Comet so she, too, could have her dish of oats and fork of hay.

❖ Memories of the Family Grain Mill ❖
by Jane L. Gilbert, Turners Falls, Massachusetts

George Washington had a water-powered grain mill, and so did my family. When Dad graduated from school, he experimented with various businesses, but soon discovered he wanted something different. My grandfather, who had been selling real estate in Bernardston, Massachusetts, realized that he wanted to go back into the grain business. Earlier he had a grain business in Northfield, Massachusetts. Grandfather had a listing for a water-powered mill in Bernardston, so it wasn't long before J.L. Dunnell & Son was begun. A sawmill came with the grainmill which was a bonus.

The mill stands quiet now, the rope tower is gone, but the memories linger. The little girl with long curls still teases to go to work with her father and grandfather. The mill boys, as the hired help called themselves, didn't seem to mind having the little girl follow them around. They did their work selling the bagged grain to customers, the bags polishing the floor every time a customer dragged one out the door.

The most exciting thing to the little girl was the sound of the mill wheels when they started to turn. The iron wheels set the mill in motion to mix the grains for bagging or grind the grains to order. When the workday ended the day's sales were added up and the mill was at rest until the next day. During the night a train might stop and push in a car of grain for the help to unload the next day.

❖ Going to Christian Hill ❖
by Jane L. Gilbert, Turners Falls, Massachusetts

The name Christian Hill brings back many memories of happy times spent there. My great grandfather lived there on a farm. My grandfather and his brother were born there. The house was just about gone, but some of the old stone fences remained.

It was in the 1930s, before the war, that I first heard of Christian Hill in Colrain, Massachusetts. Every summer my relatives would "go up on the hill" (as they called it) for a vacation and to relive old times.

"The boys" (men of all ages), as they were lovingly called, had built a four room cabin where they could relax. It had two bedrooms in the back part. In the front there was a kitchen at one end and dining area at the other end with chairs for company in between.

Water was brought in with buckets from a spring that set almost into the woods.

Every time we went "up on the hill" my mother would take food she had baked ahead and my aunt would do the same.

As the sun set in the west we would gather our belongings, load the car and Dad would drive carefully down the hill.

Good night, Christian Hill!

❖ Christmas at Apple Valley School in the Twenties ❖
by Barbara R. Graves, West Springfield, Massachusetts

In the 1920s, rural life was very different from what it is today. In Apple Valley in Ashfield, Massachusetts. Farmers had owned their farms for years, and some of them were members of the same family. Schools also were quite different, as they were very small and away from the center of town.

The Christmas party was the most exciting event of the year at the Apple Valley School. The teacher, a veteran of many years (in fact, she had taught my father when she was very young), planned a superior program and students eagerly participated. One year we wrote and decorated invitations to our parents and the school superintendent.

The occasions when I best remember these programs were in the late twenties. At this time the enrollment of the school was larger than usual, as there were at least fifteen students. All eight grades might have been represented.

Preparations started at least three weeks before the day of the party, which was the last day of school before the holidays. Each child memorized a piece, usually a poem, suitable to his or her age and ability. The teacher planned at least two skits. The music teacher helped with songs of the season. Since the music teacher did not come every week, the regular teacher shouldered most of the work. While one group was rehearsing, the remaining students did school work, read from the small library or simply watched the performers. It might seem strange to some of today's teachers that we watched in silence.

The building was entered from a porch to a small entry where stove wood was stacked. On the opposite wall were hooks for coats. A pail stood on a small table below nails that held each child's drinking cup. The water pail was filled each day when two children armed with a long stick climbed the hill to my family's home for the daily supply of fresh spring water. It was truly amazing how fast two kids with a pail held between them on a stick could run down the hill to the school and still have water left in the pail. At the end of the entry were the doors to the privy.

The class area was one large room with three rows of double-seated desks. A long black stove stood in the middle of the room with a stove pipe stretching to the outside wall where it joined the chimney. In the twenties, rural electrification was in the future. For this evening affair a large metal candelabra with sprawling arms that held small kerosene lamps provided the light. Larger lamps were fastened to the walls on either side of the room.

To prepare for the great night, a large spruce tree was brought into the main room and decorated. No candles were used. The teacher decorated the blackboards with seasonal scenes using her precious colored chalk.

At last the long-awaited day arrived. We all raced home to urge our parents to do their chores, eat their supper, and get back to the school as soon as possible. Nearby families like ours walked to the school, as the school yard was small. Groups from farther away came in sleighs, sleds, and wagons. One father was remembered for the squeaky wheel on his wagon, which always announced his arrival.

Inside the schoolhouse the candelabra was lighted and the stove was carefully stoked. Parents and friends began to arrive and were seated by the children. Boards were placed from one desk to another across the aisles, allowing more people to be seated. The children congregated in the rear of the room, whispering quietly, interspersed with an occasional giggle. Outside it was dark—no street lights and very little traffic. In those days many farmers did not take their cars out in the winter. The roads were rolled with a large horse-drawn wooden roller. This roller did not make the roads easy for cars. Thus the only break in the outer darkness was the soft light coming from the schoolhouse windows.

Finally, quiet settled over the room and the program began with welcoming words from a student, and the first song. Not surprisingly, even the little first graders did well and were roundly applauded. The recitations—all memorized—were followed by skits and more songs, which were accompanied by the teacher on her zither—a small stringed instrument that was played with a pick.

As the last song was sung, Santa Claus bounded in with a loud "Ho ho." With the help of the children, Santa distributed the really nice presents that the teacher gave each of us. The year that I was in the eighth grade the teacher gave every eighth grader an album containing a picture for each year that we had been in the school.

Earlier the children had drawn names for gift-giving, and those gifts were passed out as the recipients tried to guess who had drawn their names. By this time Santa had to leave to go on his way. With a "Merry Christmas to all" and a wave he was gone. I might note here that one year the Santa was my future husband. He remembers seeing my younger brother but apparently I made no impression on him. No doubt I sat quietly with my mouth shut.

At this point the mothers passed out the fudge, cookies, and my grandmother's popcorn balls, which they had provided. General conversation ensued as the group exchanged the news of their families while we enjoyed the only Christmas party that most of us would attend.

As the last guest left, the teacher drew a deep breath of satisfaction and with the help of the oldest boy, who built the fire in the morning and swept the floor, closed up the stove, locked the door, and Christmas vacation began.

With the passage of time, Apple Valley School was abandoned in favor of a large consolidated school. The rural neighborhood lost some of its unique character; its sense of community; a commonality of interest. The children lost the close relationship with their neighborhood friends. A bigger world had opened, but not necessarily a better one.

❖ The "Wash" ❖
by Barbara R. Graves, West Springfield, Massachusetts

Monday Washday at my grandmother's house was probably where the name "Black Monday" came from. Doing laundry Grandma's way was truly a terrible undertaking.

It all started on Sunday evening when my grandmother called me downstairs to cut up the big yellow cake of P and G soap (no soap flakes those days—too expensive) into a small copper kettle, which was filled with water and cut-up soap and set on the back of the old wood stove. Grandma put a much larger copper kettle called a "boiler," which she filled with water, on the stove, too.

My grandmother was very up-to-date. She had an electric washing machine with an electric wringer that could be swiveled from washing machine to the soapstone tubs she used for rinsing, and since she had two tubs, she had two rinses.

Starting early on Monday morning, Grandma put some of the melted soap into the big boiler, added the sheets, and moved the boiler onto the front of the stove to boil. Other soap she put into the washing machine then filled it with cold water from the soapstone tubs' faucets. To this she added a kettle of boiling water from the stove. This tub of soapy water would do at least two tubs of clothes.

She was ready to begin. If I was lucky I was on my way down the hill to the one-room schoolhouse where I went for seven years. I would not be back until time for the noon meal.

During the summer I was not always lucky and was reluctantly snatched from my book. Dragging feet, I was sent downstairs to help Grandma until my mother had reached the point where she could come down and get busy with "the wash."

Grandma was very fussy about separating the clothes into piles of white, colored, and work clothes. Into the tub of soapy water she put as many whites as she thought the tub would take, put the cover on, and turned the machine on to agitate the clothes while she tended the sheets and finished her morning breakfast dishes.

Since the laundry of two households was being done at the same time there was usually more than one tub of whites, although I must say that we did not change our clothes the way we do today, or every day would have been wash day. A greater calamity I cannot imagine happening at that time.

My turn came when the clothes were ready to be put through the wringer. The wringer swung around so that the clothes pulled through it would go into the first rinse water. When using the wringer, I had to shake each item out and carefully introduce it to the rollers that were the working part of the wringer. I had to be careful to keep my fingers out of the maw of the rollers. It was common knowledge around town that a certain lady had caught a very sensitive piece of her anatomy in the wringer when she was leaning over the tub.

A strange metal affair with four cup-like appendages, which was one of my grandmother's favorite pieces of laundry equipment, was manipulated by hand to slosh the clothes around. This required a certain amount of muscle to operate and was definitely not one of my favorite tasks. After using this gadget on the rinsing clothes, I put them through the wringer into the second tub of rinse water and from there through the rollers into a basket, ready to be hung on the line.

While this was taking place, my grandmother prepared a solution of starch to use on dress shirts, house dresses, and aprons. She also started the noon meal for the men. This meal was no light lunch, but hearty fare of potatoes, meat, vegetables, and pie.

About the fate of the sheets in the boiler, I am not certain. They were probably fished out with sticks, after which they eventually made it to the wringer. Grandma never had a bottle of bleach in the house, as she felt that it caused the sheets to wear out more quickly.

My mother and I, if I was at home and could be hauled out of the attic where I was usually reading, worked with the machine and wringer and tried to keep up with hanging the clothes.

There was nothing simple about hanging the clothes. First a long line had to be strung across the front lawn. Since we were away from the nearest neighbor, who was no doubt doing her own washing, using the front lawn was acceptable practice. In fact, some of the white items were spread out on the grass to bleach in the sun. The clothes were hung on the porch in rainy weather, and in the winter when they froze they had to be dried in the house.

Before the day was over Grandma had scrubbed by hand (using her handy-dandy scrubbing board) the worst of the men's clothes and washed and scrubbed their socks. She turned socks inside out so she could be sure to get all the dirt.

She ended this dreadful day by using the final rinse water to mop the back shed. I suspect this was to get the last bit of soapy water where it would do the most good.

At this point there was nothing left to do except change her dress and get the evening meal, which blessedly was very simple, sometimes crackers and milk with a piece of cake or a cookie.

She went to bed early, knowing that there was a lot of work on Tuesday, which was ironing day.

Footnote: As time went on and there were improvements in washing machines and my grandma became lame, my mother managed to cut out some of the more arduous steps in the process, such as boiling sheets and scrubbing socks. Remember that only the under sheet was changed each week, and clothes were not changed as often as they are today. We all survived nevertheless. Believe it or not, Grandma's laundry was always white and clean.

❖ Oh, Tithonia! ❖
by Barbara R. Graves, West Springfield, Massachusetts

One should never look a gift horse in the mouth, so the old adage goes. But sometimes the temptation is great. Such an occasion occurred this summer.

As we were taking care of the last plants in the greenhouse in May, my good friend Luci, whose judgment I can always count on, offered me a small plant in a small pot.

"Do you want this, Barbara?" asked Luci at the end of one morning's work.

Always open to more plants, I said "yes" and took what I thought was a basil. I planted it at the foot of my garden steps where I could reach it without going into the garden, gave it my usual desultory care, and it seemed to thrive.

Oh yes, it thrived all right. After about two weeks I noticed that it did not seem to be growing like a basil plant. In fact it seemed to be more like a sunflower. The next time that I saw Luci I asked what kind of plant my misnamed basil really was.

"Oh, that is a Mexican sunflower, a tithonia. It grows about four feet high."

I was a little surprised and a little perturbed, as after all, the thing was almost in the path to the regular garden. By this time the thought of moving this unexpectedly large plant was out of the question. The little plant was two feet tall and doing beautifully—a lush green and very healthy and rugged.

I left it alone, but I did check it every day or two.

By the first of August I realized that I was having to duck under a huge bush to get into the garden. Things did not get better. By September my little sunflower was six feet high and going strong. It was also beginning to blossom. At that point I was reconciled to the discomfort of pushing branches aside every time I went to pick a tomato and some string beans.

Something had happened to ease my pain—the Mexican sunflower blossomed and it was beautiful. The blossoms were not large, were a beautiful shade of burnt orange, and were widely distributed over the plant, which was now reaching its final height of at least eight feet with a comparable diameter.

I had something unusual to show my friends and neighbors. All admired it but very few wanted seeds.

On being questioned, Luci admitted that her tithonia had taken over her patio but she said that there was a smaller variety that grew only to four feet.

Next year no giant plant big enough for a two-acre garden, just a nice little four-foot Mexican sunflower.

❖ Grandfather and the Model T ❖
by Dorothy G. Hmieleski, South Deerfield, Massachusetts

In the 1920s my grandfather bought a Model T Ford. Grandfather had always been a lover of horses. There had always been horses on his farm in Sunderland, Massachusetts where he grew up, and he used horses in his logging business as well as for any traveling that he did. When he lived in Greenfield he boarded his horses at the livery stable that was located behind the present day Garden Theatre in Greenfield, Massachusetts.

Grandfather and the Model T did not get off to a very good start. He had trouble learning how to drive. One day he drove the car up a hill, and the car sputtered and coughed and shook. He didn't like that at all. His son told him, "Dad, you have to shift it."

Grandfather didn't see why he should. He said a horse could just go up hill with no trouble. He sold his Model T after a few weeks and never owned another car.

❖ Prospecting for Gold on Maple Street ❖
by Dick Hoyt, Winchedon, Massachusetts

One hot, summer day, sometime in the late 40s, Tommy Muir and I were building dams in the brook that ran up behind our house at 5 Maple Street in Shelburne Falls, Massachusetts when one of us, I forget who, spotted a shiny nugget in the stream bed.

"Hey, I bet this is gold!" one of us exclaimed.

We clambered up the clay bank of the brook and ran into our kitchen.

"Hey, Mom, look at this! Do you think it's gold?" (Moms were always home in those days.)

"I don't know. Perhaps you ought to take it down to Ben Kemp and have him take a look at it. We sure could use the money," she said excitedly.

We put our sample under the kitchen faucet, washed if off—it still shone like gold—and, our clothes still covered with mud, we began walking down Bridge Street, our ore tucked into a pocket, to Ben Kemp's jewelry store.

En route I remember talking about staking a claim and how I said to Tommy, "We better keep this a secret," and wondering how exactly to go about filing a claim. (Remember, every Saturday afternoon we watched along with half the kids in town, those serialized Westerns upstairs in

Memorial Hall, and the image of hardworking prospectors being swindled or ambushed by fast-talking, hair-slicked hustlers was fresh in our minds.)

Ben took our "gold" from a grubby hand, took out his loupe and, after turning it this way and that, put our sample on top of the thick glass counter that ran the length of the store. And such a store it was! The wood floor reeked of years of oiling and polish, there was the ticking of the myriad clocks on the shelves, and there were photos and cameras alongside the clocks and watches on those same shelves.

We shuffled our feet impatiently. Ben Kemp was not a young man then, and was slightly stooped from all the years of close work as the town's jeweler. He may have been about 5'8", tall and slender. He wore wire-rim glasses, and his thinning gray hair lay across his slightly balding head. He gently informed us with that twinkle in his eye that it was "fool's gold" or iron pyrite and that we were not the first to be so deceived by its resemblance to gold. Thus our introduction to geology.

I remember Ben's slight chuckle as he gently broke the news that we had not struck it rich. Disappointed, we left the store and went three doors down to Father's store, R. W. Hoyt Bottled Gas and Appliances, where we shared the bad news before beginning the longer, and much slower, trek back up Bridge Street and home. Father must have called Mother. When we walked into the kitchen, she had a pitcher of iced lemonade ready as we informed her of Ben's verdict and of our near miss at wealth.

We abandoned our dam building for the day. I think, by then, one of us said to the other, "Oh well, I didn't want to be rich anyway." Other adventures awaited us other days. Little did we know how rich we were in that time and place.

❖ Enjoyable Journey ❖
by Florence M. Lanfair, Turners Falls, Massachusetts

I recall a time that brings back some of my fondest memories. I was a small girl and it was the end of summer. My dad and mother would begin to make plans for a little outing. They would tell my sister and me that if it didn't rain on a certain Sunday, we would take a trip to visit our Aunt Debbie and Uncle Oscar. That would start me worrying until that special day arrived. As I remember it, the worry was for nothing, as the day would inevitably dawn bright and sunny.

Mother would pack a change of clothes and some night things. Dad would look up one of the men he knew and, if the man had extra time, Dad would hire him to take us from White River Junction, Vermont, where we lived, to Montpelier, Vermont, where Aunt Debbie and Uncle Oscar lived. Aunt Debbie was my mother's oldest sister.

It would be a lovely trip. My sister and I would be dressed up in our best dresses. Gertie was usually dressed in pink and I was dressed in blue. We'd wear large ribbon bows of matching color in our hair. I remember how proud I was of that beautiful hair ribbon!

It took quite a long time to get there, as the roads were all gravel. There was no hard top and the ride was very rough. Cars in those days were not made for speed.

Did I mention the dust? Let's forget about that!

At last we would arrive at Montpelier and drive by the Statehouse with its gold dome all aglow in the sunshine. From that point I knew it was only three more miles to Aunt Debbie's house. Aunt Debbie and Uncle Oscar lived on a farm three miles outside the city.

How happy I was as I looked in the distance and saw a trim brick farmhouse with large barns. I could hardly wait to drive into the yard where

Aunt Debbie would be waiting on the porch with a happy smile of greeting on her face. We were so happy to see one another that we all talked at once. What a happy sound!

With Aunt Debbie leading the way into the house, the first room we entered was the dining room. There was a very large table with many places set for the meal. Aunt Debbie had done lots of work, for she had her own family and two hired men and all of us, including our driver who would spend time there with us until it was time to drive us back home again.

One of the nicest things about Aunt Debbie was that she would plan to cook many of our favorite dishes. Graham Gems, for example, that she always baked in an iron gem pan. Could that be why they always came out of the oven tasting so good—the iron gem pan? Another favorite was her Maple Sugar Doughnuts (my favorite!). For breakfast she served pie besides all the other good food. I was surprised to see pie for breakfast. My mother only served pie at our house after the evening meal for dessert.

Aunt Debbie also made butter to sell and she had so many customers that she had trouble keeping enough for her own use. She had a wooden butter mold with the design of a clover blossom and leaf. It was very attractive.

There is another room in my memory that I would like to tell about. It was Aunt Debbie's parlor. It was a room set aside for weddings, funerals, and special company. Sister Gert and I must have been special company for we were always allowed to go in and enjoy all the lovely treasures. It was such a pretty room. There was an organ. Gert could play chords as we sang. We would tease Aunt Debbie to come for a short while and she would play her concertina and we would clap our hands. It was a special get together! This was before my youngest sister was born.

Night time came and it was time for bed. Aunt Debbie had so

many guests she ran out of beds, so Gert and I had to sleep upstairs in a large hallway on a mattress on the floor. Mother and Aunt Debbie carried the oil lamp up the stairs and got us all snug in our bed. When they left with the lamp it became very dark and we couldn't see each other's faces. We were just falling asleep when we heard it—rock, rock, rock—and it kept on. We were so afraid. We couldn't see and we didn't want to cry out, so we huddled together and shook. Then it stopped! We got some sleep and in the morning we rushed downstairs and told Aunt Debbie how frightened we were in the night.

"Oh my land!" she said. She rushed up the stairs and went over to a corner. There was a big, gray-blue Hubbard squash there. It was the biggest one I'd ever seen.

"This is Uncle Oscar's prize squash. He was planning to take it to the fair," she said. She moved the squash and on one side there was a large hole that had been chewed in it. We could see all the seeds were gone. Uncle Oscar was some upset! He had taken special care in growing that squash and had hoped to win a prize!

❖ Resurrection ❖
by Elisabeth Leete, Ashfield, Massachusetts

The problem when you live and work in two languages is that you don't know who you are. It's as simple as that. Some days I am English, some days I am French, some days I am both. Today I think I am French and maybe my non-poem is in French. The mountains, the lakes, the forests I imagined must have been French. When I woke up I was reciting a poem Lamartine wrote while sitting on the edge of a beautiful mountain lake, thinking of a woman he loved:

Oh temps suspends ton vol
Et vous, heures propices
Suspendez votre cours.
Laissez-nous savourer
Les rapides délices
Du plus beau de nos jours.
(Oh time suspend your flight/ and you, propitious hours/ suspend your course./ Let us savor/the passing delights/of the most beautiful of our days.)

I dreamed a poem that had everything a poem should have: Musical sounds, enchanting rhythms, momentous crescendos, mischievous diminuendos, a touch of mystery, and a tad of philosophy.

When I woke up I searched for that poem on the kitchen counter. But I could not find it.

I looked inside the wood stove, behind the bathroom door, on top of the living room desk. But it wasn't there.

I asked my soul to tell me about it but my soul didn't answer. All I found was a blank page, a multitude of blank pages.

Later that day, driving on a beautiful early spring morning, I saw an opening in the blue sky and in the opening, a magnificent, towering white mountain. I longed to climb it, to see the view from the top: green valleys cut in two by torrential blue streams from the glaciers. Layers and layers of green mountains dotted with yellow, white and purple flowers. Pastures, quiet herds of brown cows and white sheep. Forests and limpid lakes. But as I came closer the mountain became just a fluffy cloud dispersed by the wind.

When I was young, I fell in love many times and thought I saw perfection in the men I loved: intelligence, beauty, generosity, charm and gentleness. But usually that love was nothing but a crush, and the man a good-for-nothing.

One autumn, some years ago, I planted thirty-five daffodil bulbs around my pond. At the end of every winter I dreamed of a yellow explosion, an orgy of color that would make the sun jealous, but every spring when I walk around the pond I see nothing but mud and weeds.

No poem, no white mountain, no man, no daffodils.

But there are pink lilies on the table, birds singing in the trees, music in the afternoon, an infinitely blue sky, friendships, laughter, and resurrection.

❖ Lincoln School—1936 ❖
by Warren LeMon, York, Maine

Lincoln School on Lincoln Avenue in the small city of Mount Vernon, New York.

A blue piece of paper with a dripping white star. The blue of the paper is cold, and the white of the paint is cold, and together they are very cold. It is winter and there is an aroma throughout the school which smacks of Christmas.

A cold season, winter is, when your mother wraps you in long winter pants—toboggan pants—and rubbery galoshes with metal clasps that lock and unlock unless your fingers are too cold and stiff to manage and impossible to manage if you still have your mittens on. But, no bother, your good teachers—Miss Giles and Miss Swanson and Miss Elifeld and Mrs. Parker will help you in the cloak room in the back where all the hooks and snaps hung.

You are elected—or selected—to be the editor of the third grade newspaper. Also you are accused of being the loved one of a certain classmate—a girl.

You make clumsy transparent efforts to deny it. You scoff out loud:

"Why don't you print it in the papers?"

You like the sound of the question and you repeat it, eliciting giggles from your fellow third graders.

Lincoln School is a very nice school.

❖ Home to Paris ❖
by Warren LeMon, York, Maine

I was supposed to go to Spain to visit my cousin in June 1961, but became ill. I spent the entire summer in the military wing of the American Hospital in Paris at Neuilly-sur-Seine. I passed the early autumn convalescing at our base at Camp des Loges near St. Germaine-en-Laye.

But the following year, the invitation was renewed and I flew to Madrid.

And that is about all I have to say about those two weeks with my cousin and her family, because what I want to talk about concerns my return to Paris. By that time I had lived there almost two years. I did not realize her beauty had filtered so deeply into my conscious being. I had been too close to the buildings to see the city.

Unlike the sleek, plastic, antiseptic flight out to Spain, I came back by train: third class to the Iberian border, second class to Paris.

The rocking of the cars as they rolled on their wheels along the tracks was mesmerizing. Mesmerizing, too, were the broad plains of Castille, the upland climb of earth as we entered the lower Pyrenees, the sun and blue sky fading, falling, dying, a violet dusk, and then darkness.

No one to tell one to go to bed. No one to destroy the night's beauty with chatter. Some noises at the border. A transfer from Spanish to French cars. Squeak, squeak, grind, grind. Boom! as the cars were coupled.

As I sat in perfect, quiet darkness after midnight on the French car, the moment of recognition began. The design of the seats and the windows and the handles on them were Gallic. Spain was a desert, a garden, a ranch. Honest wood and humble simplicity. France was authentically cosmopolitan.

As the train races northward, one dozes and on awakening feels that one is traveling unerringly in the right direction.

At first light I saw trees, houses, fences, roads, all France. The train rocketed on, and suddenly there was the Seine, the luring river, the magnetic river. The buildings flew by and I felt a warmth, a glow, I am coming home, I am embraced by the arms of Paris, the gorgeous city, the welcoming forgiving mother.

❖ York Beach ❖
by Warren LeMon, York, Maine

There is a longing in the heart of the average man or woman which is enhanced by pleasing sights and sounds and aromas. This longing may be traced to romance, not of a sexual nature, but as it applies to wonder and glamour and curtained mysteries.

The gypsy caravans which rattled and rolled through the winding ways of Europe in centuries past held the keys to this lure: lights and shadows, smoke and fire, the thrill of the question and the thrill of the answer.

These secrets were transferred to the players of Broadway, and their myriad adherents, since the early nineteenth century. At York Beach, Maine, for more than one hundred years, the atmosphere from June to September has been pure Coney Island. It differs from York Harbor and York Village which is Victorian and Edwardian seaside.

At York Beach, the elephants bray, the tigers roar, the monkeys chatter and screech. Huge lighted marquees decorate every other doorway. The sweet-salty odor of peanuts and popcorn and sizzling franks and fried dough are at one's nose; the cries of families wandering the sidewalks in search of souvenirs and lobster rolls predominate. Madame Zeena, for a modest sum, will take you back into her beckoning private chamber and echo what she can tell is already in your heart.

The lights burn until dawn when a damp mist rolls in across the beach.

The perpetual Atlantic forms the backdrop to this summer romance. If you stare very hard straight out to sea—beyond Boon Island Light—there are—though it be thousands of miles away—the golden shores of the Spanish kingdom to dream upon. Mystery enough.

❖ Never Rarely Often Always ❖
by Warren LeMon, York, Maine

I am enrolled in a military health program which I find most satisfactory. I did, that is, until I was presented with a questionnaire which rather confounded me. I appreciate thc program is dealing with masses of people, and number-crunchers always seek to reduce costs.But I mean, really.

Each question—no matter its nature—had four possible answers:

Never, Rarely, Often, Always. Only one was to be circled.

There was no room for explanation or amplification. Or clarification.

How often did I do such-and-such? Did I experience such-and-such a reaction to such-and-such a stimuli? Will I ever answer such questions again?

Never. Rarely. Often. Always.

❖ A Day at Greenfield Pool ❖
by Eileen Marguet, Greenfield, Massachusetts

It was usually a bright, warm day in July when we would plan our family "day at the pool" in Greenfield, Massachusetts. It meant rounding up our kids, our company's kids, and a few neighbors in West Halifax, Vermont.

We'd pile into our big red station wagon with all we would need. It might have seemed a little crowded, but that didn't lessen the excitement. We all loved going to the Greenfield pool which was part of the Green River dammed up to create a swimming area.

When we'd pull into the parking area, in view of the green wooden building, all four car doors would open at once and it was every man for himself!

"Last one in is a rotten egg!" someone would yell.

"First one eats it!" another would answer.

Splashing started and children of all ages were finding their favorite activity. I had to interrupt the fun and coax the gang to carry our baggage over the bridge to find a nice empty picnic table and a cool spot for the playpen. Then they were all racing back into the river. That was the time for my husband, Bill, and I to relax a bit.

Seeing the kids going down the slide, hoping they didn't bump into each other, took some watching. They played some water games that were all fun, but very noisy.

Getting the food ready sharpened everyone's appetite and we ate heartily. Of course, there was a trip to the refreshment stand (operated by the Most twins) to find something we might have forgotten. Food always tastes so much better when picnicking.

After a short rest we were ready to go in the water again. Bill and I took turns babysitting. The swim across the pool and back was enough for me. Bill enjoyed teaching the kids how to dive from the low board and even the high board. It looked as if we might have a few Olympic hopefuls seeing how much they all improved over time.

The day couldn't end until we took a trip to the A&P and Woolworth's on Main Street in Greenfield. We had to replenish our food supply for the coming week.

It was a long time before I started coming back to the Greenfield pool. All my kids are grown. Bill is gone and life for me is very different. When I come to the Green River Swimming and Recreation area (which it is now called) my lawn chair is not as heavy as the playpen was. I can easily manage it myself. I still like to swim just across and back.

When my nieces and nephews come to visit they like to drive past the pool. The Most boys are probably grandparents now and the old green building has been replaced by a new masonry structure.

I wonder if the men of the WPA (Work Progress Administration) who built the Green River pool ever realized how much happiness they would be providing for so many, even today.

❖ The Dining Room Table ❖
by Eileen Marguet, Greenfield, Massachusetts

It was a large, oak table with three leaves. We usually only used one leaf which made the table big enough for our family.

The dining room was the largest room downstairs. It had a fireplace and doors that could be moved into the walls (pocket-doors). At the time our house was built this was the warmest room in the house.

When the dishes were cleared we sat around the table again and resumed conversations begun earlier. Sometimes there were two or three conversations going at once.

Democrats and Republicans had their spokesmen and political issues were clarified. Often a friend or two might arrive and join the party. Nobody won or lost at that time. When someone decided to read the paper it was spread out on the table. *The Brooklyn Daily Eagle* took precedence over the *New York Times*.

If my mother had sewing to do, what better place to cut out a pattern than on that table. It was large enough so you could turn the material this way and that while walking around it.

There was one night a month when my dad played poker with his cronies. When it was his turn to have the game at our house, we kids made ourselves scarce and did our homework on the floor of our bedrooms so he could have the table, and his friends, to himself.

We also did our share of card-playing and there was always another favorite, Lotto. We often put all three leaves in the table and played ping pong. We covered the chandelier so it wouldn't get hurt. Games were not rough, but respectful and fun.

I remember the dining room table mostly for the homework we did there. Often we studied out loud. I can remember my sister Peggy, reading

Latin: "Agricola, agricolae, feminine, farmer." I remember my brother Jimmy memorizing a song: "The minstrel boy to war has gone, in the ranks of death you'll find him. His father's sword he has girded on and his wild heart slung behind him."

Jimmy was the first of my brothers to be drafted in World War II. He was severely wounded there. Whenever I hear bagpipes playing it's usually the minstrel boy tune they play. It reminds me of all the people who were part of my life growing up. Perhaps all our lives are the sum of experiences we have had. In my life that includes all the times life played out at our dining room table.

❖ My First Job ❖
by Eileen Marguet, Greenfield, Massachusetts

I remember my first real job. It was back in 1936 when I was just starting at Brooklyn College. That job was like nothing I've ever experienced since.

Lord & Taylor was and is a most prestigious store. It's on Fifth Avenue and 38th Street. To work there on Saturday they gave me three days of training. I was even paid $3 a day for the training time!

I worked on the fifth floor in the Young New Yorker Shop selling coats, suits and sweaters. We were invited to wear clothes we were selling and was that ever fun! Picking out which skirt to wear with which sweater!

We got a ten minute break in the morning and the same in the afternoon. There was a restaurant across 37th Street called The Quality Shop where we had soup, a sandwich and a lavish dessert all for (you won't believe this!) twenty-five cents with a five cent tip!

Out of that magnificent $3-per-hour salary I made I seemed to have money left over for all sorts of things. One of the pluses of this job was a sale they held just before Christmas in a huge room upstairs. Everything in that room was marked down. One time I bought a corduroy jacket for myself and one for each of my four sisters during that sale. The jackets were just $1 a piece. They were beautiful! Mine was a bright turquoise with a cardigan neck and red leather buttons. I had it for years. It never wore out.

I can remember my sister Kay saying, "You'll never be this wealthy again."

"Oh," I said. "This is only the beginning of my brilliant career in retailing."

Somehow I didn't understand what my sister meant, but I know now. That money was like gold in those times. I savored every dime I spent.

❖ The Front Porch ❖
by Eileen Marguet, Greenfield, Massachusetts

Perhaps it's just part of over-all Americana. Or did the front porch have another function in the lives of those a few generations ago? It was a place between the security of home and the pressures of the outside world; a place where men left from to go to work each day.

In inclement weather folks could shake the rain or snow from their clothes on the porch—or even dust off their shoes. I remember people standing on the porch saying goodbye in war time, and the homecoming of returning servicemen. They came back to their folks waiting on a porch, too.

I can remember when I was very young and the weather was

warm, we spent so much time together on the porch. Supper was often served there. It was *the* place for socializing with neighbors and friends. For young people it was where courting took place. It was where families got to know each other.

Before TV and even radio, the news of the day was circulated just sitting there watching people going by, exchanging information, or notes of interest. Kids stayed up a little later during the summer, listening to old folks. Think of how much we learned by observing all kinds of stories and activities that were circulated.

New England was famous for the number and size of porches. Clothes were often hung out to dry there. In Vermont, before the advent of clothes dryers, you could guess the homeowner's occupation by the garments waving in the wind. One Victorian-style house told the neighbors of the man's outdoor occupation: long johns, often stiff with the cold.

Many of the three story houses had a porch on each floor. They certainly took the place of air-conditioning in the summer.

There were many large hotels where guests might stay for several weeks. Kennedy rockers were the usual furniture on the spacious front porch. Some large colonial homes added the front porch as the owners' incomes increased. Frequently it was a wrap-around porch, going halfway across the side of the house. There was the "me-to" porch, possibly added after the house was built. It was built just a few feet deep, but had the same purpose as any other porch.

Over the years, porches showed up on houses in the rear, or on the side. Patios, terraces and decks have become popular, perhaps as people today prefer privacy, but the front porch is still the hallmark of a friendly home.

❖ Childhood's End ❖
by Joseph A. Parzych, Gill, Massachusetts

The huge olive-drab Army bus cruised down the highway, gently rocking like a ship at sea. I'd never been on a ship, but that's what I imagined it would be like. The high backed seats were soft and comfortable. I enjoyed the ride until doubts crept into my mind. I wondered if I'd done the right thing.

It had all started on a pleasant summer day in June 1946 barely a month before. I was savoring the liberty of being out of school for the summer, out in the fresh air raking hay with our homemade tractor towing a one-horse dump rake. The warm sun and gentle breeze felt good. First I raked the hay into windrows, letting up on the gas as I yanked on the trip rope tied to the rake's dump lever. Then I straddled the windrows with the tractor to gather them into haycocks. I aligned the haycocks in rows, leaving room for the hay wagon to pass. I loved the aroma of new mown hay and the feeling of freedom of being out of stuffy classrooms and in the open air under sunny skies. Life couldn't get any better than this, I thought, humming a little tune. The noise of the engine seemed to harmonize with my happy song. I thought about times past when the whole family took part in the haying ritual.

Haying usually began the first part of June, and I always looked forward to the hustle and bustle that went with it. I loved the excitement and noise— the clatter of the mowing machine, its pitman arm and cutters flying to and fro in a blur of moving parts. There was always a sense of urgency once the hay was cut and drying. My father would scan the sky for signs of rain as the family hurried to get the hay raked, piled into haycocks, loaded on the wagon, and hauled into the barn before a sudden summer rain storm could spoil it.

Local Color 457

But now all the kids in our family were gone. They'd all left home except for my younger brother and me. But I didn't dwell on that. I knew we could still get the hay in, even if it took a bit more time, as long as the weather held. And nothing could ruin this perfect day.

My father came trudging out to the field and I wondered why. There was no need for him to be out here. A heart attack had slowed him and he was getting on in years. He held out a letter. I shut off the engine so we could talk.

"This came in the mail for you," he said and watched as I opened it. The letter was from Mount Hermon School in Gill, Massachusetts where I was a day student. The letter informed me that I'd passed all my subjects, but they suggested I'd be happier going to school elsewhere.

"What's it say?" my father asked.

"They don't want me to come back."

"What you gonna do?" he asked.

"I don't know, Pa," I said, starting up the engine to resume raking hay. The truth was I *really didn't know* what I was going to do. I'd felt good about being the only boy in town accepted to the school. Now they were telling me they didn't want me. I knew I could have done better. Getting that letter made me feel like a total failure. Why hadn't I tried harder and studied more? The humiliation of facing my former classmates at Turners Falls High School was not what I wanted to do. Still, I wanted to finish high school and go on to college. I tried to concentrate on pulling the trip rope so the piles would be evenly spaced. But my timing was off. All sorts of thoughts ran through my mind.

Feelings of frustration, shame and anger came over me. The sun felt hot, and hay chaff now clung to my sweaty skin in an annoying way. This is a stupid way to farm, I thought, trying to farm with a tractor made out of an old car dragging an old horse-rake when neighbors drove Farmalls or Ford-Fergusons pulling hay balers running off the power take-off, making neat bales.

When the hay was gathered into piles, I went back to the barn to get the wagon. My brother Louis, my mother, and my father came out to help get the hay in. My father drove the tractor towing the wagon through the field. I pitched hay onto the load while Louis and my mother built the load and tramped down the hay. Usually I dressed the wagonload into a neat cube by raking the sides even and pitching the hay back up on top. But today I really didn't care what the load looked like; I just wanted to get the hay in the barn and be done with it.

A few days later I drove to a gas station to have an inner tube vulcanized. Less than a year since the end of World War II, the only tire tubes available were made of brittle synthetic rubber. A regular tube patch wouldn't hold. After I put the vulcanized tube and tire back on the rim, it'd go flat, again and again. The slightest bit of rust or scale would cause a leak and I'd have to take the tire apart and patch the leak. As I went through the frustrating process of vulcanizing yet another leak and reassembling the tire, again, a friendly Army recruiter struck up a conversation.

"You look a little down in the dumps," he said.

When I confessed my school dilemma, he assured me that I could complete my education in the Army, get free room and board, medical and dental care, shoes and clothes, and $75 dollars a month besides.

"That's the perfect solution," he said. "And we got a special deal. If you sign up right now, we offer an eighteen-month enlistment. But, because you're only 17 you'll have to get your folks to sign for you."

I hadn't counted on needing my parents' signature. I was afraid they wouldn't sign for me. The next night after supper, I got up the nerve to show them the enlistment papers and tell them I wanted to join the Army. I thought I'd have to convince them it was a good idea, but they agreed without any coaxing. I'd have felt a lot better if they'd shown even the slightest hesitation.

The day soon came for me to leave. My father offered me a ride to Greenfield, Massachusetts where the recruiters had an office above the post office. My mother came with us, which surprised and pleased me. We rode along in silence. To break the silence, I said, "This would be a good day to make hay."

Then I remembered that they'd depended on me to help with the haying. How would they get the hay in, I wondered, with Pa's heart condition and Louis only thirteen? Who would pitch the hay onto the wagon and then up into the hay mow? Guilt came over me for deserting them and thinking only of myself.

At the post office, a big olive-green bus sat waiting. We got out of the car and stood, not knowing what to say or do. I shook my father's hand and gave my mother a hug. She hugged me for a long time, and then tried to smile, biting her lip to keep from crying. My eyes got a little watery and I hoped the others on the bus wouldn't notice. I climbed aboard and sat by a window to wave goodbye. But they were gone.

I didn't know it, but I was leaving my childhood behind. The big diesel bus roared away from the post office to an uncertain future in a world that I would soon discover wasn't as rosy as the recruiter had painted.

The bus stopped in Springfield. A rough looking bunch of recruits got on, including an older man wearing an Army jacket and smelling of liquor. It made me uneasy to see that everyone was much older. They talked and joked among themselves— all but the old soldier.

"I ain't one of them stupid jerks," he said to the recruiters. "I'm re-upping for another hitch."

The bus belched black smoke and roared off toward Boston. Afternoon shadows lengthened as we reached Fort Banks. I hadn't eaten much breakfast and I felt faint from hunger. They herded us into a cafeteria. The rowdy recruits jostled each other for a place in line. I hung back, letting them go first. When I got to the food servers, a grandmotherly woman working behind the counter looked at me and said, "Oh my, you're so young."

I could feel my face flushing. I picked up my tray of food and went to a table. Some of the others sat wolfing their food, talking with full mouths, and laughing loudly at their own inane remarks. One man picked up his food and ate with his fingers, wiping them on his clothes. I thought how different this was from eating in the Mount Hermon dining hall where a professor sat at the head of each table. Students dressed in suit jackets and neckties dined on white table cloths with cloth napkins, correctly used silver, ate like gentlemen and carried on a quiet dinner conversation. I felt like an outsider attending a primitive feast and hoped this was the last I'd see of this rough bunch.

After supper, our escorts herded us into a barn-like building with a room that seemed as long as a football field. Rows of beds lined each wall. The old soldier threw his satchel on the bed next to me and announced he was going to the PX for beer. The others flocked along behind him.

With the barracks empty, I got ready for bed and knelt to say my nightly prayers, glad to have the room empty. Exhausted from a long day, farther from home than I'd ever been in my life, I felt tired and lonely. I tried to swallow the lump in my throat as homesickness came over me. I visualized the folks at home around the supper table, just the three of them, now. I wondered if they felt as lonely as I did, and I hoped everything would work out for them with the haying and all.

Hours later, just as I was dozing off, the other recruits came back, drunk and rowdy. The old soldier yelled, "Everybody shaddup!" Then he flopped in his bunk, flat on his back, and fell asleep with his mouth open. I lay awake most of the night listening to him snore as I'd never heard anyone snore before. I wondered if this was the education I wanted.

❖ First Day in Church ❖
by Joseph A. Parzych, Gill, Massachusetts

I don't know exactly how old I was when my father first took me to church, though I don't think I was six yet. I do remember being puzzled he'd chosen me. He hadn't paid me a lot of attention before then. My mother and sisters may have had something to do with it. They wanted to stay home and continue fussing over our new baby Julia, bathing and dressing and cooing to her.

I was happy to go, though, especially since my younger brother, Louis, was much too little to go to such an important place as church. He had to stay home with the girls.

My father dressed up in his blue suit, white shirt, red necktie, big black overcoat and his bulb-toed hightop shoes shined bright. My sisters bundled me up in a warm jacket and put one of their berets on my head. He put his driving cap at an angle. I adjusted my beret to match. We made a dandy pair as we went out the door.

We drove off in my father's pride, his Essex automobile with the crank-up windows and bud vases on the door posts. He liked to talk about its powerful Super Six engine with aluminum pistons and adjustable louvers on the radiator. The carburetor even had a heater. Unfortunately, the passengers had none. Our breath looked like we were smoking. I was glad to have on long underwear and a heavy, woolen coat. My father sat up straight, handling the big wooden steering wheel and fiddling with the choke and knobs for the radiator control as though he were piloting a river boat on the Mississippi.

At the Polish church in Turners Falls, Massachusetts, the immense set of stone steps leading to the entrance seemed like the stairs leading to the top of an Aztec temple where priests sacrificed children. The Aztec children couldn't have been any more intimidated than me as I tried to keep up with my father striding up those steep stairs.

The huge front doors opened into a hushed interior with ceilings that seemed nearly as high as the sky. Sunlight streamed through stained glass windows and cast colored patterns where it fell. The smell of incense, statues of saints, fancy altar, and paintings of angels on the ceiling made me wonder if the stairs had somehow led us to heaven. I began to doubt that as we headed for a pew, going by statues of dead bodies with bloody wounds.

Suddenly, the beret was snatched from my head.

I looked around to see who'd taken it. No one was there. I looked up at my father. He continued walking, looking straight ahead, his hat in his hand. Apparently, he hadn't noticed what had happened. I continued to follow him.

Once seated in a pew, my father pushed a brass button on the back of the pew in front of us. A little hanger sprang open and he hung up his hat. I'd hoped he had my beret in his hand along with his hat. No such luck. I stared at the little button with an empty hook in front of me and prayed for a miracle. Ma often said she prayed for miracles.

The beret didn't appear. I didn't seem to have any better luck with praying than Ma did.

I didn't dare speak to my father for fear of getting cuffed in front of God and everybody. Maybe he wouldn't notice the beret gone, and I could throw myself on the mercy of my sisters when I got home. They might holler at me for losing their beret, but at least they wouldn't spank me. But my father was sure to notice as soon as I left the church.

Soon the priest began rattling off prayers in machine gun style getting into the swing of the mass. His voice rose and fell, and then rose again, until his hollering scared me. I hoped he wasn't hollering at me for walking in without taking off my beret.

The only thing I could think of was the mystery of the vanishing beret all during church service. I knew I was going to get a good licking for losing that nice brown beret with the little curved tail sticking up at the top, and it wasn't even my fault. Or was it? I shouldn't have been so proud of myself all dressed up. I'd been warned about being proud.

What would I tell my sisters when they asked what happened to their beret when I had no idea myself what had happened, and my father hadn't seen anything, either? Perhaps God had snatched the beret from my head. Maybe he gave it to some woman who'd forgotten to wear a hat, since all the women, I noticed, wore hats in church while the men wore none.

Here I'd felt so lucky to be the only one to go to church with my father, and now I was in a jam, again. Why hadn't he left me home and taken one of my sisters? Then I wouldn't be in all this trouble.

It wasn't even fun. My knees hurt from kneeling on the hard little wooden benches down by the floor. I couldn't see what was going on, nor understand the priest's Polish half the time. The service dragged on forever. The heavy coat I was bundled up in made me hot and my long underwear began to itch. I dared not scratch for fear I'd get cuffed. Would this church service ever end?

There seemed to be no limit to sitting, standing, kneeling, sitting, and back to standing in this strange game of silent Simon Says, which I mostly guessed wrong. Just when I felt like we were going to spend the rest of our lives jumping up and down, folks acted more lively, women picked up their pocket books and men began unsnapping their hats.

Pa got his hat from the little hanger and headed for the door. He still hadn't noticed that I wasn't carrying the beret. I followed, keeping my eyes peeled for that damned beret, hoping someone had found it and put it where I could see it, or that God might take pity on me for not knowing I was committing a sin by keeping my beret on in church and would put it back on my head just as quickly as it had vanished. No such luck. I began trying to figure out an excuse for losing the beret. Nothing came to me.

Outside the church, the long set of stone stairs looked awful steep. I hesitated. Pa reached into his pocket, slipped out the beret and put it on my head. I looked up at him and smiled. He smiled back and took my hand.

When we got home, my sisters were coaxing baby Julia to smile and kick her feet in delight. I took off the beret and waited for Pa to tell everyone what a fool I'd made of myself wearing the damn thing into church.

"How did everything go?" one of my sisters asked. Pa shrugged, "Church is church. Nothing ever happens in church."

❖ Never Too Young to Fall in Love ❖
by Jack Perry, Shutesbury, Massachusetts

I fell in love three times before I was eight years old. I don't know if this is a record—there are hardly any little kids' diaries available to check with. The passionate encounters were all unrequited, and they may have scarred me for life

The first was my Sunday school teacher, Miss Pardun, whom I recall in a sort of powder-blue haze. She always wore blue and that may be why blue has remained my favorite color to this day. The other thing I remember is that when she smiled—a very wide, expressive smile—her eyes narrowed to slits and glistened. I couldn't have been more than four or five years old and was the only boy amid a passel of girls in her class. They all babbled and squeaked but I never uttered a word.

Seeing I was the only boy and hopelessly shy, Miss Pardun would take me on her lap and hold me while she read bible stories, hugging me, patting me and kissing my little cheek. I knew when to keep my mouth shut.

The second was the mother of one of my classmates who lived two blocks away. Mrs. Littlefield. I was six years old and walking to school, first grade. All kids walked to school, even kindergartners. There were no busses unless you lived more than a mile. Crowds of little people trudged daily through the streets of Clarion, Iowa giggling and chattering and kicking cans ahead of them—or rolling a hoop, as I often did.

But instead of going to school I would pick dandelions, take them to Mrs. Littlefield's house, knock on the door and give them to her. She would clasp her hands in joy, take my offering, ask me in for a glass of milk and call my mother, who would soon arrive, take me by the arm and march me to school. However, I continued to stray, showing up regularly at Mrs. Littlefield's house (I found her most attractive).

Finally, my mother, fed up with that nonsense—since I was obviously impervious to scolding—cut a switch from a maple tree and drove me ahead of her, flicking my bare little legs smartly as she walked fast, keeping me at a run. I cried all the way to school. And I stopped picking dandelions for Mrs. Littlefield.

At age seven I became enamored of my second-grade teacher, Miss Christian. One day at recess I was picked on by some boys from the second and third grades. At recess the girls often dragged me away to play with them—and I went willingly, preferring their games to the rough games of the boys.

The boys started after me but the pack of girls drove them off. One of the girls, Ruth Salisbury, a tough tomboy, shoved a few of them over. Well, they yelled that they would get me after school. When school let out I refused to leave the classroom and go home.

Ultimately, all persuasion failing, Miss Christian said she'd walk home with me if I'd show her the way. She took my hand and walked the whole eight blocks. Halfway home, downtown, she said she thought we ought to have some refreshment for such a long walk and took me to the Corner Drug Store for a soda. She kept smiling at me across the soda fountain table and I was a goner.

Later, at home, she had tea with my mother. Before she left she hugged and kissed me and I wondered if I could ever live without her.

I also suffered many embarrassments as a child—usually, it seems, at the hands of girls or women. Sometimes it happened to me in school by teachers who embarrassed me in front of the class by favoring me. Whenever I was embarrassed I looked cross-eyed, an "escape" reaction I developed to shut out those around me.

The cross-eyed business went on for years, even in high school. Once in a football game with Hampton, a 30-yard touchdown run was nullified when I was called for clipping, which was very upsetting to our all-conference quarterback and captain Carrol Swanger. I went a whole series of downs blocking cross-eyed.

The most flagrant incident occurred when I once took a girl to a movie on a first date, then walked her home. We sat in her parlor alone on the sofa; she settled herself comfortably at one end and we talked. She started to doze off, I noticed, so I stopped talking in mid-sentence and, sure enough, she fell sound asleep—a tribute, no doubt, to my scintillating conversation.

I watched her sleep for about fifteen minutes—until she began to snore. Clearing my throat loudly didn't rouse her at all, so I got up and let myself out, being careful to close the door quietly (though there was certainly no reason for that). Standing on the walk in front of her house I could still hear her.

The embarrassment came the next night. I was in the New Home Café with three guys when she came in and headed straight for our booth. Confronting me, fists on hips, eyes blazing, she shoved her face close to mine.

"Surprised to see me?" she spat out.

"A little," I replied meekly. "I thought you were hibernating."

Not funny. She slammed her hand against the back of the booth near my head and we all recoiled. She proceeded to tell me off royally in a loud voice, really ripping into me. It was devastating. I sat there petrified and immediately began to look cross-eyed. It enraged her! She stopped suddenly mid-tirade:

"Stop doing that with your eyes!" she demanded.

"I'm not doing anything," I lied.

"Are you making fun of me?" she screamed. Without waiting for an answer, her roundhouse left caught me with the flat of her hand—wham!—and she stormed out.

Only two others have ever slapped my face—my mother and my seventh-grade music teacher—both for being "too flip, young man!"

A girl once threw a chair at me—but that's another story.

❖ The Parade of Pots ❖
by Charlotte Robinson, Turners Falls, Massachusetts

During the second semester of my sophomore year at Sargent College in Boston, one of our college instructors, Mary, asked if I would like to be a counselor at a camp where she was the director. Within a couple of days I said "yes" to her and she filled me in on what I would have to know.

The camp was located on the Clara Barton Homestead Estate and was called the "Clara Barton Camp." Clara Barton, of course, was one of the first nurses to volunteer as a battlefield nurse during the Civil War. She was "The Angel of the Battlefield" and she was also the founder of the American Red Cross. Her homestead in Oxford, Massachusetts, was the ideal place for this camp because it was established under laboratory conditions for diabetic girls. It was an alternative for girls aged 5-18 to have their diabetes regulated rather than spending a lot of dreary days at the sterile Joslin Clinic in Boston. And this camp was so much more fun for the girls!

The girls were all in a very brittle condition and we counselors had to have a roll of Lifesavers™ on our person at all times. The Lifesavers™ were just that. After a few days with the girls we could easily appraise a girl by the slightest change in her demeanor, and would know that one Lifesaver™ would provide an infinitesimal rise in her blood sugar level and perhaps prevent a reaction.

During the first pre-camp session we were assigned specific duties. I was to be the camp craft instructor. Others were assigned to art, music, games, dramatics, nature, and swimming. These designations were, of course, in addition to being cabin leaders for the 10-12 girls in the cabin. The girls were assigned to cabins by age. The youngest girls were placed in the cabin nearest the administration building, and the older girls were farther away. Each cabin had two counselors, designated #1 and #2. We had to sleep lightly to notice if any of our charges might be too low or too high in sugar. My job as #1 was to assess a problem—would I go to alert the "first responders" or would I send #2? One of us had to go for help and one would stay to control the non-involved girls whenever trouble appeared.

A select group of four counselors who had several years of experience at this camp were the only ones to answer a cabin leader's call for assistance. This tactic prevented others from gathering and creating a circus atmosphere. Any of these four could immediately have a calming effect on the cabin involved. Having already witnessed a grand mal seizure years earlier, I was pleased that I had been assigned to remain in my cabin when the trouble was in a different cabin.

Several days into the activities of camp, Mary told me about the purchase of an additional lot of land abutting the homestead. It was about 18 acres of woods and was on a slight hill. Mary instructed me to investigate the woods, find a place to make a camping area for overnight trips and, with the help of the girls, get it done! The site soon contained a fireplace with lots of wood, no underbrush, and a nice flat space for sleeping bags. We inaugurated the site with a cookout supper, a late snack after a singing session, and wonderful sleep. Although we had with us all of the food for breakfast and were soon eating heartily, a group of counselors appeared carrying cans of orange juice for the campers. Of course we didn't need the juice. Eventually all of the campers had the opportunity to sleep out under the stars. The ratio of counselors to campers for the campout was set at one counselor to three campers.

The kitchen staff had to weigh all of the food for all of the campers for the first few days, and then campers knew about how much to put on their plates from the family-style dishes.

The most difficult time for campers was the half-hour before lunch. That was when we all gathered near the mess hall and waited to be called into the hall. We had to watch the girls carefully, as most of them were so hungry. The lunches changed everything. Games or races were held after lunch, followed by a quiet time in the cabins.

Occasionally we took the girls on hikes—always on side roads, never cross-country. Everyone would be bused to an area two or three miles from camp. When the hike back to camp began, two counselors led the way. Two counselors brought up the rear of the long line and the other counselors were spaced along the line. A camp auto followed quite a distance to the rear. In the event that any of the girls had to sit and rest or sip juice and chew a Lifesaver™, one of the last counselors had to wait with her. Shortly, the trailing car would appear and the camper would be taken by car back to camp and the nurse. The girls mostly sang as they hiked, kept a steady pace and demonstrated the need to assess their own physical well-being.

When any of the girls were swimming in the small pond, many of the staff had to be lifeguards. The "Partner's Call" was heard very frequently and the campers learned to respond immediately.

Every year the girls and staff produced a play, usually a musical. One year it was "The Mikado." Most of the parents came to see their productions.

I enjoyed two years as staff at this camp. We were kept on our toes every minute. The girls tried to mix me up, like the time they brought some ping pong balls to me and told me they were turtle eggs and they wanted to see them hatch. I played their little game for a while and then we put them into the sand to "hatch." Those turtle eggs are probably still there.

Each January there was a reunion in Boston. I was invited to join the festivities for several years after I quit being a counselor.

The rules at camp were strictly followed. The responsibility of each counselor was unbelievable. The planning and follow-through that went into the success of the camp was amazing. What a wonderful experience I had during those two summers. Then I graduated from college and had to go to work.

While at the camp the girls all had to keep 24-hour specimens of their urine. The shelves in the lab held individual bottles with each girl's name. Usually the girls would go to the lab when they needed to, and would then add to their bottle. But every morning before breakfast and every afternoon after lunch we all watched the Parade of Pots to the lab.

❖ My First Job ❖
by Charlotte Robinson, Turners Falls, Massachusetts

My first paying job was as a maker of Dish Gardens at the Johnson Greenhouses. I was thirteen or fourteen-years-old and worked a couple of hours after school, two or three afternoons a week. I could walk to work because the greenhouses were only a short distance from my home in Stoneham, Massachusetts through a few backyards. The job went like this:

First: Clear a place on a workbench. Get the one-quart measuring can. Get two quarts of #1 potting soil, one quart of #2 powdered fertilizers, and one quart of #3 special additives. Pile all together in the center of the bench and mix carefully with those little wooden rakes until the various parts are totally mixed in and each has lost its identity.

Second: Select five or six different quart-size dishes from an endless supply of different shapes, colors, and designs. Divide the mixture into each of the dishes until they are two-thirds full.

Third: Select three non-blooming plants for each dish from the large selection available about ten steps away. Must have three different plants in each dish. Cannot use the same combination of plants in any two dishes. Plant the plants.

Fourth: Put green, mossy, synthetic stuff around each plant. Add colored crushed stones by the teaspoonful to represent paths, water, caves, or what have you.

Fifth: Dig through boxes of miniature ceramic animals, houses, people, birds and statuary. Select and add two or three to each dish to represent a theme of your choosing.

Sixth: Sprinkle with water. Wipe inside lip of dish and wash entire outside of dish.

Seventh: Add price tag on toothpick to each dish—$10.00. Carefully carry dishes (no more than two at a time) to retail area for selling. Go back to bench, clean up your area, and begin again.

Eighth: Pay Charlotte twenty-five cents per hour.

It is strange that there are so few dish gardens available today to buy as gifts. Hospital and nursing home patients love them. The plants last for years with minimum care and are quite a conversation piece.

I loved that job! I was working with my hands. My imagination was constantly being stressed. And best of all—nobody was checking on me except when looking at the finished project!

❖ Funerals ❖
by Charlotte Robinson, Turners Falls, Massachusetts

When my grandmother Rose Barker died she was living with her daughter, my Aunt Grace. The undertakers took her body to Keene, New Hampshire for the necessary procedures. After that they brought the body back to Aunt Grace's house and placed the casket on sawhorses in the room my grandmother had used while she lived there.

Everyone arrived to view the body, and when the time came near for the funeral, the undertakers requested that we all go outside while they removed the body. Some time later I found out that with the height of the ceiling and the size of the bedroom door and frame, it was necessary to stand the casket on end and twist it sideways and on edge to move it out of the room. How considerate they were to spare us this operation.

❖ Our Blue Jewett ❖
by Juliana Sivik Samoriski, Shelburne, Massachusetts

I remember that during my youth people walked a great deal from place to place often over long distances. Public transportation was provided by trolley cars, trains, and buses. Automobiles were owned by a few families and used on special occasions.

My parents owned a large, midnight blue Jewett automobile that resembled a huge box with four wheels and a huge tire hooked on the back. A "running board" along both sides was used as a step to get into the car. Also included was one windshield/rain wiper on the driver's side of the front windshield, a five inch visor-like piece of metal to shade the driver's eyes, and four doors—two on each side of the car. A steering wheel on the left front of the car had a horn in the center and a head light switch. A stick shift on the right side of the driver also had an emergency brake; two foot pedals were called the "clutch" and "brake" respectively.

This was a nine-passenger car and accommodated our family and guests. Three passengers could fit on the front bench seat, four in the back seat and one each could pull down a jump seat.

This "mechanical wonder" was the topic of many loud discussions within my family, mainly because one of my older brothers would invariably "forget" to put gas in the car, would let the oil run very low, or would neglect to put water in the radiator.

My oldest sister was the "designated" driver on all family trips. My dad sat next to her. The brake was easily accessible to him for emergencies and he used it often. I remember all of us were frequently displaced within the car on a regular basis during family outings especially when we drove on the Mohawk Trail.

We took two trips on the Mohawk Trail yearly: spring and fall. Each trip, the scenario was the same: the weighted down Jewett would be going up the hill nicely, when suddenly it would start sputtering and bucking. Next my father would shout the command, "Everybody out!" and we would all bail out in formation that resembled ants running from an ant hill. We would then run alongside the car until it regained its mechanical momentum. My sister would stop briefly and we would jump back into the car to continue on our journey up the Mohawk Trail. The trips to the "Summit" took all day, from daybreak to late night, because we stopped at the shops for trinkets and a picnic lunch.

Air conditioning and a heater in the car were nonexistent. Winter heating was provided by a "horse blanket." This blanket was also used to cover the hood of the car when the car was in the garage. Air conditioning

Local Color 475

in summer was an open window with grime and dust blowing in along with the air.

The Jewett was manufactured by the Jewett family only during the years of 1926, 1927 and 1928, according to information compiled by way of an Internet search. It was rated as a large sports car!

Looking back to the years of the Jewett brings to mind many happy trips and endless memories.

About the Authors

Allan D. Adie was born in Boston, Massachusetts. He joined the Civilian Conservation Corps in 1935 and was stationed in Turners Falls, Massachusetts. He has been honored to be an appointed and an elected officer in the town of Gill, Massachusetts. On September 3, 1935 he married Angelina Murley, a native of Gill. For several years he was director of the Millers Falls Drum and Bugle Corps Color Guard and has been a volunteer at his church for many years.

Helen G. Adzema was born in Greenfield, Massachusetts on November 21, 1924. She has lived in her current Linden Street home all her life and has been a watchmaker for fifty-six years.

Joanne Balzarini was born and grew up in Watertown, Massachusetts. She is married and has three adult children. She lived in China as a civilian for three years and appreciates the freedom and privileges of the U.S.A. Upon her return from China, she and her husband opened the first Dunkin' Donuts store in Greenfield and owned it for twenty-one years. She retired from her eighteen year run as Director for both Bernardston, Massachusetts and Northfield, Massachusetts senior centers. She was instrumental in getting funding for, and seeing through to completion, the renovations of the old Powers Institute into the new Bernardston Senior Center.

Edna Baublis was born in Athol, Massachusetts. After graduating from high school, she received a diploma from Frank Manning and from UMASS/Boston. She raised her family in Athol, Massachusetts and lives there today. Her work has appeared in all previous issues of *Local Color* and *The Stories of Our Lives*.

Rosalie Bolton is a graduate of UMASS when it was Massachusetts State College. She was home economist for the Franklin County Extension Service prior to her marriage. She has seven children and twelve grandchildren. Her stories have appeared in previous *Local Color* issues. A native of Montague, born at the Farren Hospital, she now lives in Greenfield, Massachusetts.

Alice Brough spent many decades of her life in Montague, Massachusetts. She held many jobs including dental assistant and assistant to a milliner. She is a great correspondent, writing many wonderful letters to all the members of her large family. She also writes stories of her life to share with them. Mrs. Brough has read her work at area readings. In 2003, Alice turned 98 years old.

Estelle Cade: "According to Socrates, "The unexamined life is not worth living," so as a "Senior Writer" with no longer any family or career responsibilities, I enjoy looking back on my life through the filter of time and experience, writing about parts of it and attempting to see who I was and who I have become. Although in the last twenty-five years or so I've traveled fairly extensively, my life since early adolescence has been tied to Franklin County. My days as a young child were far more "citified" and I bring those experiences to my writing and to my outlook on life as well. At some point I expect to tie things together in a book for my children and grandchildren so that they might know what it was like in "the Olden Days" of the 1930s – 1940s. (My eldest son, then three years old, asked me once if I'd ever seen dinosaurs. When I said, of course not, he then asked if I traveled in a covered wagon when I was little. Not quite those olden days, either!)

Guy Carey, Jr. was born and raised in Warwick, Massachusetts. He has enjoyed writing all his life and has been encouraged by his family in recent years to preserve the stories of his life. He is enjoying his retirement doing just that. His work has appeared in previous issues of *Local Color*.

Mary Ciechomski, one of ten children of Polish immigrants, was born and raised in South Hadley, Massachusetts. Mary attended public schools there and graduated from South Hadley High School in 1940. She continued her education at Northampton Commercial College (NCC) and graduated from NCC in 1941. Married to Paul "Steve" Ciechomski in 1946, Mary and Steve raised five children. Upon retirement she and her husband moved to New Hampshire for six years and the returned to Turners Falls, Massachusetts. Inspired by a request from one of her children, she began to write memories of her childhood to share with her children and grandchildren. She currently lives in Turners Falls.

Dorothy Clark was born March 10, 1923 on her grandparents' farm in Spruce Corner, Ashfield, Massachusetts. She moved to Hawley, Massachusetts when she was three. She attended Charlemont High School where she played basketball and was in the band. She graduated in 1941. Mrs. Clark belongs to various civic organizations including the Sons and Daughters of Hawley (Massachusetts) and the Senior Center.

Genevieve Clark is "just another senior citizen that enjoys writing and remembering. I was able to help instill the joy of story-telling as a teacher of Reading and Language Arts at Linden Hill School in Northfield, Massachusetts for some years before retiring and am writing now for my family."

Margaret M. "Pat" Currie was born and raised in Greenfield, Massachusetts. After marriage to Ross Currie, she moved to Turners Falls, Massachusetts. ("He was from Millers Falls and we compromised on a halfway point between the two towns.") Mrs. Currie is mother to six—three daughters and three sons. She is grandmother to sixteen—seven boys and nine girls. She is so proud of and happy with her large family as she was an only child growing up. Mrs. Currie has read her work at area readings.

Jane Daignault was born in South Boston and came to Franklin County in Western Massachusetts "the long way." She stayed in Western Massachusetts for over sixty years and raised two sons there. Mrs. Daignault read her work at the Montague Senior Center. She passed away in 2003.

Robert A. Desilets was born in Canada, but lived most of his life in the United States. This is his first published piece. He lives in Gill, Massachusetts.

Elisabeth R. Donaj: "Thanks to the caring and inspiration received from a wonderful facilitator, I became encouraged to share my memories of a long life and all my experiences by writing them down. Writing is therapy and realization. How rich and blessed one can feel when reaching into the wealth of memories. And I have learned to enjoy sharing my stories with readers who can believe them to be true experiences."

Vera Farris was born in Chelsea, Massachusetts in 1915. She spent her first seven years in Buffalo, New York and then moved to Deerfield, Massachusetts where she went to Deerfield Elementary School and Deerfield Academy. After a move to Northfield, Massachusetts she finished her schooling at Northfield High School. She has lived in her family's old Northfield homestead ever since. She has taken creative writing correspondence courses through the University of Chicago. Her writing was recognized by Dick Van Dyke in his book Faith, Hope and Hilarity. She worked at Millers Falls Paper Company before retirement. She has one son, four grandchildren and two great-grandchildren.

Rena Finch was born in Tubingen, Germany and came to the States at age nine just before the outbreak of war in 1939. She spent her teen years in Shrewsbury, Massachusetts and graduated from Clarke University in Worcester, Massachusetts. In 1951 she married Ed Finch of Northfield, Massachusetts. They have lived in Northfield for more than fifty years and raised their three children there. She taught in Leyden, Massachusetts for thirteen years and ran the Northfield Country Store. She enjoys writing and is instrumental in producing the *Northfield Community Newsletter*. She is writing her memoirs for her children and grandchildren.

Edith J. Fisher is widowed and retired. She has five children—four boys and one girl—and has done all kinds of jobs in her life: tax collector, school committee, president (twice) of her church organization (women), chairman of several committees, hayed, milked cows (by hand), worked on church suppers, put on lunches—whatever needed to be done. She turns eighty-one in 2003.

Alice (Bourdeau) Fisk was born in 1919 at home in Montague City, Massachusetts. Her family (railroad) moved often and she did not return to Montague until she married in 1937. With her husband Harry, Mrs. Fisk raised five children in Montague Center, Massachusetts—"a great place for kids." All her children belonged to Scouts, 4-H Club and church. They all went to Montague schools. After the children were grown, she traveled with her husband and moved to Greenfield. A widow now, she lives with her cat in a pleasant apartment and keeps busy volunteering doing handwork, reading and enjoying her family and friends.

William R. Fitzgerald was born in Holyoke, Massachusetts and moved to Conway, Massachusetts as a child. He was a farmer from 1952 to 1994. He has written professionally for years and his work has appeared in many publications including previous issues of *Local Color*.

Margaret "Peg" Folgmann was born in Pumpkin Hollow, Conway, Massachusetts in 1917. She graduated Sanderson Academy (Ashfield, Massachusetts), nursing school and Boston University then taught in schools of nursing for many years. She is active in civic and church affairs and continues to travel extensively. She returned to the Pioneer Valley following the death of her husband. She has one son, grandchildren and great- grandchildren. She's been writing stories of her childhood for her family for many years.

Katherine L. Forster loves to write! She also enjoys seeing her words in print. She is working on a family story at this time which she hopes to have in the next *Local Color*. She is ninety six years old and lives in Orange, Massachusetts.

Henry Gabriel is a writer living in Northfield, Massachusetts. His work has appeared in the *Northfield Community Newsletter*.

Jane L. Gilbert was born at the Farren Hospital in Turners Falls, Massachusetts and has lived in Franklin County her whole life. She has had work published by the Greenfield Recorder and New England Homestead magazine. Mrs. Gilbert lives in Turners Falls, Massachusetts.

Suzanne Gluck-Sosis has been living in Greenfield, Massachusetts since 1996. Her beloved husband, Phil, died in June 2002. She is taking a year to officially mourn his death, taking time to write about the wonder of their relationship. She plans to resume her healing work as a Rubenfeld Synergist and Reiki practitioner in the fall of 2003.

Barbara R. Graves was born on May 4, 1916 and spent her early years in Ashfield, Massachusetts in the Apple Valley section of town on the Clark Farm that is still in operation. On July 24, 1937 she married another Ashfield native, Arthur Hall Graves, and has lived all her married life in West Springfield, Massachusetts. While raising her three children, she taught in Agawam, Massachusetts schools and became an avid gardener and garden club member. Barbara has spent many hours working in the town greenhouse. Her piece "The

"Wash"" was first published in *The Ashfield News*.

Phyllis Hamilton was born in Barre, Massachusetts and moved to Franklin County in 1970. She was part of a wind and string ensemble called the Four Seasons led by Robin Stone. In addition to her writing and music work, she enjoyed Tai Chi and painting. She was also interested in the healing arts such as therapeutic touch and healing with music. Ms. Hamilton passed away in 2003.

Dorothy G. Hmieleski of South Deerfield, Massachusetts was born in Montague Center, Massachusetts. She worked for a number of years at UMASS and while there completed a BA and MA in English. She was married to Henry Hmieleski and has three children and four grandchildren.

Dick Hoyt was born and raised in Shelburne Falls, Massachusetts and recently retired after thirty-six years of teaching French, Russian, and Spanish. For a number of years, he and his wife, Jean, ran Bona Vista Farm Bed & Breakfast in Winchendon, Massachusetts. They recently moved to Lubec, Maine where they are restoring an 1800s farmhouse, watching eagles and walking the rugged coastline Down East.

Leona Jarvi has written two stories for previous *Local Color* issues about country living and city living. Her next story will be about living in a small town, then perhaps stories of her adult life.

Irmarie Jones, of Greenfield, was a reporter for *The Recorder* in Greenfield, Massachusetts from 1969 until 1990. Although she retired, she continues to write her human interest column, "Just Plain Neighbors," twice a week for *The Recorder*. She has twelve grandchildren and ten great-grandchildren.

Jean Kozlowski grew up in Portland, Maine, later graduating from Tufts University. For over thirty-four years she was a teacher in three different states. Ten years ago she and her husband moved to Northfield where she still enjoys writing reminiscences, as well as being an avid watercolorist.

Florence M. Lanfair was born in Waterbury, Vermont on March 21, 1912. She spent her early years in Vermont, moving with her family to the town of Montague, Massachusetts in 1928. She married Earle E. Lanfair on May 28, 1930. Florence and Earle have two children, Joan and Bradley, four grandchildren and five great grandchildren. She enjoys music, reading, sewing, embroidery, crocheting and indoor gardening.

Elisabeth Bourquin Leete was born and grew up in Geneva, Switzerland, the daughter of a Calvinist minister, who died of tuberculosis at age 45. She came to New York at twenty-three to "improve [her] English" and become acquainted with American relatives. She became a correspondent of *France-Soir* and covered many major stories of the 1960s. She has traveled extensively, lived in Libya and then settled at her Ashfield, Massachusetts summer home after the Ghadhafi regime expelled her and her family in 1971. Mrs. Leete is a French teacher, cellist and recorder musician when she is not working on her memoirs. Her daughter Lucy is a nurse.

Warren LeMon is a retired soldier of the US Army. He and his wife Sally lived in Montague from 1972 until 2000 when they relocated to Maine. He holds degrees from UMASS/Amherst and the Western New England College School of Law. During his active writing career, LeMon served on the staffs of the *Stars and Stripes* in Europe and the Pacific, *Soldier's Magazine* and *The Recorder* as a municipal and business reporter. Mr. LeMon was raised in the Bronx, New York and was recently invited to submit his memoirs to the Bronx Historical Society.

Janice Howard Lepore is a retired secretary, mother of four and grandmother of seven. She was raised in South Dakota and worked for the Navy Department in Washington, D.C. She has lived in Massachusetts since 1957 and graduated from Greenfield Community College. Her work has been published in The Baldwin Center Writers Group literary journal *Caboodle*, the Greenfield Senior Center publication *Pen 'n Pencil* and *Local Color*, *The Good Life* and The International Library of Poetry. She enjoys music, art, theatre, and meeting new people through volunteering and writing groups.

Betty Lockwood was born in 1913 in Hammond, Indiana. She grew up, was educated and married in the Midwest. In 1949 she and her husband moved to Boston with their five children. She moved to West County (Western Massachusetts) in 1989 and her roots were firmly set in the rural hills. She was Director of Religious Education in Unitarian Universalist churches, manager of a summer book shop on Star Island and mother to a brood of children and their children. She's been published in *The Massachusetts Review*, *This Wood Sang Out* and *Five Minute Pieces*. Mrs. Lockwood died in 2002.

Phyllis Loomis: "I have always been a teacher and have twice been a wife. The first time I was too young and the second time I was too old. Between the two, I spent almost twenty years on my own. I have GREAT children and a dozen grandchildren most of whom are taller than I. Through the years I have lived in and through surprising changes that leave me wondering if one life could have been so varied. Four years ago I began writing about what I remembered of all those lives within a life." Phyllis' collection of stories from her Peace Corp experiences in Africa is now under consideration by publishers.

Lorraine Madden is originally from Connecticut where she began writing in 1989 in the Baldwin Senior Center in Stratford. Now a resident of Greenfield, Massachusetts for several years, she enjoys the Writing Class in the Greenfield Senior Center. She has been published in previous issues of *Local Color*.

Eileen Marguet was born in Brooklyn, New York. She is a writer and artist whose work has appeared in *The Cracker Barrel, Reminisce* as well as all past *Local Color* to name just a few publications. She self-published a book called, "The Chronicles of the Civilian Conservation Corps" which is now in its second printing.

Marjorie Naida grew up in Springfield, Massachusetts and moved to Gill, Massachusetts in 1955 after she married. Mrs. Naida raised three daughters and still lives in Gill.

Louise Bowen O'Brien was born in Beverly, Massachusetts and grew up in Vermont. She graduated from Arms Academy in Shelburne Falls, Massachusetts and married Clarence O'Brien. They had a daughter and four sons. Louise has lived in Colrain for over sixty years. She served as town librarian for many years and as an officer of the Colrain Historical Society. She had a poem book published and several stories and poems published in magazines. She loves books and travel.

Joseph A. Parzych was born and raised in Gill, Massachusetts. He wrote during his military service in World War II and continued writing long after. His work appears extensively in publications like *Yankee, Hard Hat Review, Reader's Digest* and countless others. His memoir is currently ready for publication.

Jack Perry grew up in Clarion, Iowa and achieved a theater degree from Cornell College, Mount Vernon, Iowa before pursuing gradate studies at Stanford University and Yale Drama School. He wrote plays between acting in summer stock and holding down jobs to make ends meet. Several of his plays have been produced at locations up and down the east coast including New York City. An ad man for *The Daily Hampshire Gazette*, he oversold ads for a supplement that had to run into four more pages and was ordered to write something to fill the space. Thus began his memoir writing. His collection, *The Clarion Chronicles* is published by and available through *The Daily Hampshire Gazette* in Northampton, Massachusetts.

Dorothy M. Persons has been remembering her life for about eighty-three years now, most of it happening in New England. After retiring from school teaching in Vermont and Massachusetts elementary schools about twenty five years ago, she has spent time painting watercolor pictures, traveling, playing violin, gardening, reading and occasionally writing stories of her life for her descendents, children, grandchildren and great-grandchildren.

Marilyn M. Pinson: "My parents' business meant moving around a great deal, thus affording me the opportunity to attend a variety of schools and to make many, many friends. My favorite hobby is contacting people in other countries of the world as a Ham Operator, using voice or Morse code communication. Inactive on radio currently, writing, reading, crossword puzzles in addition to crocheting keep me busy these days."

Francis R. Pleasant was born in St. Anne's School apartments in Turners Falls, Massachusetts to Eva and Wayne Pleasant. He grew up attending St. Anne's School and Turners Falls High School. His next four years were with the U.S. Air Force and then twenty-three years at the family business, Pleasant Insurance Agency. His working career continued with ten years at the Treasury of the Commonwealth and now as Head of Security at Stoneleigh-Burnham School. He also spent many active years in the Town of Montague and Franklin County governments. He has been married to Helen (Delpha) for forty-four years and boasts five children and eleven grandchildren.

Charlotte Potter was born in Bowdenham, Maine on March 22, 1920. She attended Richmond High School and graduated in 1937. Charlotte received a Bachelor of Arts degree from the University of Maine in 1941 and married Edwin Potter on May 21, 1943. Charlotte and Edwin had two children, Noel and Nedine, four grandchildren and two great grandchildren. Charlotte taught school for twenty-six years—mostly English at Turners Falls High School, but also in Maine. Mrs. Potter passed away in 2000.

Nicholas Prokowich was born in Greenfield, Massachusetts and educated in Greenfield Schools. He has written as part of his work at Vermont Yankee and enjoys writing now as a way to get his experiences down on paper. Mr. Prokowich lives in Montague, Massachusetts.

Marjorie Reid came to Greenfield as a bride fifty years ago and decided to stay. She lives here with her husband, Bob. Five of her children live in Franklin County and one is in Vermont.

Theresa Richards was born in Boston, Massachusetts and came to Western Massachusetts with her family. She never thought much of writing until a friend encouraged her to write. She has been married to David for forty-nine years.

Leona Robert was born in Leverett, Massachusetts. She spent most of her life in Montague, Massachusetts and attended local schools. The mother of three, she has seven grandchildren and fifteen great-grandchildren. She started writing her memoirs for the benefit of the younger generation, hoping to give them some knowledge of what life was like for their ancestors.

Charlotte Robinson was born and brought up in Stoneham, Massachusetts. She was a physical education teacher in Turners Falls,

Massachusetts for many years. Her love of genealogy and local history has sparked a variety of projects including working on a war memorial for area soldiers who served in the Civil and Revolutionary wars.

Juliana Sivik Samoriski was a graduate of Turners Falls High School, Franklin County Public Hospital School of Nursing and George Mason University School of Social Work. She worked as the Town Nurse of Montague, in the US Navy Nurse Corps, and in Fairfax Hospital as an alcoholism counselor. She lived all over the world before she retired to Shelburne Falls, Massachusetts. She was married to Henry Samoriski and had five children. Writing for *Local Color* was her first writing experience. Mrs. Samoriski died in 2003.

Doris Shirtcliff was born in Heath, Massachusetts on Easter Sunday (March 27) 1921. She moved to Greenfield when she was four years old, attended local schools and graduated from Greenfield High School in 1939. She worked at Greenfield Tap and Die (GTD) two years and has had a variety of jobs since then. She has two daughters, four grandchildren and one great grandchild. She enjoys music, ceramics, tag sales, furniture refinishing and writing. Her work has appeared in *The Good Life* and the *Springfield Union News*.

Margaret D. Smolen was born and brought up in Northfield, Massachusetts. She graduated from Northfield Mount Hermon School in Northfield and from Green Mountain College in Putney, Vermont. She worked for thirty-one years at the Grand Union grocery stores in Brattleboro and Greenfield as a bookkeeper and cashier. She has one son living in Connecticut and three grandsons. She recently relocated to Connecticut herself.

Constance (Viens) Sokoloski was born and raised in Turners Falls, Massachusetts. She attended St. Anne's Parish School and graduated from Turners Falls High School. She spent her working years mainly in the clerical and secretarial fields. Now retired, she enjoys reading, crafts and most of all, her pets. She also lived many years in Gill, Massachusetts before moving to Greenfield, but says that growing up and living in Turners Falls was the happiest time of her life.

Helen Carey Tatro was born in Wendell, Massachusetts and grew up in Warwick, Massachusetts. She graduated from New Salem Academy in 1943. She has lived in Baldwinville, Massachusetts since 1954 where she and her husband raised four children. This is her first published piece.

Virginia Taylor was born in Hawley, Massachusetts. She was educated in a one-room schoolhouse for eight grades and had the same teacher for seven of those grades. After she graduated high school, she went to work as a telephone operator in Charlemont, Massachusetts. She has lived in Charlemont ever since with the exception of several years traveling with her husband to Oklahoma, Georgia and North Carolina when he was in the Service. Virginia was meal site manager at the Charlemont Senior Center from 1980-1991. She has been a member of the Charlemont Council on Aging for many years. She has always started her Senior Center news columns for *The Good Life* (a newspaper for seniors aged 55 and older in Franklin County and the North Quabbin area) with short musings, some of which were collected for her piece herein.

Norah (Noreen) Torrey, the daughter of an English missionary, spent the first five years of her life near Bombay, India before returning to England to enter boarding school at the age of six. She served four years in the WAAFs during WWII and moved to the US in 1949 after her marriage to an American botanist, whom she met in 1942 when they were both stationed in Northern Ireland. Since her husband's death in 1993, she has continued to live in Greenfield, Massachusetts taking an active interest in the lives of her five daughters and enjoying her grandchildren. She is an avid violinist and participates in a number of local chamber groups.

Ellen C. Tosi was born in West Northfield, Massachusetts and graduated from Northfield Seminary. She went to Emerson College for two years and is a graduate of the Hickox Secretarial School. She was a secretary in architectural and engineering firms in Boston during her working career. She enjoyed living in New York City for nearly two years during WWII. She is now retired and living in Northfield.

Priscilla Tromblay was born in 1916 in Springfield, Massachusetts. She graduated from Technical High School in Springfield in 1936 and moved to Franklin County in 1971. She graduated from Greenfield Community College in 1980 with an AA degree and has performed a variety of human service jobs including Case Manager at Franklin County Home Care, receptionist at the Greenfield Social Security Office and currently program assistant for the SHINE Health Insurance Counseling Program. Ms. Tromblay's work has appeared in the National Library of Poetry. She has also privately published a collection of poems called *Poems*. Ms. Tromblay now lives in Florida state.

Robert Viarengo was born in New York City and graduated from Columbia which he attended with the goal of becoming a writer. The need to support a family, among other distractions, led him to a career in business where he learned to prepare terse memos. After retiring several years ago he studied non-fiction writing at the New School in New York, moved to a spiritual place called Heath, Massachusetts, and began writing as a hobby. "It's been a wonderful and liberating experience."

Hélène Sullivan Walker was born in Paris in 1903. Her father, the American painter James Amory Sullivan, moved his family to Asolo, Italy in 1909 where Ms. Walker spent her girlhood among expatriate artists, local artisans and peasant farmers. She returned to the U.S. in 1914 when Italy entered WWI to begin her first formal schooling. She later married and raised four boys. After her husband died in the late 1940s, she worked in New York City for Elizabeth Arden and wrote a food column for Flair magazine. In the 1960s she moved permanently to her grandmother's farm on Hawley Road in Ashfield, Massachusetts where she had spent many childhood summers. This story is part of an unpublished memoir about her early life in Italy. Ms. Walker passed away in 2002.

Lynne Warrin taught fifth and sixth grades in public schools in New York and at Eaglebrook School, a private, boys' school, in Deerfield, Massachusetts. For twenty years she was the program director at Camp Kehonka in Wolfeboro, New Hampshire. Now that she is retired, she pursues interests including studying the viola, playing in a string quartet and in The Four Seasons Ensemble in Greenfield as well as writing, weaving and working as a member of the Friends of the Dickinson Memorial Library in Northfield, Massachusetts.

Anna Viadero is a writer and writing teacher. Her works have appeared in publications like *Yankee*, *Ms.*, *Sahara*, *The Berkshire Review* and others. She is a frequent commentator on National Public Radio in New England and New York.

> For more information on this title or on the annual printing of *Local Color,* please contact Anna Viadero at aviadero@yahoo.com or PO Box 116 Montague, MA 01351.

Photo Captions:

Cover: Author Charlotte Robinson (L) with sister Priscilla and brother Roscoe in the 1930s. See story on page 246.

Front piece: Author Elisabeth Leete with siblings in Geneva, Switzerland.

Title Page: D.O. Paul with his wife Edna and a friend on the steps of the Gill Store in Gill, Massachusetts. See story on page 154.

Stories of Our Lives chapter page: General Eisenhower reviewing the troops during WWII. Joe Viadero, Jr. is second from right.

Page 7: Author Estelle Cade in the 1930s.

Local Color #1 chapter page: Author Estelle Cade in the 1930s.

Local Color #2 chapter page: Estelle M. (Heard) Robinson (author Estelle Cade's grandmother) & daughter Gracie, 1893. See story on page 119.

Local Color #3 chapter page: Author Peg Folgmann's mother deer hunting. See story on page 78.

Page 207: Author Joe Parzych's family in their car in the 1930s.

Local Color #4 chapter page: The Warwick General Store in the 1930s. See story page 335.

Local Color #5 chapter page: Author Eileen Marguet and her husband Bill in 1943. See story on page 149.

Local Color Extras chapter page: Author Charlotte Robinson and her cousins in 1935. See story on page 159.

Page 475: Anna Maksjutenko and Ivan Tonuk, Anna Viadero's grandparents in 1954.